**Norman, Marsha.
Collected plays**

"In the absolute truthfulness of her treatment and dialogue, in the unforced poetry of her modern speech, and in her capacity to create major climaxes out of petty quotidian affairs, Miss Norman has followed the path of Chekhov, who believed that the great stakes of modern drama must emerge from under the trivial course of the daily routine...I believe Miss Norman, consciously or not, is writing in a great dramatic tradition and...has the potential to preserve and revitalize it. Nothing reinforces one's faith in the power and importance of the theatre more than the emergence of an authentic universal playwright—not a woman playwright, mind you, not a regional playwright, not an ethnic playwright, but one who speaks to the concerns and experiences of all humankind...I have grown convinced that Marsha Norman is the genuine article—an American writer with the courage to look unflinchingly into the black holes from which we normally turn our faces."

Robert Brustein
from *Who Needs Theatre*

Marsha Norman
Collected Plays

CONTEMPORARY PLAYWRIGHTS SERIES

SK
A Smith and Kraus Book

A Smith and Kraus Book
Published by Smith and Kraus, Inc.
PO Box 127, Lyme, NH 03768

First Edition: April 1998
10 9 8 7 6 5 4 3 2

The Library of Congress Cataloging-In-Publication Data
Norman, Marsha.
    [Plays. Selections]
    Collected plays / Marsha Norman. —1st ed.
    p. cm. —(Contemporary playwrights series)

    Contents: Loving Daniel Boone—Sarah and Abraham—Getting out—
    Third and oak—Traveler in the dark—Circus Valentine—The holdup.

    ISBN 1-57525-029-2
    I. Title. II. Series.
    PS3564.0623A6   1997
    812'.54—dc21   97-7665
                        CIP

CONTENTS

Getting Out.   1

Third and Oak. 59

Circus Valentine 109

The Holdup 163

Traveler in the Dark 221

Sarah and Abraham 273

Loving Daniel Boone 331

Three Speeches 393

Getting Out

Getting Out was originally produced in November 1977 by Actors Theatre of Louisville, in Louisville, Kentucky, under the direction of Jon Jory. The original cast was as follows:

Arlene	Susan Kingsley
Arlie	Denny Dillon
Guard (1) (Evans)	Brian Lynner
Bennie	Bob Burrus
Guard (2) (Caldwell)	Jim Baker
Doctor	Thurman Scott
Teacher	Nan Wray
Mother	Anne Pitoniak
Woman	Jeanne Cullen
Woman	Maggie Riley
Male Teacher	Michael Kevin
Carl	Leo Burmester
Warden	Ray Fry
Ruby	Lynn Cohen

The West Coast premiere of *Getting Out* was produced in 1978 by the Center Theatre Group of Los Angeles, Mark Taper Forum, Gordon Davidson, Artistic Director, under the direction of Mr. Davidson. The cast was as follows:

Arlene	Susan Clark
Arlie	Janette Lane Bradbury
Guard (1) (Evans)	John O'Connell
Bennie	Hugh Gillin
Guard (2) (Caldwell)	F. William Parker
Doctor	Bill Cobbs
Mother	Collin Wilcox
School Principal	Sarah Cunningham
Ronnie	Griffin Dunne
Carl	James G. Richardson
Warden	Michael Fairman
Ruby	Conchata Ferrell

Originally produced in New York in 1978 by The Phoenix Theatre, under the direction of Jon Jory.

Produced Off-Broadway in 1979 in New York City by Lester Osterman, Lucille Lortel, and Mac Howard, under the direction of Jon Jory. The original cast was as follows:

Arlene	Susan Kingsley
Arlie	Pamela Reed
Guard (1) (Evans)	John C. Capodice
Bennie	Bob Burrus
Guard (2) (Caldwell)	Fritz Sperberg
Doctor	William Jay
Mother	Madeleine Thornton-Sherwood
School Principal	Anna Minot
Ronnie	Kevin Bacon
Carl	Leo Burmester
Warden	Hansford Rowe
Ruby	Joan Pape

Getting Out was the co-winner of ATL's Great American Play Contest for 1977, and went on to receive numerous other honors, including the Oppenheimer/ Newsday Award, the John Gassner Playwriting Medallion awarded by the Outer Critics Circle, and the American Theatre Critics Association citation as the outstanding new play produced outside of New York during the 1977–78 season. The following year *Getting Out* was featured in *The Burns Mantle Theatre Yearbook* as one of the best plays of the New York season, published by Avon Books, and chosen as a Fireside Book Club Selection.

INTRODUCTION

Jon Jory told me where to look for this play. "Go back ten years in your life," he said, "to a time when you were physically frightened." I knew instantly that I would write about a violent girl I had known briefly when I worked in a state mental hospital, a girl who later went to prison for murder. What made her particularly dangerous was her complete lack of concern for consequences, and her seeming ability to escape whenever she wanted. What I wanted to write about, was what would happen if a girl like this was ever really locked up, locked up someplace she couldn't get out of.

When I learned through research that people kept in long-term solitary confinement tend to come out cold, passive, and withdrawn, I realized I had a problem. I wanted to write a hostile girl who didn't care what you did to her. But how could I write a hostile girl, if the girl who came out of prison was perfectly tame? The solution to this problem was the beginning of my life in the

2

theatre. I would have to put them *both* on stage—Arlie, the girl she had been, and Arlene, the woman she had become in captivity—and the play would uncover the relationship between them.

Years later, I would realize I wasn't writing about Arlie, I was writing about myself. I would realize that all of us are frequently mistaken for someone we used to be, but that's a subject for another day.

NOTES TO THE ACTING EDITION

Arlie is the violent kid Arlene was until her last stretch in prison. Arlie may walk through the apartment quite freely, but no one there will acknowledge her presence. Most of her scenes take place in the prison areas.

Arlie, in a sense, is Arlene's memory of herself, called up by fears, needs, and even simple word cues. The memory haunts, attacks, and warns. But mainly, the memory will not go away.

Arlie's life should be as vivid as Arlene's, if not as continuous. There must be hints of both physical type and gesture that Arlie and Arlene are the same person, though seen at different times in her life. They both speak with a country twang, but Arlene is suspicious and guarded, withdrawal is always a possibility. Arlie is unpredictable and incorrigible. The change seen in Arlie during the second act represents a movement toward the adult Arlene, but the transition should never be complete. Only in the final scene are they enjoyably aware of each other.

The life in the prison "surround" needs to convince without distracting. The guards do not belong to any specific institution, but rather to all the places where Arlene has done time.

CHARACTERS

ARLENE: a thin, drawn woman in her late twenties who has just served an eight-year prison term for murder.

ARLIE: Arlene at various times earlier in her life.

BENNIE: an Alabama prison guard in his fifties.

EVANS: guard.

CALDWELL: guard.

DOCTOR: a psychiatrist in a juvenile institution.

MOTHER: Arlene's mother.

SCHOOL PRINCIPAL: female.

RONNIE: a teenager in a juvenile institution.

CARL: Arlene's former pimp and partner in various crimes, in his late twenties.

WARDEN: superintendent of Pine Ridge Correctional Institute for Women.

RUBY: Arlene's upstairs neighbor, a cook in a diner, also an ex-con, in her late thirties.

Getting Out

PROLOGUE

Beginning five minutes before the houselights come down, the following announcements are broadcast over the loudspeaker. A woman's voice is preferred, a droning tone is essential.

LOUDSPEAKER VOICE: Kitchen workers, all kitchen workers report immediately to the kitchen. Kitchen workers to the kitchen. The library will not be open today. Those scheduled for book checkout should remain in morning work assignments. Kitchen workers to the kitchen. No library hours today. Library hours resume tomorrow as usual. All kitchen workers to the kitchen.

Frances Mills, you have a visitor at the front gate. All residents and staff, all residents and staff...Do not, repeat, do not, walk on the front lawn today or use the picnic tables on the front lawn during your break after lunch or dinner.

Your attention please. The exercise class for Dorm A residents has been canceled. Mrs. Fischer should be back at work in another month. She thanks you for your cards and wants all her girls to know she had an eight-pound baby girl.

Doris Creech, see Mrs. Adams at the library before lunch. Frances Mills, you have a visitor at the front gate. The Women's Associates' picnic for the beauty school class has been postponed until Friday. As picnic lunches have already been prepared, any beauty school member who so wishes, may pick up a picnic lunch and eat it at her assigned lunch table during the regular lunch period.

Frances Mills, you have a visitor at the front gate. Doris Creech to see Mrs. Adams at the library before lunch. I'm sorry, that's Frankie Hill, you have a visitor at the front gate. Repeat, Frankie Hill, not Frances Mills, you have a visitor at the front gate.

ACT I

The play is set in a dingy one-room apartment in a rundown section of downtown Louisville, Kentucky. There is a twin bed and one chair. There is a sink, an apartment-size combination stove and refrigerator, and a counter with cabinets above. Dirty curtains conceal the bars on the outside of the single window. There is one closet and a door to the bathroom. The door to the apartment opens into a hall.

A catwalk stretches above the apartment and a prison cell, stage right, connects to it by stairways. An area downstage and another stage left complete the enclosure of the apartment by playing areas for the past. The apartment must seem imprisoned.

Following the prologue, lights fade to black and the warden's voice is heard on tape.

WARDEN'S VOICE: The Alabama State Parole Board hereby grants parole to Holsclaw, Arlene, subject having served eight years at Pine Ridge Correctional Institute for the second-degree murder of a cab driver in conjunction with a filling station robbery involving attempted kidnapping of attendant. Crime occurred during escape from Lakewood State Prison where subject Holsclaw was serving three years for forgery and prostitution. Extensive juvenile records from the state of Kentucky appended hereto.

(As the warden continues, light comes up on Arlene, walking around the cell, waiting to be picked up for the ride home. Arlie is visible, but just barely, down center.)

WARDEN'S VOICE: Subject now considered completely rehabilitated is returned to Kentucky under interstate parole agreement in consideration of family residence and appropriate support personnel in the area. Subject will remain under the supervision of Kentucky parole officers for a period of five years. Prospects for successful integration into community rated good. Psychological evaluation, institutional history, and health records attached in Appendix C, this document.

BENNIE'S VOICE: Arlie!

(Arlene leaves the cell as light comes up on Arlie, seated down center. She tells this story rather simply. She enjoys it, but its horror is not lost on her. She may be doing some semiabsorbing activity such as painting her toenails.)

ARLIE: So, there was this little kid, see, this creepy little fucker next door. Had glasses an somethin' wrong with his foot. I don't know, seven, maybe.

Anyhow, ever time his daddy went fishin', he'd bring this kid back some frogs. They built this little fence around 'em in the backyard like they was pets or somethin'. An we'd try to go over an see 'em but he'd start screamin' to his mother to come out an git rid of us. Real snotty like. So we got sick of him bein' such a goody-goody an one night me an June snuck over there an put all his dumb ol' frogs in this sack. You never heared such a fuss. *(Makes croaking sounds.)* Slimy bastards, frogs. We was plannin' to let 'em go all over the place, but when they started jumpin' an all, we just figured they was askin' for it. So, we taken 'em out front to the porch an we throwed 'em, one at a time, into the street. *(Laughs.)* Some of 'em hit cars goin' by but most of 'em jus' got squashed, you know, runned over? It was great, seein' how far we could throw 'em, over back of our backs an under our legs an God, it was really fun watchin' 'em fly through the air then *splat (Claps hands.)* all over somebody's car window or somethin'. Then the next day, we was waitin' and this little kid comes out in his backyard lookin' for his stupid frogs and he don't see any an he gets so crazy, cryin' and everything. So me an June goes over an tells him we seen this big mess out in the street, an he goes out an sees all them frogs' legs and bodies an shit all over the everwhere, an, man, it was so funny. We 'bout killed ourselves laughin'. Then his mother come out and she wouldn't let him go out an pick up all the pieces, so he jus' had to stand there watchin' all the cars go by smush his little babies right into the street. I's gonna run out an git him a frog's head, but June yellin' at me "Arlie, git over here fore some car slips on them frog guts an crashes into you." *(Pause.)* I never had so much fun in one day in my whole life.

(Arlie remains seated as Arlene enters the apartment. It is late evening. Two sets of footsteps are heard coming up the stairs. Arlene opens the door and walks into the room. She stands still, surveying the littered apartment. Bennie is heard dragging a heavy trunk up the stairs. Bennie is wearing his guard uniform. He is a heavy man, but obviously used to physical work.)

BENNIE: *(From outside.)* Arlie?

ARLENE: Arlene.

BENNIE: Arlene? *(Bringing the trunk just inside the door.)*

ARLENE: Leave it. I'll git it later.

BENNIE: Oh, now, let me bring it in for you. You ain't as strong as you was.

ARLENE: I ain't as mean as I was. I'm strong as ever. You go on now. *(Beginning to walk around the room.)*

ARLIE: *(Irritated, as though someone is calling her.)* Lay off! *(Gets up and walks past Bennie.)*

BENNIE: *(Scoots the trunk into the room a little further.)* Go on where, Arlie?

ARLENE: I don't know where. How'd I know where you'd be goin'?

BENNIE: I can't go till I know you're gonna do all right.

ARLENE: Look, I'm gonna do all right. I done all right before Pine Ridge, an I done all right at Pine Ridge. An I'm gonna do all right here.

BENNIE: But you don't know nobody. I mean, nobody nice.

ARLENE: Lay off.

BENNIE: Nobody to take care of you.

ARLENE: *(Picking up old newspapers and other trash from the floor.)* I kin take care of myself. I been doin' it long enough.

BENNIE: Sure you have, an you landed yourself in prison doin' it, Arlie girl.

ARLENE: *(Wheels around.)* Arlie girl landed herself in prison. Arlene is out, okay?

BENNIE: Hey, now, I know we said we wasn't gonna say nuthin' about that, but I been lookin' after you for a long time. I been watchin' you eat your dinner for eight years now. I got used to it, you know?

ARLENE: Well, you kin jus' git unused to it.

BENNIE: Then why'd you ask me to drive you all the way up here?

ARLENE: I didn't, now. That was all your big ideal.

BENNIE: And what were you gonna do? Ride the bus, pick up some soldier, git yourself in another mess of trouble?

(Arlie struts back into the apartment, speaking as if to a soldier in a bar.)

ARLIE: Okay, who's gonna buy me a beer?

ARLENE: You oughta go by Fort Knox on your way home.

ARLIE: Fuckin' soldiers, don't care where they get theirself drunk.

ARLENE: You'd like it.

ARLIE: Well, Arlie girl, take your pick.

ARLENE: They got tanks right out on the grass to look at.

ARLIE: *(Now appears to lean on a bar rail.)* You git that haircut today, honey?

BENNIE: I just didn't want you given your twenty dollars the warden gave you to the first pusher you come across.

(Arlie laughs.)

ARLENE: That's what you think I been waitin' for?

(A guard appears and motions for Arlie to follow him.)

ARLIE: Yeah! I heard ya.

(The guard takes Arlie to the cell and slams the door.)

BENNIE: But God almighty, I hate to think what you'd done to the first ol' bugger

tried to make you in that bus station. You got grit, Arlie girl. I gotta credit you for that.

ARLIE: *(From the cell, as she dumps a plate of food on the floor.)* Officer!

BENNIE: The screamin' you'd do. Wake the dead.

ARLENE: Uh-huh.

BENNIE: *(Proudly.)* An there ain't nobody can beat you for throwin' plates.

ARLIE: Are you gonna clean up this shit or do I have to sit here and look at it
till I vomit?

(A guard comes in to clean it up.)

BENNIE: Listen, ever prison in Alabama's usin' plastic forks now on account of
what you done.

ARLENE: You can quit talkin' just anytime now.

ARLIE: Some life you got, fatso. Bringin' me my dinner then wipin' it off the
walls. *(Laughs.)*

BENNIE: Some of them officers was pretty leery of you. Even the chaplain.

ARLENE: No he wasn't either.

BENNIE: Not me, though. You was just wild, that's all.

ARLENE: Animals is wild, not people. That's what he said.

ARLIE: *(Mocking.)* Good behavior, good behavior. Shit.

BENNIE: Now what could that four-eyes chaplain know about wild?

(Arlene looks up sharply.)

BENNIE: Okay. Not wild, then…

ARLIE: I kin git outta here anytime I want. *(Leaves the cell.)*

BENNIE: But you got grit, Arlie.

ARLENE: I have said for you to call me Arlene.

BENNIE: Okay okay.

ARLENE: Huh?

BENNIE: Don't git riled. You want me to call you Arlene, then Arlene it is. Yes
ma'am. Now, *(Slapping the trunk.)* where do you want this? *(No response.)*
Arlene, I said, where do you want this trunk?

ARLENE: I don't care.

(Bennie starts to put it at the foot of the bed.)

ARLENE: No! *(Then calmer.)* I seen it there too long.

(Bennie is irritated.)

ARLENE: Maybe over here. *(Points to a spot near the window.)* I could put a cloth
on it and sit an look out the… *(She pulls the curtains apart, sees the bars on
the window.)* What's these bars doin' here?

BENNIE: *(Stops moving the trunk.)* I think they're to keep out burglars, you know. *(Sits on the trunk.)*

ARLENE: Yeah, I know.

(Arlie appears on the catwalk, as if stopped during a break-in.)

ARLIE: We ain't breakin' in, cop, we're just admirin' this beautiful window.

ARLENE: I don't want them there. Pull them out.

BENNIE: You can't go tearin' up the place, Arlene. Landlord wouldn't like it.

ARLIE: *(To the unseen policeman.)* Maybe I got a brick in my hand and maybe I don't.

BENNIE: Not one bit.

ARLIE: An I'm standin' on this garbage can because I like to, all right?

ARLENE: *(Walking back toward Bennie.)* I ain't gonna let no landlord tell me what to do.

BENNIE: The landlord owns the building. You gotta do what he says or he'll throw you out right on your pretty little *behind. (Gives her a familiar pat.)*

ARLENE: *(Slaps his hand away.)* You watch your mouth. I won't have no dirty talk.

ARLIE: Just shut the fuck up, cop! Go bust a wino or somethin'. *(Returns to the cell.)*

ARLENE: *(Points down right.)* Here, put the trunk over here.

BENNIE: *(Carrying the trunk over to the spot she has picked.)* What you got in here, anyhow? Rocks? Rocks from the rock pile?

ARLENE: That ain't funny.

BENNIE: Oh sweetie, I didn't mean nuthin' by that.

ARLENE: And I ain't your sweetie.

BENNIE: We really did have us a rock pile, you know, at the old men's prison, yes we did. And those boys, time they did nine or ten years carryin' rocks around, they was pret-ty mean, I'm here to tell you. And strong? God.

ARLENE: Well, what did you expect? *(Beginning to unpack the trunk.)*

BENNIE: You're tellin' me. It was dumb, I kept tellin' the warden that. They coulda killed us all, easy, anytime, that outfit. Except, we did have the guns.

ARLENE: Uh-huh.

BENNIE: One old bastard sailed a throwin' rock at me one day, woulda took my eye out if I hadn't turned around just then. Still got the scar, see? *(Reaches up to the back of his head.)*

ARLENE: You shoot him?

BENNIE: Nope. Somebody else did. I forget who. Hey! *(Walking over to the window.)*

These bars won't be so bad. Maybe you could get you some plants so's you don't even see them. Yeah, plants'd do it up just fine. Just fine.

ARLENE: *(Pulls a cheaply framed picture of Jesus out of the trunk.)* Chaplain give me this.

BENNIE: He got it for free, I bet.

ARLENE: Now, look here. That chaplain was good to me, so you can shut up about him.

BENNIE: *(Backing down.)* Fine. Fine.

ARLENE: Here. *(Handing him the picture.)* You might as well be useful fore you go.

BENNIE: Where you want it?

ARLENE: Don't matter.

BENNIE: Course it matters. Wouldn't want me puttin' it inside the closet, would you? You gotta make decisions now, Arlene. Gotta decide things.

ARLENE: I don't care.

BENNIE: *(Insisting.)* Arlene.

ARLENE: *(Pointing to a prominent position on the apartment wall, center.)* There.

BENNIE: Yeah. Good place. See it first thing when you get up.

(Arlene lights a cigarette, as Arlie retrieves a hidden lighter from the toilet in the cell.)

ARLIE: There's ways...gettin' outta bars... *(Lights a fire in the cell, catching her blouse on fire too.)*

BENNIE: *(As Arlie is lighting the fire.)* This ol' nail's pretty loose. I'll find something better to hang it with...somewhere or other...

(Arlie screams and the doctor runs toward her, getting the attention of a guard who has been goofing off on the catwalk.)

ARLIE: Let me outta here! There's a fuckin' fire in here!

(The doctor arrives at the cell, pats his pockets as if looking for the keys.)

ARLIE: Officer!

DOCTOR: Guard!

(Guard begins his run to the cell.)

ARLIE: It's burnin' me!

DOCTOR: Hurry!

GUARD (EVANS): I'm comin'! I'm comin'!

DOCTOR: What the hell were you—

GUARD (EVANS): *(Fumbling for the right key.)* Come on, come on.

DOCTOR: *(Urgent.)* For Chrissake!

(The guard gets the door open, they rush in. The doctor, wrestling Arlie to the ground, opens his bag.)

DOCTOR: Lay still, dammit.

(*Arlie collapses. The doctor gives an injection.*)

DOCTOR: (*Grabbing his hand.*) Ow!

GUARD (EVANS): (*Lifting Arlie up to the bed.*) Get bit, Doc?

DOCTOR: You going to let her burn this place down before you start payin' attention up there?

GUARD (EVANS): (*Walks to the toilet, feels under the rim.*) Uh-huh.

BENNIE: There, that what you had in mind?

ARLENE: Yeah, thanks.

GUARD (EVANS): She musta had them matches hid right here.

BENNIE: (*Staring at the picture he's hung.*) How you think he kept his beard trimmed all nice?

ARLENE: (*Preoccupied with unloading the trunk.*) Who?

BENNIE: (*Pointing to the picture.*) Jesus.

DOCTOR: I'll have to report you for this, Evans.

ARLENE: I don't know.

DOCTOR: That injection should hold her. I'll check back later. (*Leaves.*)

GUARD (EVANS): (*Walking over to the bed.*) Report me, my ass. We got cells don't have potties, Holsclaw. (*Begins to search her and the bed, handling her very roughly.*) So where is it now? Got it up your pookie, I bet. Oh, that'd be good. Doc comin' back an me with my fingers up your…roll over…don't weigh hardly nuthin', do you, dollie?

BENNIE: Never seen him without a mustache either.

ARLENE: Huh?

BENNIE: The picture.

GUARD (EVANS): Aw now… (*Finding the lighter under the mattress.*) That wasn't hard at all. Don't you know 'bout hide an seek, Arlie, girl? Gonna hide somethin', hide it where it's fun to find it. (*Standing up, going to the door.*) Crazy fuckin' someday-we-ain't-gonna-come-save-you bitch!

(*Guard slams cell door and leaves.*)

BENNIE: Well, Arlie girl, that ol' trunk's 'bout as empty as my belly.

ARLENE: You have been talkin' 'bout your belly ever since we left this mornin'.

BENNIE: You hungry? Them hotdogs we had give out around Nashville.

ARLENE: No. Not really.

BENNIE: You gotta eat, Arlene.

ARLENE: Says who?

BENNIE: (*Laughs.*) How 'bout I pick us up some chicken, give you time to clean yourself up. We'll have a nice little dinner, just the two of us.

ARLENE: I git sick if I eat this late. Besides, I'm tired.

BENNIE: You'll feel better soon's you git somethin' on your stomach. Like I always said, "Can't plow less'n you feed the mule."

ARLENE: I ain't never heard you say that.

BENNIE: There's lots you don't know about me, Arlene. You been seein' me ever day, but you ain't been payin' attention. You'll get to like me now we're out.

ARLENE: You...was always out.

BENNIE: Yes sir, I'm gonna like bein' retired. I kin tell already. An I can take care of you, like I been, only now—

ARLENE: You tol' me you was jus' takin' a vacation.

BENNIE: I was gonna tell you.

ARLENE: You had some time off an nothin' to do...

BENNIE: Figured you knew already.

ARLENE: You said you ain't never seen Kentucky like you always wanted to. Now you tell me you done quit at the prison?

BENNIE: They wouldn't let me drive you up here if I was still on the payroll, you know. Rules, against the rules. Coulda got me in big trouble doin' that.

ARLENE: You ain't goin' back to Pine Ridge?

BENNIE: Nope.

ARLENE: An you drove me all the way up here plannin' to stay here?

BENNIE: I was thinkin' on it.

ARLENE: Well what are you gonna do?

BENNIE: *(Not positive, just a possibility.)* Hardware.

ARLENE: Sell guns?

BENNIE: *(Laughs.)* Nails. Always wanted to. Some little store with bins and barrels full of nails and screws. Count 'em out. Put 'em in little sacks.

ARLENE: I don't need nobody hangin' around remindin' me where I been.

BENNIE: We had us a good time drivin' up here, didn't we? You throwin' that tomato outta the car...hit that no litterin' sign square in the middle. *(Grabs her arm as if to feel the muscle.)* Good arm you got.

ARLENE: *(Pulling away sharply.)* Don't you go grabbin' me.

BENNIE: Listen, you take off them clothes and have yourself a nice hot bath. *(Heading for the bathroom.)* See, I'll start the water. And me, I'll go get us some chicken. *(Coming out of the bathroom.)* You like slaw or potato salad?

ARLENE: Don't matter.

BENNIE: *(Asking her to decide.)* Arlene...

ARLENE: Slaw.

BENNIE: One big bucket of slaw comin' right up. An extra rolls. You have a nice bath, now, you hear? I'll take my time so's you don't have to hurry fixin' yourself up.

ARLENE: I ain't gonna do no fixin'.

BENNIE: *(A knowing smile.)* I know how you gals are when you get in the tub. You got any bubbles?

ARLENE: What?

BENNIE: Bubbles. You know, stuff to make bubbles with. Bubble bath.

ARLENE: I thought you was goin'.

BENNIE: Right. Right. Goin' right now.

> *(Bennie leaves, locking the door behind him. He has left his hat on the bed. Arlene checks the stove and refrigerator.)*

GUARD (CALDWELL): *(Opening the cell door, carrying a plastic dinner carton.)* Got your grub, girlie.

ARLIE: Get out!

GUARD (CALDWELL): Can't. Doc says you gotta take the sun today.

ARLIE: You take it! I ain't hungry.

> *(The guard and Arlie begin to walk to the downstage table area.)*

GUARD (CALDWELL): You gotta eat, Arlie.

ARLIE: Says who?

GUARD (CALDWELL): Says me. Says the warden. Says the Department of Corrections. Brung you two rolls.

ARLIE: And you know what you can do with your—

GUARD (CALDWELL): Stuff 'em in your bra, why don't you?

ARLIE: Ain't you got somebody to go beat up somewhere?

GUARD (CALDWELL): Gotta see you get fattened up.

ARLIE: What do you care?

> *(Arlene goes into the bathroom.)*

GUARD (CALDWELL): Oh, we care all right. *(Setting the food down on the table.)* Got us a two-way mirror in the shower room.

> *(She looks up, hostile.)*

GUARD (CALDWELL): And you don't know which one it is, do you? *(He forces her onto the seat.)* Yes ma'am. Eat. *(Pointing to the food.)* We sure do care if you go gittin too skinny. *(Walks away but continues to watch her.)* Yes ma'am. We care a hog-lickin' lot.

ARLIE: *(Throws the whole carton at him.)* Sons-a-bitches!

> *(Mother's knock is heard on the apartment door.)*

MOTHER'S VOICE: Arlie? Arlie girl you in there?

> *(Arlene walks out of the bathroom. She stands still, looking at the door. Arlie*

hears the knock at the same time and slips into the apartment and over to the bed, putting the pillow between her legs and holding the yellow teddy bear Arlene has unpacked. The knocking gets louder.)

MOTHER'S VOICE: Arlie?

ARLIE: *(Pulling herself up weakly on one elbow, speaking with the voice of a very young child.)* Mama? Mama?

(Arlene walks slowly toward the door.)

MOTHER'S VOICE: *(Now pulling the doorknob from the outside, angry that the door is locked.)* Arlie? I know you're in there.

ARLIE: I can't git up, Mama. *(Hands between her legs.)* My legs is hurt.

MOTHER'S VOICE: What's takin' you so long?

ARLENE: *(Smoothing out her dress.)* Yeah, I'm comin'. *(Puts Bennie's hat out of sight under the bed.)* Hold on.

MOTHER'S VOICE: I brung you some stuff but I ain't gonna stand here all night. *(Arlene opens the door and stands back. Mother looks strong but badly worn. She is wearing her cab driver's uniform and is carrying a plastic laundry basket stuffed with cleaning fluids, towels, bug spray, etc.)*

ARLENE: I didn't know if you'd come.

MOTHER: Ain't I always?

ARLENE: How are you?

(Arlene moves as if to hug her. Mother stands still, Arlene backs off.)

MOTHER: 'Bout the same. *(Walking into the room.)*

ARLENE: I'm glad to see you.

MOTHER: *(Not looking at Arlene.)* You look tired.

ARLENE: It was a long drive.

MOTHER: *(Putting the laundry basket on the trunk.)* Didn't fatten you up none, I see. *(Walks around the room, looking the place over.)* You always was too skinny.

(Arlene straightens her clothes again.)

MOTHER: Shoulda beat you like your daddy said. Make you eat.

ARLIE: Nobody done this to me, Mama. *(Protesting, in pain.)* No! No!

MOTHER: He weren't a mean man, though, your daddy.

ARLIE: Was... *(Quickly.)* my bike. My bike hurt me. The seat bumped me.

MOTHER: You remember that black chewing gum he got you when you was sick?

ARLENE: I remember he beat up on you.

MOTHER: Yeah, *(Proudly.)* and he was real sorry a coupla times. *(Looking in the closet.)* Filthy dirty. Hey! *(Slamming the closet door.)*

(Arlene jumps at the noise.)

MOTHER: I brung you all kinda stuff. Just like Candy not leavin' you nuthin'. *(Walking back to the basket.)* Some kids I got.

ARLIE: *(Curling up into a ball.)* No, Mama, don't touch it. It'll git well. It git well before.

ARLENE: Where is Candy?

MOTHER: You got her place so what do you care? I got her outta my house so whatta I care? This'll be a good place for you.

ARLENE: *(Going to the window.)* Wish there was a yard, here.

MOTHER: *(Beginning to empty the basket.)* Nice things, see? Bet you ain't had no colored towels where you been.

ARLENE: No.

MOTHER: *(Putting some things away in cabinets.)* No place like home. Got that up on the kitchen wall now.

ARLIE: I don't want no tea, Mama.

ARLENE: Yeah?

MOTHER: *(Repeating Arlene's answers.)* No...yeah?...You forgit how to talk? I ain't gonna be here all that long. Least you can talk to me while I'm here.

ARLENE: You ever git that swing you wanted?

MOTHER: Dish towels, an see here? June sent along this teapot. You drink tea, Arlie?

ARLENE: No.

MOTHER: June's havin' another baby. Don't know when to quit, that girl. Course, I ain't one to talk. *(Starting to pick up trash on the floor.)*

ARLENE: Have you seen Joey?

ARLIE: I'm tellin' you the truth.

MOTHER: An Ray...

ARLIE: *(Pleading.)* Daddy didn't do nuthin' to me.

MOTHER: Ray ain't had a day of luck in his life.

ARLIE: Ask him. He saw me fall on my bike.

MOTHER: Least bein' locked up now, he'll keep off June till the baby gits here.

ARLENE: Have you seen Joey?

MOTHER: Your daddy ain't doin' too good right now. Man's been dyin' for ten years, to hear him tell it. You'd think he'd git tired of it an jus' go ahead...pass on.

ARLENE: *(Wanting an answer.)* Mother...

MOTHER: Yeah, I seen 'im. 'Bout two years ago. Got your stringy hair.

ARLENE: You got a picture?

MOTHER: You was right to give him up. Foster homes is good for some kids.

ARLIE: Where's my Joey-bear? Yellow Joey-bear? Mama?

ARLENE: How'd you see him?

MOTHER: I was down at Detention Center pickin' up Pete. *(Beginning her serious cleaning now.)*

ARLENE: *(Less than interested.)* How is he?

MOTHER: I could be workin' at the Detention Center I been there so much. All I gotta do's have somethin' big goin' on an I git a call to come after one of you. Can't jus' have kids, no, gotta be pickin' 'em up all over town.

ARLENE: You was just tellin' me—

MOTHER: Pete is taller, that's all.

ARLENE: You was just tellin' me how you saw Joey.

MOTHER: I'm comin' back in the cab an I seen him waitin' for the bus.

ARLENE: What'd he say?

MOTHER: Oh, I didn't stop.

(Arlene looks up quickly, hurt and angry.)

MOTHER: If the kid don't even know you, Arlie, he sure ain't gonna know who I am.

ARLENE: How come he couldn't stay at Shirley's?

MOTHER: 'Cause Shirley never was crazy about washin' more diapers. She's the only smart kid I got. Anyway, social worker only put him there till she could find him a foster home.

ARLENE: But I coulda seen him.

MOTHER: Thatta been trouble, him bein' in the family. Kid wouldn't have known who to listen to, Shirley or you.

ARLENE: But I'm his mother.

MOTHER: See, now you don't have to be worryin' about him. No kids, no worryin'.

ARLENE: He just had his birthday, you know.

ARLIE: Don't let Daddy come in here, Mama. Just you an me. Mama?

ARLENE: When I git workin', I'll git a nice rug for this place. He could come live here with me.

MOTHER: Fat chance.

ARLENE: I done my time.

MOTHER: You never really got attached to him anyway.

ARLENE: How do you know that?

MOTHER: Now don't you go gettin' het up. I'm telling you…

ARLENE: But…

MOTHER: Kids need rules to go by an he'll get 'em over there.

ARLIE: *(Screaming.)* No Daddy! I didn't tell her nuthin'. I didn't! I didn't! *(Gets up from the bed, terrified.)*

MOTHER: Here, help me with these sheets. *(Hands Arlene the sheets from the laundry basket.)* Even got you a spread. Kinda goes with them curtains. *(Arlene is silent.)*

MOTHER: You ain't thanked me, Arlie girl.

ARLENE: *(Going to the other side of the bed.)* They don't call me Arlie no more. It's Arlene now.

(Arlene and Mother make up the bed. Arlie jumps up, looks around, and goes over to Mother's purse. She looks through it hurriedly and pulls out the wallet. She takes some money and runs down left, where she is caught by a school principal.)

PRINCIPAL: Arlie? You're in an awfully big hurry for such a little girl. *(Brushes Arlie's hair.)* That is you under all that hair, isn't it? *(Arlie resists this gesture.)*

PRINCIPAL: Now, you can watch where you're going.

ARLIE: Gotta git home.

PRINCIPAL: But school isn't over for another three hours. And there's peanut butter and chili today.

ARLIE: Ain't hungry. *(Struggling free.)*

(The principal now sees Arlie's hands clenched behind her back.)

PRINCIPAL: What do we have in our hands, Arlie?

ARLIE: Nuthin'.

PRINCIPAL: Let me see your hands, Arlie. Open up your hands.

(Arlie brings her hands around in front, opening them, showing crumpled dollars.)

ARLIE: It's my money. I earned it.

PRINCIPAL: *(Taking the money.)* And how did we earn this money?

ARLIE: Doin' things.

PRINCIPAL: What kind of things?

ARLIE: For my daddy.

PRINCIPAL: Well, we'll see about that. You'll have to come with me.

(Arlie resists as the principal pulls her.)

ARLIE: No.

PRINCIPAL: Your mother was right after all. She said put you in a special school. *(Quickly.)* No, what she said was put you away somewhere and I said, no, she's too young, well I was wrong. I have four hundred other children to take care of here and what have I been doing? Breaking up your fights, talking to your truant officer and washing your writing off the bathroom

wall. Well, I've had enough. You've made your choice. You *want* out of regular school and you're going to *get* out of regular school.

ARLIE: *(Becoming more violent.)* You can't make me go nowhere, bitch!

PRINCIPAL: *(Backing off in cold anger.)* I'm not making you go. You've earned it.
You've worked hard for this, well, they're used to your type over there.
They'll know exactly what to do with you. *(She stalks off, leaving Arlie
alone.)*

MOTHER: *(Smoothing out the spread.)* Spread ain't new, but it don't look so bad.
Think we got it right after we got you. No, I remember now. I was pregnant with you an been real sick the whole time.

(Arlene lights a cigarette, Mother takes one, Arlene retrieves the pack quickly.)

MOTHER: Your daddy brung me home this big bowl of chili an some jelly
doughnuts. Some fare from the airport give him a big tip. Anyway, I'd been
eatin' peanut brittle all day, only thing that tasted any good. Then in he
come with this chili an no sooner'n I got in bed I thrown up all over everwhere. Lucky I didn't throw you up, Arlie girl. Anyhow, that's how come
us to get a new spread. This one here. *(Sits on the bed.)*

ARLENE: You drivin' the cab any?

MOTHER: Any? Your daddy ain't drove it at all a long time now. Six years, seven
maybe.

ARLENE: You meet anybody nice?

MOTHER: Not anymore. Mostly drivin' old ladies to get their shoes. Guess it got
around the nursin' homes I was reliable. *(Sounds funny to her.)* You remember that time I took you drivin' with me that night after you been in a fight
an that soldier bought us a beer? Shitty place, hole in the wall?

ARLENE: You made me wait in the car.

MOTHER: *(Standing up.)* Think I'd take a child of mine into a dump like that?

ARLENE: You went in.

MOTHER: Weren't no harm in it. *(Walking over for the bug spray.)* I didn't always
look so bad, you know.

ARLENE: You was pretty.

MOTHER: *(Beginning to spray the floor.)* You could look better'n you do. Do
somethin' with your hair. I always thought if you'd looked better you
wouldn't have got in so much trouble.

ARLENE: *(Pleased and curious.)* Joey got my hair?

MOTHER: And skinny.

ARLENE: I took some beauty school at Pine Ridge.

MOTHER: Yeah, a beautician?

ARLENE: I don't guess so.

MOTHER: Said you was gonna work.

ARLENE: They got a law here. Ex-cons can't get no license.

MOTHER: Shoulda stayed in Alabama, then. Worked there.

ARLENE: They got a law there, too.

MOTHER: Then why'd they give you the trainin'?

ARLENE: I don't know.

MOTHER: Maybe they thought it'd straighten you out.

ARLENE: Yeah.

MOTHER: But you are gonna work, right?

ARLENE: Yeah. Cookin' maybe. Somethin' that pays good.

MOTHER: You? Cook? *(Laughs.)*

ARLENE: I could learn it.

MOTHER: Your daddy ain't never forgive you for that bologna sandwich.

(Arlene laughs a little, finally enjoying a memory.)

MOTHER: Oh, I wish I'd seen you spreadin' that Colgate on that bread. He'd have smelled that toothpaste if he hadn't been so sloshed. Little snotty-nosed kid tryin' to kill her daddy with a bologna sandwich. An him bein' so pleased when you brung it to him… *(Laughing.)*

ARLENE: He beat me good.

MOTHER: Well, now, Arlie, you gotta admit you had it comin' to you. *(Wiping tears from laughing.)*

ARLENE: I guess.

MOTHER: You got a broom?

ARLENE: No.

MOTHER: Well, I got one in the cab I brung just in case. I can't leave it here, but I'll sweep up fore I go. *(Walking toward the door.)* You jus' rest till I git back. Won't find no work lookin' the way you do. *(Mother leaves.)*

(Arlene finds some lipstick and a mirror in her purse, makes an attempt to look better while Mother is gone.)

ARLIE: *(Jumps up, as if talking to another kid.)* She is not skinny!

ARLENE: *(Looking at herself in the mirror.)* I guess I could…

ARLIE: And she don't have to git them stinky permanents. Her hair just comes outta her head curly.

ARLENE: Some lipstick.

ARLIE: *(Serious.)* She drives the cab to buy us stuff, 'cause we don't take no charity from nobody, 'cause we got money 'cause she earned it.

ARLENE: *(Closing the mirror, dejected, afraid Mother might be right.)* But you're too skinny and you got stringy hair. *(Sitting on the floor.)*

ARLIE: *(More angry.)* She drives at night 'cause people needs rides at night. People goin' to see their friends that are sick, or people's cars broken down an they gotta get to work at the…nobody calls my mama a whore!

MOTHER: *(Coming back in with the broom.)* If I'd known you were gonna sweep up with your butt, I wouldn't have got this broom. Get up! *(Sweeps at Arlie to get her to move.)*

ARLIE: You're gonna take that back or I'm gonna rip out all your ugly hair and stuff it down your ugly throat.

ARLENE: *(Tugging at her own hair.)* You still cut hair?

MOTHER: *(Noticing some spot on the floor.)* Gonna take a razor blade to get out this paint.

ARLENE: Nail polish.

ARLIE: Wanna know what I know about your mama? She's dyin'. Somethin's eatin' up her insides piece by piece, only she don't want you to know it.

MOTHER: *(Continuing to sweep.)* So, you're callin' yourself Arlene, now?

ARLENE: Yes.

MOTHER: Don't want your girlie name no more?

ARLENE: Somethin' like that.

MOTHER: They call you Arlene in prison?

ARLENE: Not at first when I was bein' hateful. Just my number then.

MOTHER: You always been hateful.

ARLENE: There was this chaplain, he called me Arlene from the first day he come to talk to me. Here, let me help you. *(She reaches for the broom.)*

MOTHER: I'll do it.

ARLENE: You kin rest.

MOTHER: Since when?

(Arlene backs off.)

MOTHER: I ain't hateful, how come I got so many hateful kids? *(Sweeping harder now.)* Poor dumb-as-hell Pat, stealin' them wigs, Candy screwin' since day one, Pete cuttin' up ol' Mac down at the grocery, June sellin' dope like it was Girl Scout cookies, and you…thank God I can't remember it all.

ARLENE: *(A very serious request.)* Maybe I could come out on Sunday for…you still make that pot roast?

MOTHER: *(Now sweeping over by the picture of Jesus.)* That your picture?

ARLENE: That chaplain give it to me.

MOTHER: The one give you your "new name."

ARLENE: Yes.

MOTHER: It's crooked. *(Doesn't straighten it.)*

ARLENE: I liked those potatoes with no skins. An that ketchup squirter we had, jus' like in a real restaurant.

MOTHER: People that run them institutions now, they jus' don't know how to teach kids right. Let 'em run around an get in more trouble. They should get you up at the crack of dawn an set you to scrubbin' the floor. That's what kids need. Trainin'. Hard work.

ARLENE: *(A clear request.)* I'll probably git my Sundays off.

MOTHER: Sunday…is my day to clean house now.

(Arlene gets the message, finally walks over to straighten the picture. Mother now feels a little bad about this rejection, stops sweeping for a moment.)

MOTHER: I woulda wrote you but I didn't have nuthin' to say. An no money to send, so what's the use?

ARLENE: I made out.

MOTHER: They pay you for workin'?

ARLENE: 'Bout three dollars a month.

MOTHER: How'd you make it on three dollars a month? *(Answers her own question.)* You do some favors?

ARLENE: *(Sitting down in the chair under the picture, a somewhat smug look.)* You jus' can't make it by yourself.

MOTHER: *(Pauses, suspicious, then contemptuous.)* You play, Arlie?

ARLENE: You don't know nuthin' about that.

MOTHER: I hear things. Girls callin' each other "mommy" an bringin' things back from the canteen for their "husbands." Makes me sick. You got family, Arlie, what you want with that playin'? Don't want nobody like that in my house.

ARLENE: You don't know what you're talkin' about.

MOTHER: I still got two kids at home. Don't want no bad example. *(Not finishing the sweeping. Has all the dirt in one place, but doesn't get it up off the floor yet.)*

ARLENE: I could tell them some things.

MOTHER: *(Vicious.)* Like about that cab driver.

ARLENE: Look, that was a long time ago. I wanna work, now, make somethin' of myself. I learned to knit. People'll buy nice sweaters. Make some extra money.

MOTHER: We sure could use it.

ARLENE: An then if I have money, maybe they'd let me take Joey to the fair, buy him hot dogs an talk to him. Make sure he ain't foolin' around.

MOTHER: What makes you think he'd listen to you? Alice, across the street? Her sister took care her kids while she was at Lexington. You think they pay any attention to her now? Ashamed, that's what. One of 'em told me his mother done died. Gone to see a friend and died there.

ARLENE: Be different with me and Joey.

MOTHER: He don't even know who you are, Arlie.

ARLENE: *(Wearily.)* Arlene.

MOTHER: You forgot already what you was like as a kid. At Waverly, tellin' them lies about that campin' trip we took, sayin' your daddy made you watch while he an me… you know. I'd have killed you then if them social workers hadn't been watchin'.

ARLENE: Yeah.

MOTHER: Didn't want them thinkin' I weren't fit. Well, what do they know? Each time you'd get out of one of them places, you'd be actin' worse than ever. Go right back to that junkie, pimp, Carl, sellin' the stuff he steals, savin' his ass from the police. He follow you home this time, too?

ARLENE: He's got four more years at Bricktown.

MOTHER: Glad to hear it. Here… *(Handing her a bucket.)* Water.
(Arlene fills up the bucket and Mother washes several dirty spots on the walls, floor, and furniture. Arlene knows better than to try to help. The doctor walks downstage to find Arlie for their counseling session.)

DOCTOR: So you refuse to go to camp?

ARLIE: Now why'd I want to go to your fuckin' camp? Camp's for babies. You can go shit in the woods if you want to, but I ain't goin'.

DOCTOR: Oh, you're goin'.

ARLIE: Wanna bet?

MOTHER: Arlie, I'm waitin'. *(For the water.)*

ARLIE: 'Sides, I'm waitin'.

DOCTOR: Waiting for what?

ARLIE: For Carl to come git me.

DOCTOR: And who is Carl?

ARLIE: Jus' some guy. We're goin' to Alabama.

DOCTOR: You don't go till we say you can go.

ARLIE: Carls got a car.

DOCTOR: Does he have a driver's license to go with it?

ARLIE: *(Enraged, impatient.)* I'm goin' now.

(Arlie stalks away, then backs up toward the doctor again. He has information she wants.)

DOCTOR: Hey!

ARLENE: June picked out a name for the baby?

MOTHER: Clara…or Clarence. Got it from this fancy shampoo she bought.

ARLIE: I don't feel good. I'm pregnant, you know.

DOCTOR: The test was negative.

ARLIE: Well, I should know, shouldn't I?

DOCTOR: No. You want to be pregnant, is that it?

ARLIE: I wouldn't mind. Kids need somebody to bring 'em up right.

DOCTOR: Raising children is a big responsibility, you know.

ARLIE: Yeah, I know it. I ain't dumb. Everybody always thinks I'm so dumb.

DOCTOR: You could learn if you wanted to. That's what the teachers are here for.

ARLIE: Shit.

DOCTOR: Or so they say.

ARLIE: All they teach us is about geography. Why'd I need to know about Africa. Jungles and shit.

DOCTOR: They want you to know about other parts of the world.

ARLIE: Well, I ain't goin' there so whatta I care?

DOCTOR: What's this about Cindy?

ARLIE: *(Hostile.)* She told Mr. Dawson some lies about me.

DOCTOR: I bet.

ARLIE: She said I fuck my daddy for money.

DOCTOR: And what did you do when she said that?

ARLIE: What do you think I did? I beat the shit out of her.

DOCTOR: And that's a good way to work out your problem?

ARLIE: *(Proudly.)* She ain't done it since.

DOCTOR: She's been in traction, since.

ARLIE: So, whatta I care? She say it again, I'll do it again. Bitch!

ARLENE: *(Looking down at the dirt Mother is gathering on the floor.)* I ain't got a can. Just leave it.

MOTHER: And have you sweep it under the bed after I go? *(Wraps the dirt in a piece of newspaper and puts it in her laundry basket.)*

DOCTOR: *(Looking at his clipboard.)* You're on unit cleanup this week.

ARLIE: I done it last week!

DOCTOR: Then you should remember what to do. The session is over. *(Getting up, walking away.)* And stand up straight! And take off that hat! *(Doctor and Arlie go offstage as Mother finds Bennie's hat.)*

MOTHER: This your hat?

ARLENE: No.

MOTHER: Guess Candy left it here.

ARLENE: Candy didn't leave nuthin'.

MOTHER: Then whose is it?

(Arlene doesn't answer.)

MOTHER: Do you know whose hat this is?

(Arlene knows she made a mistake.)

MOTHER: I'm askin' you a question and I want an answer.

(Arlene turns her back.)

MOTHER: Whose hat is this? You tell me right now, whose hat is this?

ARLENE: It's Bennie's.

MOTHER: And who's Bennie?

ARLENE: Guy drove me home from Pine Ridge. A guard.

MOTHER: *(Upset.)* I knew it. You been screwin' a goddamn guard. *(Throws the hat on the bed.)*

ARLENE: He jus' drove me up here, that's all.

MOTHER: Sure.

ARLENE: I git sick on the bus.

MOTHER: You expect me to believe that?

ARLENE: I'm tellin' you, he jus'—

MOTHER: No man alive gonna drive a girl five hundred miles for nuthin'.

ARLENE: He ain't never seen Kentucky.

MOTHER: It ain't Kentucky he wants to see.

ARLENE: He ain't gettin' nuthin' from me.

MOTHER: That's what you think.

ARLENE: He done some nice things for me at Pine Ridge. Gum, funny stories.

MOTHER: He'd be tellin' stories all right, tellin' his buddies where to find you.

ARLENE: He's gettin' us some dinner right now.

MOTHER: And how're you gonna pay him? Huh? Tell me that.

ARLENE: I ain't like that no more.

MOTHER: Oh you ain't. I'm your mother. I know what you'll do.

ARLENE: I tell you I ain't.

MOTHER: I knew it. Well, when you got another bastard in you, don't come cryin' to me, 'cause I done told you.

ARLENE: Don't worry.

MOTHER: An I'm gettin' myself outta here fore your boyfriend comes back.

ARLENE: *(Increasing anger.)* He ain't my boyfriend.

MOTHER: I been a lotta things, but I ain't dumb, Arlene. *("Arlene" is mocking.)*

ARLENE: I didn't say you was. *(Beginning to know how this is going to turn out.)*

MOTHER: Oh no? You lied to me!

ARLENE: How?

MOTHER: You took my spread without even sayin' thank you. You're hintin' at comin' to my house for pot roast just like nuthin' ever happened, an all the time you're hidin' a goddamn guard under your bed. *(Furious.)* Uh-huh.

ARLENE: *(Quietly.)* Mama?

MOTHER: *(Cold, fierce.)* What?

ARLENE: What kind of meat makes a pot roast?

MOTHER: A roast makes a pot roast. Buy a roast. Shoulder, chuck…

ARLENE: Are you comin' back?

MOTHER: You ain't got no need for me.

ARLENE: I gotta ask you to come see me?

MOTHER: I come tonight, didn't I, an nobody asked me?

ARLENE: Just forget it.

MOTHER: *(Getting her things together.)* An if I hadn't told them about this apartment, you wouldn't be out at all, how 'bout that!

ARLENE: Forgit it!

MOTHER: Don't you go talkin' to me that way. You remember who I am. I'm the one took you back after all you done all them years. I brung you that teapot. I scrubbed your place. You remember that when you talk to me.

ARLENE: Sure.

MOTHER: Uh-huh. *(Now goes to the bed, rips off the spread and stuffs it in her basket.)* I knowed I shouldn't have come. You ain't changed a bit.

ARLENE: Same hateful brat, right?

MOTHER: *(Arms full, heading for the door.)* Same hateful brat. Right.

ARLENE: *(Rushing toward her.)* Mama…

MOTHER: Don't you touch me.

(Mother leaves. Arlene stares out the door, stunned and hurt. Finally, she slams the door and turns back into the room.)

ARLENE: No! Don't you touch Mama, Arlie.

(Ronnie, a fellow juvenile offender, runs across the catwalk, wearing a necklace and being chased by Arlie.)

RONNIE: Arlie got a boyfriend, Arlie got a boyfriend. *(Throws the necklace downstage.)* Whoo!

ARLIE: *(Chasing him.)* Ronnie, you ugly mother, I'll smash your fuckin'—

ARLENE: *(Getting more angry.)* You might steal all—

RONNIE: *(Running down the stairs.)* Arlie got a boyfriend…

ARLIE: Gimme that necklace or I'll—

ARLENE: —or eat all Mama's precious pot roast.

RONNIE: *(As they wrestle downstage.)* You'll tell the doctor on me? And get your private room back? *(Laughing.)*

ARLENE: *(Cold and hostile.)* No, don't touch Mama, Arlie. 'Cause you might slit Mama's throat. *(Goes into the bathroom.)*

ARLIE: You wanna swallow all them dirty teeth?

RONNIE: Tell me who give it to you.

ARLIE: No, you tell me where it's at.

(Ronnie breaks away, pushing Arlie in the opposite direction, and runs for the necklace.)

RONNIE: It's right here. *(Drops it down his pants.)* Come an git it.

ARLIE: Oh now, that was really ignorant, you stupid pig.

RONNIE: *(Backing away, daring her.)* Jus' reach right in. First come, first served.

ARLIE: Now, how you gonna pee after I throw your weenie over the fence?

RONNIE: You ain't gonna do that, girl. You gonna fall in love.

(Arlie turns vicious, pins Ronnie down, attacking. This is no longer play. He screams. The doctor appears on the catwalk.)

DOCTOR: Arlie! *(Heads down the stairs to stop this.)*

CARL'S VOICE: *(From outside the apartment door.)* Arlie!

DOCTOR: Arlie!

ARLIE: Stupid, ugly—

RONNIE: Help!

(Arlie runs away and hides down left.)

DOCTOR: That's three more weeks of isolation, Arlie. *(Bending down Ronnie.)* You all right? Can you walk?

RONNIE: *(Looking back to Arlie as he gets up in great pain.)* She was tryin' to kill me.

DOCTOR: Yeah. Easy now. You should've known, Ronnie.

ARLIE: *(Yelling at Ronnie.)* You'll get yours, crybaby.

CARL'S VOICE: Arlie…

ARLIE: Yeah, I'm comin'!

CARL'S VOICE: Bad-lookin' dude says move your ass an open up this here door, girl.

(Arlene does not come out of the bathroom. Carl twists the door knob violently, then kicks in the door and walks in. Carl is thin and cheaply dressed. Carl's walk and manner are imitative of black pimps, but he can't quite carry it off.)

CARL: Where you at, mama?

ARLENE: Carl?

CARL: Who else? You 'spectin' Leroy Brown?

ARLENE: I'm takin' a bath!

CARL: *(Walking toward the bathroom.)* I like my ladies clean. Matter of professional pride.

ARLENE: Don't come in here.

CARL: *(Mocking her tone.)* Don't come in here. I seen it all before, girl.

ARLENE: I'm gittin' out. Sit down or somethin'.

CARL: *(Talking loud enough for her to hear him through the door.)* Ain't got the time. *(Opens her purse, then searches the trunk.)* Jus' come by to tell you it's tomorrow. We be takin' our feet to the New York street. *(As though she will be pleased.)* No more fuckin' around with these jiveass southern turkeys. We're goin' to the big city, baby. Get you some red shades and some red shorts an' the johns be linin' up fore we hit town. Four tricks a night. How's that sound? No use wearin' out that cute ass you got. Way I hear it, only way to git busted up there's be stupid, an I ain't lived this long bein' stupid.

ARLENE: *(Coming out of the bathroom wearing a towel.)* That's exactly how you lived your whole life—bein' stupid.

CARL: Arlie... *(Moving in on her.)* be sweet, sugar.

ARLENE: Still got your curls.

CARL: *(Trying to hug her.)* You're looking okay yourself.

ARLENE: Oh, Carl. *(Noticing the damage to the door, breaking away from any closeness he might try to force.)*

CARL: *(Amused.)* Bent up your door, some.

ARLENE: How come you're out?

CARL: Sweetheart, you done broke out once, been nabbed and sent to Pine Ridge and got yourself paroled since I been in. I got a right to a little free time too, ain't that right?

ARLENE: You escape?

CARL: Am I standin' here or am I standin' here? They been fuckin' with you, I can tell.

ARLENE: They gonna catch you.

CARL: *(Going to the window.)* Not where we're going. Not a chance.

ARLENE: Where you goin' they won't git you?

CARL: Remember that green hat you picked out for me down in Birmingham? Well, I ain't ever wore it yet, but I kin wear it in New York 'cause New York's where you wear whatever you feel like. One guy tol' me he saw this dude wearin' a whole ring of feathers roun' his leg, right here *(Grabs his leg above the knee.)* an he weren't in no circus nor no Indian neither.

ARLENE: I ain't seen you since Birmingham. How come you think I wanna see you now?

(Arlie appears suddenly, confronts Carl.)

ARLIE: *(Pointing as if there is a trick waiting.)* Carl, I ain't goin' with that dude, he's weird.

CARL: 'Cause we gotta go collect the johns' money, that's "how come."

ARLIE: I don't need you pimpin' for me.

ARLENE: *(Very strong.)* I'm gonna work.

CARL: Work?

ARLENE: Yeah.

CARL: What's this "work"?

ARLIE: You always sendin' me to them ol' droolers...

CARL: You kin do two things, girl—

ARLIE: They slobberin' all over me.

CARL: Breakin' out an hookin'.

ARLIE: They tyin' me to the bed!

ARLENE: I mean real work.

ARLIE: *(Now screaming, gets further away from him.)* I could git killed working for you. Some sicko, some crazy drunk...

(Arlie goes offstage. A guard puts her in the cell sometime before Bennie's entrance.)

CARL: You forget, we seen it all on TV in the day room, you bustin' outta Lakewood like that. Fakin' that palsy fit, then beatin' that guard half to death with his own key ring. Whoo-ee! Then that spree you went on... stoppin' at that fillin' station for some cash, then kidnappin' the old dude pumpin' the gas.

ARLENE: Yeah.

CARL: Then that cab driver comes outta the bathroom an tries to mess with you and you shoots him with his own piece. *(Fires an imaginary pistol.)* That there's nice work, mama. *(Going over to her, putting his arms around her.)*

ARLENE: That gun...it went off, Carl.

CARL: *(Getting more determined with his affection.)* That's what guns do, doll. They go off.

BENNIE'S VOICE: *(From outside.)* Arlene? Arlene?

CARL: Arlene? *(Jumping up.)* Well, la-de-da.

(Bennie opens the door, carrying the chicken dinners. He is confused, seeing Arlene wearing a towel and talking to Carl.)

ARLENE: Bennie, this here's Carl.

CARL: You're interruptin', Jack. Me an Arlie got business.

BENNIE: She's callin' herself Arlene.

CARL: I call my ladies what I feel like, chicken man, an you call yourself "gone."

BENNIE: I don't take orders from you.

CARL: Well, you been takin' orders from somebody, or did you git that outfit at the army surplus store?

ARLENE: Bennie brung me home from Pine Ridge.

CARL: *(Walking toward him.)* Oh, it's a guard now, is it? That chicken break out or what? *(Grabs the chicken.)*

BENNIE: I don't know what you're doin' here, but—

CARL: What you gonna do about it, huh? Lock me up in the toilet? You an who else, Batman?

BENNIE: *(Taking the chicken back, walking calmly to the counter.)* Watch your mouth, punk.

CARL: *(Kicks a chair toward Bennie.)* Punk!

ARLENE: *(Trying to stop this.)* I'm hungry.

BENNIE: You heard her, she's hungry.

CARL: *(Vicious.)* Shut up! *(Mocking.)* Ossifer.

BENNIE: Arlene, tell this guy if he knows what's good for him…

CARL: *(Walking to the counter where Bennie has left the chicken.)* Why don't you write me a parkin' ticket? *(Shoves the chicken on the floor.)* Don't fuck with me, dad. It ain't healthy.

(Bennie pauses. A real standoff. Finally, Bennie bends down and picks up the chicken.)

BENNIE: You ain't worth dirtyin' my hands.

(Carl walks by him, laughing.)

CARL: Hey, Arlie. I got some dude to see. *(For Bennie's benefit as he struts to the door.)* What I need with another beat-up guard? All that blood, jus' ugly up my threads. *(Very sarcastic.)* Bye y'all.

ARLENE: Bye, Carl.

(Carl turns back quickly at the door, stopping Bennie, who was following him.)

CARL: You really oughta shine them shoes, man. *(Vindictive laugh, slams the door in Bennie's face.)*

BENNIE: *(Relieved, trying to change the atmosphere.)* Well, how 'bout if we eat? You'll catch your death dressed like that.

ARLENE: Turn around then. *(Arlene gets a shabby housecoat from the closet. She puts it on over her towel, buttons it up, then pulls the towel out from under it. This has the look of a prison ritual.)*

BENNIE: *(As she is dressing.)* Your parole officer's gonna tell you to keep away from guys like that…for your own good, you know. Those types, just like the suckers on my tomatoes back home. Take everything right outta you. Gotta pull 'em off, Arlie, uh, Arlene.

ARLENE: Now, I'm decent now.

BENNIE: You hear what I said?

ARLENE: *(Going to the bathroom for her hairbrush.)* I told him that. That's exactly what I did tell him.

BENNIE: Who was that anyhow? *(Sits down on the bed, opens up the chicken.)*

ARLENE: *(From the bathroom.)* Long time ago, me an Carl took a trip together.

BENNIE: When you was a kid, you mean?

ARLENE: I was at this place for kids.

BENNIE: And Carl was there?

ARLENE: No, he picked me up an we went to Alabama. There was this wreck an all. I ended up at Lakewood for forgery. It was him that done it. Got me pregnant too.

BENNIE: That was Joey's father?

ARLENE: Yeah, but he don't know that. *(Sits down.)*

BENNIE: Just as well. Guy like that, don't know what they'd do.

ARLENE: Mother was here while ago. Says she's seen Joey. *(Taking a napkin from Bennie.)*

BENNIE: Wish I had a kid. Life ain't, well, complete, without no kids to play ball with an take fishin'. Dorrie, though, she had them backaches an that neuralgia, day I married her to the day she died. Good woman though. No drinkin', no card playin', real sweet voice…what was that song she used to sing?…Oh, yeah…

ARLENE: She says Joey's a real good-lookin' kid.

BENNIE: Well, his mom ain't bad.

ARLENE: At Lakewood, they tried to git me to have an abortion.

BENNIE: They was just thinkin' of you, Arlene.

ARLENE: *(Matter-of-fact, no self-pity.)* I told 'em I'd kill myself if they done that. I would have too.

BENNIE: But they took him away after he was born.

ARLENE: Yeah.

(Bennie waits, knowing she is about to say more.)

ARLENE: An I guess I went crazy after that. Thought if I could jus' git out an find him...

BENNIE: I don't remember any of that on the TV.

ARLENE: No.

BENNIE: Just remember you smilin' at the cameras, yellin' how you tol' that cab driver not to touch you.

ARLENE: I never seen his cab. *(Forces herself to eat.)*

ARLIE: *(In the cell, holding a pillow and singing.)* Rock-a-bye baby, in the tree top, when the wind blows, the cradle will... *(Not remembering.)* cradle will... *(Now talking.)* What you gonna be when you grow up, pretty boy baby? You gonna be a doctor? You gonna give people medicine an take out they... no, don't be no doctor...be...be a preacher...sayin' Our Father who is in heaven...heaven, that's where people go when they dies, when doctors can't save 'em or somebody kills 'em fore they even git a chance to...no, don't be no preacher neither...be...go to school an learn good *(Tone begins to change.)* so you kin...make everbody else feel so stupid all the time. Best thing you to be is stay a baby 'cause nobody beats up on babies or puts them... *(Much more quiet.)* that ain't true, baby. People is mean to babies, so you stay right here with me so nobody kin git you an make you cry an they lay one finger on you *(Hostile.)* an I'll beat the screamin' shit right out of 'em. They even blow on you an I'll kill 'em.

(Bennie and Arlene have finished their dinner. Bennie puts one carton of slaw in the refrigerator, then picks up all the paper, making a garbage bag out of one of the sacks.)

BENNIE: Ain't got a can, I guess. Jus' use this ol' sack for now.

ARLENE: I ain't never emptyin' another garbage can.

BENNIE: Yeah, I reckon you know how by now. *(Yawns.)* You 'bout ready for bed?

ARLENE: *(Stands up.)* I s'pose.

BENNIE: *(Stretches.)* Little tired myself.

ARLENE: *(Dusting the crumbs off the bed.)* Thanks for the chicken.

BENNIE: You're right welcome. You look beat. How 'bout I rub your back. *(Grabs her shoulders.)*

ARLENE: *(Pulling away.)* No. *(Walking to the sink.)* You go on now.

BENNIE: Oh come on. *(Wiping his hands on his pants.)* I ain't all that tired.

ARLENE: *I'm* tired.

BENNIE: Well, see then, a back rub is just what the doctor ordered.

ARLENE: No. I don't... *(Pulling away.)*

(Bennie grabs her shoulders and turns her around, sits her down hard on the trunk, starts rubbing her back and neck.)

BENNIE: Muscles git real tightlike, right in here.

ARLENE: You hurtin' me.

BENNIE: Has to hurt a little or it won't do no good.

ARLENE: *(Jumps, he has hurt her.)* Oh, stop it! *(She slips away from him and out into the room. She is frightened.)*

BENNIE: *(Smiling, coming after her, toward the bed.)* Be lot nicer if you was layin' down. Wouldn't hurt as much.

ARLENE: Now, I ain't gonna start yellin'. I'm jus' tellin' you to go.

BENNIE: *(Straightens up as though he's going to cooperate.)* Okay then. I'll jus' git my hat.

(He reaches for the hat, then turns quickly, grabs her and throws her down on the bed. He starts rubbing again.)

BENNIE: Now, you just relax. Don't you go bein' scared of me.

ARLENE: You ain't gettin' nuthin' from me.

BENNIE: I don't want nuthin', honey. Jus' tryin' to help you sleep.

ARLENE: *(Struggling.)* Don't you call me honey.

(Bennie stops rubbing, but keeps one hand on her back. He rubs her hair with his free hand.)

BENNIE: See? Don't that feel better?

ARLENE: Let me up.

BENNIE: Why, I ain't holdin' you down.

ARLENE: Then let me up.

BENNIE: *(Takes hands off.)* Okay. Git up.

(Arlene turns over slowly, begins to lift herself up on her elbows. Bennie puts one hand on her leg.)

ARLENE: Move your hand. *(She gets up, moves across the room.)*

BENNIE: I'd be happy to stay here with you tonight. Make sure you'll be all right. You ain't spent a night by yourself for a long time.

ARLENE: I remember how.

BENNIE: Well how you gonna git up? You got a alarm?

ARLENE: It ain't all that hard.

BENNIE: *(Puts one hand in his pocket, leers a little.)* Oh yeah it is. *(Walks toward her again.)* Gimme a kiss. Then I'll go.

ARLENE: *(Edging along the counter, seeing she's trapped.)* You stay away from me. *(Bennie reaches for her, clamping her hands behind her, pressing up against her.)*

BENNIE: Now what's it going to hurt you to give me a little ol' kiss?

ARLENE: *(Struggling.)* Git out! I said git out!

BENNIE: You don't want me to go. You're jus' beginning to git interested. Your ol' girlie temper's flarin' up. I like that in a woman.

ARLENE: Yeah, you'd love it if I'd swat you one. *(Getting away from him.)*

BENNIE: I been hit by you before. I kin take anything you got.

ARLENE: I could mess you up good.

BENNIE: Now, Arlie. You ain't had a man in a long time. And the ones you had been no-count.

ARLENE: Git out!

(She slaps him. He returns the slap.)

BENNIE: *(Moving in.)* Ain't natural goin' without it too long. Young thing like you. Git all shriveled up.

ARLENE: All right, you sunuvabitch, you asked for it!

(She goes into a violent rage, hitting and kicking him. Bennie overpowers her capably, prison-guard style.)

BENNIE: *(Amused.)* Little outta practice, ain't you?

ARLENE: *(Screaming.)* I'll kill you, you creep!

(The struggle continues, Bennie pinning her arms under his legs as he kneels over her on the bed. Arlene is terrified and in pain.)

BENNIE: You will? You'll kill ol' Bennie...kill ol' Bennie like you done that cab driver?

(A cruel reminder he employs to stun and mock her. Arlene looks as though she has been hit. Bennie, still fired up, unzips his pants.)

ARLENE: *(Passive, cold and bitter.)* This how you got your Dorrie, rapin'?

BENNIE: *(Unbuttoning his shirt.)* That what you think this is, rape?

ARLENE: I oughta know.

BENNIE: Uh-huh.

ARLENE: First they unzip their pants.

(Bennie pulls his shirttail out.)

ARLENE: Sometimes they take off their shirt.

BENNIE: They do huh?

ARLENE: But mostly, they just pull it out and stick it in.

(Bennie stops, finally hearing what she has been saying. He straightens up, obviously shocked. He puts his arms back in his shirt.)

BENNIE: Don't you call me no rapist. *(Pause, then insistent.)* No, I ain't no rapist, Arlie. *(Gets up, begins to tuck his shirt back in and zip up his pants.)*

ARLENE: And I ain't Arlie.

(Arlene remains on the bed as he continues dressing.)
BENNIE: No I guess you ain't.
ARLENE: *(Quietly and painfully.)* Arlie coulda killed you.

END OF ACT I

PROLOGUE

These announcements are heard during the last five minutes of the intermission.

LOUDSPEAKER VOICE: Garden workers will, repeat, will, report for work this afternoon. Bring a hat and raincoat and wear boots. All raincoats will be checked at the front gate at the end of work period and returned to you after supper.

Your attention please. A checkerboard was not returned to the recreation area after dinner last night. Anyone with information regarding the black and red checkerboard missing from the recreation area will please contact Mrs. Duvall after lunch. No checkerboards or checkers will be distributed until this board is returned.

Betty Rickey and Mary Alice Wolf report to the laundry. Doris Creech and Arlie Holsclaw report immediately to the superintendent's office. The movie this evening will be *Dirty Harry* starring Clint Eastwood. Doris Creech and Arlie Holsclaw report to the superintendent's office immediately.

The bus from St. Mary's this Sunday will arrive at 1:00 P.M. as usual. Those residents expecting visitors on that bus will gather on the front steps promptly at 1:20 and proceed with the duty officer to the visiting area after it has been confirmed that you have a visitor on the bus.

Attention all residents. Attention all residents. *(Pause.)* Mrs. Helen Carson has taught needlework classes here at Pine Ridge for thirty years. She will be retiring at the end of this month and moving to Florida where her husband has bought a trailer park. The resident council and the superintendent's staff has decided on a suitable retirement present. We want every resident to participate in this project—which is—a quilt, made from scraps of material collected from the residents and sewn together by residents and staff alike. The procedure will be as follows. A quilting room has been set up in an empty storage area just off the infirmary. Scraps of fabric will be collected as officers do evening count. Those residents who would enjoy cutting up old uniforms and bedding no longer in use should sign up for this detail with your dorm officer. If you would like to sign your name or send Mrs. Carson some special message on your square of fabric, the officers will have tubes of embroidery paint for that purpose. The backing for the quilt has been donated by the Women's Associates as well as the refreshments for the retirement party to be held after lunch on the thirtieth.

Thank you very much for your attention and participation in this worth-while tribute to someone we are all very fond of here. You may resume work at this time. Doris Creech and Arlie Holsclaw report to the superin-tendent's office immediately.

ACT II

Lights fade. When they come up, it is the next morning. Arlene is asleep on the bed. Arlie is locked in a maximum-security cell. We do not see the officer to whom she speaks.

ARLIE: No, I don't have to shut up, neither. You already got me in seg-re-ga-tion, what else you gonna do? I got all day to sleep, while everybody else is out bustin' ass in the laundry. *(Laughs.)* Hey! I know…you ain't gotta go do no dorm count, I'll just tell you an you jus' sit. Huh? You 'preciate that? Ease them corns you been moanin' about…yeah…okay. Write this down. *(Pride, mixed with alternating contempt and amusement.)* Startin' down by the john on the back side, we got Mary Alice. Sleeps with her pillow stuffed in her mouth. Says her mom says it'd keep her from grindin' down her teeth or somethin'. She be suckin' that pillow like she gettin' paid for it. *(Laughs.)* Next, it's Betty the Frog. Got her legs all opened out like some fuckin'… *(Makes croaking noises.)* Then it's Doris eatin' pork rinds. Thinks somebody gonna grab 'em outta her mouth if she eats 'em during the day. Doris ain't dumb. She fat, but she ain't dumb. Hey! You notice how many girls is fat here? Then it be Rhonda, snorin', Marvene, wheezin', and Suzanne, coughin'. Then Clara an Ellie be still whisperin'. Family shit, who's gettin' outta line, which girls is gittin' a new work 'signment, an who kin git extra desserts an for how much. Them's the two really run this place. My bed right next to Ellie, for sure it's got some of her shit hid in it by now. Crackers or some crap gonna leak out all over my sheets. Last time I found a fuckin' grilled cheese in my pillow. Even had two of them little warty pickles. Christ! Okay. Linda and Lucille. They be real quiet, but they ain't sleepin'. Prayin', that's them. Linda be sayin' them Hell Marys till you kin just about scream. An Lucille, she tol' me once she didn't believe in no God, jus' some stupid spirits whooshin' aroun' everwhere makin' people do stuff. Weird. Now, I'm goin' back down the other side, there's… *(Screams.)* I'd like to see you try it! I been listenin' at you for the last three hours. Your husband's gettin' laid off an your lettuce is gettin' eat by rabbits. Crap City. *You* shut up! Whadda I care if I wake everybody up? I want the nurse...I'm gittin' sick in here...an there's bugs in here!

(The light comes up in the apartment. Faint morning traffic sounds are heard. Arlene does not wake up. The warden walks across the catwalk. A guard catches up with him near Arlie's cell. Bennie is stationed at the far end of the walk.)

LOUDSPEAKER VOICE: Dorm A may now eat lunch.

GUARD (EVANS): Warden, I thought 456... *(Nodding in Arlie's direction.)* was leavin' here.

WARDEN: Is there some problem?

GUARD (EVANS): Oh, we can take care of her all right. We're just tired of takin' her shit, if you'll pardon the expression.

ARLIE: You ain't seen nuthin' yet, you mother.

WARDEN: Washington will decide on her transfer. Till then, you do your job.

GUARD (EVANS): She don't belong here. Rest of—

LOUDSPEAKER VOICE: Betty Rickey and Mary Alice Wolf report to the laundry.

GUARD (EVANS): Most of these girls are mostly nice people, go along with things. She needs a cage.

ARLIE: *(Vicious.)* I need a knife.

WARDEN: *(Very curt.)* Had it occurred to you that we could send the rest of them home and just keep her? *(Walks away.)*

LOUDSPEAKER VOICE: Dorm A may now eat lunch. A Dorm to lunch.

GUARD (EVANS): *(Turning around, muttering to himself.)* Oh, that's a swell idea. Let everybody out except bitches like Holsclaw. *(She makes an obscene gesture at him, he turns back toward the catwalk.)* Smartass warden, thinks he's runnin' a hotel.

BENNIE: Give you some trouble, did she?

GUARD (EVANS): I can wait.

BENNIE: For what?

GUARD (EVANS): For the day she tries gettin' out an I'm here by myself. I'll show that screechin' slut a thing or two.

BENNIE: That ain't the way, Evans.

GUARD (EVANS): The hell it ain't. Beat the livin'—

BENNIE: Outta a little thing like her? Gotta do her like all the rest. You got your shorts washed by givin' Betty Rickey Milky Ways. You git your chairs fixed givin' Frankie Hill extra time in the shower with Lucille Smith. An you git ol' Arlie girl to behave herself with a stick of gum. Gotta have her brand, though.

GUARD (EVANS): You screwin' that wildcat?

BENNIE: *(Starts walk to Arlie's cell.)* Watch.

(Arlie is silent as he approaches, but is watching intently.)

BENNIE: Now, *(To nobody in particular.)* where was that piece of Juicy Fruit I had in this pocket. Gotta be here somewhere. *(Takes a piece of gum out of his pocket and drops it within Arlie's reach.)* Well, *(Feigning disappointment.)* I guess I already chewed it.

(Arlie reaches for the gum and gets it.)

BENNIE: Oh, *(Looking down at her now.)* how's it goin', kid?

ARLIE: Okay.

(Arlie says nothing more, but unwraps the gum and chews it. Bennie leaves the cell area, motioning to the other guard as if to say, "See, that's how it's done." A loud siren goes by in the street below the apartment. Arlene bolts up out of bed, then turns back to it quickly, making it up in a frenzied, ritual manner. As she tucks the spread up under the pillow, the siren stops and so does she. For the first time, now, she realizes where she is and the inappropriateness of the habit she has just played out. A jackhammer noise gets louder. She walks over to the window and looks out. There is a wolf whistle from a worker below. She shuts the window in a fury. She looks around the room as if trying to remember what she is doing there. She looks at her watch, now aware that it is late and that she has slept in her clothes.)

ARLENE: People don't sleep in their clothes, Arlene. An people git up fore noon.

(Arlene makes a still-disoriented attempt to pull herself together—changing shoes, combing her hair, washing her face—as prison life continues on the catwalk. The warden walks toward Arlie, stopping some distance from her but talking directly to her, as he checks files or papers.)

WARDEN: Good afternoon, Arlie.

ARLIE: Fuck you.

(Warden walks away.)

ARLIE: Wait! I wanna talk to you.

WARDEN: I'm listening.

ARLIE: When am I gittin' outta here?

WARDEN: That's up to you.

ARLIE: The hell it is.

WARDEN: When you can show that you can be with the other girls, you can get out.

ARLIE: How'm I supposed to prove that bein' in here?

WARDEN: And then you can have mail again and visitors.

ARLIE: You're just fuckin' with me. You ain't ever gonna let me out. I been in this ad-just-ment room four months, I think.

WARDEN: Arlie, you see the other girls in the dorm walking around, free to do whatever they want? If we felt the way you seem to think we do, everyone would be in lockup. When you get out of segregation, you can go to the records office and have your time explained to you.

ARLIE: It won't make no sense.

WARDEN: They'll go through it all very slowly...when you're eligible for parole, how many days of good time you have, how many industrial days you've earned, what constitutes meritorious good time...and how many days you're set back for your write-ups and all your time in segregation.

ARLIE: I don't even remember what I done to git this lockup.

WARDEN: Well, I do. And if you ever do it again, or anything like it again, you'll be right back in lockup where you will stay until you forget how to do it.

ARLIE: What was it?

WARDEN: You just remember what I said.

ARLENE: Now then... (*Sounds as if she has something in mind to do. Looks as though she doesn't.*)

ARLIE: What was it?

WARDEN: Oh, and Arlie, the prison chaplain will be coming by to visit you today.

ARLIE: I don't want to see no chaplain!

WARDEN: Did I ask you if you wanted to see the chaplain? No, I did not. I said, the chaplain will be coming by to visit you today. (*To an unseen guard.*) Mrs. Roberts, why hasn't this light bulb been replaced?

ARLIE: (*Screaming.*) Get out of my hall!

(*The warden walks away. Arlene walks to the refrigerator and opens it. She picks out the carton of slaw Bennie put there last night. She walks away from the door, then turns around, remembering to close it. She looks at the slaw, as a guard comes up to Arlie's cell with a plate.*)

ARLENE: I ain't never eatin' no more scrambled eggs.

GUARD (CALDWELL): Chow time, cutie pie.

ARLIE: These eggs ain't scrambled, they's throwed up! And I want a fork!

(*Arlene realizes she has no fork, then fishes one out of the garbage sack from last night. She returns to the bed, takes a bite of slaw and gets her wallet out of her purse. She lays the bills out on the bed one at a time.*)

ARLENE: That's for coffee...and that's for milk and bread...an that's cookies... an cheese and crackers...and shampoo an soap...and bacon an livercheese.

No, pickle loaf…an ketchup and some onions…an peanut butter an jelly…and shoe polish. Well, ain't no need gettin' everything all at once. Coffee, milk, ketchup, cookies, cheese, onions, jelly. Coffee, milk… oh, shampoo…

(There is a banging on the door.)

RUBY'S VOICE: *(Yelling.)* Candy, I gotta have my five dollars back.

ARLENE: *(Quickly stuffing her money back in her wallet.)* Candy ain't here!

RUBY'S VOICE: It's Ruby, upstairs. She's got five dollars I loaned her…Arlie? That Arlie? Candy told me her sister be…

(Arlene opens the door hesitantly.)

RUBY: It is Arlie, right?

ARLENE: It's Arlene. *(Does not extend her hand.)*

RUBY: See, I got these shoes in layaway… *(Puts her hand back in her pocket.)* she said you been…you just got…you seen my money?

ARLENE: No.

RUBY: I don't get 'em out today they go back on the shelf.

ARLENE: *(Doesn't understand.)* They sell your shoes?

RUBY: Yeah. Welcome back.

ARLENE: Thank you.

RUBY: She coulda put it in my mailbox.

(Ruby starts to leave. Arlene is closing the door when Ruby turns around.)

RUBY: Uh…listen…if you need a phone, I got one most of the time.

ARLENE: I do have to make this call.

RUBY: Ain't got a book though…well, I got one but it's holdin' up my bed. *(Laughs.)*

ARLENE: I got the number.

RUBY: Well, then…

ARLENE: Would you…wanna come in?

RUBY: You sure I'm not interruptin' anything?

ARLENE: I'm s'posed to call my parole officer.

RUBY: Good girl. Most of them can't talk but you call 'em anyway.

(Arlene does not laugh.)

RUBY: Candy go back to that creep?

ARLENE: I guess.

RUBY: I's afraid of that. *(Looking around.)* Maybe an envelope with my name on it? Really cleaned out the place, didn't she?

ARLENE: Yeah. Took everything.

(They laugh a little.)

RUBY: Didn't have much. Didn't do nuthin' here 'cept...sleep.

ARLENE: Least the rent's paid till the end of the month. I'll be workin' by then.

RUBY: You ain't seen Candy in a while.

ARLENE: No. Think she was in the seventh grade when—

RUBY: She's growed up now, you know.

ARLENE: Yeah. I was thinkin' she might come by.

RUBY: Honey, she won't be comin' by. He keeps all his... *(Starting over.)* his place is pretty far from here. But... *(Stops, trying to decide what to say.)*

ARLENE: But what?

RUBY: But she had a lot of friends, you know. *They* might be comin' by.

ARLENE: Men, you mean.

RUBY: Yeah. *(Quietly, waiting for Arlene's reaction.)*

ARLENE: *(Realizing the truth.)* Mother said he was her boyfriend.

RUBY: I shouldn't have said nuthin'. I jus' didn't want you to be surprised if some john showed up, his tongue hangin' out an all. *(Sits down on the bed.)*

ARLENE: It's okay. I shoulda known anyway. *(Now suddenly angry.)* No, it ain't okay. Guys got their dirty fingernails all over her. Some pimp's out buyin' green pants while she...Goddamn her.

RUBY: Hey now, that ain't your problem.

(Moves toward her, Arlene backs away.)

ARLIE: *(Pointing.)* You stick you hand in here again Doris an I'll bite it off.

RUBY: She'll figure it out soon enough.

ARLIE: *(Pointing to another person.)* An you, you ain't my mama, so you can cut the mama crap.

ARLENE: I wasn't gonna cuss no more.

RUBY: Nuthin' in the parole rules says you can't get pissed. My first day outta Gilbertsville I done the damn craziest...

(Arlene looks around, surprised to hear she has done time.)

RUBY: Oh yeah, a long time ago, but...hell, I heaved a whole gallon of milk right out the window my first day.

ARLENE: *(Somewhat cheered.)* It hit anybody?

RUBY: It bounced! Made me feel a helluva lot better. I said, "Ruby, if a gallon of milk can bounce back, so kin you."

ARLENE: That's really what you thought?

RUBY: Well, not exactly. I had to keep sayin' it for 'bout a year fore I finally believed it. I's moppin' this lady's floor once an she come in an heard me sayin' "gallon a milk, gallon a milk," fired me. She did. Thought I was too crazy to mop her floors.

(Ruby laughs, but is still bitter. Arlene wasn't listening. Ruby wants to change the subject now.)

RUBY: Hey! You have a good trip? Candy said you was in Arkansas.

ARLENE: Alabama. It was okay. This guard, well he used to be a guard, he just quit. He ain't never seen Kentucky, so he drove me. *(Watching for Ruby's response.)*

RUBY: Pine Ridge?

ARLENE: Yeah.

RUBY: It's coed now, ain't it?

ARLENE: Yeah. That's dumb, you know. They put you with men so's they can git you if you're seen with 'em.

RUBY: S'posed to be more natural, I guess.

ARLENE: I guess.

RUBY: Well, I say it sucks. Still a prison. No matter how many pictures they stick up on the walls or how many dirty movies they show, you still gotta be counted five times a day. *(Now beginning to worry about Arlene's silence.)* You don't seem like Candy said.

ARLENE: She tell you I was a killer?

RUBY: More like the meanest bitch that ever walked. I seen lots worse than you.

ARLENE: I been lots worse.

RUBY: Got to you, didn't it?

(Arlene doesn't respond, but Ruby knows she's right.)

RUBY: Well, you jus' gotta git over it. Bein' out, you gotta—

ARLENE: Don't you start in on me.

RUBY: *(Realizing her tone.)* Right, sorry.

ARLENE: It's okay.

RUBY: Ex-cons is the worst. I'm sorry.

ARLENE: It's okay.

RUBY: Done that about a year ago. New waitress we had. Gave my little goin'-straight speech, "No booze, no men, no buyin' on credit," shit like that, she quit that very night. Stole my fuckin' raincoat on her way out. Some speech, huh? *(Laughs, no longer resenting this theft.)*

ARLENE: You a waitress?

RUBY: I am the Queen of Grease. Make the finest french fries you ever did see.

ARLENE: You make a lot of money?

RUBY: I sure know how to. But I ain't about to go back inside for doin' it. Cookin' out's better'n eatin' in, I say.

ARLENE: You think up all these things you say?

RUBY: Know what I hate? Makin' salads—cuttin' up all that stuff 'n floppin' it in a bowl. Some day…some day…I'm gonna hear "tossed salad" an I'm gonna do jus' that. Toss out a tomato, toss out a head a lettuce, toss out a big ol' carrot. *(Miming the throwing and enjoying herself immensely.)*

ARLENE: *(Laughing.)* Be funny seein' all that stuff flyin' outta the kitchen.

RUBY: Hey Arlene! *(Gives her a friendly pat.)* You had your lunch yet?

ARLENE: *(Pulling away immediately.)* I ain't hungry.

RUBY: *(Carefully.)* I got raisin toast.

ARLENE: No. *(Goes over to the sink, twists knobs as if to stop a leak.)*

ARLIE: Whaddaya mean, what did she do to me? You got eyes or is they broke? You only seein' what you feel like seein'. I git ready to protect myself from a bunch of weirdos an then you look.

ARLENE: Sink's stopped up. *(Begins to work on it.)*

ARLIE: You ain't seein' when they's leavin' packs of cigarettes on my bed an then thinking I owe 'em or somethin'.

RUBY: Stopped up, huh? *(Squashing a bug on the floor.)*

ARLIE: You ain't lookin' when them kitchen workers lets up their mommies in line nights they know they only baked half enough brownies.

RUBY: Let me try.

ARLIE: You ain't seein' all the letters comin' in an goin' out with visitors. I'll tell you somethin'. One of them workmen buries dope for Betty Rickey in little plastic bottles under them sticker bushes at the water tower. You see that? No, you only seein' me. Well, you don't see shit.

RUBY: *(A quiet attempt.)* Gotta git you some Drano if you're gonna stay here.

ARLIE: I'll tell you what she done. Doris brung me some rollers from the beauty-school class. Three fuckin' pink rollers. Them plastic ones with the little holes. I didn't ask her. She jus' done it.

RUBY: Let me give her a try.

ARLENE: I can fix my own sink.

ARLIE: I's stupid. I's thinkin' maybe she were different from all them others. Then that night everbody disappears from the john and she's wantin' to brush my hair. Sure, brush my hair. How'd I know she was gonna crack her head open on the sink. I jus' barely even touched her.

RUBY: *(Walking to the bed now, digging through her purse.)* Want a Chiclet?

ARLIE: You ain't asked what she was gonna do to me. Huh? When you gonna ask that? You don't give a shit about that 'cause Doris such a good girl.

ARLENE: *(Giving up.)* Don't work.

RUBY: We got a dishwasher quittin' this week if you're interested.

ARLENE: I need somethin' that pays good.

RUBY: You type?

ARLENE: No.

RUBY: Do any clerk work?

ARLENE: No.

RUBY: Any keypunch?

ARLENE: No.

RUBY: Well, then I hate to tell you, but all us old-timers already got all the good cookin' and cleanin' jobs. *(Smashes another bug, goes to the cabinet to look for the bug spray.)* She even took the can of Raid! Just as well, empty anyway. *(Arlene doesn't respond.)* She hit the bugs with it. *(Still no response.)* Now, there's that phone call you was talkin' about.

ARLENE: Yeah.

RUBY: *(Walking toward the door.)* An I'll git you that number for the dishwashin' job, just in case.

(Arlene backs off.)

RUBY: How 'bout cards? You play any cards? Course you do. I get sick of beatin' myself all the time at solitaire. Damn borin' bein' so good at it.

ARLENE: *(Goes for her purse.)* Maybe I'll jus' walk to the corner an make my call from there.

RUBY: It's always broke.

ARLENE: What?

RUBY: The phone…at the corner. Only it ain't at the corner. It's inside the A&P.

ARLENE: Maybe it'll be fixed.

RUBY: Look, I ain't gonna force you to play cards with me. It's time for my programs anyway.

ARLENE: I gotta git some pickle loaf an…things.

RUBY: Suit yourself. I'll be there if you change your mind.

ARLENE: I have some things I gotta do here first.

RUBY: *(Trying to leave on a friendly basis.)* Look, I'll charge you a dime if it'll make you feel better.

ARLENE: *(Takes her seriously.)* Okay.

RUBY: *(Laughs, then realizes Arlene is serious.)* Mine's the one with the little picture of Johnny Cash on the door.

(Ruby leaves. Singing to the tune of "I'll Toe the Line," Bennie walks across the catwalk carrying a tray with cups and a pitcher of water. Arlene walks toward the closet. She is delaying going to the store, but is determined to go. She checks little things in the room, remembers to get a scarf, changes shoes, checks her wallet.)

Finally, as she is walking out, she stops and looks at the picture of Jesus, then moves closer, having noticed a dirty spot. She goes back into the bathroom for a tissue, wets it in her mouth, then dabs at the offending spot. She puts the tissue in her purse, then leaves the room when noted.)

BENNIE: I keep my pants up with a piece of twine. I keep my eyes wide open all the time. Da da da da-da da da da da da. If you'll be mine, please pull the twine.

ARLIE: You can't sing for shit.

BENNIE: *(Starts down the stairs toward Arlie's cell.)* You know what elephants got between their toes?

ARLIE: I don't care.

BENNIE: Slow natives. *(Laughs.)*

ARLIE: That ain't funny.

GUARD (EVANS): *(As Bennie opens Arlie's door.)* Hey, Davis.

BENNIE: Conversation is rehabilitatin', Evans. Want some water?

ARLIE: Okay.

BENNIE: How about some Kool-Aid to go in it? *(Gives her a glass of water.)*

ARLIE: When does the chaplain come?

BENNIE: Want some gum?

ARLIE: Is it today?

BENNIE: Kool-Aid's gone up, you know. Fifteen cents and tax. You get out, you'll learn all about that.

ARLIE: Does the chaplain come today?

BENNIE: *(Going back up the catwalk.)* Income tax, sales tax, property tax, gas and electric, water, rent—

ARLIE: Hey!

BENNIE: Yeah, he's comin', so don't mess up.

ARLIE: I ain't.

BENNIE: What's he tell you anyway, get you so starry-eyed?

ARLIE: He jus' talks to me.

BENNIE: I talk to you.

ARLIE: Where's Frankie Hill?

BENNIE: Gone.

ARLIE: Out?

BENNIE: Pretty soon.

ARLIE: When.

BENNIE: Miss her don't you? Ain't got nobody to bullshit with. Stories you gals tell…whoo-ee!

ARLIE: Get to cut that grass now, Frankie, honey.

BENNIE: Huh?

ARLIE: Stupidest thing she said. *(Gently.)* Said first thing she was gonna do when she got out—

(Arlene leaves the apartment.)

BENNIE: Get laid.

ARLIE: Shut up. First thing was gonna be going to the garage. Said it always smelled like car grease an turpur...somethin'.

BENNIE: Turpentine.

ARLIE: Yeah, an gasoline, wet. An she'll bend down an squirt oil in the lawn-mower, red can with a long pointy spout. Then cut the grass in the back-yard, up an back, up an back. They got this grass catcher on it. Says she likes scoopin' up that cut grass an spreadin' it out under the trees. Says it makes her real hungry for some lunch. *(A quiet curiosity about all this.)*

BENNIE: I got a power mower, myself.

ARLIE: They done somethin' to her. Took out her nerves or somethin'. She...

BENNIE: She jus' got better, that's all.

ARLIE: Hah. Know what else? They give her a fork to eat with last week. A fork. A fuckin' fork. Now how long's it been since I had a fork to eat with?

BENNIE: *(Getting ready to leave the cell.)* Wish I could help you with that, honey.

ARLIE: *(Loud.)* Don't call me honey.

BENNIE: *(Locks the door behind him.)* That's my girl.

ARLIE: I ain't your girl.

BENNIE: *(On his way back up the stairs.)* Screechin' wildcat.

ARLIE: *(Very quiet.)* What time is it?

(Arlene walks back into the apartment. She is out of breath and has some trou-ble getting the door open. She is carrying a big sack of groceries. As she sets the bag on the counter, it breaks open, spilling cans and packages all over the floor. She just stands and looks at the mess. She takes off her scarf and sets down her purse, still looking at the spilled groceries. Finally, she bends down and picks up the package of pickle loaf. She starts to put it on the counter, then turns sud-denly and throws it at the door. She stares at it as it falls.)

ARLENE: Bounce? *(In disgust.)* Shit.

(Arlene sinks to the floor. She tears open the package of pickle loaf and eats a piece of it. She is still angry, but is completely unable to do anything about her anger.)

ARLIE: Who's out there? Is anybody out there? *(Reading.)* Depart from evil and do good. *(Yelling.)* Now, you pay attention out there 'cause this is right out of the Lord's mouth. *(Reading.)* And dwell, that means live, dwell for-ever-more. *(Speaking.)* That's like for longer than I've been in here or longer than…this Bible the chaplain give me's got my name right in the front of it. Hey! Somebody's s'posed to be out there watchin' me. Wanna hear some more? *(Reading.)* For the Lord for… *(The word is forsaketh.)* I can't read in here, you turn on my light, you hear me? Or let me out and I'll go read it in the TV room. Please let me out. I won't scream or nuthin'? I'll just go right to sleep, okay? Somebody! I'll go right to sleep. Okay? You won't even know I'm there. Hey! Goddammit, somebody let me out of here, I can't stand it in here anymore. Somebody! *(Her spirit finally broken.)*

ARLENE: *(She draws her knees up, wraps her arms around them, and rests her head on her arms.)* Jus' gotta git a job an make some money an everything will be all right. You hear me, Arlene? You git yourself up an go find a job. *(Continues to sit.)* An you kin start by cleanin' up this mess you made 'cause food don't belong on the floor.

(Arlene still doesn't get up. Carl appears in the doorway of the apartment. When he sees Arlene on the floor, he goes into a fit of vicious, sadistic laughter.)

CARL: What's happenin', mama? You havin' lunch with the bugs?

ARLENE: *(Quietly.)* Fuck off.

CARL: *(Threatening.)* What'd you say?

ARLENE: *(Reconsidering.)* Go away.

CARL: You watch your mouth or I'll close it up for you.

(Arlene stands up now. Carl goes to the window and looks out, as if checking for someone.)

ARLENE: They after you, ain't they?

(Carl sniffs, scratches at his arm. He finds a plastic bag near the bed, stuffed with brightly colored knitted things. He pulls out baby sweaters, booties, and caps.)

CARL: What the fuck is this?

ARLENE: You leave them be.

CARL: You got a baby hid here somewhere? I found its little shoes. *(Laughs, dangling them in front of him.)*

ARLENE: *(Chasing him.)* Them's mine.

CARL: Aw sugar, I ain't botherin' nuthin'. Just lookin'. *(Pulls more out of the sack, dropping one or two booties on the floor, kicking them away.)*

ARLENE: *(Picking up what he's dropped.)* I ain't tellin' you again. Give me them.

CARL: *(Turns around quickly, walking away with a few of the sweaters.)* How much these go for?

ARLENE: I don't know yet.

CARL: I'll jus' take care of 'em for you—a few coin for the trip. You *are* gonna have to pay your share, you know.

ARLENE: You give me them. I ain't goin' with you. *(She walks toward him.)*

CARL: You ain't?

(Mocking, Arlene walks up close to him now, taking the bag in her hands. He knocks her away and onto the bed.)

CARL: Straighten up, girlie. *(Now kneels over her.)* You done forgot how to behave yourself. *(Moves as if to threaten her, but kisses her on the forehead, then moves out into the room.)*

ARLENE: *(Sitting up.)* I worked hard on them things. They's nice, too, for babies and little kids.

CARL: I bet you fooled them officers good, doin' this shit. *(Throws the bag in the sink.)*

ARLENE: I weren't—

CARL: I kin see that scene. They sayin'… *(Puts on a high southern voice.)* "I'd jus' love one a them nice yella sweaters."

ARLENE: They liked them.

CARL: Those turkeys, sure they did. Where else you gonna git your free sweaters an free washin' an free step-right-up-git-your-convict-special-shoe-shine. No, don't give me no money, officer. I's jus' doin' this 'cause I likes you.

ARLENE: They give 'em for Christmas presents.

CARL: *(Checks the window again, then peers into the grocery sack.)* What you got sweet, mama? *(Pulls out a box of cookies and begins to eat them.)*

ARLIE: I'm sweepin', Doris, 'cause it's like a pigpen in here. So you might like it, but I don't, so if you got some mops, I'll take one of them too.

ARLENE: You caught another habit, didn't you?

CARL: You turned into a narc or what?

ARLENE: You scratchin' an sniffin' like crazy.

CARL: I see a man eatin' cookies an that's what you see too.

ARLENE: An you was laughin' at me sittin' on the floor! You got cops lookin' for you an you ain't scored yet this morning. You better get yourself back to prison where you can git all you need.

CARL: Since when Carl couldn't find it if he really wanted it?

ARLENE: An I bought them cookies for me.

CARL: An I wouldn't come no closer if I's you.

ARLENE: *(Stops, then walks to the door.)* Then take the cookies an git out.

CARL: *(Imitating Bennie.)* Oh, please, Miss Arlene, come go with Carl to the big city. We'll jus' have us the best time.

ARLENE: I'm gonna stay here an git a job an save up money so's I kin git Joey. *(Opening the door.)* Now, I ain't s'posed to see no ex-cons.

CARL: *(Big laugh.)* You don't know nobody else. Huh, Arlie? Who you know ain't a con-vict?

ARLENE: I'll meet 'em.

CARL: And what if they don't wanna meet you? You ain't exactly a nice girl, you know. An you gotta be jivin' about that job shit. *(Throws the sack of cookies on the floor.)*

ARLENE: *(Retrieving the cookies.)* I kin work.

CARL: Doin' what?

ARLENE: I don't know. Cookin', cleanin', somethin' that pays good.

CARL: You got your choice, honey. You can do cookin' an cleanin' or you can do somethin' that pays good. You ain't gonna git rich working on your knees. You come with me an you'll have money. You stay here, you won't have shit.

ARLENE: Ruby works an she does okay.

CARL: You got any Kool-Aid? *(Looking in the cabinets, moving Arlene out of his way.)* Ruby who?

ARLENE: Upstairs. She cooks. Works nights an has all day to do jus' what she wants.

CARL: And what, exactly, do she do? See flicks take rides in cabs to pick up see-through shoes?

ARLENE: She watches TV, plays cards, you know.

CARL: Yeah, I know. Sounds just like the day room in the fuckin' joint.

ARLENE: She likes it.

CARL: *(Exasperated.)* All right. Say you stay here an *finally* find yourself some job. *(Grabs the picture of Jesus off the wall.)* This your boyfriend?

ARLENE: The chaplain give it to me.

CARL: Say it's dishwashin', okay?

(Arlene doesn't answer.)

CARL: Okay?

ARLENE: Okay. *(Takes the picture, hangs it back up.)*

CARL: An you git maybe seventy-five a week. Seventy-five for standin' over a sink full of greasy gray water, fishin' out blobs of bread an lettuce. People puttin' pieces of chewed-up meat in their napkins and you gotta pick it out. Eight hours a day, six days a week, to make seventy-five lousy pictures of Big Daddy George. Now, how long it'll take you to make seventy-five workin' for me?

ARLENE: A night.

(She sits on the bed, Carl pacing in front of her.)

CARL: Less than a night. Two hours maybe. Now, it's the same fuckin' seventy-five bills. You can either work all week for it or make it in two hours. You work two hours a night for me an how much you got in a week?

(Arlene looks puzzled by the multiplication required. He sits down beside her, even more disgusted.)

CARL: Two seventy-five's is a hundred and fifty. Three hundred-and-fifties is four hundred and fifty. You stay here you git seventy-five a week. You come with me an you git four hundred and fifty a week. Now, four hundred and fifty, Arlie, is more than seventy five. You stay here you gotta work eight hours a day and your hands git wrinkled and your feet swell up. *(Suddenly distracted.)* There was this guy at Bricktown had webby toes like a duck. *(Back now.)* You come home with me you work two hours a night an you kin sleep all mornin' an spend the day buyin' eyelashes and tryin' out perfume. Come home, have some guy openin' the door for you sayin', "Good evenin', Miss Holsclaw, nice night now ain't it?" *(Puts his arm around her.)*

ARLENE: It's Joey I'm thinkin' about.

CARL: If you was a kid, would you want your mom to git so dragged out washin' dishes she don't have no time for you an no money to spend on you? You come with me, you kin send him big orange bears an Sting Ray bikes with his name wrote on the fenders. He'll like that. Holsclaw. *(Amused.)* Kinda sounds like coleslaw, don't it? Joey be tellin' all his friends 'bout his mom livin' up in New York City an bein' so rich an sendin' him stuff all the time.

ARLENE: I want to be with him.

CARL: *(Now stretches out on the bed, his head in her lap.)* So, fly him up to see you. Take him on that boat they got goes roun' the island. Take him up to the Empire State Building, let him play King Kong. *(Rubs her hair, unstudied tenderness.)* He be talkin' 'bout that trip his whole life.

ARLENE: *(Smoothing his hair.)* I don't want to go back to prison, Carl.

CARL: *(Jumps up, moves toward the refrigerator.)* There any chocolate milk? *(Distracted again.)* You know they got this motel down in Mexico named after me? Carlsbad Cabins. *(Proudly.)* Who said anything about goin' back to prison? *(Slams the refrigerator door, really hostile.)* What do you think I'm gonna be doin'? Keepin' you out, that's what!

ARLENE: *(Stands up.)* Like last time? Like you gettin' drunk? Like you lookin' for kid junkies to beat up?

CARL: God, ain't it hot in this dump. You gonna come or not? You wanna wash dishes, I could give a shit. *(Yelling.)* But you comin' with me, you say it right now, lady! *(Grabs her by the arm.)* Huh?
(There is a knock on the door.)

RUBY'S VOICE: Arlene?

CARL: *(Yelling.)* She ain't here!

RUBY'S VOICE: *(Alarmed.)* Arlene! You all right?

ARLENE: That's Ruby I was tellin' you about.

CARL: *(Catches Arlene's arm again, very rough.)* We ain't through!

RUBY: *(Opening the door.)* Hey! *(Seeing the rough treatment.)* Goin' to the store. *(Very firm.)* Thought maybe you forgot somethin'.

CARL: *(Turns Arlene loose.)* You this cook I been hearin' about?

RUBY: I cook. So what?

CARL: Buys you nice shoes, don't it, cookin'? Why don't you hock your watch an have somethin' done to your hair? If you got a watch.

RUBY: Why don't you drop by the coffee shop. I'll spit in your eggs.

CARL: They let you bring home the half-eat chili dogs?

RUBY: You...You got half-eat chili dogs for brains. *(To Arlene.)* I'll stop by later. *(Contemptuous look for Carl.)*

ARLENE: No. Stay.
(Carl gets the message. He goes over to the sink to get a drink of water out of the faucet, then looks down at his watch.)

CARL: Piece a shit. *(Thumps it with his finger.)* Shoulda took the dude's hat, Jack. Guy preachin' about the end of the world ain't gonna own a watch that works.

ARLENE: *(Walks over to the sink, bends over Carl.)* You don't need me. I'm gittin' too old for it, anyway.

CARL: I don't discuss my business with strangers in the room. *(Heads for the door.)*

ARLENE: When you leavin'?

CARL: Six. You wanna come, meet me at this bar. *(Gives her a brightly colored matchbook.)* I'm havin' my wheels delivered.

ARLENE: You stealin' a car?

CARL: Take a cab. *(Gives her a dollar.)* You don't come...well, I already laid it out for you. I ain't never lied to you, have I girl?

ARLENE: No.

CARL: Then you be there. That's all the words I got. *(Makes an unconscious move toward her.)* I don't beg nobody. *(Backs off.)* Be there.
(He turns abruptly and leaves. Arlene watches him go, folding up the money in the matchbook. The door remains open.)

ARLIE: *(Reading, or trying to, from a small Testament.)* For the Lord forsaketh not his saints, but the seed of the wicked shall be cut off.
(Ruby walks over to the counter, starts to pick up some of the groceries lying on the floor, then stops.)

RUBY: I 'magine you'll want to be puttin' these up yourself.
(Arlene continues to stare out the door.)

RUBY: He do this?

ARLENE: No.

RUBY: Can't trust these sacks. I seen bag boys punchin' holes in 'em at the store.

ARLENE: Can't trust anybody. *(Finally turning around.)*

RUBY: Well, you don't want to trust him, that's for sure.

ARLENE: We spent a lot of time together, me an Carl.

RUBY: He live here?

ARLENE: No, he jus' broke outta Bricktown near where I was. I got word there sayin' he'd meet me. I didn't believe it then, but he don't lie, Carl don't.

RUBY: You thinkin' of goin' with him?

ARLENE: They'll catch him. I told him but he don't listen.

RUBY: Funny ain't it, the number a men come without ears.

ARLENE: How much that dishwashin' job pay?

RUBY: I don't know. Maybe seventy-five.

ARLENE: That's what he said.

RUBY: He tell you you was gonna wear out your hands and knees grubbin' for nuthin', git old an be broke an never have a nice dress to wear? *(Sitting down.)*

ARLENE: Yeah.

RUBY: He tell you nobody's gonna wanna be with you 'cause you done time?

ARLENE: Yeah.

RUBY: He tell you your kid gonna be ashamed of you an nobody's gonna believe you if you tell 'em you changed?

ARLENE: Yeah.

RUBY: Then he was right. *(Pauses.)* But when you make your two nickels, you can keep both of 'em.

ARLENE: *(Shattered by these words.)* Well, I can't do that.

RUBY: Can't do what?

ARLENE: Live like that. Be like bein' dead.

RUBY: You kin always call in sick…stay home, send out for pizza an watch your Johnny Carson on TV…or git a bus way out Preston Street an go bowlin'.

ARLENE: *(Anger building.)* What am I gonna do? I can't git no work that will pay good 'cause I can't do nuthin'. It'll be years fore I have a nice rug for this place. I'll never even have some ol' Ford to drive around, I'll never take Joey to no fair. I won't be invited home for pot roast and I'll have to wear this fuckin' dress for the rest of my life. What kind of life is that?

RUBY: It's outside.

ARLENE: Outside? Honey I'll either be *inside* this apartment or *inside* some kitchen sweatin' over the sink. Outside's where you get to do what you want, not where you gotta do some shit job jus' so's you can eat worse than you did in prison. That ain't why I quit bein' so hateful, so I could come back and rot in some slum.

RUBY: *(Word "slum" hits hard.)* Well, you can wash dishes to pay the rent on your "slum," or you can spread your legs for any shit that's got the ten dollars.

ARLENE: *(Not hostile.)* I don't need you agitatin' me.

RUBY: An I don't live in no slum.

ARLENE: *(Sensing Ruby's hurt.)* Well, I'm sorry…it's just…I thought… *(Increasingly upset.)*

RUBY: *(Finishing her sentence.)* …it was gonna be different. Well, it ain't. And the sooner you believe it, the better off you'll be.

(A guard enters Arlie's cell.)

ARLIE: Where's the chaplain? I got somethin' to tell him.

ARLENE: They said I's…

GUARD (CALDWELL): He ain't comin'.

ARLENE: …he tol' me if…I thought once Arlie…

ARLIE: It's Tuesday. He comes to see me on Tuesday.

GUARD (CALDWELL): Chaplain's been transferred, dollie. Gone. Bye-bye. You know.

ARLENE: He said the meek, meek, them that's quiet and good…the meek…as soon as Arlie…

RUBY: What, Arlene? Who said what?

ARLIE: He's not comin' back?

ARLENE: At Pine Ridge there was…

ARLIE: He woulda told me if he couldn't come back.

ARLENE: I was…

GUARD (CALDWELL): He left this for you.

ARLENE: I was…

GUARD (CALDWELL): Picture of Jesus, looks like.

ARLENE: …this chaplain…

RUBY: *(Trying to call her back from this hysteria.)* Arlene…

ARLIE: *(Hysterical.)* I need to talk to him.

ARLENE: This chaplain…

ARLIE: You tell him to come back and see me.

ARLENE: I was in lockup…

ARLIE: *(A final, anguished plea.)* I want the chaplain!

ARLENE: I don't know…years…

RUBY: And…

ARLENE: This chaplain said I had…said Arlie was my hateful self and she was hurtin' me and God would find some way to take her away…and it was God's will so I could be the meek…the meek, them that's quiet and good an git whatever they want…I forgit that word…they git the earth.

RUBY: Inherit.

ARLENE: Yeah. And that's why I done it.

RUBY: Done what?

ARLENE: What I done. 'Cause the chaplain he said…I'd sit up nights waitin' for him to come talk to me.

RUBY: Arlene, what did you do? What are you talkin' about?

ARLENE: They tol' me…after I's out an it was all over…they said after the chaplain got transferred…I didn't know why he didn't come no more till after…they said it was three whole nights at first, me screamin' to God to come git Arlie an kill her. They give me this medicine an thought I's better…then that night it happened, the officer was in the dorm doin' count…an they didn't hear nuthin' but they come back out where I was an I'm standin' there tellin' 'em to come see, real quiet I'm tellin' 'em, but there's all this blood all over my shirt an I got this fork I'm holdin' real tight in my hand… *(Clenches one hand now, the other hand fumbling with the front of her dress as if she's going to show Ruby.)* this fork, they said Doris stole it from the kitchen an give it to me so I'd kill myself and shut up botherin' her…an there's all these holes all over me where I been stabbin' myself an I'm sayin' Arlie is dead for what she done to me, Arlie is dead an it's God's will…I didn't scream it, I was jus' sayin' it over and over…Arlie is dead, Arlie is dead…they couldn't git that fork outta my hand till…I woke up in the infirmary an they said I almost died. They said they's glad I didn't.

(Smiling.) They said did I feel better now an they was real nice, bringing me chocolate puddin'…

RUBY: I'm sorry, Arlene.

(Ruby reaches out for her, but Arlene pulls away sharply.)

ARLENE: I'd be eatin' or jus' lookin' at the ceiling an git a tear in my eye, but it'd jus' dry up, you know, it didn't run out or nuthin'. An then pretty soon, I's well, an officers was sayin' they's seein' such a change in me an givin' me yarn to knit sweaters an how'd I like to have a new skirt to wear an sometimes lettin' me chew gum. They said things ain't never been as clean as when I's doin' the housekeepin' at the dorm. *(So proud.)* An then I got in the honor cottage an nobody was foolin' with me no more or nuthin'. An I didn't git mad like before or nuthin'. I jus' done my work an knit…an I don't think about it, what happened, 'cept… *(Now losing control.)* people here keep callin' me Arlie an… *(Has trouble saying "Arlie".)* I didn't mean to do it, what I done…

RUBY: Oh, honey . . .

ARLENE: I did… *(This is very difficult.)* I mean, Arlie was a pretty mean kid, but I did… *(Very quickly.)* I didn't know what I…

(Arlene breaks down completely, screaming, crying, falling over into Ruby's lap.)

ARLENE: *(Grieving for this lost self.)* Arlie!

(Ruby rubs her back, her hair, waiting for the calm she knows will come.)

RUBY: *(Finally, but very quietly.)* You can still… *(Stops to think of how to say it.)* …you can still love people that's gone.

(Ruby continues to hold her tenderly, rocking as with a baby. A terrible crash is heard on the steps outside the apartment.)

BENNIE'S VOICE: Well, chicken-pluckin', hog-kickin' shit!

RUBY: Don't you move now, it's just somebody out in the hall.

ARLENE: That's—

RUBY: It's okay Arlene. Everything's gonna be just fine. Nice and quiet now.

ARLENE: That's Bennie that guard I told you about.

RUBY: I'll get it. You stay still now. *(She walks to the door and looks out into the hall, hands on hips.)* Why you dumpin' them flowers on the stairs like that? Won't git no sun at all! *(Turns back to Arlene.)* Arlene, there's a man plantin' a garden out in the hall. You think we should call the police or get him a waterin' can?

(Bennie appears in the doorway, carrying a box of dead-looking plants.)

BENNIE: I didn't try to fall, you know.

RUBY: *(Blocking the door.)* Well, when you git ready to try, I wanna watch!

ARLENE: I thought you's gone.

RUBY: *(To Bennie.)* You got a visitin' pass?

BENNIE: *(Coming into the room.)* Arlie… *(Quickly.)* Arlene. I brung you some plants. You know, plants for your window. Like we talked about, so's you don't see them bars.

RUBY: *(Picking up one of the plants.)* They sure is scraggly-lookin' things. Next time, git plastic.

BENNIE: I'm sorry I dropped 'em, Arlene. We kin get 'em back together an they'll do real good. *(Setting them down on the trunk.)* These ones don't take the sun. I asked just to make sure. Arlene?

RUBY: You up for seein' this petunia killer?

ARLENE: It's okay. Bennie, this is Ruby, upstairs.

BENNIE: *(Bringing one flower over to show Arlene, stuffing it back into its pot.)* See? It ain't dead.

RUBY: Poor little plant. It comes from a broken home.

BENNIE: *(Walks over to the window, getting the box and holding it up.)* That's gonna look real pretty. Cheerful-like.

RUBY: Arlene ain't gettin' the picture yet. *(Walking to the window and holding her plant up too, posing.)* Now.

(Arlene looks, but is not amused.)

BENNIE: *(Putting the plants back down.)* I jus' thought, after what I done last night…I jus' wanted to do somethin' nice.

ARLENE: *(Calmer now.)* They is nice. Thanks.

RUBY: Arlene says you're a guard.

BENNIE: I was. I quit. Retired.

ARLENE: Bennie's goin' back to Alabama.

BENNIE: Well, I ain't leavin' right away. There's this guy at the motel says the bass is hittin' pretty good right now. Thought I might fish some first.

ARLENE: Then he's goin' back.

BENNIE: *(To Ruby as he washes his hands.)* I'm real fond of this little girl. I ain't goin' till I'm sure she's gonna do okay. Thought I might help some.

RUBY: Arlene's had about all the help she can stand.

BENNIE: I got a car, Arlene. An money. An… *(Reaching into his pocket.)* I brung you some gum.

ARLENE: That's real nice, too. An I 'preciate what you done, bringin' me here an all, but…

BENNIE: Well, look. Least you can take my number at the motel an give me a ring if you need somethin'. *(Holds out a piece of paper.)* Here, I wrote it down for you.

(Arlene takes the paper.)

BENNIE: Oh, an somethin' else, these towel things... *(Reaching into his pocket, pulling out a package of towelettes.)* they was in the chicken last night. I thought I might be needin' 'em, but they give us new towels every day at that motel.

ARLENE: Okay then. I got your number.

BENNIE: *(Backing up toward the door.)* Right. Right. Any ol' thing, now. Jus' any ol' thing. You even run outta gum an you call.

RUBY: Careful goin' down.

ARLENE: Bye Bennie.

BENNIE: Right. The number now. Don't lose it. You know, in case you need somethin'.

ARLENE: No.

(Bennie leaves, Arlene gets up and picks up the matchbook Carl gave her and holds it with Bennie's piece of paper. Ruby watches a moment, sees Arlene trying to make this decision, knows that what she says now is very important.)

RUBY: We had this waitress put her phone number in matchbooks, give 'em to guys left her nice tips. Anyway, one night this little ol' guy calls her and comes over and says he works at this museum an he don't have any money but he's got this hat belonged to Queen Victoria. An she felt real sorry for him so she screwed him for this little ol' lacy hat. Then she takes the hat back the next day to the museum thinkin' she'll git a reward or somethin' an you know what they done? *(Pause.)* Give her a free membership. Tellin' her thanks so much an we're so grateful an wouldn't she like to see this mummy they got downstairs...an all the time jus' stallin'...waiting 'cause they called the police.

ARLENE: You do any time for that?

RUBY: *(Admitting the story was about her.)* County jail.

ARLENE: *(Quietly, looking at the matchbook.)* County jail. *(She tears up the matchbook and drops it in the sack of trash.)* You got any Old Maids?

RUBY: Huh?

ARLENE: You know.

RUBY: *(Surprised and pleased.)* Cards?

ARLENE: *(Laughs a little.)* It's the only one I know.

RUBY: Old Maid, huh? *(Not her favorite game.)*

ARLENE: I gotta put my food up first.

RUBY: 'Bout an hour?

ARLENE: I'll come up.

RUBY: Great. *(Stops by the plants on her way to the door, smiles.)* These plants is real ugly.

(Ruby exits. Arlene watches her, then turns back to the groceries still on the floor. Slowly, but with great determination, she picks up the items one at a time and puts them away in the cabinet above the counter. Arlie appears on the catwalk. There is one light on each of them.)

ARLIE: Hey! You 'member that time we was playin' policeman an June locked me up in Mama's closet an then took off swimmin'? An I stood around with them dresses itchin' my ears an crashin' into that door tryin' to git outta there? It was dark in there. So, finally, *(Very proud.)* I went around an peed in all Mama's shoes. But then she come home an tried to git in the closet only June taken the key so she said, "Who's in there?" an I said, "It's me!" and she said, "What you doin' in there?" an I started gigglin' an she started pullin' on the door an yellin', "Arlie, what you doin' in there?" *(Big laugh.)*

(Arlene has begun to smile during the story. Now they speak together, both standing as Mama did, one hand on her hip.)

ARLIE AND ARLENE: Arlie, what you doin' in there?

ARLENE: *(Still smiling and remembering, stage dark except for one light on her face.)* Aw shoot.

(Light dims on Arlene's fond smile as Arlie laughs once more.)

THE END

Third and Oak

Third and Oak was originally produced by Actors Theatre of Louisville in March 1978, under the direction of Jon Jory. The cast was as follows:

The Laundromat

        Alberta . . . . Anne Pitoniak

        Deedee . . . . Dawn Didawick

The Pool Hall

        Alberta . . . . Anne Pitoniak

        Deedee . . . . Dawn Didawick

        Shooter . . . . Joe Morton

        Willie . . . . John Hancock

Third and Oak: The Laundromat was presented in New York City in December 1979 as part of Ensemble Studio Theatre's One-Act Marathon, Curt Dempster, Artistic Director. The production was directed by Kenneth Frankel. The cast was as follows:

        Alberta . . . . Regina David

        Deedee . . . . Dawn Didawick

In 1984 *Third and Oak: The Laundromat* was filmed for HBO by Robert Altman, starring Carol Burnett and Amy Madigan.

In 1989 *Third and Oak: The Pool Hall* starring James Earl Jones and Mario Van Peebles was filmed by Nederlander Television & Film and aired on General Motors Theatre. *The Pool Hall* was directed by Fielder Cook and was produced by Gladys Nederlander.

INTRODUCTION

These two plays are about the same thing: why we lie to protect ourselves when we could tell the truth and be saved. Not that the plays answer this question. Plays don't answer questions, they simply preserve them, they pass them on.

And though each act is frequently performed by itself, I prefer that the two acts be seen together. Rather like the right foot following the left.

CHARACTERS

ALBERTA: a reserved woman in her late fifties.
DEEDEE: a restless twenty-year-old.
SHOOTER: a black disc jockey in his late twenties.
WILLIE: a black man in his late fifties.

TIME AND PLACE

The time is the late seventies. The two acts of this play take place in a laundromat and the pool hall next door, at the corner of Third and Oak, in the middle of the night.

Third and Oak

ACT I

THE LAUNDROMAT

Lights come up on a standard, dreary laundromat. There are tile floors, washers, dryers, laundry baskets on wheels, and coin-op vending machines for soaps, soft drinks, and candy bars. There is a bulletin board on which various notices are posted. There is a table for folding clothes, a low table covered with dirty ashtrays and some ugly chairs littered with magazines. A clock on the wall reads three o'clock and should continue to run throughout the show. One side of the laundromat will be used as a window looking out onto the street. The song "Stand By Your Man" is playing over the radio. The door to the attendant's room is slightly ajar.

SHOOTER'S VOICE: *(On the radio, over the final chords of the song.)* And that's all for tonight, night owls. This is your Number One Night Owl saying it's three o'clock, all right, and time to rock your daddy to dreams of de-light. And mama, I'm comin' home. And the rest of you night owls gonna have to make it through the rest of this night by *yourself* or with the help of *your* friends, if you know what I mean. And you know what I mean.

(The radio station goes dead, music replaced by an irritating static. Alberta opens the door tentatively, looks around and walks in. She has dressed carefully and her laundry basket exhibits the same care. She checks the top of a washer for dust or water before putting her purse and basket down. She takes off her coat and hat. She walks back to the door marked Attendant, and is startled briefly when she looks in.)

ALBERTA: Hello? *(Steps back, seeing that the attendant is asleep.)* Sleep? Is that how you do your job? Sleep? What they pay you to do, sleep? Listen, it's fine with me. Better, in fact. I'm glad, actually. *(She leans in and turns off the radio. She walks back toward the basket, talking to herself.)* Do you want him out here talking to you? *(Procrastinating.)* You came to do your wash so do your wash. No, first… *(She takes an index card out of her purse. She tacks it up on the bulletin board. We must see that it is very important to her.)* There. Good. *(She opens a washer lid and runs her fingers around the soap tray, taking*

61

out lint and depositing it in one of the coffee cans. As she does this, she acci-
dentally knocks over her purse.) It's okay. Nothing breakable. Clean it up,
that's all. You've been up this late before. Nothing the matter with you, just
nerves…and gravity.

(Alberta bends down and begins to put the things back in her purse. She can-
not see as Deedee backs in the door of the laundromat. Deedee is a wreck. She
carries her clothes tied up in a man's shirt. She trips over a wastebasket and falls
on her laundry as it spills out of the shirt.)

DEEDEE: Well, poo-rats!

(Alberta stands up, startled, hesitates, then walks over to where Deedee is still
sprawled on the floor.)

ALBERTA: Are you all right? *(She is angry that Deedee is there at all, but polite nev-*
ertheless.)

DEEDEE: *(Grudgingly.)* Cute, huh?

ALBERTA: *(Moving the wastebasket out of the way.)* Probably a wet spot on the
floor. *(Goes back to her wash.)*

DEEDEE: I already picked these clothes off the floor once tonight. *(No response*
from Alberta.) We been in our apartment two years and Joe still ain't found
the closets. He thinks hangers are for when you lock your keys in your car.
(Still no response, though she is expecting one.) I mean, he's got this coat made
of sheep's fur or somethin' and my mom came over one day and asked
where did we get that fuzzy little rug. *(She is increasingly nervous.)* Joe works
at the Ford plant. I asked him why they call it that. I said, "How often do
you have to water a Ford plant?" It was just a little joke, but he didn't think
it was very funny.

ALBERTA: *(Her good manners requiring her to say something.)* They probably do
have a sprinkler system.

DEEDEE: Shoulda saved my breath and just tripped over the coffee table. He'd
laughed at that. *(No response.)* Well, *(Brightly.)* I guess it's just you and me.

ALBERTA: Yes. *(Makes a move to get back to her wash.)*

DEEDEE: Guess not too many people suds their duds in the middle of the night.

ALBERTA: Suds their duds?

DEEDEE: I do mine at Mom's. *(She begins to put her clothes in two washers, imi-*
tating Alberta.) I mean, I take our stuff over to Mom's. She got matching
Maytags. She buys giant-size Cheer and we sit around and watch the soaps
till the clothes come out. Suds the duds, that's what she says. Well, more
than that. She wrote it on a little card and sent it in to Cheer so they could
use it on their TV ads.

ALBERTA: *(Pleasantly.)* Gives you a chance to talk, I guess. Visit.

DEEDEE: She says, "Just leave 'em, I'll do 'em," but that wouldn't be right, so I stay. Course she don't ever say how she likes seeing me, but she holds back, you know. I mean, there's stuff you don't have to say when it's family.

ALBERTA: Is she out of town tonight?

DEEDEE: No, probably just asleep. *(Alberta nods. She reads from the top of the washer.)* Five cycle Turbomatic Deluxe. *(Punching buttons.)* Hot wash warm rinse, warm wash warm rinse, warm wash cold rinse, cold wash cold rinse, cold wash, delicate cycle. *(Now lifts the lid of the washer.)* What's this? Add laundry aids.

ALBERTA: Your mother does your laundry.

DEEDEE: You don't have a washer either, huh?

ALBERTA: *(Too quickly.)* It's broken.

DEEDEE: Get your husband to fix it. *(Looking at Alberta's mound of shirts.)* Got a heap of shirts, don't he?

ALBERTA: It can't be fixed.

DEEDEE: Where are *your* clothes?

ALBERTA: Mine are mostly hand wash.

DEEDEE: We just dump all our stuff in together.

ALBERTA: That's nice.

DEEDEE: Joe can fix just about anything. He's real good with his hands. *(Relaxing some now.)* I've been saying that since high school. *(Laughs.)* He makes trucks. God, I'd hate to see the truck I'd put together. *(Now a nervous laugh.)* He had to work the double shift tonight. *(Going on quickly.)* They do all kinds out there. Pickups, dump trucks…they got this joke, him and his buddies, about what rhymes with pickle truck, but I don't know the end of it, you know, the punch line. Goes like… "I'll come to get you baby in a pickle truck, I'll tell you what I'm wantin' is a— *(Stops, but continues the beat with her foot or by snapping her fingers.)* See, that's the part I don't know. The end. *(Shrugs.)*

ALBERTA: Overtime pays well, I imagine.

DEEDEE: It's all-the-time, here lately. He says people are buyin' more trucks 'cause farmers have to raise more cows 'cause we got a population explosion going on. Really crummy, you know? People I don't even know having babies means Joe can't come home at the right time. Don't seem fair.

ALBERTA: Or true.

DEEDEE: Huh?

ALBERTA: The population explosion is over. The birthrate is very stable now.

DEEDEE: Oh.

ALBERTA: Still, it's no fun to be in the house by yourself.

DEEDEE: See, we live right over there, on top of the Mexican restaurant. *(Going over to the window.)* That window with the blue light in it, that's ours. It's a bunch of blueberries on a stalk, only it's a light. Joe gave it to me. He thinks blue is my favorite color.

ALBERTA: So the restaurant noise was bothering you.

DEEDEE: They got this bar that stays open till four. That's how Joe picked the apartment. He hates to run out for beer late. He don't mind running down. *(Broadly.)* Old Mexico Taco Tavern. Except Joe says it's supposed to be Olé Mexico, like what they say in bullfights.

ALBERTA: Bullfights are disgusting.

DEEDEE: You've seen a real bullfight?

ALBERTA: We used to travel quite a bit.

DEEDEE: *(Excited, curious, demanding.)* Well, tell me about it.

ALBERTA: There's not much to tell. The bull comes out and they kill it.

DEEDEE: What for? *(Putting her clothes in the washer.)*

ALBERTA: *(Pleased at the question.)* Fun. Doesn't that sound like *fun* to you?

DEEDEE: *(Encouraged.)* Your husband works nights too?

ALBERTA: Herb is out of town. Did you mean to put that in there?

DEEDEE: *(Peering into her washer.)* Huh?

ALBERTA: Your whites will come out green.

DEEDEE: *(Retrieving the shirt.)* Joe wouldn't like that. No sir. Be like when Mom's washer chewed this hole in his bowling shirt. Whoo-ee! Was he hot. Kicked the chest of drawers, broke his toe. *(No response from Alberta.)* And the chest of drawers too. *(No response.)* Is Herb picky like that?

ALBERTA: Herb likes to look nice. *(Reaches for her soap.)*

DEEDEE: Hey! You forgot one. *(Picking the remaining shirt out of Alberta's basket.)* See? *(Opens it out, showing an awful stain.)* Yuck! Looks like vomit.

ALBERTA: It's my cabbage soup.

DEEDEE: Well, *(Helping.)* in it goes. *(Opening one of Alberta's washers.)*

ALBERTA: No!

DEEDEE: The other one? *(Reaching for the other washer.)*

ALBERTA: *(Taking the shirt away from her.)* I don't want to…it's too…that stain will never… *(Enforcing a calm now.)* It needs to presoak. I forgot the Woolite.

DEEDEE: Sorry.

ALBERTA: That's quite all right. *(Folding the shirt carefully, putting it back in the basket. Wants Deedee to vanish.)*

DEEDEE: One of those machines give soap?

(Alberta points to the correct one and Deedee walks over to it.)

DEEDEE: It takes nickels. I only got quarters.

ALBERTA: The attendant will give you change. *(Pointing to the open attendant door, putting her own coins in her washers.)*

DEEDEE: *(Looking in the door.)* He's asleep.

ALBERTA: Ah.

DEEDEE: Be terrible to wake him up just for some old nickels. Do you have any change?

ALBERTA: No.

DEEDEE: Looks like he's got a pocket full of money. Think it would wake him up if I stuck my hand in there? *(Enjoys this idea.)*

ALBERTA: *(Feeling bad about not helping and also not wanting the attendant awake.)* Twenty years ago, maybe. *(Deedee laughs.)* Here, I found some. *(Deedee walks back, gives Alberta the quarters; she counts out the change.)*

ALBERTA: That's ten, twenty, thirty, forty, fifty.

DEEDEE: *(Putting the nickels in the soap machine.)* He shouldn't be sleeping like that. Somebody could come in here and rob him. You don't think he's dead or anything, do you? I mean, I probably wouldn't know it if I saw somebody dead.

ALBERTA: You'd know. *(Starts her washers.)*

DEEDEE: *(Pushing in the coin trays, starting her washers.)* Okay. Cheer up! *(Laughs.)* That's what Mom always says, "Cheer Up" *(Looks at Alberta.)* Hey, my name is Deedee. Deedee Johnson.

ALBERTA: Nice to meet you.

DEEDEE: What's yours?

ALBERTA: Alberta.

DEEDEE: Alberta what?

ALBERTA: *(Reluctantly.)* Alberta Johnson.

DEEDEE: Hey! We might be related. I mean, Herb and Joe could be cousins or something.

ALBERTA: I don't think so.

DEEDEE: Yeah. I guess there's lots of Johnsons.

ALBERTA: *(Looking down at the magazine.)* Yes.

DEEDEE: I'm botherin' you, aren't I? *(Alberta smiles.)* I'd talk to somebody else, but there ain't nobody else. 'Cept Sleepy back there. I talk in *my* sleep sometimes, but him, he looks like he's lucky to be breathin' in his. *(Awkward.)* Sleep, I mean.

ALBERTA: Would you like a magazine?

DEEDEE: No thanks. I brought a Dr. Pepper. *(Alberta is amazed.)* You can have it if you want.

ALBERTA: No thank you.

DEEDEE: Sleepy was one of the seven dwarfs. I can still name them all. I couldn't tell you seven presidents of the United States, but I can say the dwarfs. *(Very proud.)* Sleepy, Grumpy, Sneezy, Dopey, Doc, and Bashful. *(Suddenly very low.)* That's only six. Who's the other one?

ALBERTA: *(Willing to help.)* You could name seven presidents.

DEEDEE: Oh no.

ALBERTA: Try it.

DEEDEE: Okay. *(Takes a big breath.)* There's Carter, Nixon, Kennedy, Lincoln, Ben Franklin, George Washington...uh...

ALBERTA: Eleanor Roosevelt's husband.

DEEDEE: Mr. Roosevelt.

ALBERTA: Mr. Roosevelt. That's seven. Except Benjamin Franklin was never president.

DEEDEE: You're a teacher or something, aren't you?

ALBERTA: I was. Say Mr. Roosevelt again.

DEEDEE: Mr. Roosevelt.

ALBERTA: There. Teddy makes seven.

DEEDEE: Around here? *(Alberta looks puzzled.)* Or in the county schools?

ALBERTA: Ohio. Columbus.

DEEDEE: Great!

ALBERTA: Do you know Columbus?

DEEDEE: Not personally.

ALBERTA: Ah.

DEEDEE: I better be careful. No ain'ts or nuthin'.

ALBERTA: You can't say anything I haven't heard before.

DEEDEE: Want me to try?

ALBERTA: No.

DEEDEE: What does Herb do?

ALBERTA: *(Too quickly.)* Is Deedee short for something? Deirdre, Deborah?

DEEDEE: No. Just Deedee. The guys in high school always kidded me about my name. *(Affecting a boy's voice.)* Hey, Deedee, is Deedee your name or your bra size?

ALBERTA: That wasn't very nice of them.

DEEDEE: That ain't the worst. Wanna hear the worst? *(Alberta doesn't respond.)* Ricky Baker, Icky Ricky Baker and David Duvall said this one. They'd come up to the locker bank, David's locker was right next to mine and Ricky'd say, "Hey, did you have a good time last night?" And David would say, "Yes. In Deedee." Then they'd slap each other and laugh like idiots.

ALBERTA: You could've had your locker moved.

DEEDEE: I guess, but see, the basketball players always came down that hall at the end of school. Going to practice, you know.

ALBERTA: One of the basketball players I taught… *(Begins to chuckle.)*

DEEDEE: *(Anxious to laugh with her.)* Yeah?

ALBERTA: …thought Herbert Hoover invented the vacuum cleaner.

(Alberta waits for Deedee to laugh. When she doesn't, Alberta steps back a few steps. Deedee is embarrassed.)

DEEDEE: Why did you quit…teaching.

ALBERTA: Age.

DEEDEE: You don't look old enough to retire.

ALBERTA: Not my age. Theirs.

DEEDEE: Mine, you mean.

ALBERTA: Actually, Mother was very sick then.

DEEDEE: Is she still alive?

ALBERTA: No.

DEEDEE: I'm sorry.

ALBERTA: It was a blessing, really. There was quite a lot of pain at the end.

DEEDEE: For her maybe, but what about you?

ALBERTA: She was the one with the pain.

DEEDEE: Sounds like she was lucky to have you there, nursing her and all.

ALBERTA: I read her *Wuthering Heights* five times that year. I kept checking different ones out of the library, you know, *Little Women, Pride and Prejudice,* but each time she'd say, "No, I think I'd like to hear *Wuthering Heights.*" Just like she hadn't heard it in fifty years. But each time, I'd read the last page and look up, and she'd say the same thing.

DEEDEE: What thing?

ALBERTA: She'd say, "I still don't see it. They didn't have to have all that trouble. All they had to do was find Heathcliff someplace to go every day. The man just needed a job. *(Pause.)* But maybe I missed something. Read it again."

DEEDEE: My mom thinks Joe's a bum.

(Somehow she thinks this is an appropriate response, and Alberta is jolted back to the present.)

DEEDEE: No really, she kept paying this guy that worked at Walgreen's to come over and strip our wallpaper. She said, "Deedee, he's gonna be manager of that drugstore someday." Hell, the only reason he worked there was getting a discount on his pimple cream. She thought that would get me off Joe. No way. We've been married two years last month. Mom says this is the itch year.

ALBERTA: The itch year?

DEEDEE: When guys get the itch, you know, to fool around with other women. Stayin' out late, comin' in with stories about goin' drinkin' with the boys or workin' overtime or…somethin'. Is that clock right?

ALBERTA: I think so.

DEEDEE: Bet Herb never did that, huh?

ALBERTA: Be unfaithful, you mean? *(Deedee nods.)* No.

DEEDEE: How can you be so sure like that? You keep him in the refrigerator?

ALBERTA: Well, I suppose he could have… *(Doesn't believe this for a minute.)*

DEEDEE: Like right now, while he's up in wherever he is…

ALBERTA: Akron. *(Surprised at her need to say this.)*

DEEDEE: Akron, he could be sittin' at the bar in some all-night bowling alley polishin' some big blonde's ball.

ALBERTA: No.

DEEDEE: That's real nice to trust him like that.

ALBERTA: Aren't you afraid Joe will call you on his break and be worried about where you are?

DEEDEE: You got any kids?

ALBERTA: No.

DEEDEE: Didn't you want some?

ALBERTA: Oh yes.

DEEDEE: Me too. Lots of 'em. But Joe says he's not ready. Wants to be earning lots of money before we start our family.

ALBERTA: That's why he works this double shift.

DEEDEE: Yeah. Only now he's fixin' up this '64 Chevy he bought to drag race. Then when the race money starts comin' in, we can have them kids. He's really lookin' forward to that—winnin' a big race and havin' me and the kids run out on the track and him smilin' and grabbin' up the baby and pourin' beer all over us while the crowd is yellin' and screamin'…

ALBERTA: So all his money goes into this car.

DEEDEE: Hey. I love it too. Sundays we go to the garage and work on it. *(Gets a picture out of her wallet.)* That devil painted there on the door, that cost two hundred dollars!

ALBERTA: You help him?

DEEDEE: He says it's a real big help just havin' me there watchin'.

ALBERTA: I never understood that, men wanting you to watch them do whatever it is…I mean…Well *(Deciding to tell this story, a surprise both to her and to us.)* every year at Thanksgiving, Herb would watch over me, washing the turkey, making the stuffing, stuffing the turkey. Made me nervous.

DEEDEE: You coulda told him to get lost. *(Offers fabric softener.)* Downy?
(Alberta nods yes, accepting Deedee's help, but is still nervous about it.)

ALBERTA: Actually, the last ten years or so, I sent him out for sage. For the dressing. He'd come in and sit down saying "Mmm boy was this ever going to be the best turkey yet" and rubbing his hands together and I'd push jars around in the cabinet and look all worried and say "Herb, I don't think I have enough sage." And he'd say, "Well, Bertie, my girl, I'll just go to the store and get some."

DEEDEE: *(Jittery when someone else is talking.)* I saw white pepper at the store last week. How do they do that?

ALBERTA: I don't know.

DEEDEE: Is Dr. Pepper made out of pepper?

ALBERTA: I don't know.

DEEDEE: And what did Herb do, that you had to watch, I mean.

ALBERTA: He gardened. I didn't have to watch him plant the seeds or weed the plants or spray for pests or pick okra. But when the day came to turn over the soil, that was the day. Herb would rent a rototiller and bring out a lawn chair from the garage. He'd wipe it off and call in the kitchen window, "Alberta, it's so pleasant out here in the sunshine." And when he finished, he'd bring out this little wooden sign and drive it into the ground.

DEEDEE: What'd it say?

ALBERTA: Herb Garden. *(Pauses.)* He thought that was funny.

DEEDEE: Did you laugh?

ALBERTA: Every year.

DEEDEE: He's not doing one anymore? *(Walking to the window.)*

ALBERTA: No.

DEEDEE: *(Looks uneasy, still staring out the window.)* Why not?

ALBERTA: What's out there?

DEEDEE: Oh nothing.

ALBERTA: You looked like—

DEEDEE: Joe should be home soon. I turned out all the lights except the blueberries so I could tell if he comes in, you know, when he turns the lights on.

ALBERTA: When is the shift over?

DEEDEE: *(Enforced cheer now.)* Oh, not for a long time yet. I just thought…He might get through early, he said. And we could go have a beer. Course, he might stop off and bowl a few games first.

(Alberta gets up to check on her wash. Deedee walks to the bulletin board.)

DEEDEE: *(Reading.)* "Typing done, hourly or by the page. Cheer." What on earth?

ALBERTA: Must be cheap. *(Laughs a little.)* It better be cheap.

DEEDEE: *(Taking some notices down.)* Most of this stuff is over already. Hey! Here's one for Herb. "Gardening tools, never used. Rake, hoe, spade and towel."

ALBERTA: Trowel.

DEEDEE: *(Aggravated by the correction.)* You got great eyes, Alberta. *(Continues reading.)* "459-4734. A. Johnson." You think this A. Johnson is related to us? *(Laughs.)* No, that's right, you said Herb wasn't doing a garden anymore. No, I got it! This A. Johnson is you. And the reason Herb ain't doin' a garden is you're selling his rakes. But this says "never used." Alberta, you shouldn't try to fool people like that. Washin' up Herb's hoe and selling it like it was new. Bad girl.

ALBERTA: Actually, that is me. I bought Herb some new tools for his birthday and then he…gave it up…gardening.

DEEDEE: Before his birthday?

ALBERTA: What?

DEEDEE: Did you have time to go buy him another present?

ALBERTA: Yes…well, no. I mean, he told me before his birthday, but I didn't get a chance to get him anything else.

DEEDEE: He's probably got everything anyhow.

ALBERTA: Just about.

DEEDEE: Didn't he get his feelings hurt?

ALBERTA: No.

DEEDEE: Joe never likes the stuff I give him.

ALBERTA: Oh, I'm sure he does. He just doesn't know how to tell you.

DEEDEE: No. He doesn't. For our anniversary, I planned real far ahead for this one, I'm tellin' you. I sent off my picture, not a whole body picture, just my face real close up, to this place in Massachusetts, and they painted, well

I don't know if they really painted, but somehow or other they *put* my face on this doll. It was unbelievable how it really looked like me. 'Bout this tall *(Indicates about two feet.)* with overalls and a checked shirt. I thought it was real cute, and I wrote this card sayin' "From one livin' doll to another. Let's keep playin' house till the day we die."

ALBERTA: And he didn't like it?

DEEDEE: He laughed so hard he fell over backward out of the chair and cracked his head open on the radiator. We had to take him to the emergency room.

ALBERTA: I'm sorry.

DEEDEE: We was sittin' there waitin' for him to get sewed up and this little kid comes in real sick and Joe he says to me, *(Getting a candy bar out of her purse and taking a big anxious bite out of it.)* I brought this doll along, see, I don't know why, anyway Joe says to me…"Deedee, that little girl is so much sicker than me. Let's give her this doll to make her feel better." And they were takin' her right on in to the doctors 'cause she looked pretty bad, and Joe rushes up and puts this doll in her arms.

ALBERTA: They let her keep it?

DEEDEE: Her mother said, "Thanks a lot." Real sweet like they didn't have much money to buy the kid dolls or something. It made Joe feel real good.

ALBERTA: But it was your present to him. It was your face on the doll.

DEEDEE: Yeah, *(Pause.)* but I figure it was his present as soon as I gave it to him, so if he wanted to give it away, that's his business. But *(Stops.)* he didn't like it. I could tell. *(Walks to the window again.)* They need to wash this window here.

ALBERTA: I gave Herb a fishing pole one year.

DEEDEE: *(Not interested.)* He fishes.

ALBERTA: No, but I thought he wanted to. He'd cut out a picture of this husky man standing in water practically up to his waist, fishing. I thought he left it out so I'd get the hint.

DEEDEE: But he didn't?

ALBERTA: Oh, it was a hint all right. He wanted the hat.

DEEDEE: Right.

ALBERTA: *(Seeing that Deedee is really getting upset.)* Do you like the things Joe gives you?

DEEDEE: I'd like it if he came home, that's what I'd like.

ALBERTA: He'll be back soon. You'll probably see those lights go on as soon as your clothes are dry.

DEEDEE: Sure.

ALBERTA: People just can't always be where we want them to be, when we want them to be there.

DEEDEE: Well, I don't like it.

ALBERTA: You don't have to like it. You just have to know it.

DEEDEE: *(Defensive.)* Wouldn't you like for Herb to be home right now?

ALBERTA: I certainly would.

DEEDEE: 'Cause if they were both home where they should be, we wouldn't have to be here in this crappy laundromat washin' fuckin' shirts in the middle of the night!

(Deedee kicks a dryer. Alberta is alarmed and disturbed at the use of the word "fuckin'.")

DEEDEE: I'm sorry. You probably don't use language like that, well, neither do I, very often, but I'm *(Now doing it on purpose.)* pissed as hell at that sunuvabitch.

(Alberta picks up a magazine, trying to withdraw completely. She is offended, but doesn't want to appear self-righteous. Now, Shooter pushes open the front door. Deedee turns sharply and sees him. She storms back and sits down beside Alberta. Both women are somewhat alarmed at a black man entering this preserve so late at night. Shooter is poised and handsome. He is dressed neatly, but casually. He is carrying an army duffel bag full of clothes, a cue case, and a sack of tacos. He has a can of beer in one pocket. He moves toward a washer, sets down the duffel bag, opens the cap on the beer. He is aware that he has frightened them. This amuses him, but he understands it. Besides, he is so goddamned charming.)

SHOOTER: *(Holding the taco sack so they can see it.)* Would either of you two ladies care to join me in a taco?

ALBERTA: *(Finally.)* No thank you.

SHOOTER: *(As though in an ad.)* Freshly chopped lettuce, firm vine-ripened New Jersey beefsteak tomatoes, a-ged, shred-ded, ched-dar cheese, sweet slivers of Bermuda onion and Ole Mexico's very own, very hot taco sauce.

DEEDEE: That's just what they say on the radio.

SHOOTER: That's because I'm the "they" who says it on the radio.

DEEDEE: You are?

SHOOTER: *(Walking over.)* Shooter Stevens. *(Shakes her hand.)*

ALBERTA: *(As he shakes her hand.)* Nice to meet you.

DEEDEE: You're the Number One Night Owl?

SHOOTER: *(As he said it at the beginning of the act.)* …sayin' it's three o'clock, all right, and time to rock your daddy to dreams of de-light.

DEEDEE: You are! You really are! That's fantastic! I always listen to you!

SHOOTER: *(Walking back to his laundry.)* Yeah?

DEEDEE: Always. Except when…I mean, when I get to pick, I pick you. I mean, your station. You're on late.

SHOOTER: You got it.

DEEDEE: *(To Alberta.)* Terrific. *(Disgusted with herself.)* I'm telling him he's on late. He knows he's on late. He's the one who's on late. Big news, huh?

SHOOTER: You a reporter?

DEEDEE: *(Pleased with the question.)* Oh no. *(Stands up, stretches.)* Gotten so stiff sitting there. *(Walks over.)* Don't you know what they put in those things?

SHOOTER: The tacos?

DEEDEE: Dog food.

SHOOTER: *(Laughing.)* Have to eat 'em anyway. Good business. I keep stoppin' in over there, they keep running the ad. Gonna kill me.

DEEDEE: No kidding. We take our… *(Quickly.)* My garbage cans are right next to theirs and whatta theirs got in 'em all the time? Dog-food cans.

SHOOTER: *(He smiles.)* Maybe they have a dog.

ALBERTA: It could be someone else in the building.

SHOOTER: See?

DEEDEE: She didn't mean they have a dog. She meant some old person in the building's eatin' dog food. It happens. A lot around here.

SHOOTER: *(To Alberta.)* You her mom?

ALBERTA: No.

DEEDEE: We just met in here. She's Alberta Johnson. I'm Deedee Johnson.

ALBERTA: Shooter is an unusual name.

SHOOTER: *(Nodding toward the pool hall next door.)* I play some pool.

DEEDEE: *(Pointing to the cue case.)* What's that?

SHOOTER: My cue.

DEEDEE: You any good?

SHOOTER: At what?

DEEDEE: At pool, dummy.

SHOOTER: *(Putting his clothes in the washer.)* I do okay.

DEEDEE: You must do better than okay or else why would you have your own cue?

SHOOTER: Willie says, Willie's the guy who owns the place, Willie says pool cues are like women. You gotta have your own and you gotta treat her right.

DEEDEE: *(Seeing a piece of clothing he's dropped in.)* Did you mean to put that in there?

SHOOTER: *(Pulling it back out.)* This?

DEEDEE: Your whites will come out green.

SHOOTER: *(Dropping it back in the washer.)* Uh-uh. It's nylon.

ALBERTA: Your work sounds very interesting.

SHOOTER: Yes, it does.

DEEDEE: What's your real name?

SHOOTER: G.W.

DEEDEE: That's not a real name.

SHOOTER: I don't like my real name.

DEEDEE: Come on…

SHOOTER: *(Disgusted.)* It's Gary Wayne. Now do I look like Gary Wayne to you?

DEEDEE: *(Laughs.)* No.

SHOOTER: Mom's from Indiana.

ALBERTA: From Gary or Fort Wayne?

DEEDEE: Alberta used to be a teacher.

SHOOTER: It coulda been worse. She coulda named me Clarksville.

  (Deedee laughs.)

SHOOTER: Hey! Now why don't the two of you come over and join us for a beer?

ALBERTA: No thank you.

SHOOTER: *(Pouring in the soap.)* It's just Willie and me this time of night.

ALBERTA: No.

DEEDEE: *(With a knowing look at Alberta.)* And watch you play pool?

SHOOTER: Actually, what we were planning to do tonight was whip us up a big devil's food cake and pour it in one of the pool tables to bake. Turn up the heat real high…watch it rise and then pour on the creamy fudge icing with lots of nuts.

DEEDEE: *You're* nuts.

SHOOTER: Get real sick if we have to eat it all ourselves…

DEEDEE: I've never seen anybody play pool.

SHOOTER: The key to pool's a… *(Directly seductive now.)* real smooth stroke… the feel of that stick in your hand…

DEEDEE: Feels good?

SHOOTER: You come on over, I'll show you just how it's done.

DEEDEE: Pool.

SHOOTER: Sure. *(Smiles, then turns sharply and walks back to Alberta, depositing an empty soap box in the trash can.)* Willie always keeps hot water. You could have a nice cup of tea.

ALBERTA: *(A pointed look at Deedee.)* No.

DEEDEE: Our wash is almost done. We have to—

SHOOTER: We'll be there quite a while. Gets lonesome this late, you know.

DEEDEE: We know.

(And suddenly, everybody feels quite uncomfortable.)

SHOOTER: *(To Alberta.)* It was nice meeting you. Hope I didn't interrupt your reading or anything.

DEEDEE: She used to be a teacher.

SHOOTER: That's what you said. *(Walking toward the door.)* Right next door, now. Can't miss it. *(To Deedee.)* Give you a piece of that fudge cake.

DEEDEE: Yeah, I'll bet you would.

SHOOTER: *(Closing the door.)* Big piece.

(Alberta watches Deedee watch to see which direction Shooter takes.)

DEEDEE: *(After a moment.)* I thought we'd had it there for a minute, didn't you? *(Visibly cheered.)* Coulda been a murderer, or a robber or a rapist, just as easy! *(Increasingly excited.)* We coulda been hostages by now!

ALBERTA: To have hostages you have to commit a hijacking. You do not hijack a laundromat.

DEEDEE: Depends how bad you need clean clothes.

ALBERTA: I didn't like the things he said to you.

DEEDEE: He was just playin'.

ALBERTA: He was not playing.

DEEDEE: Well, what does it hurt? Just words.

ALBERTA: Not those words.

DEEDEE: You don't miss a thing, do you?

ALBERTA: I'm not deaf.

DEEDEE: Just prejudiced.

ALBERTA: That's not true.

DEEDEE: If that was a white DJ comin' in here, you'd still be talkin' to him, I bet. Seein' if he knows your "old" favorites.

ALBERTA: If you don't want to know what I think, you can stop talking to me.

DEEDEE: What you think is what's wrong with the world. People don't trust each other just because they're some other color from them.

ALBERTA: And who was it who said he could be a murderer? That was you, Deedee. Would you have said that if he'd been white?

DEEDEE: It just makes you sick, doesn't it. The thought of me and Shooter over there after you go home.

ALBERTA: It's not my business.

DEEDEE: That's for sure.

(Alberta goes back to reading her magazine. Deedee wanders around.)

DEEDEE: You don't listen to him on the radio, but I do. And you know what he says after "rock your daddy to dreams of de-light"? He says, "And mama, I'm comin' home." Now, if he has a "mama" to go home to, what's he doing washing his own clothes? So he don't have a "mama," and that means lonely. And he's loaded, too. So if he's got a wife, she's got a washer, so don't say maybe they don't have a washer. Lonely.

ALBERTA: All right. He's a nice young man who washes his own clothes and is "friendly" without regard to race, creed, or national origin.

DEEDEE: I mean, we're both in here in the middle of the night and it don't mean we're on the make, does it?

ALBERTA: It's perfectly respectable.

DEEDEE: You always do this when Herb is out of town?

ALBERTA: No.

DEEDEE: You don't even live in this neighborhood, do you?

ALBERTA: No.

DEEDEE: Know how I knew that? That garden. There ain't a garden for miles around here.

ALBERTA: You've been reading Sherlock Holmes.

DEEDEE: *(Knows Alberta was insulting her.)* So why did you come over here?

ALBERTA: *(Knows she made a mistake.)* I came for the same reason you did. To do my wash.

DEEDEE: In the middle of the night? Hah. It's a big mystery, isn't it? And you don't want to tell me. Is some man meetin' you here? Yeah, and you can't have your meetin' out where you live 'cause your friends might see you and give the word to old Herb when he gets back.

ALBERTA: No. *(Pauses.)* I'm sorry I said what I did. Go on over to the pool hall. I'll put your clothes in the dryer.

DEEDEE: *(Easily thrown off the track.)* And let him think I'm all hot for him. No sir. Besides, Joe might come home.

ALBERTA: That's right.

DEEDEE: Might just serve him right, though. Come in and see me drinkin' beer and playin' pool with Willie and Shooter. Joe hates black people. He says even when they're dancin' or playin' ball, they're thinkin' about killin'. Yeah, that would teach him to run out on me. A little dose of his own medicine. Watch him gag on it.

ALBERTA: So he *has* run out on you.

DEEDEE: He's workin' the double shift.

ALBERTA: That's what you said.

DEEDEE: And you don't believe me. You think he just didn't come home, is that it? You think I was over there waitin' and waitin' in my new nightgown and when the late show went off I turned on the radio and ate a whole pint of chocolate ice cream, and when the radio went off I couldn't stand it anymore so I grabbed up all these clothes, dirty or not, and got outta there so he wouldn't come in and find me cryin'. Well, *(Firmly.)* I wasn't cryin'!

ALBERTA: *(After a considerable pause.)* I haven't cried in forty years.

DEEDEE: Just happy I guess.

ALBERTA: *(With a real desire to help now.)* I had an Aunt Dora, who had a rabbit, Puffer, who died. I cried then. I cried for weeks.

DEEDEE: And it wasn't even your rabbit.

ALBERTA: I loved Aunt Dora and she loved that rabbit. I'd go to visit and she'd tell me what Puffer had done that day. She claimed he told her stories, Goldilocks and the Three Hares, The Rabbit Who Ate New York. Then we'd go outside and drink lemonade while Puffer ate lettuce. She grew lettuce just for him. A whole backyard of it.

DEEDEE: Little cracked, huh?

ALBERTA: I helped her bury him. Tears were streaming down my face. "Bertie," she said, "stop crying. He didn't mean to go and leave us all alone and he'd feel bad if he knew he made us so miserable." But in the next few weeks, Aunt Dora got quieter and quieter till finally she wasn't talking at all and Mother put her in a nursing home.

DEEDEE: Where she died.

ALBERTA: Yes.

DEEDEE: Hey! Our wash is done. *(Alberta seems not to hear her.)* Look, I'll do it. You go sit.

ALBERTA: *(Disoriented.)* No, I…

DEEDEE: Let me, really. I know this part. Mom says you can't blow this part, so I do it. She still checks, though, finds some reason to go downstairs and check the heat I set. I don't mind, really. Can't be too careful.

(Deedee unloads the washers and carries the clothes to the dryers. Alberta walks to the window, seeming very far away.)

DEEDEE: *(Setting the heat.)* Regular for you guys, warm for permos and undies. Now Herb's shirts and shorts get hot. Pants and socks get…

ALBERTA: Warm.

DEEDEE: What's Herb got left to wear anyhow?

ALBERTA: His gray suit.

DEEDEE: *(Laughs at how positive Alberta is about this.)* What color tie?

ALBERTA: Red with a silver stripe through it.

DEEDEE: *(Still merry.)* Shirt?

ALBERTA: White.

DEEDEE: Shoes?

ALBERTA: *(Quiet astonishment.)* I don't know.

DEEDEE: Well I'm glad. Thought you were seeing him all the way to Akron, X-ray eyes or something weird. Alberta...

ALBERTA: Yes? *(Worried, turning around to face her now, afraid Deedee will know her secret.)*

DEEDEE: You got any dimes?

ALBERTA: *(Relieved.)* Sure. *(Walks to her purse.)* How many do we need?

DEEDEE: Two each, I guess. Four dryers makes eight.

(As Alberta is getting them out of her wallet.)

DEEDEE: I don't know what I'd have done if you hadn't been here. I didn't think...before I...

ALBERTA: You'd have done just fine. Don't forget Sleepy back there.

DEEDEE: I wish Mom were more like you.

ALBERTA: Stuck up?

DEEDEE: Smart. Nice to talk to.

ALBERTA: Thank you, but...

DEEDEE: No, really. You've been to Mexico and you've got a good man.

(Alberta takes off her glasses, still very upset.)

DEEDEE: Mom's just got me and giant-size Cheer. And she don't say two words while I'm there. Ever. I don't blame her I guess.

ALBERTA: Well...

DEEDEE: Yeah.

ALBERTA: *(Back in balance now.)* But you're young and pretty. You have a wonderful sense of humor.

DEEDEE: Uh-huh.

ALBERTA: And you'll have those children someday.

DEEDEE: Yeah, I know. *(Gloomily.)* I have my whole life in front of me.

ALBERTA: You could get a job.

DEEDEE: Oh, I got one. This company in New Jersey, they send me envelopes and letters and lists of names and I write on the names and addresses and Dear Mr. Wilson or whatever at the top of the letter. I do have nice handwriting.

ALBERTA: I'm sure.

DEEDEE: I get so bored doing it. Sometimes I want to take a fat orange crayon and scribble *(Making letters in the air.)* EAT BEANS, FATSO, and then draw funny faces all over the letter.

ALBERTA: I'm sure the extra money comes in handy.

DEEDEE: Well, Joe don't know I do it. I hide all the stuff before he comes home. And I keep the money at Mom's. She borrows from it sometimes. She says that makes us even for the water for the washing machine. See, I can't spend it or Joe will know I got it.

ALBERTA: He doesn't want you to work.

DEEDEE: *(Imitating Joe's voice.)* I'm the head of this house.

ALBERTA: He expects you to sit around all day?

DEEDEE: I guess. *(With good-humored rage.)* Oh, I can wash the floor if I want.

ALBERTA: You should tell him how you feel.

DEEDEE: He'd leave me.

ALBERTA: Maybe.

DEEDEE: *(After a moment.)* So what, right?

ALBERTA: I just meant, if you give him the chance to understand—

DEEDEE: But what would I say?

ALBERTA: You'd figure something out. I'm sure.

DEEDEE: I don't want to start it. I don't want to say I want a real job, 'cause then I'll say the reason I want a real job is I gotta have something to think about besides when are you coming home and how long is it gonna be before you don't come home at all. And he'll say what do you mean don't come home at all and I'll have to tell him I know what you're doing, I know you're lying to me and going out on me and he'll say what are you gonna do about it. You want a divorce? And I don't want him to say that.

ALBERTA: Now...you don't know—

DEEDEE: *(Firmly.)* I called the bowling alley and asked for him and the bartender said, "This Patsy? He's on his way, honey." I hope he falls in the sewer.

ALBERTA: Deedee!

DEEDEE: I hope he gets his shirt caught in his zipper. I hope he wore socks with holes in 'em. I hope his Right Guard gives out. I hope his baseball cap falls in the toilet. I hope she kills him. *(Pushing one of the carts, hard.)*

ALBERTA: Deedee!

DEEDEE: I do. Last night, I thought I'd surprise him and maybe we'd bowl a few games? Well, I was gettin' my shoes and I saw them down at lane twelve, laughin' and all. He had one of his hands rubbing her hair and the other one rubbing his bowling ball. Boy did I get out of there quick. I've seen her there before. She teaches at the Weight Control upstairs, so she's probably not very strong but maybe she could poison him or something. She wears those pink leotards and even her hair looks thin. I hate him.

ALBERTA: I'm sure you don't really.

DEEDEE: He's mean and stupid. I thought he'd get over it, but he didn't. Mean and stupid. And I ain't all that smart, so if I know he's dumb, he must really be dumb. I used to think he just acted mean and stupid. Now, I know he really *is*...

ALBERTA: ...mean and stupid.

DEEDEE: Why am I telling you this? You don't know nuthin' about bein' dumped.

ALBERTA: At least you have some money saved.

DEEDEE: For what?

ALBERTA: And your mother would let you stay with her till you got your own place.

DEEDEE: She's the *last* person I'm tellin'.

ALBERTA: I'll bet you'd like being a telephone operator.

DEEDEE: But how's he gonna eat? The only time he ever even fried an egg, he flipped it over and it landed in the sink. It was the last egg, so he grabbed it up and ate it in one bite.

ALBERTA: One bite?

DEEDEE: I like how he comes in the door. Picks me up, swings me around in the air...

ALBERTA: *(Incredulous.)* He stuffed a whole egg in his mouth?

DEEDEE: You're worse than Mom. *(Angrily.)* He's gonna be a famous race car driver someday and I want to be there.

ALBERTA: To have him pour beer all over you.

DEEDEE: Yes, to have him pour beer all over me.

ALBERTA: *(Checking the clothes in one of her dryers, knowing she has said too much.)* He could have come in without turning on the lights. If you want to go check, I'll watch your things here.

DEEDEE: You want to get rid of me, don't you?

ALBERTA: I do not want to get rid of you.

DEEDEE: So why don't *you* go home? Go get the Woolite for that yucky shirt you didn't wash. You not only don't want to talk to me, you didn't even want me to touch that shirt. Herb's shirt is too nice for me to even touch. Well, I may be a slob, but I'm clean.

ALBERTA: I didn't want to wash it.

DEEDEE: That ain't it at all. Herb is so wonderful. You love him so much. You wash his clothes just the right way. I could never drop his shirt in the washer the way you do it. The stain might not come out and he might say what did you do to my shirt and you might fight and that would mess up your little dream world where everything is always sweet and nobody ever gets mad and you just go around gardening and giving each other little pecky kisses all the time. Well, you're either kidding yourself or lying to me. Nobody is so wonderful that somebody else can't touch their shirt. You act like he's a saint. Like he's dead and now you worship the shirts he wore.

ALBERTA: What do I have to do to get you to leave me alone?

DEEDEE: *(Feeling very bad.)* He is dead, isn't he?

ALBERTA: Yes.

DEEDEE: I'm so stupid.

ALBERTA: You...

DEEDEE: What? Tell me. Say something horrible.

ALBERTA: *(Slowly, but not mean.)* You just don't know when to shut up.

DEEDEE: Worse than that. I don't know how. *(Hates what she has done.)*

ALBERTA: But you are not dumb, child. And don't let anybody tell you you are, okay? *(Takes off her glasses and rubs her eyes.)*

DEEDEE: I'm sorry, Mrs. Johnson, I really am sorry. You probably been plannin' this night for a long time. Washin' his things. And I barged in and spoiled it all.

ALBERTA: I've been avoiding it for a long time.

(Deedee feels terrible, she wants to ask questions, but is trying very hard, for once, to control her mouth.)

ALBERTA: Herb died last winter, the day before his birthday.

DEEDEE: When you got him the rakes.

ALBERTA: He was being nosy, like I told you before, in the kitchen. I was making his cake. So I asked him to take out the garbage. He said, "Can't we wait till it's old enough to walk?"

DEEDEE: How...

ALBERTA: I didn't miss him till I put the cake in the oven. Guess I thought he was checking his seedbeds in the garage. I yelled out, "Herb, do you want butter cream or chocolate?" And then I saw him. Lying in the alley, covered in my cabbage soup. It was his heart.

DEEDEE: Did you call the...

ALBERTA: I picked up his head in my hand and held it while I cleaned up as much of the stuff as I could. A tuna can, coffee grounds, eggshells...

DEEDEE: *(Carefully.)* You knew he was dead, not just knocked out?

ALBERTA: He'd hit his head when he fell. He was bleeding in my hand. I knew I should get up, but the blood was still so warm.

DEEDEE: I'm so sorry.

ALBERTA: I don't want you to be alone, that's not what I meant before.

DEEDEE: Looks like I'm alone anyway.

ALBERTA: That's what I meant.

DEEDEE: Sometimes I bring in a little stand-up mirror to the coffee table while I'm watching TV. It's my face over there when I look, but it's a face just the same.

ALBERTA: Being alone isn't so awful. I mean, it's awful, but it's not that awful. There are hard things.

(The dryers stop. Deedee watches Alberta take a load of clothes from the dryer, holding them up to smell them.)

DEEDEE: I'd probably eat pork and beans for weeks.

ALBERTA: *(Her back to Deedee.)* I found our beachball when I cleaned out the basement. I can't let the air out of it. It's *(Turning around now.)* his breath in there. *(Sees Deedee is upset.)* Get your clothes out. They'll wrinkle. That's amazing about the shoes.

DEEDEE: The shoes?

ALBERTA: Remember I was telling you what Herb had on? Gray suit...

DEEDEE: ...white shirt, red tie with a silver stripe through it...

ALBERTA: I hang onto the shirt he died in, and I don't even know if he's got shoes on in his coffin.

DEEDEE: Well, if he's flyin' around heaven, he probably don't need 'em. *(Pauses.)* You bought him all black socks.

ALBERTA: It was his idea. He thought they'd be easier to match if they were all the same color.

DEEDEE: Is it?

ALBERTA: No. Now I have to match by length. They may be all black, but they don't all shrink the same. I guess I don't really have to match them now, though, do I? *(Continues to match them.)*

DEEDEE: I'd like to lose all Joe's white ones. *(Holding them up over the trash can, then thinking maybe it's not such a good idea.)*

ALBERTA: *(Going back for her last load of clothes, looking toward the window.)* Deedee...your lights are on. In your apartment. All the lights are on now.

DEEDEE: You sure?

ALBERTA: Come see.

(Deedee walks over to the window.)

DEEDEE: You're right.

ALBERTA: Yes.

DEEDEE: So what do I do now?

ALBERTA: I don't know.

DEEDEE: Should I rush right home? Ask Joe did he have a good time bowling a few games after his double shift? Listen to him brag about his score? His score he didn't make in the games he didn't bowl after the double shift he didn't work? Well I don't feel like it. I'm going next door. Play some pool. Make him miss me.

ALBERTA: You should go home before you forget how mad you are. You don't have to put up with what he's doing. You can if you want to, if you think you can't make it without him, but you don't have to.

DEEDEE: But what should I say? Joe, if you don't stop going out on me, I'm not ever speaking to you again? That's exactly what he wants.

ALBERTA: What you say isn't that important. But there is something you have to remember while you say it.

DEEDEE: Which is?

ALBERTA: Your own face in the mirror is better company than a man who would eat a whole fried egg in one bite.

(Deedee laughs.)

ALBERTA: But it won't be easy.

DEEDEE: *(Cautiously.)* Are you gonna wash that other shirt ever?

ALBERTA: The cabbage-soup shirt? No, I don't think so.

DEEDEE: Yeah.

ALBERTA: *(Loading up her basket.)* Maybe, in a few months or next year some-time, I'll be able to give these away. They're nice things.

DEEDEE: People do need them. Hey! *(Leaving her laundry and going to the bulletin board.)* I told you there ain't a garden for miles around here. You better hang onto these hoes. It's gettin' about time to turn over the soil, isn't it?

ALBERTA: Another two weeks or so, yes it is. Well, *(Taking the card.)* that's every-thing. I'll just get my soap and…

DEEDEE: *(Hesitantly.)* Mrs. Johnson?

ALBERTA: Alberta.

DEEDEE: Alberta.

ALBERTA: Yes?

DEEDEE: I'm really lonely.

ALBERTA: I know.

DEEDEE: How can you stand it?

ALBERTA: I can't. *(Pauses.)* But I have to, just the same.

DEEDEE: How do I...how do you do that?

ALBERTA: I don't know. You call me if you think of something. *(Gives her a small kiss on the forehead.)*

DEEDEE: I don't have your number.

ALBERTA: *(Backing away toward the door.)* I really wanted to be alone tonight.

DEEDEE: I know.

ALBERTA: I'm glad you talked me out of it.

DEEDEE: Boy, you can count on me for that. Hey! Don't go yet. I owe you some money.

ALBERTA: No. *(Fondly.)* Everybody deserves a free load now and then.

DEEDEE: *(Trying to reach across the space to her.)* Thank you.

ALBERTA: Now, I suggest you go wake up Sleepy back there and see if there's something he needs to talk about.

DEEDEE: Tell you the truth, I'm ready for a little peace and quiet.

ALBERTA: Good night. *(Leaves.)*

DEEDEE: *(Reaching for the Dr. Pepper she put on the washer early on.)* Yeah, peace and quiet. *(Pops the top on the Dr. Pepper.)* Too bad it don't come in cans. *(Lights go down as she stands there looking out the window.)*

END OF ACT I

ACT II

THE POOL HALL

The pool hall is small and seedy. Plastic beer ads cover the walls. Talc is kept in empty candy-bar boxes along the window sills. There is an old bar with sacks of potato chips and other snacks. Tacky ashtrays and calendars litter the room. There is one television set and one pool table. "The Star-Spangled Banner" is playing on the television as the lights come up.

Willie is wiping off the bar. As the song ends, he turns off the TV and opens a beer. He pulls out a racing form and sits down. He looks at the clock. Shooter enters, carrying a sack of tacos, his cue case, and a beer.

SHOOTER: *(In greeting.)* Willie.

WILLIE: *(Not looking up from the form.)* It's the man from the radio.

SHOOTER: How's it goin'?

WILLIE: Gets any busier I'll have to stand up.

SHOOTER: Or at least *look* up.

WILLIE: *(Looking up now.)* Sondra just called.

SHOOTER: She knows when I get off.

WILLIE: She sure does.

SHOOTER: Where else would I be?

WILLIE: Somethin' like that.

SHOOTER: Somebody did one helluva job teaching that girl to tell the time. Tells me the time to come home, tells me the time to eat, tells me the time to go to bed.

WILLIE: Well, I told her I'd send you on soon's you finished your beer.

SHOOTER: *(Indicating the racing form.)* Got any winners tomorrow?

WILLIE: Till tomorrow, they're all winners.

SHOOTER: Still betting those grays?

WILLIE: Yeah, the older I get, the more I love them gray horses.

SHOOTER: Trouble is, most of the ones you pick, gray isn't so much their color as an indication of their age.

WILLIE: Yeah, that one horse, Dusty Days, he's still runnin' from the first time I bet on him. *(Laughs.)* 'Bout eight years now. I sit here and handicap 'em, he always comes out the winner. I can't figure it out.

SHOOTER: It's some other dude does the handicappin', Willie. Back in the stable. Finds out which ones you're layin' your money on, then ties lead weights to their legs. That's handicappin', man.

WILLIE: You're tellin' me.

SHOOTER: George go home already?

WILLIE: Sick.

SHOOTER: Bad?

WILLIE: You know any that's good? Doc says circulation.

SHOOTER: I thought I improved his circulation with that wheelchair I gave him.

WILLIE: Callin' himself the stick-shift cripple. That was nice, boy. End of the world wouldn't keep ol' George from comin' in here every night, but he sure does like havin' that motor do the work. Last six months, he gets real tired, real quick.

SHOOTER: Sondra said he wouldn't even know it was real leather, but I figured, what the hell, it's only money.

WILLIE: Oh he knew. Said, "Willie, cows got it rough, don't they? Folks lookin' at 'em seein' steak dinners and upholstery." You shoulda seen him, George doin' this dumb cow voice, "Hey, man, you don't love me for what I am. You love me for what I'm gonna be—your suede leather shoes that walk you to get your all-beef cheeseburger which you pay for outta your genuine cowhide wallet."

SHOOTER: This dude at the surgical supply says, "Who's this for, son?" I started into this whole number like I had to explain, "Well, George, see, he's Sondra's father. Sondra, that's my wife. But George, he's also, well, my dad and George and this other man Willie, Willie he owns a pool hall, the three of them were real tight, and since Dad's gone now, one helluva pool player, my dad, anyway, George and Willie are like, well, George is family about five ways, see?" And on and on like that till finally he was givin' me this crazy look so I slapped down all those hundreds and said, "Hey, man, just give me the chair, okay?"

WILLIE: White boy in here the other night wouldn't let me lift George up to the rail to shoot. Said he had to keep one wheel on the floor.

SHOOTER: Just letting anybody in here these days.

WILLIE: Yeah. Even DJs.

SHOOTER: Little kid called me up tonight, wanted to talk to the record player. I said it don't talk, kid. He said, "No, man, you man, the record player." Over the air he said that. *(And he sets his cue case on the bar.)*

WILLIE: The record player.

SHOOTER: Very funny.

WILLIE: Oh come on, boy, it don't matter what you say over the air.

SHOOTER: Thanks.

WILLIE: Folks turn on the radio to hear the music, remember?

SHOOTER: *(Opening the cue case.)* I'll try to keep that in mind.

WILLIE: *(Closing the cue case.)* You're hidin' out tonight, aren't you? Well, you ain't hidin' *here.*

SHOOTER: *(Getting his cue out of the case.)* What you mean is you don't want nobody else hidin' in your hole. Well, the "hole" population looks pretty sparse to me.

WILLIE: Then what are you doin' here? Run outta skinny white girls?

SHOOTER: What's with you, man?

WILLIE: Go home, boy. Get outta my hall. Go home. See your wife.

SHOOTER: Ah, now we're gettin'—

WILLIE: Yeah, we're gettin'—

SHOOTER: *(Looking for the felt brush.)* Nowhere, man. I've had enough of this mother-hen shit.

WILLIE: Then quit playin' rooster.

(A big laugh from Shooter.)

SHOOTER: Oh I'm so sorry. Did I interrupt your nap? Did I disturb your dust?

WILLIE: You're sorry all right. Did I pay for you to be born? Did I scrape up what was left of your old man when he died? Now you go home when I tell you.

SHOOTER: I'm what's left of my old man.

WILLIE: Yeah. *(Unfortunately.)*

SHOOTER: And I didn't plan to be in Miami Beach when he died, it just happened. So, I'd have done it.

WILLIE: But you didn't. I identified him. I carried him to the ambulance. I bought his buryin' suit. I paid for his funeral.

SHOOTER: You got a plot out back for George when he goes? Way you tell it, those guys can't even die without you.

WILLIE: Man in here the other night said you better not die without payin' him his six thousand dollars you owe him. Said he'd come to hell to get it. Left you this note.

SHOOTER: *(Crumpling up the note.)* Least thanks to me, you won't have to carry George. Just dig the hole, then wheel him outta here some night, bury him wheelchair and all.

WILLIE: You can have your chair back, boy. He don't need your four-speed charity.

SHOOTER: Listen to you, giving away the cripple's chair. And charity, my man, is building a ramp *(Pointing to the door.)* up to a pool hall.

WILLIE: *(Pointing to the cue.)* What you think you're doin' with that?

SHOOTER: *(Swinging it around in a showy move.)* Gonna pick my teeth.

WILLIE: Might as well, G.W., 'cause you sure as hell don't know nothin' else to do with it.

SHOOTER: Least I ain't forgot what it's for. (*And he sets the cue ball on the head spot, taps it down to the foot rail so it rolls back to hit the tip of the cue in follow-through position.*)

WILLIE: And I ain't tryin' to be somethin' I ain't.

SHOOTER: I'm his kid.

WILLIE: You got his name.

SHOOTER: Yes sir. I've got the prize-winning best of the Three Blind Mice. I've got ol' Shooter's name, I've got George's only child, Sondra. And now I've got my own private pool palace.

WILLIE: Think so, huh?

SHOOTER: But not for long, right, Willie? You ain't the only nigger got spies. Man down at the station owns a part of Baskin-Robbins told me the chain needs a downtown shop and they got their eye on this place. I hear Mr. Rum Raisin makes a nice offer.

WILLIE: You heard wrong. I ain't sellin'.

SHOOTER: The hell you ain't. Come on, Willie, all the old pool players go to Asbury Park to die. Pool player's paradise. Big tournaments, best players coming through all the time. Then just eight miles up the Jersey coast you got the ponies running at Monmouth Park. And gambling in Atlantic City. Don't blame you for goin', Willie.

WILLIE: This place is a firetrap. Who'd want it?

SHOOTER: You might as well tell me, Willie, 'cause I got the picture already. Wake up about noon, spend a coupla hours with the racing form, then go for a swim, well, more like a walk in the pool. Then drive up to Monmouth, catch the daily double, collect your money and get back in time to see the hustlers do business down at Hopkins Billiards. Yes sir, racing, roulette and rack 'em up, boys, Willie's retirin' to Asbury Park. I hear they even got green felt carpet in the nursing homes.

WILLIE: I'd sell this place in a minute just to keep you outta here, get you home at night.

SHOOTER: This place, got your "friend" Shooter's tracks all over the floor? This place, the only place your "friend" George got to go every night? You'd sell the only thing you got to show for your whole life just to keep me paying Sondra's cleaning lady?

WILLIE: I sure would.

SHOOTER: *(As he puts the balls on the table.)* Married her to please Dad and George and now I gotta keep her 'cause of you?

WILLIE: Catch right on, don't you.

SHOOTER: You're talking crazy, man.

WILLIE: You talk crazy for a living. Man gets famous talking to the air.

SHOOTER: I'm not famous.

WILLIE: But you do talk to the air.

SHOOTER: And get paid for it.

WILLIE: Well, it ain't improved your personality.

SHOOTER: When you *are* a personality, you don't have to *have* a personality.

WILLIE: Good thing.

SHOOTER: What's between Sondra and me is between Sondra and me. What do you care? She's not your baby.

WILLIE: She's George's baby and that's enough for me. And if Shooter was here—

SHOOTER: He'd be shootin' pool and that's all. 'Cause he knew—

WILLIE: 'Cause that's all he could do. Never had a job in his life. I paid for you to be born.

SHOOTER: We know.

WILLIE: *(Refuses to stop.)* George paid the electric, and I paid the phone bill. George kept the grocery sendin' ham hocks, and I bought his beer.

SHOOTER: So what's that come to? I'm good for my old man's bills. *(Getting out his wallet.)* You take MasterCharge?

WILLIE: It comes to more than you'll ever have.

SHOOTER: I'm rich, remember?

WILLIE: Too bad you ain't blond. I hear that's a terrific combination.

SHOOTER: Couldn't you take care of that for me, Willie? I mean, you're takin' care of George and takin' care Sondra gets her new Lincoln every year.

WILLIE: Whatever she wants. *(Then quickly.)* Don't you rack those balls, boy.

SHOOTER: Uh-uh. *(Racking the balls.)* What she wants, my man, is everything there is. Sable coats, suede chairs, a Cuisinart and a cook to run it, trips to wherever-it-is Hong Kong, five-hundred-dollar shoes, and fourteen carat-gold fingernails.

WILLIE: Just things, kid. Everybody needs some things. You, you could even do with a few things.

SHOOTER: I don't need any things.

WILLIE: Your things are how you know it's your house.

SHOOTER: Then my house…is one of her things. I bought myself a recliner…

WILLIE: Yeah?

SHOOTER: She gave it away. *(Pauses.)* Said it didn't go with the rest of the "things" I paid for. Marrying her was like cosigning for the national debt.

WILLIE: Marrying her was what you did.

SHOOTER: Unfortunately.

WILLIE: And you are going to stay married to her or you are going to have to answer to me.

SHOOTER: Well, the answer is no.

WILLIE: And you are going to keep her happy or you are gonna stay outta my sight. You gonna grow up if it kills you. And don't you think you can get away with one thing because I know every move you make. You screw a sheep and I'll know it.

SHOOTER: Sure you will. What else you got to do?

WILLIE: You're the one needs somethin' else to do. Somethin' else besides that gambling or dope or whatever you s'posed to owe that greasy white boy that six thousand dollars for. He shows up again, I'll kill him.

SHOOTER: It's an investment, man.

WILLIE: The hell it is.

SHOOTER: Yeah. I'm buying a mountain, a great big mountain covered in pretty red flowers. None of your business.

WILLIE: You're my business. You want somethin' I can get for you, I'll get it. Till then, I'm keepin' you from makin' the mistake of your life. You lose Sondra…she's a real classy lady and you like the way she looks and you know it. She reminds you where you want to get to in this world. You lose her and you're gonna lose it all. Then all you'll have left is some lousy grams of cocaine and pictures of your daddy.

SHOOTER: And won't you be happy then?

WILLIE: I will be happy—no, happy ain't got nuthin' to do with it. I will let you back in here when you stop messin' around and stay where you belong. At home. With Sondra. Your wife.

SHOOTER: Till depth do us part.

WILLIE: Now that is all I have to say to you. Get outta my hall.

SHOOTER: I don't believe you. I mean, did somebody make you Resident Caretaker and Marvelous Little Yard Man for the whole world?

WILLIE: If you don't get outta my hall—

SHOOTER: What? Huh? *(Taking his practice strokes.)* What you gonna do, man? You gonna prune my hedge and trim the edges of my mile-long circular driveway? *(Now gets up quickly, poses, in an old move of his father's.)* Give me a break! *(And he gets in position just as quickly and breaks the racked balls with a powerful stroke.)*

WILLIE: *(Has to laugh.)* Give me a break.

SHOOTER: *(Pleased with his shot.)* Yeah.

WILLIE: Shooter always said that.

SHOOTER: *(After a moment.)* Yeah. Give me a break.

WILLIE: Hadn't been funny for years.

SHOOTER: He's probably still sayin' it. *(And now he proceeds to run the balls in rotation.)*

WILLIE: *(Starting to clean up now.)* Yeah. Beer's probably hot in hell, but they got all the best pool players down there. Greenleaf, Hoppe…Shooter takin' 'em all on, dollar a game and the loser runs up to heaven for the cold Falls City. *(Laughs.)* He was the best.

SHOOTER: Nobody even close.

WILLIE: One night he puts on this cowboy hat and glasses, wraps his left arm in a sling, rents a tux, figures to hop on down to South Side, Owensboro, pick up some fast cash. Borrows George's car, gets the word about the short-stop* there, how much money he's carrying, where he'll be standin' in the room—

SHOOTER: Who's runnin' that place now?

WILLIE: Lookin' for some one-pocket, see? So he's got on this rig. I swear he looks so strange, and walks in this joint and the bartender, swingin' a pret-zel around his finger and openin' a beer, looks up, sees this bifocaled, bro-ken-armed cowboy wearin' a tux, and says, "Hey boys, it's Shooter Stevens!" Like to died. He like to died. Got on all that crap and the first guy sees him says, "Hey boys, it's Shooter Stevens! Trip the alarm, the rob-ber has arrived." *(Shakes his head.)* Nothin', but nothin' so goddamned sad as a pool player can't get a game.

SHOOTER: *(Referring to the fact that Willie won't play with him.)* Know what you mean.

WILLIE: But God, the thing he said the last night he…well…

SHOOTER: You can say it. You can say "the last night before the leap." Before the final, flyin' leap of his life.

WILLIE: Walked in. Right by a big money nine-ball goin' over there. *(Points.)* Whistlin'. Not a good sign, whistlin'. Meant trouble when he was shootin', but just walkin' whistlin', I didn't worry, see?

SHOOTER: Wish you had, Willie.

The shortstop is the best local player, the hustler's target.

WILLIE: Gets a Falls City and goes back to the nine-ball. Man with white shoes and his own stick, blue knitty pants says, "You in, buddy?" Man, I heard that word, "buddy," and I knew it was all over. Shooter backs up to the cues there, picks a stick not even lookin'. Mr. White Shoes says, "You don't even look?" Your ol' man gives him the ugliest scariest straight-on stare you ever seen in your life and says, "Buddy, if you can't play with any of 'em, you can't play with any of 'em." *(He laughs.)* Whole place cracked up.

SHOOTER: And sure enough that night…

WILLIE: He couldn't play with any of 'em.

SHOOTER: Well, it had to be something else, Willie. My old man did not jump off of that bridge because of a lousy run here.

WILLIE: Sorry, boy. He did. He really did. Oh sure, maybe he knew he was losin' it, shaky stroke, no games. Hell, George was even beatin' him. So no, it wasn't this one night, but it was this goddamn game and you can bet all your fancy DJ bucks on that.

SHOOTER: All right, then, since you know so much about my old man, why'd he pick that side? *(He has been wanting to know the answer to this for a long time, but would prefer to have Willie think he has asked out of anger.)*

WILLIE: Go for the salvage yard instead of the water?

SHOOTER: Why did he land on the '56 Chevy?

WILLIE: I got a thought about it.

SHOOTER: Well, let's hear it, Willie.

WILLIE: He was a helluva swimmer.

SHOOTER: Nice try, man.

WILLIE: I'm tellin' you, boy, your old man was so stubborn, I mean, he didn't want to give himself the slightest chance of pullin' outta that dive alive. He'd never lived it down. George'd been on him somethin' awful.

(Shooter takes a shot and misses. Willie laughs.)

SHOOTER: What's so funny?

WILLIE: I'm sorry. See, they called me to come get him. One of the cops knew us. Got there, nice bright mornin', spotted him soon's I got outta the car. Been layin' there all night, flat on his back, arms stretched out, legs hangin' down over the windshield. That far away, I swear to God, he looked like he was gettin' himself a suntan.

SHOOTER: Just what he always wanted.

WILLIE: Close up was different.

(Points but Shooter doesn't see him.)

WILLIE: Needed a shorter bridge.

SHOOTER: That's enough about it, okay?

WILLIE: I'm talkin' your bridge, not his. *(Starts to walk over.)* Six inches, fingers to cue tip.

SHOOTER: You start playing again, I'll start listening.

WILLIE: Shooter was the only game I had in this town. So he's gone, so why bother?

SHOOTER: It's your game, man.

WILLIE: It was his game. It killed him.

SHOOTER: You don't keep in shape, he'll be ashamed of you down at hell's pool hall. Make you watch. "But I been waitin' to play you, Shooter," you'll say, and he'll say, "Willie, I'm real glad to see you and you look real good for an old man, but this is a serious game, you know?"

WILLIE: I'll keep this place open, I'll tell you to bend from the knees and stroke from the shoulder, but unless I get some all-fired good reason, like my life depended on it, I ain't playin'.

SHOOTER: It's gonna kill you to play with me?

WILLIE: You want a beer?

SHOOTER: You just couldn't stand losin' to me.

WILLIE: What I couldn't stand, is a game that didn't mean nothin'. Don't take it personal, boy, but I went fifteen rounds with the champ, so I ain't got nothin' to prove to the challengers. Now do you want a beer or not?

SHOOTER: *(Miscues.)* No.

WILLIE: Boy.

SHOOTER: *(Belligerent, expecting more advice.)* Yeah?

WILLIE: What are you doing here?

(Shooter doesn't answer. Willie turns away.)

SHOOTER: *(Finally.)* Workin' on this bank shot.

WILLIE: *(Louder.)* Boy...

SHOOTER: *(Stands up, leans on his stick.)* What?

WILLIE: Look... *(Then deciding not to go on with this.)* Don't lean on your... *(Tired of this too.)* Oh hell. Did you ever see him shoot with an umbrella?

SHOOTER: *(Going back to his game.)* No.

WILLIE: *(Laughs.)* He lost your crib one night before he figured it out.

SHOOTER: Huh?

WILLIE: Havin' us a helluva storm, your old man comes in soaked, carryin' his umbrella, still all folded up perfect. George busts out laughin', says, "Why didn't you use that thing? Shooter you the dumbest nigger." And Shooter says, just like always, first thing popped into his head, says, "'Cause I'm runnin' the rack with it, mother." So George says, "Let's see your green, man." Well, Shooter didn't have any, of course, so he says, "Bet the boy's bed, buddy." Now he goes real good for a while, but then he gets to the seven, and it's plumb froze to the rail. He looks it over, checks the line, sets him a sweet rail bridge, pulls back to shoot. George waits for just the right moment and says, "Do de name Ruby Begonia ring a bell?"

SHOOTER: And Dad miscued.

WILLIE: Then he hit George upside of the head.

SHOOTER: Then George went over and got my crib.

WILLIE: Bet's a bet, boy. Came draggin' it back in here, said your mama said, "George I am so tired of seein' your face carryin' out my furniture."

SHOOTER: Uh-huh.

WILLIE: So then Shooter has to learn how to shoot with that umbrella 'cause that's the only way George will give the crib back. Run the rack you get it back. Run the rack, you get it back. Wonder old George didn't die off of that bet. He could be awful mean, your daddy.

SHOOTER: The Three Blind Mice.

WILLIE: Well that's what your mama thought all right.

SHOOTER: (Singing.) They all ran after the farmer's wife.

WILLIE: You use a wafer on that tip?

SHOOTER: (Still singing.) She cut off their tails with a carving knife.

WILLIE: Need about five more pounds over your right foot.

SHOOTER: (Singing.) Did you ever see such a sight in your life as three blind mice.

WILLIE: God, your mama, that night down at the jail. (Laughing.) God almighty.

SHOOTER: I heard that story so many times. I don't know anything like I know that story.

WILLIE: So do it.

SHOOTER: (As Mama did it, more music than narration.) See, I'm pregnant with you, boy, and paintin' on your crib one night, while your daddy and George and Willie are busy beatin' up on each other down at Willie's pool hall.

WILLIE: (Loving this.) Yeah!

SHOOTER: And I pick up the phone and, Lord have mercy, it's the police and they say they got three beat-up black men, all callin' my name. And they said would I gather up some money and come relieve them of their prisoners. And they said, it's gonna be dark when you get here, honey, 'cause the 'lectric's knocked out and the stoves ain't workin', but we fed 'em Velveeta just to hold 'em till you get here, girl.

WILLIE: She took one look at us, drunk as shit, sittin' on the floor, in the dark, eatin' cheese. She said, "I drive myself all the way down here, I give them all my money, and what do I get?"

SHOOTER AND WILLIE: *(As Mama said it.)* The Three Blind Mice. *(They laugh.)*

WILLIE: Shooter turns on the radio on the way home and she says, "I ain't through screamin' at you yet, turn that thing off. And George, if you don't stop bleedin' on my Buick, you gonna walk!"

SHOOTER: It's a wonder she didn't drive him straight to the Red Cross, sayin', "George here's so anxious to give blood, he done started without you. Just catch a coupla pints and send him over to Willie's when he dries up."

WILLIE: *(Beginning to recover from the laughing.)* I'd like to see your mama again. Maybe she'll come visit. She would've walked to China for your daddy. Nearly did a coupla times. But God, did she hate George.

SHOOTER: Remember George's stick at the wedding?

WILLIE: And that big fudge cake sittin' on the table here?

SHOOTER: Mom wanted the reception at the church.

WILLIE: Sure she did.

SHOOTER: Sondra wanted it at the Palm Room.

WILLIE: Not a bad place.

SHOOTER: Her mom wanted it at the Galt House.

(They both laugh.)

WILLIE: *(Proudly.)* But we had it…here.

SHOOTER: Got a great picture of Dad and George holdin' their cues lookin' down real serious at this what was always their table, but what is now a high-rise fudge cake, you pourin' champagne on their heads.

WILLIE: Oh, Sondra was beautiful that day. She's the best shot ol' George ever made.

SHOOTER: She's still beautiful, man. That's not the problem.

WILLIE: She really wants a new Lincoln?

SHOOTER: Silver.

WILLIE: Used to look like the Lincoln dealership in front of this place.

SHOOTER: We can't even go to Sears driving my BMW. Gotta arrive in her Linc.

WILLIE: *(Proudly.)* She just looks like money.

SHOOTER: Which is why I don't have any.

WILLIE: George says they raised you to thirty grand.

SHOOTER: *(Opening his sack of tacos.)* Want a taco?

WILLIE: Says you can expect sixty maybe seventy in five years.

SHOOTER: And then what? You ever seen any old DJs man? You watch those records go around long enough, you start thinkin' in circles, walkin' in circles, talkin' in circles. All I learned in five years is the names of eight hundred and ninety-two singing groups and how many people don't have anybody to talk to late at night so they call up the "record player."

WILLIE: So quit.

SHOOTER: And do what?

WILLIE: You tell me.

SHOOTER: I don't know.

WILLIE: There's gotta be somethin' you like to do.

SHOOTER: I like to play pool.

WILLIE: That's not what I mean. Somethin' else.

SHOOTER: There isn't anything else.

WILLIE: Then you got a real problem, boy, 'cause pool just ain't your game.

SHOOTER: I see.

WILLIE: I mean, you do okay, but I gotta tell you—

SHOOTER: *(Quietly.)* No you don't.

WILLIE: Good. So tell me somethin' else you like to do.
(And Willie's helpful tone only intensifies Shooter's realization.)

SHOOTER: *(In complete emotional panic.)* There isn't anything else I like to do.
(Willie backs off stunned, but knows not to wait too long before he starts to talk again.)

WILLIE: There's about a billion jobs in this world. You think there ain't one or two might make you happy?

SHOOTER: *(Angry now.)* How am I supposed to know what makes me happy? And what difference does it make? You don't work to be happy. You work to make money. Happy, my man…was one of the seven dwarfs.

WILLIE: Well, either you really do like what you do, in which case you can shut up bitchin' about it, or you hate what you do so you quit.

SHOOTER: I don't like it and I don't hate it. It pays the bills.

WILLIE: Fryin' fish would pay the bills.

SHOOTER: Not her bills.

WILLIE: I'm sick to death of you blaming her for spendin' the money you make. You quit makin' it, she'll quit spendin' it. She'd do anything for you, but you ain't told her anything except don't buy fur coats. So she's doin' what she can. Makin' you look good, and makin' your house look good. You quit work, she'll make poor look good. So you shut up about you have to work to pay her bills. Her bills are all you got to show for your work... *(Pauses.)* best I can tell.

SHOOTER: *(Stops shooting.)* Well, I got something to tell you. *(Calm but firm.)* And I got the chain burns to prove it. I am a certified, wholly owned, shipped-to-the-plantation slave boy, property of...MasterCharge. *(And he takes a bite of his taco now.)*

WILLIE: You shouldn't eat that crap.

SHOOTER: Girl next door says they're made out of dog food.

WILLIE: White girl?

SHOOTER: Come on, man, I stopped in the laundromat next door, put my clothes in the wash, and this white girl talked to me, okay?

WILLIE: Makes me sick just to look at those tacos. But George eats so many of 'em, he starts speakin' Spanish around midnight.

SHOOTER: I keep tellin' Sondra to come see him.

WILLIE: She should. He's her father. She should come in here some night and see him.

SHOOTER: I know. I told her.

WILLIE: Yeah? So tell her not to. Tell her this is the last place you want to see her sweet face. Look ugly mean. Hit the table. She'll sneak right over soon's you look the other way.

SHOOTER: Yeah. Like this other routine she's got asking should I wear the green or should I wear the red. I say green, she puts on the red. I say red—

WILLIE: On go the green.

SHOOTER: I mean, why does she bother to ask?

WILLIE: It ain't just her, boy. They all do it.

SHOOTER: Yeah, but why?

WILLIE: Well if I knew that, I'd be on Johnny Carson 'stead of runnin' this place.

SHOOTER: Yeah.

WILLIE: You get Sondra down here to see George. He needs it, but he won't ask for it, and he won't get himself over to her...your place, 'cause he don't feel...he hates that white rug.

SHOOTER: Who doesn't?

WILLIE: I know she don't feel safe comin' down, and I don't exactly blame her, it ain't safe, and she is good about callin', but you bring her down here, you hear?

SHOOTER: *(Throwing away the taco sack.)* Right.

(Willie watches him, perhaps begins to feel a little of Shooter's pain. Suddenly, Willie shouts.)

WILLIE: Shooter! Shooter Stevens! *(And now he lines up the balls.)* Wipe the sweat outta your eyes and pay attention up here, man. The boy's gonna try your favorite trick! Shooter! Hey!
(Shooter doesn't understand at first, then sees that Willie is preparing one of his father's old shots.)

SHOOTER: Come on...

WILLIE: I'll set it up for you. You can do it.

SHOOTER: This ain't my game, remember?

WILLIE: *(Pointing out what should happen.)* Cue ball here, hit top center, like a clean follow. No English. Hit the one about half-ball, it goes here... *(Points to the middle left-hand pocket.)* while the two is rotatin' its way up there. *(Points to the top right-hand pocket.)* And, not to leave anybody out in the cold, the cue ball rolls across the table and drops the three in the middle. *(Middle right-hand pocket.)* And, don't scratch.

SHOOTER: Of course.

WILLIE: *(Reviewing.)* One to here, two up there, three over there.

SHOOTER: Yeah. *(Studying the shot.)* Okay. I'm ready.

WILLIE: *(As Shooter is about to shoot.)* Now, what about kids?

SHOOTER: Christ! You got a shopping list for my life. Milk, bread, wife, kids...

WILLIE: Then read me your list. What do you want?

SHOOTER: Her exact words, Willie, about kids? Her exact words, "I'm gonna blow up like a whale? Not this body, baby. Uh-uh, honey." I mean, if you could buy 'em, she'd have 'em, but she ain't buyin' havin' 'em.

WILLIE: Probably thinks she'd have to raise it by herself.

SHOOTER: If she'd have a baby, I'd stay.

WILLIE: Does she know that?

SHOOTER: But how long am I supposed to wait? If she had the boy today, I'd be forty when he's ten. He's ready to go play ball and I'm workin' up a sweat gettin' outta my chair.

WILLIE: And what you're doin' now, goin' out on her all over town, that's supposed to convince her to have your boy for you?

SHOOTER: Whoever's playing records in your head's asleep at the deck, man. Got a broken one, goin' around and around.

WILLIE: You shape up, you'll get your boy.

SHOOTER: Wanna bet?

WILLIE: Wanna try?

SHOOTER: I want to try this shot, okay?

WILLIE: Keep your stick level.

SHOOTER: All right. One for the old man. *(Shoots and misses.)* Shit.

WILLIE: One to nothin', favor of the ol' man.

SHOOTER: He really could make this?

WILLIE: This shot bought you strained carrots, boy. Lotta folks thought he couldn't make this shot. Lotta folks and lotta their money said he'd miss. But he never did.

SHOOTER: Then we'll just give it another shot.

(And Shooter goes around, replacing the balls. Willie adjusts them so they're in the right positions.)

WILLIE: *(Trying another approach.)* There's nothin' wrong, I mean, with you or Sondra? Doctor's got all kinds of—

SHOOTER: No.

WILLIE: There's tests.

SHOOTER: Look, Willie, she's taking the pill, using a diaphragm, I have to wear a rubber. Keeps foam just in case, I mean, this lady does not want any kids, okay?

WILLIE: Then you gotta change her mind. George needs a grandbaby.

SHOOTER: Tell that to her. Have George tell that to her.

WILLIE: Shooter needs a grandbaby.

SHOOTER: Shooter is dead. *(Now turning to face him.)* Willie needs the grand-baby.

WILLIE: *(As Shooter is ready to try the shot again.)* You don't have any children, it's the end of the line for the Three Blind Mice.

SHOOTER: You're talking to the wrong person, Willie. I want kids. But I'll tell you something, Sondra could care less about the Three Blind Mice. Here we go. *(Shoots and misses again.)*

WILLIE: That's two. Three and the ol' man crosses you off his visitin' list.

SHOOTER: Have your own kid. You got a coupla good shots left, huh?

WILLIE: I'm old, G.W.

SHOOTER: Ain't a question of old. It's a question of aim. Concentration. Bend from the hips, steady stroke, you know.

WILLIE: *(Laughs.)* I know.

SHOOTER: How long's it been?

WILLIE: None of your damned business.

SHOOTER: That long, huh?

(Willie gets out his keys and walks to the door.)

SHOOTER: Okay. Here goes. Watch.

WILLIE: I'm watchin'.

SHOOTER: *(As he misses again.)* Shit.

WILLIE: That's three.

(As Willie gets to the back door, it opens, and Deedee steps in carrying a stack of folded clothes.)

DEEDEE: Hello?

WILLIE: Laundry's next door, miss.

DEEDEE: *(Steps in, very uncomfortable.)* Yeah, but I'm lookin' for the pool hall.

WILLIE: We're closed.

DEEDEE: Are you Willie?

WILLIE: *(Grudgingly.)* Yes.

DEEDEE: See? I got Shooter Stevens's clothes. Shooter Stevens? He put 'em in over there and I figured since I didn't really have—

WILLIE: Shooter Stevens? *(Turning around to look at Shooter.)* You got Shooter Stevens's clothes?

DEEDEE: It's his nickname.

WILLIE: Girl's got your old man's clothes, Gary Wayne. *(Very bitter.)* Shooter Stevens's clothes.

SHOOTER: *(Walking over.)* Hey, thanks.

(Shooter takes the clothes from her. Deedee follows him into the room, then stops as though Willie had grabbed her.)

DEEDEE: I thought they were yours, oh well, guess it don't matter now.

WILLIE: Nope. It don't matter now.

SHOOTER: You didn't have to bring me these.

DEEDEE: Your dad has nice stuff.

SHOOTER: They're mine.

DEEDEE: Can I come in?

SHOOTER: Sure. I invited you, didn't I?

DEEDEE: Don't you just love the way they smell when they come out of the dryer?

SHOOTER: You thirsty?

DEEDEE: I put in a Cling-Free. That's the smell. There any tacos left?

SHOOTER: *(Walking toward the bar.)* Sorry. Chips though.

WILLIE: Dollar a bag.

(Shooter stops. Willie shouldn't have said that.)

DEEDEE: Mind if I look around?

WILLIE: Not much to see.

SHOOTER: Sure. I'll set up so you can see how the game goes.

DEEDEE: *(To Willie.)* My name's Deedee. *(No response from Willie.)* Hard to tell what year it is in here. *(Picking up an ashtray.)* Hey! I been there! *(Reading from the ashtray.)* See Rock City! *(Then remembering.)* It wasn't much. Only thing I really wanted to see, we couldn't stop for. On the way there, kept seein' these signs…Giant Jungle Rat. Sure wish I coulda seen that Giant Jungle Rat.

WILLIE: *(In Shooter's direction.)* Oh we got 'em come in here all the time.

SHOOTER: Really just old jungle mice.

DEEDEE: Shooter, are you hungry? There's this pancake place down on Broadway…

WILLIE: His name is Gary Wayne.

SHOOTER: I always wondered if that place was any good. I haven't had any pancakes since—

DEEDEE: You'd love it. They're open all night too.

WILLIE: Oh, I thought the Board of Health closed it down.

SHOOTER: Now, first you have to break.

(Gets into position, Deedee comes over to watch.)

SHOOTER: Like this.

WILLIE: Or somethin' like that. Stop by some day when we're open, you'll see what a real—

(Shooter gives her the cue, and gives Willie a fierce look.)

SHOOTER: This is a game of rotation. You have to hit the one ball first. Then every shot after that, you have to hit the lowest numbered ball on the table. You can sink other balls with the shot, but if you don't hit the low ball first, the other balls come out and you lose your turn. *(Now showing her how to stand.)* Bend like this, let the cue just rest in your hand, somewhere around here, or so. Now…stand up a minute. *(Showing her a beginner's bridge.)* Put your hand out on the table flat like this. Ease it up, like how an inchworm…

DEEDEE: *(Doing it.)* That?

SHOOTER: Perfect. Now curl your index finger and slip the cue through it. *(Reaching around her to show her how it's done.)* Take some practice strokes. Eye on the ball.

DEEDEE: *(Straightening up suddenly.)* I got it! Your dad's name was the same as yours.

SHOOTER: Yeah.

DEEDEE: Shooter.

WILLIE: No. Stevens.

SHOOTER: And he was one helluva pool player. *(Trying to appease Willie.)* Dad and Willie, here, and this other man, George—

WILLIE: The father of G.W.'s wife—

SHOOTER: Were real tight.

(Deedee gets back in position and takes practice strokes.)

DEEDEE: Friends.

SHOOTER: More like triplets. I ever needed anything, lunch money, rubbers, anything, didn't matter which one I asked. Seemed like it all came out of the same pocket.

WILLIE: *(Not to Deedee.)* It did.

SHOOTER: Gave the same advice, wore the same clothes, drove the same cars, drank the same beer, 'bout the same age, called themselves the Three Blind Mice.

(Willie does not appreciate Shooter giving away this information. That name was something they called themselves, not something they would let anybody else call them.)

DEEDEE: *(A little bored by this information.)* This place we did stop in, on that trip where we didn't stop in to see the Giant Jungle Rat, this place, Pete's, had this three-headed mouse in a jar. It was dead, though. A freak. *(Now concentrating on the table.)* I'm ready. *(She shoots and miscues.)* What happened?

SHOOTER: Aim for the middle of the ball. Loosen up your finger a little.

DEEDEE: They said it had, I mean, they, the heads…only had one heart. That's what killed them, it, the mouse.

SHOOTER: Yeah.

(And Deedee tries to shoot on her own now, Shooter backing off a little to watch.)

DEEDEE: How does this end, this rotation?

WILLIE: I could turn out the lights.

SHOOTER: First person to get sixty-one points wins the game.

DEEDEE: Could be real soon, huh?

SHOOTER: What kind of pancakes do you like?

DEEDEE: Strawberry, with whipped cream.

SHOOTER: I'll just call and have them save us some. Wouldn't want them running out before we get there.

DEEDEE: *(Handing him the cue.)* Here. You get the rest of them, okay?

WILLIE: Her mother's probably worried about her, G.W.

DEEDEE: It must feel real good to like somethin' this much.

(And Shooter is putting on a real show now, getting all the balls in as quickly as possible.)

DEEDEE: Mom likes TV.

SHOOTER: Yeah?

DEEDEE: Joe loves his '56 Chevy.

WILLIE: *(In Shooter's direction.)* Joe loves his '56 Chevy.

DEEDEE: I must love somethin'.

WILLIE: Miss…

SHOOTER: *(Indicating, somehow, himself.)* Giant Jungle Rats?

WILLIE: Deedee…that's your name, Deedee?

DEEDEE: Yes.

WILLIE: Go home.

SHOOTER: Willie!

WILLIE: The pool hall is closed. And Gary Wayne has a wife to go home to, and I'm gonna see that he gets there. Now go home.

DEEDEE: No, see, we're gonna—

WILLIE: Good night.

(Deedee looks at Shooter as if asking whether she should go or not. Shooter looks at Willie, then back to Deedee. This is an awkward moment, to say the least. Finally, Shooter shrugs his shoulders.)

SHOOTER: It's his hall.

DEEDEE: Yeah.

SHOOTER: Need a cab?

DEEDEE: *(As she walks to the door.)* I just live across the street.

SHOOTER: I'll watch you out the window.

DEEDEE: That's us. *(Pointing.)* See those blueberries in the window? It's a light. They're a light. I mean, I like blue, it's not my favorite color, but I like it a lot, and somebody gave it to me for, well, if the other lights were out, then you could see it real good, no, not it, them, no, it, the light better, the vines on it and everything. *(She's really chattering here.)* I can't ever, well, I have to hunt all over town to find blue bulbs. I tried painting one blue, but something in the paint, I guess, made the bulb break. No, it didn't break, but it got these little holes all over the… *(Smacks herself to stop talking.)* Don't you ever shut up, Deedee? *(Embarrassed laugh.)* Mom says I could find somethin' to say to a head of cabbage.

SHOOTER: You got a cabbage at home to talk to?

DEEDEE: Yeah. I do. *(She laughs.)* 'Night.

SHOOTER: *(Stepping back in, door still open.)* Thanks again for the laundry. Good
night.

*(Shooter closes the door, but he is still watching her. He yells at Willie, who is
returning the pool cue to its place on the wall.)*

SHOOTER: *(Fiercely.)* Just who do you think you are, man?

WILLIE: Messed up your plans, huh, boy?

SHOOTER: I can make them again, you know.

WILLIE: Not in here.

SHOOTER: It's a free country.

WILLIE: Not in here.

SHOOTER: And who knows, if she'd stayed here a little longer, you might have
even picked up a cue and played with me. Anything, you'd have done just
about anything to keep me from sharing a stack of strawberry pancakes
with a dumb little blonde who talks to cabbages. I mean, you tell me why
it is I am not allowed to talk to other people in this world without you
standing there like Moses heaving your stone-tablet ten commandments
down on my head. You do this to Dad? That your deal with him? I'll pay
your bills, you do what I say? And when he couldn't make your trick shots
anymore, he had to jump off that bridge because he never found anything
else satisfying in his life 'cause you already done it all for him. Is that the
real story?

WILLIE: Shooter was my friend. And I don't see that you got any friends, so you
don't know nothin' about friends, so you shut up.

SHOOTER: He was my father and I'll say whatever I want. And I'll call myself
Shooter if I want. And I'll dump Sondra if I want and I'll screw white
women if I want.

WILLIE: *(Very cold.)* Go to hell.

SHOOTER: I mean, what gives you the right to run my life?

WILLIE: I'll tell you what it is, you little—

SHOOTER: *(Boiling.)* The Gospel According to Willie:

Thou shalt not call thyself by thy father's name because it is a holy name.

Thou shalt not try to play thy father's game because it is a holy game.

Thou shalt not give thy father-in-law George a motorized wheelchair
because I, Willie, am the giver of all good things.

Thou shalt not make thy living at a radio station.

Thou shalt not refuse thy wife a new Lincoln or any other damn fool
thing she wants.

Thou shalt not go home at night except that thou go straight home.

Thou shalt not talk to any other women.

Thou shalt especially not talk to white women.

WILLIE: Eight.

SHOOTER: Thou shalt not get old enough to make thy own decisions.

WILLIE: *(Almost a dare.)* Nine?

SHOOTER: *(Particularly intense.)* That's all of your gospel, Willie. The last two are mine. The last two are for you. Thou shalt not forsake, desert, skip out on, run away from, break promises to, or leave behind to die…thy friends.

WILLIE: *(Truly confused.)* What?

SHOOTER: What do you mean "What?" Thou shalt not sell this pool hall!

WILLIE: I told you—

(But Shooter can't stop now. He's been wanting to deliver this lecture ever since he got here tonight. This is why he came here.)

SHOOTER: Don't you know what it's going to do to George when you split for New Jersey? It's going to kill him. Where's he got to go? Nowhere. What's he got to do? Nothing. Who does he care about in the world? Nobody…except you. And you're selling this place, and too cheap at that, so you can go live it up at Asbury Park. *(Now as if Willie were saying it.)* Well, George, old friend, I hate to leave you like this, in the wheelchair and all, but listen, you call me up sometime and we'll talk about the good old days.

WILLIE: *(Calmly.)* George…

SHOOTER: George will understand? George will not understand! Only two of the Three Blind Mice left as it is, and Willie wants to sell the hole. And you were giving me that shit about Sondra. Do your duty, keep your promises. Hang in there with those commitments, G.W., and all the time, you're deciding whether to pack your black shoes and wondering if they got Senior Citizens swimming pools.

WILLIE: Are you through?

SHOOTER: No. All my life I watched Dad and George depend on you. And maybe you got a rest coming, but you can't do it yet. If you leave now, while he's sick, then all that friends talk was just talk, and all those friends stories must be made up, and all that you-be-good-to-Sondra because-she's-my-friend-George's-little-girl lecture is nothing but lies, because if you leave him all alone, you are not his friend and you never were.

WILLIE: My friend, George…

SHOOTER: Your "friend," George…

WILLIE: My…friend…George…is…dying.

SHOOTER: No.

WILLIE: Yes. And I am not going to Asbury Park. I am going to stay here and watch my friend George die.

SHOOTER: You said sick.

WILLIE: Yeah I said sick. Why didn't you go home when I first told you to, boy?

SHOOTER: *(More gentle now.)* I didn't want to.

WILLIE: *(Wearily.)* Would you go home now?

SHOOTER: No. *(Walks behind the bar.)* Beer?

WILLIE: Yeah.

(And Shooter opens two beers, puts one in front of Willie.)

WILLIE: And a bag of chips. *(As Shooter gets one.)* Uh-uh. The one at the top.

SHOOTER: *(Reaching for it.)* This one?

WILLIE: Yeah. *(Taking the bag and looking at it.)* We been watchin' this bag, me and George. *(Pauses.)* We figure it's about a year old now.

SHOOTER: How long does he have?

WILLIE: Six months, maybe.

SHOOTER: That's not much.

WILLIE: Nope.

SHOOTER: Hospital?

WILLIE: Friday. They said he'd be more comfortable.

SHOOTER: That bad.

WILLIE: Right.

SHOOTER: And this place...selling this place...is going to pay for it.

WILLIE: Just about. *(Pause.)* If he really drags his feet, it might take my car, too. *(Then standing up.)* Shit, the pool hall on the mall's gettin' all the business anyway. Got pinball machines and air hockey.

SHOOTER: *(With contempt.)* Pink felt tables and a ladies' john.

WILLIE: *(Laughs.)* Real clean.

SHOOTER: Safe.

WILLIE: Then there's the jukebox, here. Don't exactly draw the crowd, you know.

SHOOTER: Huh?

WILLIE: Day George got his first wheelchair, hit him pretty hard, you know. I thought I told you this.

(Shooter shakes his head no.)

WILLIE: Had me stop by Vine Records, buy all his favorites, coupla Chubby Checkers, lotta Tennessee Ernie Ford, Christ!

(Shooter laughs.)

WILLIE: Filled up the jukebox with 'em. Left on the labels, up top here, like they were, just changed the records. Now, see, no matter what somebody picks out, they get one of George's oldies but goodies. Makes people mad. Makes me mad. Got lousy taste in music, George. Likes real crap, you know. *(Pats the machine.)* Isn't all that bad, though. Funny sometimes. People punchin' up Aretha Franklin, gettin' Pat Boone.

SHOOTER: Pat Boone?

WILLIE: I told you he was sick.

SHOOTER: Know what he told me the day we got married?

WILLIE: Little fatherly advice?

SHOOTER: He said, "Boy, there's somethin' you got to know about women. *(Conspiratorial tone.)* You want 'em to act nice, you want to stay outta trouble with 'em, you want 'em to love you forever?" *(Now in his own voice.)* "Yeah," I'm sayin', "yeah, George, how do I do that?" And he says, "Well, when you get undressed at night…you got to hang up your clothes."

WILLIE: Goddamn him.

SHOOTER: Sondra must've guessed. She said George was smelling funny and that's why she wouldn't come see him.

WILLIE: She's just scared of it.

SHOOTER: Aren't you?

WILLIE: George ain't got a smell on him I ain't smelled. *(Shooter laughs.)* She just don't want to know about it.

SHOOTER: Maybe.

WILLIE: She's afraid she'll be with him when it happens. He'll say somethin' smart like, "If you'll excuse me, girl, I gotta be goin'." Close his eyes and split. Go. Die.

SHOOTER: Maybe. *(Gentler about her now.)* And maybe she's just a selfish, silly girl who started buying grown-up clothes but never grew into them.

WILLIE: She'll get there.

SHOOTER: I could help, with George.

WILLIE: Save it.

SHOOTER: For you?

WILLIE: I want a table, set right next to my casket, so right after "Don't he look nice," I'll hear "Little nine-ball?" I mean, if I gotta lay there dyin' for a beer, least I can have a game to watch. Boys cussin' and carryin' on, balls flyin' off the table, crushin' carnations in my wreath I'm wearin' says "Bartender."

SHOOTER: If that's the way you want it.

WILLIE: You know what I want. I want you and Sondra—

SHOOTER: Yeah, I know.

WILLIE: Right.

SHOOTER: I heard you, okay?

WILLIE: So?

SHOOTER: So what?

WILLIE: So are we gonna play or not?

(Willies offer is so unexpected, it triggers an overwhelming emotional response in both of them. They embrace, acknowledging at last their desperate need, their mutual loss, and their pure and lasting love for each other.)

SHOOTER: Oh man.

WILLIE: Thought you were too old to hug me, didn't you.

SHOOTER: *(Fondly.)* Just get off my neck and chalk your cue. Nine-ball. Dollar a game.

WILLIE: You're on, buddy.

(Shooter gets out the balls and racks them in silence as Willie gets his cue and chalks it. Willie takes his practice, then looks up at Shooter.)

WILLIE: I got to see this dollar, boy.

SHOOTER: Give me a break. *(And he slaps his dollar down on the table.)*

WILLIE: What did you say? *(And he stands up, assumes old Shooter's pose.)*

WILLIE AND SHOOTER: *(As Shooter would have said it.)* Give me a break.

(And Willie breaks the balls with a powerful shot and the lights come down immediately. We hear the beginning of ad-lib exchanges as the game starts.)

THE END

Circus Valentine

Circus Valentine was first produced at Actors Theatre of Louisville as part of the 1979 Humana Festival of New American Plays. It was directed by Jon Jory with the following cast:

Fred . . . . Jim Baker
Goldie. . . . . Diane Tarleton
Eva . . . . Lynn Cohen
Trina . . . . Sherry Steiner
Oz . . . . Kent Broadhurst
Tony . . . . Bob Burrus
Kelly . . . . Leo Burmester
Reeves . . . . Michael Kevin

INTRODUCTION

This play has never been published before, or produced again since its premiere, a night of humiliation and failure so complete as to almost destroy my ability to remain in the theatre.

I hadn't believed it could happen to me. (I should've known.) What saved me was the certainty that it would never happen again. (Are you laughing yet?) Never again would I read such terrible things about a play I had written. (About half would go down, actually.) Never again would I have to go backstage and visit a cast about to go out and perform a play that had been so badly reviewed. (Still the worst part.)

As it has turned out, *Circus Valentine* was only my first failure. But from those failures have come my other work, what the world calls my "best" work. Knowing you still have plays to write doesn't make it easier to survive a critical catastrophe. It simply makes it necessary.

We survive receiving hideous reviews by admitting that it happened, talking to fellow playwrights about how much it hurts, and by realizing that even on the very day the critics thrash us in public, we'd still rather be us than them. Small comfort, I know. But hey.

CHARACTERS

FRED VALENTINE: a heavy set man in his 40s. The ringmaster and manager of the circus.

GOLDIE VALENTINE: Fred's wife, Trina's mother, Eva's sister. Fortune-teller and cook with the circus, out of shape and in her 40s.

TRINA VALENTINE: Fred and Goldie's daughter, Eva's protégé on the trapeze and bareback ponies, 19 or so.

OZ VALENTINE: Fred's brother, the elephant keeper, close to Fred in age and size.

EVA VLADIMIROV: Goldie's sister, Tony's ex-wife, a small, wild-haired aerialist. She is in her late 30s and speaks in a fake Russian accent most of the time.

TONY NAVARRO: the lion tamer. Eva's former husband. He is handsome and in his late 30s. He is not Spanish.

REEVES: an efficient but sweaty, successful but unenlightened businessman. He owns the shopping center where the circus is performing.

LEROY: a thief in his early 20s. He is restless and hungry, but not uncivilized.

TIME AND PLACE

The play takes place in the wardrobe tent, in the center ring, and in areas outside the circus tent during the first matinee performance in the back parking lot of a rather ordinary and unimpressive shopping center.

Circus Valentine

ACT I

The circus band begins to play and general hubbub is heard from the crowd coming up to the ticket window. Colored lights sweep the stage and roustabouts may be seen setting up various pieces of equipment.

FRED: *(In his spotlight.)* Ladies and Gentlemen! Only ten minutes left to buy tickets to the uniquely fabulous and gloriously original 1978 edition of Circus Valentine.

Bring those little ones to see the circus the way the circus should be seen, under an acre of canvas sky. Smell that sawdust and slide onto those genuine wooden seats, for you are about to experience the most fearless and fantastic performers, both animal and human.

You'll see the courageous and daring Antonio Navarro, whose ferocious lions and tigers are not tamed or trained, but held captive by his hypnotic gaze.

You'll thrill to the death-defying flight of Countess Eva Vladimirov, the rebellious darling of the Moscow Circus.

You'll warm to the sight of Grace Kelly, seven thousand pounds of elephantine elegance, pirouetting delicately on her jeweled ball.

But I know who you really came to see. Brad and Bill Evans. Circus Valentine's very own set of authentic Siamese twins, their inside arms joined fingertip to shoulder, standing and sleeping side by side, walking arm in arm for life. And juggling. Yes, juggling. You won't believe it. Even when you see it you won't believe it. But it's absolutely true. Welcome to Circus Valentine, the most awe-inspiring and spellbindingly superlative little circus in the entire world.

Step right up. Just a few good seats left.

IN THE WARDROBE TENT

Goldie and Eva are inside the wardrobe tent, just before the show begins. Goldie is wearing one half of the Siamese twin clown costume, Eva is avoiding getting in the other half.

GOLDIE: Get your ass in this costume, Eva.

EVA: No.

GOLDIE: The crowd paid to see the twins.

EVA: And where are the twins?

GOLDIE: I don't know. But if the crowd doesn't see the twins in the opening number, they'll want their money back.

EVA: So give it to them.

GOLDIE: Give their money back and cancel the show?

EVA: *(Submitting, but complaining.)* What I do for that idiot you married!

GOLDIE: Freddie is not an idiot.

EVA: He's cheap. He's fat. He's got a thing for freaks. And he got you pregnant and stopped you from flying.

GOLDIE: I was never good enough to fly with you.

EVA: I wanted us to be together.

GOLDIE: Well. This is your chance. Get in here.

EVA: I hate you.

GOLDIE: Lift your foot.

(Eva steps into the costume.)

EVA: You should never have married Freddie.

GOLDIE: What's the matter with Freddie? He hauls your trapeze from town to town, he hires your websitters and feeds your ponies.

EVA: They need a bath.

GOLDIE: Tell Oz.

EVA: Not the ponies need a bath. The twins need a bath. This costume stinks. *(Getting more disgusted by the minute.)* What kind of mud show asks the aerialist to dress up as half of the freak brothers?

(They should both be in the costume now, except that Eva isn't wearing her mask.)

TRINA: *(Calling from outside.)* Mother!

EVA: She's in here.

(Trina enters, but doesn't see Goldie in the costume.)

TRINA: Where?

EVA: *(Pointing to the other half of the costume.)* In there.

TRINA: What's going on? Where are Brad and Bill?

GOLDIE: *(Taking off her mask.)* Daddy took them somewhere, honey. I think they hurt their foot.

TRINA: Brad or Bill's?

EVA: It's all right, darling. They've still got three left.

TRINA: Eva, how can you—

GOLDIE: So Eva and I are doing the opening number in their costume. Do you need something?

TRINA: Not really. I just wanted to tell you that some limpster broke into your tent and stole your crystal ball.

GOLDIE: I told Freddie not to book this town. We don't know this town.

TRINA: It's O.K., though. He ran around by the menagerie and tripped over Grace Kelly's chain, and the ball went flying out of his hands and landed in a big pile of elephant shit.

GOLDIE: Oh good.

(Goldie puts on her mask, so that they look like the twins now.)

FRED: *(From offstage.)* Five minutes.

(The band begins to play. Oz Valentine walks in, dragging a long heavy chain.)

OZ: Brad? Bill?

TRINA: It's not them.

(Eva takes off her mask.)

EVA: And here is the man whose future was always in the elephant shit.

(Goldie takes off her mask.)

TRINA: Oz. What happened to the twins?

OZ: Your Dad says they had an accident.

EVA: They did not have an accident. They are an accident.

OZ: And they find you hopelessly disconnected. *(To Goldie.)* Oh, and Goldie, I caught the guy who stole your ball and chained him to the fence. He'll dig it out for you when he wakes up.

EVA: Leave it there. That's where it belongs. It's where this whole show belongs. Mangy ponies, frayed ropes, freaks, fatsos and fortune-tellers!

GOLDIE: *(Slaps Eva.)* Eva!

(Eva kicks her back and what looks like a girlhood fight breaks out, both sides of the Siamese twin costume on the attack.)

TRINA: Oz. Stop them!

(Tony enters, dressed for the opening number.)

TONY: Brad! Bill! What are you—

TRINA: It's not them, Tony.

TONY: My darling…

(Eva flips up her mask.)

EVA: It's us, bear brain.

(Goldie flips up her mask.)

GOLDIE: And my daughter is not your darling.

TONY: Oh, but she's everyone's darling. Where are the twins?

TRINA: They got hurt, but it's nothing serious.

TONY: If they're hurt, it's serious.

TRINA: They went bowling.

TONY: They're weird.

EVA: Freaks are weird. Thank you, lion tamer.

OZ: Tony. I found some mint growing under the lions tunnel. I think I got it all, but be careful.

TONY: You know what will happen if the cats smell mint!

OZ: I got it all, O.K.?

EVA: But there's always hope. Maybe one little sprig left…maybe your Sheba will smell it, and…

TONY: If the cats kill me out there, Eva, I'll steal your show.

EVA: Just don't bleed too much. I don't want to mess up my shoes.

TRINA: You're making me sick, all of you. Brad and Bill are hurt and all you're thinking of is yourselves…

(Fred enters, dressed in his Ringmaster costume.)

TONY: Fred. Where are the twins?

FRED: They're at General Hospital. Oz will go pick them up during the show. We might have to hold the second act for a few minutes, but…

TONY: You took them to a charity hospital?

FRED: It's the best emergency room in town. But it was just a precaution. They're going to be fine. They'll take some aspirin and—

EVA: Do they take two aspirin or four?

FRED: Shut up, Eva.

EVA: That's two accidents, Freddie darling. First the twins, then Goldie's ball. The third one will be the worst.

TRINA: That's an old wives' tale.

EVA: So I am an old wife. You wait. Maybe my old husband will be clawed to death by his lions.

TONY: *(To Fred.)* Fire her or I quit.

EVA: Fire him or I quit.

FRED: Fine. You're both fired.

TRINA: You can't fire Tony, Daddy.

FRED: The only people I can't fire are the twins and Grace Kelly.

GOLDIE: And me.

OZ: And me.

TRINA: And me.

EVA: And me.

TONY: And me. You owe me money.

FRED: Right. Now. Can we do this show?

(Suddenly, everyone relaxes and begins to get ready to do the show.)

OZ: I need to see you during the first clown stop, Fred.

FRED: Sure.

TONY: I said…you owe me money.

FRED: I'll pay you tonight. As soon as I meet this local presenter guy, I forget what his name is…Reeves. I'll pay you as soon as he pays me.

(Tony exits, followed by Trina.)

TRINA: Tony!

(Fred notices Trina's interest in Tony. But decides not to do anything about it today. He pulls a flower pot out of his coat sleeve, and turns to Goldie and Eva.)

FRED: All right, girls. It's not enough just to have the twins' costume, you have to do their walkabout. So. Goldie, you start taking the pot up to somebody in the crowd. Then just as they get it in their hands, Eva, you grab it away. Then Goldie you get it back somehow—point to something in the sky, hit Eva over the head, something—then it starts all over. Goldie's so glad to get the pot, and to give it away, only Eva takes it right out of their hands. Got it?

EVA: No. I won't do it.

GOLDIE: Shut up, Eva.

(They walk off toward their entrance into the tent, and lights begin to swirl.)

FRED: *(In his spotlight.)* Ladies and Gentlemen, boys and girls, the moment you've all been waiting for! Lights down, please. Welcome to the wonderful world of Circus Valentine!

(We hear applause and music for the opening number, the parade that precedes the first act.)

IN THE ANIMAL AREA

Lights come up on Oz, brushing one of the elephant blankets. The thief wakes up and finds himself chained to the fence.

LEROY: Hey!

OZ: Nice nap?

LEROY: What the hell? Chains are for animals, man.

OZ: Dig that ball out and you can go. It's under all that shit somewhere. Use my shovel.

LEROY: You can't make me do that.

OZ: Yeah, and you can't make me unlock your chain.

LEROY: *(Takes the shovel, begins to dig.)* It's Leroy.

OZ: Nice to meet you. Name's Oz.

(Suddenly, a businessman approaches. Not happy.)

REEVES: Where's Valentine?

OZ: Show's on.

REEVES: I know that. I just watched the start of that "parade"…

OZ: It's good, huh.

REEVES: It was a joke. Whoever that is in that Siamese costume, it's not those boys. Now, I told Valentine, as long as this show had those Siamese twins, we had a deal. But no boys, no deal. And that's not only for here, that's for every one of the dates I set up for him for the next four weeks. Where are the twins?

OZ: How'd you know it wasn't them?

REEVES: I saw them in Owensboro. Those boys can juggle. Whoever this is, they're doing good to walk.

OZ: Well. I wouldn't know, Mr…

REEVES: It's Reeves. You tell Valentine he better have those twins when I catch up to him. I do not like to lose money.

OZ: Hard on your heart, I guess.

REEVES: You just tell him. It takes more than a dozen gypsies to fool me.

LEROY: How many does it take?

(Oz laughs. Reeves ignores him.)

REEVES: And you. Do something about this smell. *(Reeves storms off.)*

(Oz goes back to work.)

LEROY: Where are the twins?

OZ: Are you hungry?

LEROY: Hey, great. Thanks.

OZ: I'm offering you a job, not a meal. The countess needs a websitter, some-body to hold her ropes. Pays 42 bucks a week, plus a bed, plus the cook-house. *(Smiles.)* Put you in the center ring.

LEROY: You only got one ring.

OZ: Is that so?

LEROY: You got one elephant, a coupla worn out ponies and a pack of scrappy lookin' dogs, one cute chick that's getting it on with the lion tamer, and a bunch of chickens under that ticket booth. What's her name?

OZ: Eva? Trina? The elephant?

LEROY: Trina.

OZ: You stay away from Trina. The last towner that fell for her, Freddie put him in the hospital.

LEROY: And the twins. I guess you've got the twins. Do you honest-to-God shovel animal shit for a living?

OZ: I shovel elephant shit. I don't like animals.

LEROY: Elephants are animals.

OZ: Nope. Animals are smaller.

LEROY: Where'd you get her? I mean, you guys can't afford an elephant, right? I bet you can't even afford to feed her, am I right?

OZ: A petting zoo left her in Marietta. She had colic, some idiot fed her cold water, she coulda died from that. Anyway, we were in Dalton, I read about it in the paper. Fred took everybody else on to Decatur, and I went to her. The U-Haul wouldn't rent me a truck when she got well. So you know how we caught up with them? We walked. And... *(Angrily.)* you'd think nobody in the whole state of Georgia had ever seen an elephant before!

LEROY: O.K. You've got yourself a boy, a what's it? A websitter? But just for today.

OZ: We don't hire by the day.

LEROY: Well, I don't work any other way. Do you want me or not?

OZ: *(Wearily.)* The animals all need fresh, lukewarm water, when you're through here. *(He walks off.)*

LEROY: *(Calling after him.)* She does the trapeze too, right? That Trina chick? *(He mimes a lion tamer cracking a whip.)* Back! Back!
(Lights down on Leroy. Swirling lights in the center ring. Spanish music is heard as offstage, Fred begins the intro.)

FRED: *(In his spotlight.)* And now, in the steel arena, vicious beasts from the wilds of Africa and Asia, under the hypnotic domination of the dashing, daring, death-tempter from Madrid, Antonio Navarro.

IN THE CENTER RING

Tony runs into the spotlight. He bows and snaps the whip for the "lions" to be let into the arena. Growls and roars are heard. We may see pedestals and hurdles, a huge ball, and a large ring. During his "Act" he will imitate the positions the lions take on these objects. This must not look funny, but as though he is doing it without thinking about it. As though he is the one who is trained. Tony is extremely intelligent and well-educated. He has not come from a circus family, and no one is more surprised than he to find himself traveling with this circus.

TONY: *(In a mock Spanish accent.)* You have maybe noticed the tightness of my pants. It is so the lions will not catch them in their teeth. Or maybe for some other reason having to do with the young girls in the audience, eh? *(Dropping the accent.)* I'm thinking of dropping the accent. What do you think? *(Cracking the whip.)* Back! *(A moment.)* Eva bought me these pants. Only decent thing she ever…No, there was one other thing, although I didn't think it was so decent at the time. She was only 19 then. Calling herself Eva Sparrow. Tiny little body, tiny little feet. I learned this from her. It's a bluff. The whole thing's a bluff. You can stay alive if you can keep the lions from making a correct appraisal of the situation. *(Remembering to talk about animals.)* Cats start to go bad at about ten years old. If a cat chews on one side, it's probably got a toothache. Have to watch for that. Feeding a live chicken will pick up a sick cat's appetite. And bears are not afraid of gunfire.

Eva worked snakes when she was a girl. They'd get these baths in milk to keep their skins shiny. You ever watch a wild-haired woman wash a snake? Tiny white hands stroking up that scaly hide? Still gives me chills, dammit. I was a private person then. In school, in fact. University of Florida, animal husbandry. Thought I was giving all that up to marry Eva. Wrong. *(Back to the animals.)* Right. O.K. You can't let the cats hide meat in their cages after a feeding. They bring that meat into the arena with them, and you don't break up that fight. You just hope like hell you can get out before it's too late. *(Angrily.)* All I ever wanted from Eva was one of those milk baths. Like the snakes. So I fed her ponies and fed her dogs and rubbed her feet, but that wasn't enough. So I taught lions to tell left from right and tigers to roll over and bears to ride bicycles and finally she married me. *(A moment.)* But I never got that milk bath. I never even got what the snakes got from Eva. I asked. Oh, yes. I had to ask. The snakes didn't have to ask, but I did, and she said, *(Imitating her accent.)* "Don't be silly" for years. It was silly. I knew it was silly. Oh for God's sake, this whole thing is silly. *(Calmer.)* I understand now. I didn't get a milk bath because I wasn't part of the act, and I wasn't dangerous. I was just useful. But not useful enough, so she divorced me. But by that time I was a animal trainer so what the hell. I am a good animal trainer. One of the best. *(Back to the bravado.)* I have quite the footwork, eh? Yes. I do have a way with them, animals. But I do not be their husband any more! *(Tony stands for his final applause.)*

FRED: Ladies and Gentlemen! Antonio Navarro!

(Tony jumps down from the platform, then turns once more to the audience. Casually.)

TONY: I gave Eva's snakes to a Chinese family. They were tough old snakes, but they ate them anyway. *(Tony exits.)*

(Offstage in blackout, we hear a fire engine siren start up for the clowns' Fire Brigade stunt.)

FRED: *(In his spotlight.)* Help! Help! There's a house on fire! And look! There's someone at the third story window and I think…Oh no! She has a baby in her arms! Someone must help her! Hurry! Save that poor woman and her baby! Wait! Stop! That's not the Louisville Fire Department! Those are the famous Cardwell Clowns!

(We hear screams of hysterical laughter as the clown stunt starts.)

OUTSIDE THE TENT

Fred rushes out to meet Oz, his tone changing drastically from the clown intro.

FRED: Can't this wait til intermission?

OZ: I need ninety pounds of horsemeat.

FRED: So buy it.

OZ: There's no money in the safe.

FRED: Oh, yeah. I paid off the tow trucks. Damn Owensboro mud cost us everything we took in.

OZ: So how are we gonna make payroll?

FRED: That's my business.

OZ: Fine. I need ninety pounds of horsemeat.

FRED: Take one of Eva's ponies.

OZ: Feed one of Eva's ponies to Tony's cats?

FRED: Dogs then.

OZ: What's with you?

FRED: You seen a guy named Reeves around here?

OZ: Yeah. And he's looking for you, too.

FRED: He's got your feed money. We're doing four weeks for him.

OZ: Not unless he sees the twins, we aren't. He saw the opening of the show. He knows they're gone.

FRED: They're not gone.

OZ: Whatever. Look. I need ninety pounds of horsemeat, one hundred pounds of hay, twenty pounds of grain, and twenty pounds of whatever you want to feed the dogs today.

FRED: What we should've done, was salt down the chimps when they died.

OZ: This is not a joke.

FRED: Of course it's a joke. This whole thing's a joke. I spend my entire day every day hustling money to buy horsemeat for the cats to eat so they'll be strong enough to tear up their cat wagon, which I then have to pay to have repaired, and then have to pay to have hauled out of the mud because the water truck can't pull it because it needs new tires. But I gotta have horse-meat every day, because if the cats don't eat, we've got no reason to buy new tires for the seat wagon, or a new drive shaft for the stake puller so it can get this show on down the road where the cats will need to eat again. Yes sir, this better be a joke Oz or I'm dumber than I thought.

(Oz finds the piece of paper Fred gave him earlier. He studies it.)

OZ: Did you already pay the Emergency Room for the twins?

FRED: All you gotta do is pick them up.

OZ: Is there something you're not telling me about this? No. Are you gonna *tell* me what you're not telling me about this?

FRED: I'll tell you later.

IN THE WARDROBE TENT

Eva and Goldie enter getting out of the Siamese twin costume.

EVA: We didn't fool them. They knew we weren't the twins.

GOLDIE: You didn't even try. You kept running away from me.

EVA: I'm ashamed I agreed to do it in the first place.

GOLDIE: You're ashamed of me. Even disguised, you're ashamed of me.

EVA: I am not ashamed of you. It's just that…

GOLDIE: You wish I were more like you. You wish I were exactly like you. You'd like me so much better if I weren't so deep down ordinary. How can somebody like me be your sister? Just doesn't seem fair, does it, Eva.

EVA: That's ridiculous.

GOLDIE: It's the truth. Well. I'm not you. I'm not as pretty as you. I don't have any talent on the trapeze…

EVA: You do have talent. You should…

GOLDIE: The men never lined up to see me. Even Trina likes you better. I'm not you. But I'm used to not being you, so you can please quit feeling so sorry for me.

EVA: Are you happy?

GOLDIE: Sure. Why not? You?

EVA: A triple somersault would make me happy. Other than that, I really don't care.

GOLDIE: It's all you've ever wanted, that triple. You and every other flyer I know.

EVA: But I'll get mine someday.

GOLDIE: What happens if that's all you ever get?

EVA: Then I'll have two things. Right now, I just have one. You. *(She makes some small affectionate, but not mushy gesture.)*
(Trina enters.)

TRINA: I think something is the matter with the twins.

EVA: They're coming unglued?

GOLDIE: Stop it. Just stop it.

TRINA: I'm serious. They were drinking yesterday. And fighting. And Brad didn't want to play chess and Bill didn't whistle once, all day.

GOLDIE: It's just hard, that's all.

EVA: They have a sick relationship.

GOLDIE: And you've had such healthy ones, Eva.

EVA: Their relationship makes me sick.

TRINA: Dad says they're pretty good bowlers.

EVA: And every town we play, Freddie's got to pay who knows how much to get some bowling alley to open early so they can be alone, together. I need new harnesses and Fred spends the money I earn renting them bowling shoes.

TRINA: They just want to go be ordinary.

GOLDIE: Well, they're not doing it any more, not if I have anything to say about it. They get hurt and where are we? Beached til they get well.

EVA: We could go on without them.

GOLDIE: No we couldn't. Everybody else has everything we have except them. Nobody else has them.

EVA: Nobody else has me.

GOLDIE: No, Eva. Everybody else has you. Only the you they have is Trina's age.

EVA: And I guess you think you could tell fortunes for Ringling.

TRINA: I hate this argument. It's always the same, stupid, boring thing.

GOLDIE: It's all we have. She's ashamed of me and I feel sorry for her.

EVA: Don't ever have any sisters, darling.

GOLDIE: If she had some sisters, maybe we could keep this show going without the twins.

EVA: But why should Freddie want to make babies when the flyer he married grew up to be a fortune-teller and cook?

GOLDIE: And if you hadn't dumped every man who ever loved you....

EVA: I can't be having babies. I have to fly.

TRINA: If this is the new argument, I'll take the old one back.

GOLDIE: We don't have much family.

EVA: So we don't have much circus.

TRINA: I could get married.

EVA AND GOLDIE: No!

TRINA: What do you mean, no. I guess I can get married if I want. I guess I can kill myself if I want. And if you don't think I can, do whatever I want, you just watch me.

EVA: Why do you want to get married, darling?

TRINA: I didn't say I wanted to get married. I didn't say what I want to do. I only said I want to do what I want to do.

EVA: You just keep working.

GOLDIE: You have real natural talent, honey.

EVA: Later, there will be time for men. Now. There is only time for the trapeze. There are some timing things that you have to learn right now or you'll never get them right. In a few years, after a bad marriage, it will be too late to come back to the trapeze.

TRINA: Tony said he would teach me how to eat fire.

GOLDIE: Tony is not for you.

EVA: And his fire is not so hot.

GOLDIE: (To Eva.) It was when you *met* him. *You* put it out!

TRINA: He said there were just four little rules. Don't eat fire in a high wind. Don't eat fire if you have a beard. Don't eat fire when you have a cold that would make you sneeze or cough. And don't use...something, I forgot what. Some kind of fuel...Don't use it. It turns you blue.

GOLDIE: We'll find you somebody nice. You're a special girl. You can't have just anybody.

TRINA: I like Tony.

GOLDIE: He's too old.

TRINA: He's just going to teach me how to eat fire. I don't mean to marry him.

EVA: I didn't either.

(Offstage, Fred's intro begins.)

FRED: *(In his spotlight.)* The first people on Earth wanted to fly.

TRINA: What's for dinner?

FRED: Wanted to soar with the birds over the primeval forests and swamps below. Sure, we built airplanes, but they're no more than passenger electric room fans. Eva Vladimirov flies.

TRINA: What's for dinner?

GOLDIE: I heard you the first time. I don't know.

EVA: We won't even know while we're eating it.

GOLDIE: You cook it then. And I'll ride your precious ponies in the second act.

EVA: You'd break their backs.

GOLDIE: *(As she walks off.)* And we'd all die of ptomaine.

FRED: Eva Vladimirov flies. With her young protégé, Trina Valentine, she dares the seagull to be more graceful, dares the hawks to be more powerful, dares the eagles to be more serene. You will never see, this side of Heaven, a more dazzling aerial display.

(Eva and Trina wait in the wings to go on.)

EVA: I love your Mother's pancakes.

TRINA: She has neat hair.

EVA: It runs in the family. Smile, darling.

FRED: And now, ladies and gentlemen, directing your attention first to the shimmering rope ladder, then to the tiny platform at the very top of the Big Top...Trina Valentine, and the incomparable Countess Eva Vladimirov.

IN THE CENTER RING

Eva watches quietly as Trina steps into the spotlight and does her act.

TRINA: You can't just decide you want to be circus people. If you're not born to it, you won't ever be it, really, no matter how hard you try. I was born to it. And when you're born to it, you don't ever have to worry about what you're going to do because it's going to be the same thing you've been doing since you could ever remember doing anything.

I don't go to high school. I take correspondence courses from the Calvert School in Baltimore, it's the law. Sometimes I think it would be fun to go to high school, but my arms are real muscular, you know, so I might feel funny out taking pictures for the yearbook or something.

I'm working the trapeze now. Eva and Mama did a great double trap turn when they were young. The Sparrow Sisters—da da. Eva did a triple somersault once. It was in practice, but she did it just the same. It's all Time, see, and knowing how to fall, cause you're going to fall, that's for sure. Most of the time, something breaks and that's why you fall. But sometimes people just let go. It's "casting," that's what we call it. And nobody knows why people do it. One minute they're fine and the next minute they just let go. And it's not when they're doing something hard, they could be doing some little flying return or something and it just happens. Their fingers just unwrap and straighten out all relaxed and they've let go, only they didn't mean to. It's not a mistake. They don't lose their concentration or anything. It's weird. They just let go.

If they tuck and fall right, they'll be O.K. though. You have to know how to fall right. Oh, I already said that. Lillian Leitzel once fell 55 feet from the top of the tent, and she didn't use a net either. The swivel on her wrist ring broke and she fell all the way, but she lived. She stood right up and took a bow. She died in the hospital a coupla days after that, but she looked just fine right after. Can you believe that, she stood up after that fall and took a bow.

Oz has this motorboat and we go waterskiing sometimes. My arms are real strong, like I said, so I'm kinda good at it. The best part, the very best part is at the end of the ride when one minute you're skiing along and the next minute you just open up your fingers and the bar goes flying off after the boat and you just sink down so slow into the water. And that water feels so cold on your hands where they've been holding the bar for so long.

Oz says we could probably ski straight home from here. Down the Ohio to the Mississippi and across the Gulf and right into Tampa Bay and be home. And it probably wouldn't take more than...I don't know... (*Laughing at herself.*) Forever.

IN THE OFFICE TRAILER

Goldie is changing into ordinary clothes so she can start supper. Outside, Reeves pounds on the door angrily.

REEVES: Valentine!

GOLDIE: *(Calling out.)* Not here!

REEVES: Where is he?

GOLDIE: Doesn't travel with the show. Just a name, Circus Valentine.

REEVES: I don't know who you are in there, but I brought you here whoever you are and I own this mall so you open up this door.

GOLDIE: O.K. O.K.

(Goldie opens the door. Reeves offers a stern handshake.)

REEVES: It's Reeves. I own this mall. Where's Valentine?

GOLDIE: He's not here.

REEVES: I didn't ask you where he isn't. I asked you where he is.

GOLDIE: Show's on.

REEVES: You people! What's the matter with you people? You think you're too good to talk to anybody or what? Show's on. Show's on. Your elephant man said show's on, and now you say show's on. I *know* the show's on.

GOLDIE: We say that because it's true. Freddie is announcing the show and the show is...on. O.K.?

REEVES: Where are the twins?

GOLDIE: The twins?

REEVES: I give up.

GOLDIE: I'm the cook. What do I know?

REEVES: You were the fortune-teller this morning.

GOLDIE: Yeah. Somebody stole my ball, you know. Now, if you're so in charge, you owe us some security.

REEVES: I don't owe you anything but a place to park and I'm having second thoughts about that!

GOLDIE: You owe us bathrooms.

REEVES: They're inside.

GOLDIE: If we go inside and people see the costumes, they got no reason to come to the show. Also. If you make us use the ones inside, we steal the toilet paper and write on the walls. Our lion tamer, he steals faucets. I know, but we're collectors. Picture postcards, little glass bottles, lightbulbs, display tables, popcorn machines...

REEVES: How many bathrooms do you want?

GOLDIE: Two would be nice.

(Fred opens the door, sees Reeves, hesitates a moment.)

GOLDIE: Fred. Mr. Reeves is here to see you.

(Fred slaps on a big, confident smile and steps into the trailer.)

REEVES: Valentine.

FRED: Mr. Reeves. Good to be here.

REEVES: Where are the twins?

FRED: They went bowling…They dropped a ball on their foot.

REEVES: I want them in the show.

FRED: So do we. I just sent my brother to the hospital to get them. You know. Accidents happen.

REEVES: Either they're in the evening show or you can get this zoo off my property.

FRED: Of course they'll be in the show. Unless they can't walk or something, and in that case, it might be another day or so before…

REEVES: If they can't walk, you put them on that elephant and parade them around, or if they can't be lifted up, they you put them on a stretcher.

FRED: Don't have a double stretcher.

REEVES: I don't care if they're unconscious. You put them on, I don't care how you put them on, but you show tonight's audience those Siamese twins and you show that they're hooked together absolutely real and forever, or that is it! No bathrooms, no parking lot, no four weeks of big malls, nothing to do with me or my friends again, ever, and I have a lot of friends.

FRED: Don't worry about the boys, Mr. Reeves. Brad and Bill are born entertainers. They'll be back as soon as is humanly—

REEVES: I've had posters printed and advertising. I've told the people that we'll have a circus with Siamese twin clowns and I will have a circus with Siamese twin clowns or I will have no circus.

FRED: You see the show yet?

REEVES: I've seen enough to know…

FRED: Got some great acts. The twins aren't really that talented.

REEVES: Oh for Christ's sake. They're Siamese. I'm a businessman, Valentine. And a fair man. And we could do a lot of business for a long time, you and me. But it's gotta all be real simple. We make an agreement. Then I keep my part of the agreement, and you keep your part of the agreement. Or else I haul your ass into court and you spend the rest of your life in jail while I cut up your tent and sell it for sailboats.

FRED: Good. We understand each other.

REEVES: No, Valentine. You understand me.

FRED: Right.

(*Reeves exits. Fred closes the door behind him and sits down. There is a considerable pause.*)

GOLDIE: You should've told him to shove it, Freddie.

FRED: How could I do that?

GOLDIE: He treated you like shit. Why do you let people do that?

FRED: Get off my back, Goldie. We've had this conversation.

GOLDIE: No. We've started this conversation. When we get really close to having this conversation, you always say we've had this conversation.

FRED: I let people treat me like shit because I have to.

GOLDIE: You do not.

FRED: I do. Because that's how your sister gets to keep flying and her ex-husband gets to keep subjugating the ferocious beasts. Because that's how my brother gets to hide behind his elephant and how we keep our daughter from marrying some jerk that pumps gas.

(*She is angrier than she knows. She plunges into forbidden territory.*)

GOLDIE: It's also how you forget that you grew up in the side show. It's also how you forget that you're the son of the Fat Lady.

FRED: (*Grabs her by the arm.*) I didn't hear that. And you didn't say it.

GOLDIE: I'm sorry.

FRED: I'm going to watch Eva's somersaults. See you later.

GOLDIE: Freddie. I don't know what made me say that, what I said about your mother. I don't know what's the matter with me today. I can't get going somehow. I need to start thinking about supper but I keep wandering around like I'm in a big grocery I haven't been to before and I can't find where they put the raisins. Freddie. I want to have a baby.

FRED: No.

GOLDIE: No? You just say no?

FRED: We can't afford it. The doctor and the hospital and the clothes and the baby food and the playpen. It could cost a thousand dollars, Goldie, and that would put new tires on all the trucks.

GOLDIE: We're going to make good money playing these big malls, aren't we?

FRED: Goldie. Baby me, Goldie. I need it.

GOLDIE: Are the twins going to be all right?

FRED: You just leave them to me.

GOLDIE: That's what we've always done, honey. We're just worried, that's all.

FRED: I gotta go.

(Fred runs out, as we hear applause coming from inside the circus tent. A drum roll begins and continues through Fred's offstage intro.)

FRED: *(In his spotlight.)* Ladies and Gentlemen, we must ask for absolute quiet, please. Even the smallest whisper can shatter the total concentration a flyer needs at this moment. *(A pause.)* The spotlight will find and follow her for you, fifty-five feet in the air…Countess Eva Vladimirov, performing the double twisting somersault on the flying trapeze.

IN THE CENTER RING

Spotlight on Eva. The Russian Accent is somehow softer and more believable.

EVA: Flying. Oh Flying. I do not have much to say about flying. Except this. The day will come when I will fly for the last time. But when that day comes, I pray God I do not know it is that day. It is like the grandparents making love. The last time does come. But they do not want to know it is the last time they will be together in that way. It is the same with flying. Oh Flying.

(Eva takes a proud bow over enthusiastic applause. The spotlight goes out quickly, allowing her to disappear from the stage.)

IN THE OFFICE TRAILER

Trina enters the office trailer, quite excited.

TRINA: We were fabulous. Did you hear the applause?

GOLDIE: No.

TRINA: Eva wanted to try the triple. I could tell. She was just dying to try it.

GOLDIE: You can't do a triple somersault in a tent, you know it and she knows it. There's not enough room over your head. And it's also very hot up there. If the ropes stretch just this much, we could lose her. So don't you encourage her. And Trina…

TRINA: Yeah?

GOLDIE: Stay away from Tony.

TRINA: But you were already married to Daddy when you were my age.

GOLDIE: There are some nice boys at home.

TRINA: They won't look twice at me. We're not with the Big Show so they don't care what I can do or who I am, even.

GOLDIE: There's that Christiani cousin, and the Rock-Smith Flyers have— There's Jorge Barrada.

(Apparently a very handsome young lion tamer.)

TRINA: Sure.

GOLDIE: Don't you worry. There's somebody out there waiting for you. Somebody just perfect.

TRINA: Daddy's not perfect.

GOLDIE: He was when I married him.

TRINA: He's such a cheapskate. Eva can't have new ropes this year, and Tony has to pull the cats' teeth himself because Daddy won't pay for a vet. Sometimes I think Daddy hates the circus.

GOLDIE: Sometimes I hate it.

TRINA: Then what are you doing here? You could've gone to college. Daddy could own a deep-sea boat and take tourists out to catch marlins. He could be an anchorman on TV. You could have your hair done in a beauty shop, and maybe start a boutique or a plant shop. Yeah, selling orchids or something.

GOLDIE: You wish I sold plants.

TRINA: Sometimes. Yeah. Sometimes I wish you sold plants.

GOLDIE: And your Daddy were an accountant and you got an allowance and I signed your report card. You wish we were normal people. Well. We're not normal and you should be proud of it. If being normal were any fun, people wouldn't be so happy to see the circus.

TRINA: I guess.

GOLDIE: I don't want to sell plants, honey.

(There is a moment.)

TRINA: I had this great idea. I told the twins they should write a book and go on TV. Do variety shows and Christmas specials and stuff. In the off season, I mean. They don't look so weird they'd scare people. Wouldn't that be terrific? Go on the late show, even.

GOLDIE: They don't want to be stars, sweetie.

TRINA: But think of the money they could make.

GOLDIE: If they were interested in money, they'd be gone already. Besides, that would be like being back in the sideshow. Your daddy rescued them from that a long time ago, and I don't think they want to go back to it, even if it means lots of money.

TRINA: I'm gonna work real hard this winter.

GOLDIE: Good.

TRINA: If I worked really hard…

GOLDIE: You could do anything you wanted.

TRINA: I could do a triple.

GOLDIE: You could do anything you wanted.

(There is a knock at the door. Goldie goes to open it.)

LEROY: You Goldie? Oz said to tell you I'm one more for supper. But I'm not really one more cause your websitter or whatever you call it blew the show and I'm just taking his place for today. It's Leroy. *(Extends his hand.)* Hi.

GOLDIE: Supper's at six. Have to wear a clean shirt. And there's no snacks between meals so don't ask.

(She starts to close the door on him.)

LEROY: So what do I do?

GOLDIE: Trina can tell you. I'm in the kitchen if you want me, honey.

TRINA: O.K.

(Goldie leaves, Trina sits down, takes off her headpiece, primps, very aware that he is watching, but is very condescending about it.)

LEROY: Well?

TRINA: You sit on the floor and hold our ropes. Just the ones for the sliding descent. The others are on stakes.

LEROY: What do I do during the act?

TRINA: Watch, I guess. I don't know what the last guy did during the act. I don't see anything once I'm up there.

LEROY: You don't see how far down it is?

TRINA: I *know* how far down it is.

LEROY: You couldn't pay me enough money to get up there.

TRINA: You probably don't have the arms for it anyway.

LEROY: Well, you sure do. Punched anybody out lately?

(Trina moves toward the door.)

TRINA: Get out of my way.

LEROY: *(Catches her.)* Hey, I'm sorry. I really only came over here to meet *you.* That supper business was an excuse. You are one great looking girl.

TRINA: Thank you.

LEROY: So what are you doing messing around with that lion tamer? He could be your father. Unless that's your thing, you know, a father thing.

TRINA: It's none of your business.

LEROY: No, I know that. But what are you doing with this two-bit show? You're swimming in the wrong pond, baby.

TRINA: This is no two-bit show.

LEROY: You could do better.

TRINA: My Daddy owns this show. I couldn't ever leave the circus.

LEROY: Who said anything about leaving the circus. I just meant go with a big show. Ringling doesn't use hand-me-down costumes, I bet. I'd like to see you in something that really fit. Whose is this, anyway?

TRINA: Who are you, anyway?

LEROY: They've got you locked up here like some fairytale princess.

TRINA: What do you want?

LEROY: I don't know.

TRINA: Well if you think I'm gonna believe you're some talent scout or something, you're wrong. And I'm not about to run away with you either.

LEROY: Honey, I didn't ask you to run way with me, O.K.?

TRINA: You were about to.

LEROY: No I wasn't either. I want one night, that's all. What time are you through?

TRINA: Is this how you get girls? You just walk right up and say I want to go to bed with you?

LEROY: Sure is.

TRINA: And they go for it?

LEROY: How about 10:30?

TRINA: Why should I go anywhere with you? You came busting in here to tell me I'm pretty only the way you said it was I must not be any good or I wouldn't be afraid to try out for Ringling.

LEROY: When's the next try-out?

TRINA: Sometime in February, the 14th, I think.

LEROY: You should be there.

TRINA: I have to get ready for intermission.

LEROY: 10:30. Yes or no?

TRINA: Maybe.

LEROY: That's the spirit. Tell your lion tamer you're going out for some exercise. *(Tony enters without knocking.)*

LEROY: Hey man. How'd it go out there?

TONY: Do I know you?

LEROY: Must take a lot of guts to get in there with those cats. This outfit got a good retirement plan? *(Tony opens the door for Leroy.)*

TONY: The best. You work til you die. We'll see you later. *(Tony takes Leroy by the arm, ushers him out.)*

LEROY: Sorry I can't stay and talk.

TONY: We understand.

LEROY: See you guys later.

(*Tony closes the door behind Leroy.*)

TRINA: Hi.

TONY: Come here, you pretty girl.

TRINA: Mother says to stay away from you. She says you're not for me.

TONY: (*Embracing her.*) And what do you say?

TRINA: I told her you were teaching me to eat fire.

TONY: Bet she loved that idea.

TRINA: When can we go, Tony?

TONY: Your Daddy owes me money, baby.

TRINA: I have some money.

TONY: He owes me my bonus from last season. I mean, I'm glad he didn't pay me then or I wouldn't have signed on for another season, and then I wouldn't have been here when you…grew up…

TRINA: Am I good enough for Ringling?

TONY: Tell me you love me.

TRINA: I want to go to Spain.

TONY: It would hurt your mother.

TRINA: I know. We're worse than the twins. You poke *me* in the middle of the night, and *she* wakes up.

TONY: Your father would kill me

TRINA: Not if we were far enough away.

TONY: Look. This is a bigger town than we've played before, and we're doing these malls for the next four weeks. That's got to mean money. Your Daddy will pay me and we'll just blow this old show.

TRINA: Tell me you love me.

TONY: We'll be inseparable.

TRINA: Like the twins.

(*They laugh and kiss. Trina is giggling rather than laughing. They do not see the door open.*)

TRINA: Eva!

EVA: Get dressed.

TONY: The Countess Vladimirov.

EVA: (*To Trina.*) Leave us, darling.

(*Tony pats her affectionately.*)

TONY: Go on, Trina.

(Trina exits.)

EVA: What are you doing with my Trina?

TONY: Trina is a big girl now.

EVA: What are you doing with my Trina?

TONY: She's not your Trina. She's her very own Trina, and the only reason she's stayed with you this year is because *I'm* here.

EVA: You think you're keeping her here?

TONY: I know it!

EVA: You with your slimy charm? With your boring experience? All you're really good at is taking off your shirt. And then…you don't even have any good scars to show her. She ever ask you how you made it through fifteen years as a lion trainer without a single scratch? It's easy enough to figure out. You never got close enough. Your act is all show…And anybody who knows anything about lions knows it. You're still working here because all Freddie knows about lions is what they eat.

TONY: Speaking of which, could you excuse me

EVA: Does she know you hate the circus? That you look down on all circus people, and that includes her, because we're not smart enough for you? You could've been a marine biologist. You could've been a plastic surgeon. How many times did I have to hear what you could've been. Well, you can't be either one of those things or anything else any more. You had your straight-A life and you ran off with the circus. And now all you are is a flashy old man with six mouths to feed.

TONY: *(Tries again.)* Speaking of which, could you—

EVA: And if you try to take Trina away from us…if you talk her into leaving the circus and going to middle-age with you…if you destroy all that we have worked for…if she stops flying…If I find out that you have even touched her, I will kill you.

TONY: Are you through?

EVA: You will be in the cage with the cats and I will shoot you in the legs and let the cats tear you apart. You may live long enough to see quite a bit of it, this killing of you.

TONY: Yeah, yeah.

EVA: Or I'll brush your hair with pepper. You won't even know it. Sheena will sneeze and bite your head off.

TONY: Eva…

EVA: Accidents happen.

TONY: I believe you.

EVA: You'd better.

TONY: I also remember Count Vladimirov.

EVA: You touch Trina and I will kill you.

TONY: Poor Court Vladimirov. Shall I tell your darling Trina about the last days of the rich, old, and very foolish Count Vladimirov? Shall I tell your precious protégé and niece that her has-been aerialist goddess drugged her invalid husband and pushed him down the stairs, and then had the nerve to keep his name *and* his money!

EVA: There was no money.

TONY: I could've told you that when you married him. Look, Eva, the guy was gonna kick off pretty soon anyway, so I don't much care that you killed him or not—

EVA: It was an accident and you know it!

TONY: —but what bugs the shit out of me is that you even kept his accent. *(Now in a different tone.)* I think I'll tell her.

EVA: She won't believe you.

TONY: She believes everything I say.

(Eva picks up the starters pistol he uses in his lion-taming act.)

EVA: You're also going to be deaf in a few years from shooting this. Does she know that?

TONY: It's loaded.

EVA: Do you remember how many shots you fired in the ring? You started with five blanks. *(She fires two shots.)* Did you shoot three out there so the next one is the bullet? Or was it two, so the next one is still a blank. Or was one so you have two more chances? A younger man would remember.

TONY: One.

(She fires another shot.)

TONY: There's one more blank.

EVA: Or was it two? Or was that yesterday you only shot one? If it was two today, this next one is for real.

TONY: Give me the gun.

EVA: *(Backing toward the door.)* You were wrong. You shot one yesterday and two today. This one will kill you. I always count. Still think you're right? One little squeeze… *(She hands him the gun.)*

TONY: Thank you.

EVA: Don't touch her.

TONY: Don't kill me.

(The door opens and Oz and Goldie enter, very upset and disturbed to find anyone in here.)

GOLDIE: *(To Eva and Tony.)* Get out!

EVA: Get out?

GOLDIE: You were going out. So go.

TRINA: What's up?

OZ: Nothing.

TONY: Something is up all right.

(Offstage, Fred makes the intermission announcement.)

FRED: *(In his spotlight.)* And that, ladies and gentlemen, brings us to the end of the first half of today's performance of Circus Valentine. So take a few minutes, get some popcorn and a soft drink, and hurry right back for the experience of a lifetime—

OZ: I have to see Fred.

TONY: We all have to see Fred. It's the price we pay to work here. You have to see Fred about what?

FRED: *(Continuing offstage.)* —hurry right back for the experience of a lifetime, those brilliant Siamese twins, Brad and Bill Evans, right here in the center ring, along with Grace Kelly, Ella and Elvira Esterhazy, and a whirl of other attractions.

TONY: What's going on?

GOLDIE: It's none of your business.

FRED: Ladies and Gentlemen, boys and girls. It's intermission.

(We hear the intermission music over the continuing argument.)

EVA: Everything that happens here is our business. We are the show.

TONY: Shut up, Eva. *(To Oz.)* How are the twins?

OZ: I don't know.

TONY: What do you mean, you don't know?

EVA: You didn't bring them back?

OZ: No.

TONY: You just left them down there or what? You had something else to do or what? You had a flat tire? What, Oz?

TRINA: Hey! What's going on in here? It's intermission. I need change for the cotton candy and people are stealing the programs and *(Now seeing how upset they are.)* What's going on in here?

GOLDIE: Get Leroy to help you, and the tent crew. Don't worry about the programs. Just drinks and cotton candy and popcorn. You know what to do.

TRINA: Forget about the programs?

GOLDIE: Just go.

TRINA: O.K., O.K. *(She leaves.)*

(Tony turns to Oz)

TONY: Tell us about the twins, Oz.

GOLDIE: I think we better wait for Fred.

TONY: Oz?

OZ: They didn't go bowling. There wasn't any accident.

TONY: Then where are they? If they left us for some other show, I will personally…

(Fred opens the door, sees them all, tries to get back out, but Goldie stops him.)

TONY: Fred. What is this?

OZ: You took them to a hospital all right, but it wasn't General, it was Jewish.
And it wasn't because of any accident.

FRED: They asked me not to tell.

GOLDIE: To tell what? What's wrong with them?

EVA: What do you mean, what's wrong with them? They're Siamese twins!

OZ: Well not for long. The surgery to separate them is scheduled for tomorrow
morning. That's why they're in the hospital.

GOLDIE: Oh no.

OZ: Seven, tomorrow morning. Take all day, the nurse said.

FRED: God no.

TONY: They can't do that!

OZ: They wouldn't see me, but I found them. The hospital has the best hand
surgeon in the country. That's why they picked it. They're trying for five
fingers on each hand. Never been done, the nurse said.

TONY: We have to stop them!

EVA: I could've told you. I could've told all of you.

TONY: No you couldn't either, so shut up. Now. Fred. I say we cancel the second act and get down to that hospital and spring them out of there.

FRED: We're doing the second act.

TONY: But the twins *are* the second act.

FRED: Not today, they're not. Now what we have to do is get ourselves together and give Mr. Reeves a second act he will like even better than the twins.

GOLDIE: The only thing he'd like more than the twins is if we all went out there
and killed ourselves.

FRED: Tony can do his old springboard act.

EVA: That will kill *him*, anyway.

FRED: Goldie can juggle. *(To her.)* What was that name you used to call your-self?

GOLDIE: Dumbbell...Moron?

TRINA: Mom hasn't juggled for years.

FRED: She taught the twins to juggle, and they're great at it. How bad can she be? And you and Eva will do the long version of the pony act, and the clowns will do three turns instead of two and...

EVA: And I could try the triple.

EVERYONE: No.

EVA: Why not? If I made it, we would be history.

TRINA: And if you didn't make it?

TONY: Well then, only *she* would be history.

FRED: Nobody is going to be history. Not us, not the twins, and not this circus.

TONY: We have got to stop them from having this surgery.

FRED: We can do that after the show.

GOLDIE: We can't do the show while the twins are in—

FRED: If we do a second act that Mr. Reeves likes, then maybe we can still have a circus, even without the twins. If that's how it turns out.

GOLDIE: Are you telling us everything, Freddie?

FRED: It's going to be O.K. The twins are going to be fine, and we're going to be fine.

EVA: The show must go on?

FRED: Yes.

TONY: Why?

FRED: Because it's our job. Because this is how it works. We are the clowns and they are the farmers, and if we make them laugh, they will feed us.

TONY: You hope.

FRED: We don't have any choice. Now. Five minutes to the top of Act II. Everybody.

(All around, there are looks of crisis and despair. A combination of fear and urgency about the upcoming second act and the much longer future that will follow it. The sky has fallen, and the house lights with it.)

END OF ACT I

ACT II

OUTSIDE THE MAIN TENT

FRED: *(In his spotlight.)* Ladies and Gentlemen, boys and girls, welcome back to the greatest little show on earth, the one, the only, the original, old fashioned, orchestrated oscillation of arms and legs, balls and pegs, and men and beasts and beauties... *(Seeming to forget where he is.)* Not the *least* of which is our very own African Queen, performing without a master for she has none, seven thousand pounds of grace in motion. Here she is, Ladies and Gentlemen, Circus Valentine's great, gray, grand dame, Grace Kelly. *(Oz comes out of the tent, having just sent Grace Kelly into the ring to perform.)*

OZ: She knows something is wrong, all right.
   (Tony jumps up and down trying to warm up for his springboard act.)

TONY: I think you're in love with that elephant.

OZ: You should be so lucky.
   (Leroy and Trina come up together.)

LEROY: Hey man, I hate to tell you, but somebody stole your trampoline.

TONY: I've got one chance of not killing myself on the springboard and that's to get warm, so shut up!
   (Leroy just stands there.)

TONY: I *said* get out of here.

LEROY: No, you didn't. You said shut up.

OZ: Watch it, Leroy!
   (Leroy begins to jump up and down, shadowboxing.)

LEROY: *(Laughs.)* Here's the world famous boxing kangaroo. Coming right up, folks. Throw the left, throw the right—
   (Eva and Goldie walk up, Eva dressed for the bareback act, Goldie juggling some oranges.)

EVA: The lion tamer demonstrates the law of gravity.

TONY: Shut up! Shut up! Shut up!
   (Fred enters talking.)

FRED: O.K. Tony will do his springboard act, then Goldie will go on and juggle, then Eva and Trina will do the bareback act, then—

TRINA: *(Interrupting him.)* You can't let Tony do the springboard, Daddy. He'll get hurt.

FRED: Then he better be careful, hadn't he.

TRINA: Daddy!

FRED: You're going on with him.

GOLDIE: No!

TRINA: Doing what?

FRED: You're the assistant. The drums will roll, Tony will do some leap or other and when he lands on his feet—

TONY: If he lands on his feet…

FRED: You raise your arms in the air, and go "da-da."

TRINA: I just stand there?

FRED: You got a better idea?

TRINA: He's going to get hurt. Anything is better than somebody getting hurt.

FRED: No. Anything is better than no second act. Now get ready. Everybody! Goldie are you set?

GOLDIE: How long do I have to stay out there?

FRED: *(Turning to Tony.)* Come on, Tony!

TRINA: Be careful, Tony.

LEROY: *(To Tony.)* Should I call the ambulance now, or wait?

FRED: *(To Leroy.)* Just clear the springboard as soon as he's done.

LEROY: Got it.

(Fred, Trina and Tony exit.)

GOLDIE: He'll kill himself.

EVA: *(Unconcerned.)* Well, crippled, anyway. Even when he could do it he wasn't good at it.

(Everybody stands and watches the beginning of Tony's act.)

LEROY: *(To Oz.)* Want me to feed the cats?

OZ: We don't have anything for them to eat.

GOLDIE: What are you talking about?

OZ: Fred spent the feed money.

GOLDIE: On what?

OZ: Tow trucks.

EVA: How many did he buy?

FRED: *(In his spotlight.)* Ladies and Gentlemen, Circus Valentine is proud to present a brand new act, making his appearance for the first time anywhere in the world, with a fabulous display of jumps, turns, and spins from the springboard. This young leaper is destined to hurl himself into international fame. And you saw him first. Ladies and Gentlemen, boys and girls, Alberto Ajanian.

OZ: *(As he exits.)* I'm going after Grace.

LEROY: Anybody ever fall from Grace?

GOLDIE: Look, buster. We need you to clear the ring and hold the ropes and set up for the ponies, but most of all we need you to shut your mouth.

EVA: Who are you anyway?

LEROY: Nobody.

EVA: That's what I thought.

LEROY: You got a whole bunch a nobodies who paid to see this show, lady. I'd be nice to me if I were you.

(We hear the first "da-da" and it is received with only scattered applause.)

LEROY: What's he doing out there?

EVA: Not much.

GOLDIE: Do you *want* him to kill himself?

EVA: It would save me the trouble.

LEROY: That ain't a happy crowd.

GOLDIE: They have no idea how long it would take them to learn to somersault as poorly as Tony. They don't care that we risk our lives for their money. They think we enjoy it. Karl Wallenda took his last walk for sixty lousy people.

LEROY: Hey, it's not their fault. They don't ask you to get out there.

GOLDIE: The hell they don't. If nobody came, we wouldn't have to perform.

LEROY: So quit if it makes you so miserable.

EVA: We can't quit. They need us. They love us.

GOLDIE: They feel something for us, but it isn't love. Nobody loves someone who really would die for them.

EVA: They come to see us *fly.*

GOLDIE: Oh for God's sake. They come to see us fall. I hate them.

EVA: I don't.

GOLDIE: You need them.

EVA: You don't?

LEROY: You people are very strange.

GOLDIE AND EVA: Leave us alone.

IN THE ANIMAL AREA
Oz catches up to Fred.

OZ: You lied to me.

FRED: We'll do this later.

OZ: You lied to me! You sent me all the way down there and you knew I wasn't going to find the twins at that hospital. Now I want the whole story.

FRED: I had to do it. Later, O.K.?

OZ: You forget who owns this show.

FRED: Right this minute Reeves owns this show. Unless we can convince him to help us out.

OZ: He won't do it.

FRED: When he sees the second act he might.

OZ: He won't.

FRED: It's our only chance.

OZ: It's *your* only chance. I can sell my tent, and sell my trucks and sell my costumes, and move to Iowa.

FRED: And leave Grace Kelly?

OZ: And take Grace Kelly and go to Iowa.

FRED: What the hell is there to do in Iowa?

OZ: It's not what there is to do in Iowa, it's what there is to eat.

FRED: Hay.

OZ: *(Pointing to the tent.)* $40,000 will buy a lot of hay.

FRED: But she won't get to perform.

OZ: She'll get to stay alive. You keep running my show and she's going to starve to death.

FRED: We're in this together, Oz.

OZ: Not any more.

FRED: You've never wanted anything to do with running this show! You just want a cover for your love affair with that elephant.

OZ: Dad gave *me* the money. I can take it back.

FRED: You couldn't *wait* to get rid of Dad's money. You said, "Take it, Freddie. I don't want to be tied down by it." That's exactly what you said. Put on your boots and went to work at the zoo. Only now that I've spent it for you, you want it back. Terrific.

OZ: I've changed my mind.

FRED: No you haven't, either. Do you own a car? Do you read magazines? Do you date women? Men? Better yet. People? No. You live for that damn elephant.

And all you want to do is brush her blankets and clean out her ears and hose her down when she gets hot. And as long as the two of you stay in the circus, you can get away with that. But if you go set up housekeeping in some Iowa town, I'll be able to hear them laughing wherever I am in this country. You take your elephant to Iowa and you'll be a class A freak, Oz.

OZ: So I'll be a freak.

FRED: I've taken care of you since you were twelve years old.

OZ: You've taken my money is how I see it.

(Fred realizes he needs to apologize and fast.)

FRED: *(Calling after him.)* Oz!

OZ: What?

FRED: If the twins go through with this operation…

OZ: What do you mean, "IF"?

FRED: If we lose the twins, "your" circus is going to need "your" elephant.

OZ: Are you asking me not to abandon you?

FRED: Yes, Oz. I am.

OZ: O.K. I'll think about it.

FRED: And there's one other thing. Goldie thinks I own the tent.

OZ: You lied to her too, huh? Well that's not my problem.

FRED: I was going to tell her someday.

OZ: Maybe.

FRED: Oz, I had to tell her something. I wanted her to marry me. Why should she marry me unless I had a tent. How could I be the ringmaster unless I had a tent? I wanted her to marry me, Oz.

OZ: You don't lie to people you love.

FRED: That's easy for you to say. The person you love doesn't understand English.

OZ: The hell she doesn't.

FRED: OK. O.K.

OZ: Goldie is too good for you.

FRED: I loved her, Oz. I just wanted to be with her.

OZ: I understand that.

FRED: You won't tell her?

OZ: I won't lie to her if she asks me.

FRED: But you won't go find her right now and tell her?

OZ: No.

FRED: All right. Good. Thanks.

OUTSIDE THE MAIN TENT
Goldie and Eva are standing just outside of the tent as Fred intros Goldie.

GOLDIE: *(Still practicing juggling.)* This is going to be ridiculous.

EVA: Your juggling isn't going to keep their money in our pocket, if that's what you mean.

GOLDIE: Just ridiculous!

EVA: The only way to do that is for me to try a triple.

GOLDIE: Now that's really ridiculous.

EVA: It is not. They've never seen one.

GOLDIE: And you've never done one.

EVA: It would save the show.

GOLDIE: That's all we need, Eva. The twins in the hospital, and you dead in the sawdust.

EVA: The fall might not kill me.

GOLDIE: If you're going to kill yourself, will you please do it sometime when I'm not watching.

EVA: I might make it, you know.

GOLDIE: It wouldn't matter. These people wouldn't even know what they were seeing. They'd think it was some kind of a trick!

EVA: I'm not scared of it, if that's what you're thinking.

GOLDIE: *(Realizes she is serious.)* Wait til this winter. Outside. There'll be enough room for your spin. You'll be rested. You won't be mad at Tony or me or Freddie or anybody. You'll be in Florida. You'll be home. That will make all the difference.

(Eva doesn't answer. We hear Fred's intro.)

FRED: *(In his spotlight.)* And now, Ladies and Gentlemen, boys and girls, the marvelous Margobella, manipulating a myriad of rings, balls and pins. She will amaze you. She will amuse you! Here she is…Mademoiselle Margobella!

(Goldie runs on. Eva watches her begin her act.)

EVA: *(Imitating Fred's style.)* Ladies and Gentlemen. You are about to see something really stupid. *(Really down.)* Watch the cook drop the oranges.

IN THE WARDROBE TENT

Trina and Tony enter from the tent, Tony is limping, Trina is helping him.

TRINA: Is it bad? Does it hurt much? Tony…say something. Are you all right?

TONY: It's broken.

> *(Eva enters.)*

TRINA: He was great! Did you see him?

TONY: *(Louder.)* My ankle is broken. *(He doesn't say this to Eva, but rather to the air.)*

TRINA: It's probably just a little twisted. You were wonderful.

EVA: They booed him.

TRINA: They're stupid. What do they know about acrobats? They didn't understand what he was trying to do.

EVA: Neither did he.

TONY: I made a fool of myself.

TRINA: Well I thought you were terrific. I'll kiss it.

> *(Tony looks away from both of them as Trina bends to kiss the ankle.)*

EVA: You were a fool.

TONY: Shut up.

EVA: I never shut up.

TONY: I know.

TRINA: *(Standing up.)* There now.

EVA: *(To Trina.)* Get a bucket of ice from the snow cone machine and then get dressed.

> *(Trina leaves.)*

EVA: *(To Tony.)* Sit down.

TONY: Leave me alone.

EVA: Your tucks weren't tight enough. What you should've done was our old Risley act.

TONY: With Trina?

EVA: With somebody.

TONY: Trina doesn't know it.

TRINA: *(Enters with ice.)* Trina doesn't know what?

TONY: The Risley we used to do.

TRINA: *(Bending down.)* I didn't know you did that. That's hard.

TONY: Eva had the hard part.

> *(Eva reaches for the ice and begins to pack Tony's ankle.)*

EVA: Go get dressed Trina.

(Trina reaches for the ice.)

TRINA: I'll do it.

TONY: Let Eva do it.

TRINA: Just tell me what to do.

TONY: *(Very sharp.)* I don't have time to teach you. I'm hurt *now.*

TRINA: But she hates you.

TONY: She knows where I need the ice.

EVA: *(To Trina.)* Go on, baby. Go watch your mother.

(Eva bends down and takes off the shawl she has been wearing. She starts to bandage Tony's ankle as the spot comes up for Goldie's act.)

IN THE CENTER RING

GOLDIE: *(Very embarrassed, but still trying to juggle.)* It's very nice to be here. I'm Goldie Sparrow Valentine. Isn't that silly, Mother named me Golden Sparrow. Everybody knows there aren't any golden sparrows. Well mother's have the right to hope, I guess. I'm not a juggler. I imagine you can see that for yourself. I'm only out here because…
(The balls all fall to the floor.)

IN THE WARDROBE TENT

Lights come up on Eva and Tony. She is now taking a ribbon out of her hair to tie up the bandage. This tenderness is in direct contrast with their talk.

TONY: What am I supposed to do now? I can't go into the ring with the cats like this. I have to get my money from Fred.

EVA: He spent it.

TONY: But it might be weeks before I can find another show. How am I supposed to feed the cats in the meantime?

EVA: You could turn them loose. The police would round them up…

TONY: They'd shoot them.

EVA: Exactly. Then you wouldn't have to feed them.

TONY: I could sell them to a zoo, then buy them back when I got on my feet again.

EVA: Zoos already have lions. That's how they got to be zoos…having lions already.

TONY: I could sell them to…

EVA: Everybody who already wants lions already has lions.

TONY: I'll make some calls.

EVA: To whom?

IN THE CENTER RING
Goldie struggles on.

GOLDIE: Mademoiselle Margobella. I knew Fred would make up some name or other, but Margobella! Margobella! Know where he got that? *(Pause.)* Margobella is the name you can still read on the back of the pink plastic plates we eat off of, Miraclewear's Margobella. The miracle, as in mira-clewear, is that they won't wear out. That's what will survive the nuclear disaster at the end of the world—pink plastic plates. *(Slowly.)* What I would give for plates that would break. Some plates so nice I could worry about breaking them. And while you're at it, *(Speaking as if to some unseen benefactor.)* I'd like some hooks on the walls for pots and pans. I can't hang my pots on the walls now, because every night of my life, my walls roll 100 miles down some road to some other town. And once, before I die, I'd like to open my kitchen window and not smell horses. Is that too much?

IN THE WARDROBE TENT
Eva and Tony continue.

TONY: And I suppose you know exactly what you're going to do?

EVA: I do.

TONY: What?

EVA: Circus people *know* me.

TONY: *Who* knows you? All your boyfriends died. Their sons, no, their accoun-tants are running their circuses now. And accountants don't care about fake Russian accents and beautiful legs. This was your last tour anyway and you know it. This was your home run, sweetheart.

EVA: You think my legs are beautiful?

TONY: Your legs are beautiful, yes.

EVA: Why didn't you ever say it?

TONY: I didn't want to wait in line.

EVA: They were nothing, those men.

TONY: *They* were nothing. *I* was nothing. Everything is nothing to you.

EVA: No.

TONY: Yes. You are everything for yourself. Well, you should be happy now because you are all you are going to have left. Oh, I know! Maybe the Smithsonian would take you. Rig up your trap right next to the Wright Brothers plane. Little bronze plaque with black letters. Miss Eva Sparrow Navarro Vladimirov, The World's Oldest Living Flying Machine.

EVA: I hate you.

TONY: I know.

EVA: Do you hate me because of all those men?

TONY: I don't hate you. I hate me. I love you.

EVA: *(Pretending not to be touched, but she is.)* You are a fool.

TONY: Yes.

EVA: But you are not stupid.

TONY: Oh no. Never been stupid.

IN THE CENTER RING
Goldie continues. The crowd is booing now.

GOLDIE: The only thing we own…That's worth anything, is this tent.

IN THE WARDROBE TENT
(Reeves storms up to Tony and Eva. He indicates the treatment.)

REEVES: Somebody get hurt?

TONY: It's nothing.

REEVES: Where's Valentine? *(Tony starts to point.)* No. Where are the twins?

EVA: *(A little threatening, but not belligerent.)* Who are you?

REEVES: Name is Reeves. I own this mall. Where are the twins?

EVA: *(Very nearly coy.)* You must be a very busy man.

REEVES: I can handle it.

TONY: It's a real nice set up you have here.

REEVES: Just have to know what you're doing. Are the twins going on?

TONY: I hear these malls are a good investment. You don't make money with work, you make money with money.

REEVES: Where are the—

EVA: *(Seeing that Reeves wants an answer.)* The twins keep pretty much to themselves. Is there anything else we could do for you?

TONY: Seen the show?

REEVES: No.

(Reeves looks inside the tent. The crowd is laughing now. Tony and Eva are worried about that.)

TONY: One of the finest little circuses in the world.

EVA: I wouldn't fly for anybody else. Fred is the best.

(Trina enters, dressed exactly like Eva for their bareback act.)

TRINA: Is your ankle broken?

EVA: Trina, darling, this is Mr. Reeves.

(Trina curtsies, as the laughter continues outside.)

IN THE CENTER RING

Goldie continues. The crowd is booing louder now.

GOLDIE: Fred bought this tent because he wanted to be somebody. Well this time, Fred Valentine, *I* want to be somebody. I'm not some no-talent rope girl who's afraid of heights. I'm a middle-aged fortune-teller who's sick of cheap. I'm tired of secondhand, discount, giant economy-sized plastic plate cheap! I want a house, I want a mailbox and neighbors. I want an inside telephone. *(Picking up the balls.)* I'm sorry about this. But…I never said I could juggle.

(There is a smattering of unenthusiastic applause, and a couple of boos. Goldie leaves the spotlight without bowing. There is one final laugh from the audience, and then we hear Fred's voice.)

FRED: *(In his spotlight.)* Ladies and Gentlemen, the Marvelous, the Hilarious, Mademoiselle Margobella!

IN THE WARDROBE TENT

Goldie bursts into the room, hopping mad. Eva, Tony, and Trina hold their breath as she enters.

GOLDIE: You're going to be sorry, Freddie, you sunuvabitch. You're going to be sorry you made me do this.

LEROY: *(Following her, carrying all her juggling things.)* We took some real heavy shit out there, folks.

GOLDIE: I've never been so humiliated in all my life.

EVA: Goldie, darling, this is Mr. Reeves.

GOLDIE: We've met.

EVA: He owns this mall.

TRINA: Mother!

GOLDIE: They laughed at me. They thought I was a clown. I'm in there being laughed at while you're out here cozying up to this bozo because you think he can save you.

REEVES: You shouldn't have said that.

LEROY: She can say whatever she wants, buddy.

GOLDIE: It wasn't smart.

REEVES: No it wasn't.

GOLDIE: Well, I didn't get where I am today by being smart.

TONY: Obviously.

GOLDIE: It's all over anyway. Your precious twins, Mr. Reeves, your cute little Siamese freaks that you want paraded around in front of your mall so your people will spend more money in your mall, well those twins are in the hospital today. Some doctors are going to cut them apart.

TRINA: Mother!

REEVES: Cut them apart?

GOLDIE: Two for the price of one.

EVA: Shut up, Goldie.

REEVES: I knew it! I knew it!

(Offstage, Fred begins to introduce Eva and Trina's bareback act.)

FRED: *(In his spotlight.)* No circus would be complete without two beautiful ladies on horseback.

EVA: Trina, get up here! We're on.

FRED: *(Continuing offstage.)* And here they are, in an exhilarating exercise in equine equilibrium...

REEVES: *(To Goldie.)* I hope this is one of your little jokes.

GOLDIE: *(Straightening Trina's costume.)* I already did my clown act, buster.

FRED: *(Continuing offstage.)* Excitement unequaled west of Eastern Europe...

TRINA: *(To Reeves.)* Don't pay any attention to her. She always says stuff like that when she's mad at daddy. Come watch our act.

FRED: *(In his spotlight.)* Ladies and Gentlemen, boys and girls, the enchanting Ella and the electrifying Elvira Esterhazy.

(Horse music starts up and Eva and Trina exit.)

REEVES: *(To Goldie.)* I guess you know what this means?

GOLDIE: Yes, I do. Brad and Bill could die in that operation.

REEVES: That's not what I meant.

GOLDIE: *(To Reeves.)* Of course it's not what you meant. You're going to cancel our tour. Because you don't think enough people will spend enough money if they don't see enough freaks. Well, you're the freak, mister.
(Tony shakes his head in disbelief and despair.)

GOLDIE: The only thing you have in this world is money.

REEVES: While you, on the other hand, can juggle.

GOLDIE: So tell me something your money does for you.

REEVES: Do you give away tickets to this show? No. If people don't have the money, they don't see the elephant. If they don't pay you the money, you don't feed the elephant. You have to have money. You went out there and juggled for money. I run this mall for money and it's the same damn thing.

GOLDIE: But I don't do what I do for the money. It happens to be my life. The only reason you own this mall is to make money.

REEVES: Oh shit! People like me keep the world going while people like you act like you're doing us a favor by enjoying yourselves in it. You'd starve to death without us. We paved your playground, little girl. We dug up the rocks and put in the swings.

GOLDIE: Yeah well, your money is dead and so are you.

LEROY: That's telling him.

TONY: You're going to shut up or I'm going to…
(Tony restrains Leroy, who is trying to get closer to Reeves and Goldie. As Reeves talks, Tony and Leroy ad-lib, Leroy determined to get loose and Tony muscling him to stay out of it.)

REEVES: O.K. My money is dead and so am I. But your little show is about to be dead because that's the price for not keeping your part of our deal.

GOLDIE: No twins, no show.

REEVES: That's right. And when your show is gone and all your animals starve and all your people are out of work and all that's left is a worthless piece of rotten canvas, when your show is over, I'll still have my money and my show will go on.

GOLDIE: Fuck off.

REEVES: *(Grabbing her.)* What'd you say?

LEROY: *(Breaking away from Tony.)* I told you to lay off the lady.

REEVES: This is no lady. Ladies don't…

(Leroy grabs Reeves, turning him around, freeing Goldie in the process.)
LEROY: Listen you..
(Tony rushes over, but doesn't arrive in time.)
TONY: Leroy!
REEVES: Take your hands off me, hobo.
(Leroy throws a swift punch, which knocks Reeves out cold. Goldie gasps. Tony shakes his head. And they stand in shocked silence as the equestrian act comes to an end.)
FRED: *(In his spotlight.)* Didn't I say they were exhilarating? Didn't I say they were enchanting and electrifying? Ladies and Gentlemen, Ella and Elvira Esterhazy, two extraordinary equestriennes. Coming up next, the Cardwell Clowns and their hysterical hounds.
TONY: *(Backing away from Leroy.)* Oh shit!
(Eva and Trina run out of the tent and into the silence surrounding Reeves.)
TRINA: *(Before she sees Reeves.)* Leroy, you're supposed to clear the ring!
TONY: He's not touching one more piece of this show.
TRINA: *(Now she sees Reeves.)* What on Earth?
GOLDIE: *(To Leroy.)* Why did you hit him? This had nothing to do with you.
TRINA: *(To Leroy.)* You knocked him out?
GOLDIE: Who the hell do you think you are?
LEROY: Yeah, well…
TONY: Get out of here.
LEROY: Guess it is about time. *(To Trina.)* Guess I can't make it tonight, princess.
TRINA: Get out of here!
(Fred rushes into the scene, passing Leroy on his way out.)
FRED: I just announced the clowns. Where are they?
TRINA: *(Running offstage.)* I'll find them.
GOLDIE: *(As Fred sees Reeves.)* Don't ask, honey. Go on back in there.
FRED: And do what?
GOLDIE: I don't know. It's your turn. *(Then turning away from him.)* Get me some water, Tony.

IN THE CENTER RING
Act lighting comes up on Fred, taking him somewhat by surprise.

FRED: *(In act lighting.)* Oh. Yes. All right. Well. While we're waiting for the clowns, well, maybe you wondered why my picture wasn't in the souvenir program book.

(Goldie takes the water Tony brings her and begins to bathe Reeves face, holding his head.)

FRED: No, no. Let's see. Well would anybody like to know how I keep my top hat shiny? I brush it in a clean cloth dipped in beer, that's how. Now, What else…uh…Did you see my silver trailer out there? That's circus tradition, the manager's wagon is always silver.

(Reeves comes to, now, and sits up shakily. Then as Fred continues, he tries to stand, resisting Goldie's offers of help.)

FRED: There's just not much to say about me. My mother was a Fat Lady in a Freak Show. They paid her pretty well and she invested it well, and Dad gave all the money to Oz when she died and we had to have a special coffin made to carry her and it took twelve pallbearers at the funeral. She couldn't stand up for the last fifteen years of her life and I bought her this hand mirror so she could see her feet. All that money she had and the only thing she'd buy for herself was shoes.

(Reeves stands, straightens his suit, and wipes the blood from his mouth.)

FRED: She had more pairs of shoes. Oz put them on for her, but if I hadn't given her that mirror, she wouldn't have even been able to see them. She really liked that mirror, but she never looked at her face. I tried to tell her she should look because she was pretty, but she said she didn't want to know because she thought it would kill her if it were true, that she was pretty.

(The spotlight moves to Reeves as he walks up to Fred.)

REEVES: Ladies and Gentlemen, I hate to interrupt this…

FRED: I'm not finished. What are you doing?

REEVES: Get out!

FRED: I'm not finished talking about my mother. They paid their money and I'm gonna tell them—

REEVES: The management of this mall has just learned that the Siamese twins we promised you in our advertising, will not be appearing with Circus Valentine. We have, therefore, decided to return your money.

FRED: You can't do that! That's our money. We did the show.

REEVES: You may receive a cash refund in my office on the second floor of the mall. Or, you may come to the table my assistants are setting up just outside the main entrance to the tent.

FRED: That's all the money we have.

REEVES: You may trade your ticket stub for two chances on the Honda moped being given away next Saturday at the Arvin's Amusements Old-Fashioned Fair right here in this same location, or you may receive a free pass to the Elvis Presley Automobile Show, beginning next Sunday in the front parking lot. The Show features every car owned by Elvis on the sad day of his departure from the Earth. Sit where he sat, see the pictures of his mother framed in the door of the built-in medicine cabinet...

FRED: We did the show.

REEVES: *(Looking up as if to the light booth.)* Cut the lights on this man please. *(The light goes out on Fred.)* I apologize for disappointing you today and I take full responsibility for what has happened here. The Midtown Mall deeply regrets the inconvenience we have caused you, but we hope our refund offers will convince you of our sincere desire to deal honestly with you, whether you are in our stores or enjoying one of our attractions. Thank you for your attention. This is the end of the show.

OUTSIDE THE MAIN TENT

TONY: He can't close the show!

EVA: He already did.

TONY: You should've shut up, Goldie.

GOLDIE: You should've held on to Leroy.

EVA: Where were you Oz? You know better than to leave the back door during the show.

TRINA: It's Mother's fault. She started it.

GOLDIE: You all made me sick, out there buttering him up when I came off.

TRINA: He's going to keep all our money.

GOLDIE: He better not touch that tent.

TRINA: People are taking all the programs!

EVA: He has no right to do this!

TONY: I should've killed him when I had the chance.

EVA: *(Starting to run into the arena.)* That's my rigging. My rigging stays up. *(Fred catches her on his way out of the tent.)*

GOLDIE: I'm calling the police. He can't throw us out.

FRED: Nobody calls nobody.

GOLDIE: Freddie, do something!

OZ: He did.

TONY: I want my money.

EVA: You owe me ten more weeks.

TRINA: Daddy, you have to give Tony his money.

FRED: I have to find Reeves. I'll be back.

GOLDIE: No you don't.

EVA: He can't see you right now. He's giving away our money.

TONY: This is all your fault, Valentine. It's *all* your fault.

TRINA: Daddy didn't start the fight.

TONY: The fight was just an accident. Reeves was going to close the show anyway cause we don't have the twins. And Daddy made that deal, doll. *(Vicious.)* Now talk Valentine.

GOLDIE: Say something, Freddie.

FRED: I've told you everything I know.

GOLDIE: Who's doing the surgery?

FRED: I don't know.

EVA: They had to plan this.

OZ: You don't just drop into town and lie down on the table.

TONY: Tell us where they got the money, Freddie, you no good sunuvabitch, tell us where they got the money.

OZ: Be thousands of dollars.

TONY: No, don't tell me where they got the money. I know where they got the money. It was our money. Tell us how they got the doctor. They don't drive and we haven't been here before.

EVA: Didn't they come here about a month ago to have some new poster pictures taken?

GOLDIE: They did! And you came with them!

FRED: I came to talk to Reeves. I dropped them off at the bowling alley.

OZ: Reeves never saw you before today.

GOLDIE: So the three of you came up here…

OZ: And saw the doctor. You didn't see Reeves and they didn't go bowling.

GOLDIE: You set up the surgery and then you booked us into this town.

EVA: And who paid the fee?

TONY: *(Screaming.)* We paid the fee! Tell them Freddie. We paid the fee! *(Reeves breaks into the group.)*

REEVES: I want this lot cleared by the morning. I want your lions gone and all their shit shoveled up. I want your posters down and your ticket booth out. And your power lines are being disconnected right now and if anybody tries to hook them back up, for any reason, I'll have them thrown in jail.

They're coming after the tent at 7:00 and I want all of you out…gone. And
I don't want to hear from you or any of your friends ever again.

OZ: You're not taking that tent.

GOLDIE: That's our tent, Bozo.

REEVES: It's my tent. And if you signed a contract with this man, *(Indicating
Fred.)* I'd sue him if I were you. Oh, and don't come in to use my bathrooms. There's a gas station three blocks down.

EVA: Just who do you think you are?

REEVES: You set foot inside my mall and I'll have you arrested.

TONY: You miserable sunuvabitch.

GOLDIE: Get out!

REEVES: You still don't understand, do you? You're the one who's getting out. No
more talk, just out. Now, I have other things to do. *(Reeves exits.)*

OZ: You sold my tent?

GOLDIE: It was our tent.

FRED: It was his tent, Goldie. It was the only deal I could make, Oz. He didn't
want to take us. The tent was like collateral. Against our losses. I guaran-
teed him we'd make him a thousand bucks a week or he could take the
tent.

EVA: How could you be so stupid?

FRED: I didn't have any choice.

GOLDIE: I want to know how you thought this was going to work out. You
hocked our tent to pay for destroying our main attraction?

FRED: I thought if we were all here together…

GOLDIE: *(Nearly hysterical.)* Freddie? How did you think we were going to get
out of this? If the operation was a success, the twins would be separated
and we would lose our tent because we have no twins. But if the operation
was a failure and the twins died, we would lose our tent because we have
no twins. And with no twins and no tent, there's no circus.

FRED: I thought they might change their minds.

EVA: Their mind.

FRED: I thought they'd…

TRINA: But what about us?

TONY: You're gonna do fine, Trina. We're the ones with no place to go. We're
not going to find other shows, Fred. It's the middle of the season, so even
if we knew somebody who needed us, we wouldn't know where they were.
And even if we knew where they were, you've spent all our money, so we
couldn't get there. At our age, you're either a star and you get by on reputation,

or you're out. We're out. You've destroyed what we like to think of as our
lives, Fred. What are we going to do?

FRED: I don't know what you're all going to do. I don't know what I'm going to
do. Oz can get a lawyer and get his tent back from Reeves. Reeves can sue
me. You can all sue me, but I don't have anything. All I really had was all
of you. But I only had that as long as those boys kept on being Siamese.

TRINA: They didn't mind.

GOLDIE: That's stupid, Trina. *(To Fred.)* Go on.

FRED: There really was never any reason for them to stay together. Except of
course that they'd always been that way.

EVA: Are you telling us this was *your* idea?

FRED: The operation is tricky, of course, and maybe they'll each lose partial
mobility in one hand, but I heard about this surgeon in town here...

TONY: *(Interrupting.)* You've lost your mind, Fred. Lost your mind.

FRED: I don't think so. I told the twins about the surgeon and asked them what
they thought. And do you know what they said? They said the only reason
they were staying together was because of me. Because I was kind to them.
Because we played pinochle. Because I never laughed at them. Because I
took them out of the sideshow and Goldie taught them to juggle. Because
we were a show. They stayed together all this time because of us!

OZ: Oh man.

TONY: What is that supposed to mean?

FRED: Well I wasn't about to be the reason that they stayed together. And *(To
Goldie.)* I don't know how I thought we'd get out of this. I didn't think
about it. It didn't seem important. What I did for them, that seems important. I think it's the only important thing I ever did and if it means I never
see any of you again, well, I'll miss you.

TONY: *(Slowly.)* It was your idea. You found the surgeon. You told the twins
about it and brought them up here for the consultation. You scheduled the
surgery and booked us into this town. You checked them into the hospital
this morning and you took every penny any of us has in the world and you
paid the doctors' fee.

FRED: Yes.

TONY: And you think they're gonna *like* what you've done to them? They've
been together for twenty-five years. Are they supposed to break up just
because you've decided they shouldn't be freaks anymore? How will they
earn a living now? Sure, they can juggle, but they only know how to do it

Siamese. They'll never perform again. That's a pretty heavy decision to make for somebody else, Freddie.

OZ: Easy, Tony.

FRED: I wanted them to have a choice.

TONY: You made it for them, Fred. It was simply not acceptable to you that they should remain…they way they were.

FRED: No, it wasn't. And I think they felt the same way.

GOLDIE: You think.

TRINA: Wow.

EVA: Well, I say…

FRED: *(Still calm.)* Yes?

EVA: Well, I say, 'Good for you, Freddie.'

OZ: *(After a while.)* Yeah, so do I.

GOLDIE: Me too. I'm glad you didn't ask us, Freddie. We'd still be arguing about it, and it's really pretty simple after all. How could we live on them for so long. They'll do just fine, Tony. They'll be normal people and that'll be just fine.

TRINA: But what are *we* going to do? Are we going to be fine?

(There is a moment.)

OZ: Of course we are. What did you think, we were going to starve to death because we lost our tent?

GOLDIE: We couldn't play towns like this.

OZ: Couldn't even play fairs until we got another tent.

GOLDIE: *(To Fred.)* Do we still have the trucks?

FRED: We'd have to sell one to repair the others.

OZ: And sell another one to feed the animals.

EVA: The animals have to go. We can't afford them.

TONY: So what do we have? An aerialist and a fortune-teller? That's not a show.

FRED: *(To Oz.)* Do we still have an elephant?

OZ: We have an elephant.

GOLDIE: We'll keep the animals.

OZ: We need some new acts. Make some calls.

FRED: We couldn't pay them.

TRINA: I bet some newspaper would pay us for the twins' story. They could go on talk shows.

TONY: No.

TRINA: It would help them get a new start, you know? Make them some money.

TONY: Only freaks go on talk shows. They want to stop being freaks. That's why they're having the operation. We're the ones who ought to go on talk shows. We actually want to stay freaks.

FRED: There's an amusement park, here, down in the west end. They have a pavilion, we could set up there.

GOLDIE: An amusement park?

OZ: We'll put everything in one truck. Set up at big gas stations on the turnpikes, or state parks. Yeah, state parks is better.

EVA: State parks? Without the tent, it's not the circus.

FRED: O.K. County fairs. We can sell the stake puller and sell the generator truck. Keep the microphones and hook up to their system. Strip the concessions truck cause they'll already have them.

OZ: The lions won't move in with Grace Kelly if that's what you're about to say.

FRED: Well, they might not like it, but we could do it. And the ponies too, all in the bull truck.

GOLDIE: And we all sleep in the office trailer?

FRED: And we'll go back to county fairs where we know people.

EVA: Who've seen us already.

TONY: Who'll wonder what happened to our tent.

GOLDIE: And where, since there's no tent, everybody can see the show so there's no point in selling tickets.

FRED: So we have to play inside somewhere.

EVA: Like where?

FRED: Like industrial shows, I guess. Mobile home shows, Lawn and Patio shows, Recreational Vehicle shows. Three or four half hour spots a day, set up at one end of the exhibition hall. Or, You know, Ladies' Entertainment things at insurance conventions.

TONY: Birthday Parties...

TRINA: It might not be so bad.

GOLDIE: Trapeze in the backyard and lions in the garage? Birthday parties? It would be the end.

(There is a long moment.)

GOLDIE: It is the end.

TONY: *(Very calmly.)* Damn television. Damn Ringling and spaceships. Damn electric corn poppers and Wild Kingdom and zoos and damn me. It's alright about the twins, Freddie, I just wish it was 1910.

GOLDIE: *(After a while.)* Will the trucks get us home, Freddie?

(Freddie doesn't answer. There is dead silence. Finally, Oz takes the bottle Trina

has given him earlier, out of his back pocket. He takes off the top and takes a drink.)

OZ: Give me your gun, Tony.

EVA: Here. *(Hands it to him, from the pocket of her bathrobe.)*

OZ: All right, Fred.

TRINA: Oz. Don't do this.

OZ: Stand back everybody.

GOLDIE: Oz. This is stupid.

(Oz sights down the pistol, aiming at Fred.)

FRED: Ready.

OZ: Aim. *(Takes his stance.)* I've been thinking about the tent.

FRED: Yeah?

(Oz uses the tip of the pistol to push his hat back on his head. A gesture he has seen in the movies sometime. He smiles.)

OZ: I think we should spread the tent out in the front parking lot, and drive the stake puller and the concessions truck and the generator truck and the cookhouse up on it. And take the keys with us. And Mr. Reeves can have his tent if he can figure out how to get it out from under 95,000 pounds of beat-up trucks.

(Oz hands the gun to Tony. Tony looks at it a moment. He uses it for some other he-man gesture, as he thinks.)

TONY: Yeah. Maybe I'll just leave my lions in the mall.

GOLDIE: Be fair, now, at least leave the empty cages at the front door just as a little warning, you know.

TONY: Happy to. Be happy to. What do we do about the rather large amount of elephant shit out there?

OZ: What do you mean? I think it's real attractive right where it is.

TONY: So. We go see the twins and come back and stage our little going away party, and then we'll just blow this old show.

EVA: There is, however, one last act in this circus.

(Eva takes off her bathrobe, and walks away from them all, back into the tent. The others chase her.)

TRINA: Where's she going.

GOLDIE: To try the triple.

TRINA: She wouldn't.

TONY: Come on, Eva. Stop this.

FRED: What the hell?

IN THE CENTER RING
Tony gets to her first.

TONY: Just can't be out of the spotlight, can you. Not even now.

EVA: Don't touch me. *(She starts walking toward the rope ladder.)*

OZ: This isn't going prove anything, Eva.

EVA: *(Stops and turns around.)* I'm going to do a triple. Somebody can catch me, or you can all just stand there and watch. I really don't care.

TRINA: Mother!

(Fred, Oz, and Tony exchange glances. Then Tony moves.)

TONY: I'll catch her.

TRINA: You hurt your ankle. You'll fall too. I'll do it.

GOLDIE: She's my sister. I'm going.

FRED: You haven't flown for years. You'll go down with her.

GOLDIE: She's my sister. I want to be the...

TONY: The last one to touch her alive? Thanks. I'll do it. Trina doesn't know the timing. And your fear of heights isn't going to disappear just to save your sister's life. I'll catch her up there. And if I miss, well, you catch her down here.

(Goldie slaps him and heads for the rope ladder at the side of the ring.)

EVA: *(At the same time as the slap.)* Get up here, Goldie.

TRINA: *(In near hysterics.)* She'll kill herself.

TONY: Eva!

OZ: *(Catching Tony as he tries to run after Eva.)* Let her go. Tony.

(Tony drops to his knees, he would pray if he could close his eyes or if he believed it would help.)

OZ: Well, come on, Valentine. Run this show.

(Fred straightens his coat, puts on his top hat and picks up a microphone. The lights dim and there is one spotlight on Eva, at the top of the ladder, and another one on Goldie, climbing her ladder. The others wait below, quite afraid for them, but quite aware that she has the right to do this. Oz holds Trina.)

OZ: She knows what she's doing, honey.

TRINA: She did it in practice, she told me.

FRED: *(A drum roll starts.)* Ladies and Gentlemen, when a performer attempts the dreaded triple somersault, she walks straight into the cold mouth of death itself. As her hands release the trapeze, Eva Sparrow's tiny body will be traveling at 60 miles and hour. She will tuck and spin, once, twice...By now she is nearly unconscious and only as she straightens out at the end of the third somersault will her brain fight back the blackness for one desperate stretch toward the catcher's hands. She cannot see the catcher's hands for her eyes will not focus at such speeds. Those hands, that life giving lock, arm in arm, simply must be there. Their wrists must slap. Their fingers close around each other and hold. There is no second chance with the triple.

AT THE TOP OF THE TENT

EVA: Are you ready?

GOLDIE: Are you scared?

FRED: So now, directing your attention to the very top of the Big Top, Ladies and Gentlemen, the most daring, the most beautiful, the most graceful aerial genius in the world today. Performing the triple somersault from the flying trapeze, Ladies and Gentlemen, the lovely Miss Eva Sparrow.

(The drum roll peaks, Eva and Goldie raise their hands in a salute. The trapeze, previously unseen, swings toward Eva. She grasps it with both hands and the lights hold on the sisters.)

EVA: What are you doing up here?

GOLDIE: What do you think I'm doing? Talking you down.

EVA: *(After a moment.)* So talk.

GOLDIE: It's a pretty short speech, Eva. It's either die or go on.

EVA: I think it's pretty much the same thing.

GOLDIE: It is not and you know it. For one thing, if you die, you won't have me to feel superior to.

EVA: I envy you.

GOLDIE: I know that. Jesus it's scary up here. Can we go down now? I mean, you can jump if you want to, but you will really miss me. *(Goldie starts down the ladder.)*

(Eva calls after her.)

EVA: I hate you.

GOLDIE: I hate you more.

(Eva starts down the ladder.)

EVA: You do not.

GOLDIE: What do *you* know?

(Lights come up on the group gathered below. And as the familiar argument begins, Oz and Fred start to argue, and Tony and Trina begin to argue.)

FRED: You should've taken down her rigging already. You knew she try something like this.

OZ: Yeah, well, I thought maybe you sold it.

TRINA: You don't even like the circus, do you?

TONY: I don't no. I only like the costumes.

TRINA: Daddy. Did you hear what he said.

(By now Goldie and Eva are down, and they turn and exit without ever looking at the others. The others follow them offstage, arguing, and we have...)

THE END

The Holdup

Written with the support of a grant from the Guggenheim Foundation, *The Holdup* was first developed in a 1980 Actors Theatre of Louisville workshop directed by Ms. Norman. The cast was as follows:

The Outlaw	Ken Jenkins
Archie Tucker	Timothy Busfield
Henry Tucker	Dierk Toporzysek
Lily	Adale O'Brien

It was then featured in Circle Repertory Company's 1982 summer residency in Saratoga, New York, in a production directed by Rod Marriott. The cast was as follows:

The Outlaw	Ed Seaman
Archie Tucker	Timothy Busfield
Henry Tucker	Michael Ayr
Lily	Stephanie Gordon

The Holdup had its first full production at American Conservatory Theater in April 1983 under the direction of Edward Hastings. The cast was as follows:

The Outlaw	Peter Donat
Archie Tucker	Tom O'Brien
Henry Tucker	Lawrence Hecht
Lily	Barbara Dirickson

INTRODUCTION

When I was growing up, my grandfather would tell the same five stories every night after supper. it wasn't a problem that they were the same stories. We were kids, we were trapped, we didn't have TV, Grandaddy was a master, and the stories were very good. Each one was about him in his youth in New Mexico, the pale well-behaved brother in a family of loud-mouthed ranch hands. The stories are for me, a kind of personal folklore, or anti-folklore, because in these tales, my hero, Grandaddy, usually runs away, rather than staying around to slay the enemy.

Over the years, sometimes I've thought his actions were cowardly. Now I think his actions were simply what they were. And if I grew up in Kentucky instead of New Mexico because he didn't want to stay and fight for his inheritance, well, that was just my tough luck. Maybe New Mexico in his day, in his house, was something I'd have run from too.

Anyway, I wrote this play based on his stories, so he could read about himself in the newspaper before he died. And though the critics thought the play was too funny—("Who does she think she is, Neil Simon?") I like it, and Grandaddy said the cookshack on the A.C.T. set looked exactly the way he remembered it. Grandaddy also said Tim Busfield, in the Circle Rep production, looked exactly the way he did as a boy. Except Grandaddy was taller. Of course.

CHARACTERS

THE OUTLAW: a worn, grizzled desperado, now approaching fifty. He is fearless and mean-tempered, a wily survivor of the Hole-in-the-Wall era, who never says more than is necessary and who generally gets what he wants because he knows how to stand there and mean business.

LILY: a frontier beauty, a little past her prime. She has graciously accepted the wisdom and perspective that have replaced her once startling appearance. In the old days she was a dance-hall favorite. Now she owns the finest hotel east of Albuquerque.

ARCHIE TUCKER: a green Clovis boy of seventeen. Archie's open face and simple enthusiasm seem quite out of place in this barren country. He talks too much and smiles too much and complains too much and, all in all, doesn't belong here. He's eager to find a way out but is held back by his mother and his age and his fear.

HENRY TUCKER: Archie's hothead rancher brother. Henry is mean and tough, a foul-mouthed, heavy-drinking cattleman, a bit embarrassed to be supplementing his income by working this wheat-threshing crew. He is thirty years old but still lives at home. His youth was baked dry in the sun of too many days doing his endless, lifeless work. His sole entertainment is reading outlaw books. He is an expert in their methods and manners.

TIME AND PLACE

The play takes place around a cookshack belonging to a wheat-threshing crew working a field in northern New Mexico in the fall of 1914. It is miles from nowhere and long past sundown.

The Holdup

ACT I

Night in New Mexico is dark and flat. And if you are alone, you are always lost, even if you think you know where you are going.

There are two strays in this night, headed straight for each other, but they don't know that. We see their faces but we didn't know where they are. We only know that they are alone, and they are dealing with their respective problems as best they can, determined to reach what they think is a safe place, the company of other humans.

The Outlaw takes his saddle off the horse and ties up the cinches so he can carry it. And he talks.

OUTLAW: Well, old girl, I've shot better horses than you, but never one I felt so kin to, at the moment.

(And now, from another part of the blackness comes a terrified voice, a shaky praying voice.)

ARCHIE: Jesus God in heaven, it's Archie Tucker from Clovis, New Mexico. I know you can see me, so I know you can see that coyote that's following me and I don't know if he's alone, but I'm alone and I need you to keep him back there till I can run for the cookshack, which shouldn't be too much longer, now, thank you so much, Amen.

OUTLAW: *(Taking off the bridle.)* I just don't have any choice about shootin' you, see. I can't just leave you here to die by *yourself.* And I can't hobble along with you or I'll miss Lily. I told her I'd be there at midnight, sharp. Nice and easy, girl, here it comes.

(And we hear the gunshot, and Archie hears it too, but he has other concerns.)

ARCHIE: Uh, Lord, you gave me a gun, I know, but Henry, that's my brother, he's got it standing guard back at the cookshack. So it's just you and me and that coyote. I'd stand and fight him but I imagine I'd die, if you know what I mean. People die out here all the time and nobody ever knows. Tell you what, I'll run when I can.

OUTLAW: You know who I miss? That gelding. Suzy. Snaggletooth horse. She was! Who am I talking to. Just pick up your gear and walk, old man. Just

166

another mile, buddy. Lily always had an eye for horseflesh, didn't she? She'll bring you somethin' sweet to ride, you can count on that, at least. *(And we hear him begin to walk.)*

ARCHIE: Uh, Lord, in case you saw me ride into town today, maybe you got me mixed up with the rest of the boys stayed in town to…all right, but I don't like to even *say* it. They stayed in town to drink beer and abuse women. I am *not* one of them, I am *saved* and I need some help here. Oh boy. I bet you hear that a lot. Well, listen, forget about everybody else for a while. This is serious.

OUTLAW: Well what have we got up here? Looks like some kind of cookshack, some wheat-threshing crew I guess. Well sure it is. It's the water hole, isn't it? Only water for twenty miles, as I remember. Think she's here yet? Think she's as old as you are? Think she's gonna show up at all? What do you do if she don't, huh?

ARCHIE: *(His voice showing his relief.)* Oh now, there's the cookshack, I can just about make it now. Thank you so much. *(Screaming.)* Run, Archie!

OUTLAW: *(Hearing Archie.)* What the hell?

(And now we see the cookshack and the barrels and benches that huddle around it. It is a small wood building on wheels with one door, one window, and a metal chimney for ventilation. There are heavy cloth flaps hanging down to the ground on all sides protecting the sleeping area underneath it. You wonder how it continues to stand up, but you have no doubt that it does. There are some curiously modern-looking machine parts lying around, but otherwise, the scene looks almost pre-Civil War. And Archie runs up to the cookshack terrified.)

ARCHIE: Henry! Hey in there, Henry Tucker! *(Banging on the cookshack door.)* You gotta hear what just happened to me when I'm coming back from town just now. *(Jumps up to the window, trying to wake Henry.)* Henry! Wake up! I know you're in there, Henry, and you know who this is so you open this door, Henry. *(Still no answer.)* Did you know they were gonna stay in town all night? Get cleaned up, that's what they said. But then… *(Screaming.)* Henry!

(And the door finally opens.)

ARCHIE: Nobody acts right out here. I hate this place!

HENRY: So leave, priss, the train runs both ways, Archie.

ARCHIE: You're not gonna believe what happened, Henry!

HENRY: *(Starting to build the fire back up, not eager to hear anything.)* It won't be worth wakin' up for, I can tell that already.

ARCHIE: I jumped off the train, only right away I'm not alone, see. I turn around and there he was, standing sideways in the road, the biggest coyote I ever saw. So I started up walking again, but when I speeded up, he speeded up and when I slowed down, he slowed down and finally, I got where I could see the cookshack and took off running and here I am.

HENRY: And that's your big story?

ARCHIE: I mean, I could hardly breathe there for a while.

HENRY: You ran away? Damn right it's your big story. Got a problem? Call Henry or run away. Runt coward. You make me sick, Archie. I don't know what I was doing, bringing you along. Dad's probably still laughing at me stuck out here with you.

ARCHIE: I've got as much right to be here as you do. They hired us both. Mr. White says I'm a good worker.

HENRY: They hired you because they couldn't get me unless they took you. What do you know about threshing wheat, Archie? They all laugh at you, you know. You're a joke, Archie.

ARCHIE: Well just how hard do you think the boys would laugh if they saw your pillow full of outlaw books, huh? Every spare minute you get, sneaking off to ride with the Wild Bunch, fighting the Johnson County War.

HENRY: The Wild Bunch didn't fight the Johnson County War.

ARCHIE: Well who cares whether they did or they didn't? That stuff is made up, Henry. People write those books just to find out if anybody's dumb enough to believe it.

HENRY: 'Bout like the Bible, I guess.

ARCHIE: The Bible is the truth.

HENRY: People walk out on the water and get swallowed by whales, Archie?

ARCHIE: It has to be the truth, Henry. What do you think God's trying to do, entertain?

HENRY: Just leave me alone, okay. Just go to bed, Diddly.

ARCHIE: Don't call me that!

HENRY: Just don't say one more word to me, you think you can do that? I get rid of you for one night in my whole life and what do you do? Take the train right on back here.

ARCHIE: You're just mad about Corbin in town spendin' all your pay you gambled off last night. It serves you right, pulling your gun like one of your outlaws, for God's sake. I hope you learned your lesson.

HENRY: They've had it in for me since the beginning of this job, Archie. I don't know who they think they are, these cowboys, they're just as dumb and just as worn out as everybody else I know. Bunch of sheepherders, if you ask me. So I showed 'em, that's all. Now, you just watch and see if anybody ever tries to cheat Henry Tucker again. What do I want to go into town for anyway? Have a good time with that bunch of know-it-alls? Fat chance.

ARCHIE: Oh I almost forgot! Guess what else I saw in town? Marines signing up men for the war. It's all over the papers too. Some Archduke Somebody-or-other got killed and it's all about to blow up!

HENRY: *(Not the least bit interested.)* What is?

ARCHIE: The world, Henry! Unless we get there in time!

HENRY: So why didn't you join up?

ARCHIE: Mother would *kill* me!

HENRY: So would a war, Archie.

ARCHIE: You could go! You're exactly who they're lookin' for! They're gonna fly airplanes in this war, Henry! You'd like that, zoomin' around the sky. You could be The Outlaw of the Air, Henry!

HENRY: Well, they better not take you, Archie. You'd be out there on the front lines, walk over to the enemy and say, "Hi there, my name is Archie and these are my buddies, this is Ralph and this is Joey and we're from New Mexico," and you'd be the first marine who ever died in the middle of a sentence.

(Archie turns away.)

HENRY: What's the matter with you? Guys like us go to war and we don't get to fly airplanes. We just stand on the ground and get shot. Don't make any sense at all, Archie. I can do that here.

ARCHIE: He told me I could learn to fly a plane. I asked him and he said, "Come on."

HENRY: Just shut up. You don't know what you're talking about.

ARCHIE: Okay. Okay.

(And then, in a moment of silence, they hear a twig break just behind the cook-shack.)

ARCHIE: *(Whispering.)* What was that?

HENRY: *(Covering his fear.)* Well, it sure as hell ain't the marines.

(Henry picks up a stick of wood from the fire and Archie backs away, toward Henry for protection. The Outlaw appears, gun raised, from the other direction, surprising them both. The Outlaw looks quite different than when we saw him before. Maybe it's the effect of the gun in his hand. Maybe he likes horses better than people. Whatever it is, this is somebody you don't want to fool around with. This man looks dangerous.)

OUTLAW: Keep on talking, boy. *(Waving the pistol at Henry.)* Hands high, cowboy. *(Henry is reluctant. Archie raises his hands.)*

OUTLAW: Not you, boy. You sit. Over there. Him. Up.

ARCHIE: Henry!

OUTLAW: That's better. Don't need any heroes here. Just a little hospitality. *(Starts to search Henry.)*

HENRY: What do you want, gramps?

OUTLAW: *(Not easing the tension one bit.)* Oh, I don't know. What have you got?

ARCHIE: Anything you want. You just name it.

HENRY: *(Turning quickly.)* Shut up, Archie.

OUTLAW: *(Poking Henry with the gun, not liking that fast turn.)* Careful, cowboy.

ARCHIE: His name's Henry.

HENRY: Shut up, Archie! *(Then quickly.)* How long have you been out there?

OUTLAW: *(Still very threatening.)* Long enough. You don't look a thing alike.

ARCHIE: He takes after Dad. That whole side of the family is—

HENRY: Shut up, Archie. The man's not here to get a family history. What do you want, mister?

OUTLAW: Eggs. Cooked.

HENRY: No.

ARCHIE: I'll make 'em, Henry, if you want me to.

HENRY: I said no.

OUTLAW: Yes. And if you got a gun in the cookshack, there, you just bring it right on out here.

HENRY: Maybe I will.

OUTLAW: Yeah, you go get it and then you'll draw on me and I'll kill you. Won't be anything personal, just how it happens to me anymore. I get what I want. Now, I want some eggs.

HENRY: Any man can walk in hungry and ask for eggs and I'll make 'em, any day, but you ain't asked.

OUTLAW: Are we gonna fight over a mess of eggs?

ARCHIE: *(Trying to be reasonable.)* I said I'd make the eggs. The man's a stranger here and we should—

HENRY: *(Stops him, rough.)* Don't you move. You do what I say.

ARCHIE: Then you do what he says.

HENRY: Don't tell me what to do!

ARCHIE: I'm not. What do I know? It's just…you do see the gun, don't you, Henry? We're just talking about some old eggs, Henry.

OUTLAW: Don't you want to get your gun?

HENRY: I'll cook. *(And he heads for the cookshack.)*

OUTLAW: And bring me some whiskey.

ARCHIE: We don't have any whiskey. We got a rule about it.

OUTLAW: If you didn't have any whiskey, you wouldn't have a rule about it.

(And now, the Outlaw walks behind the water barrels to retrieve his saddle and a leather satchel. He puts the saddle over a bale of hay to make a kind of seat, but he doesn't sit on it. Archie watches as long as he can before he talks.)

ARCHIE: Are you gonna kill us?

OUTLAW: I'm gonna eat first.

ARCHIE: That's not fair! We're minding our own business. It's Saturday night. We threshed wheat all week, we work hard. Then we get a night off and you come up and shoot us. It's not fair. It's not civilized. We're a state now. It's 1914.

OUTLAW: Do you know what a joke is? You know, one person says a funny thing to some other person and the other person laughs?

(No response.)

OUTLAW: Do you? Joke? Ha-ha?

ARCHIE: I know that.

OUTLAW: Then why didn't you laugh at my joke?

ARCHIE: Are you gonna kill us or not?

OUTLAW: Are you always like this?

(No response.)

OUTLAW: What time is it?

ARCHIE: Oh, you're meeting somebody here! What a good idea. It's a perfect place for it. Why didn't you say that in the first place. Maybe we've seen 'em already. Nope. Nobody for hours now, well, what do I know? I just got back myself. Maybe Henry saw somebody. Who're we lookin' for? Tall? Thin?

OUTLAW: I just asked you what time it was.

ARCHIE: Oh. Right. I don't know. Dark.

OUTLAW: What does Henry do? How come he's out here with everybody else on the town for the night?

ARCHIE: The crew could come back anytime, you know. There's twenty-five or more. Big men.

OUTLAW: *(Screaming.)* I want those eggs, cowboy! *(Then normally.)* They call you Archie?

ARCHIE: Or Doc. Some of 'em call me Doc.

(The Outlaw nods, but doesn't ask why.)

ARCHIE: I was sweet on Doc Porter's girl, Sarah. They started calling me Doc because, well, Doc Porter runs the drugstore in Clovis. I'm courting a Doc's daughter so they call me Doc. It's a joke.

OUTLAW: It isn't very funny for a joke.

ARCHIE: Or fork-pitcher. It's what I do. I fork up the wheat and—

OUTLAW: —pitch it on the wagon, I know. What's that big machine out there?

ARCHIE: It's a brand-new separator. Thing threshes ten times as much wheat as the old one in half the time. Gonna change everything.

OUTLAW: It takes up too much room. It's ugly.

(Henry comes out of the cookshack carrying a steaming plate of eggs, and now wearing a light jacket.)

HENRY: *(Heartily, as though he'd cooked for a friend.)* Six eggs. Hot and ready!

ARCHIE: I told you he'd make the eggs.

OUTLAW: *(Referring to the coat.)* Got your gun, I see.

HENRY: Cold out here. Eat up. That's a clean fork.

OUTLAW: *(Walking toward Archie, picking up a forkful of eggs.)* I was asking Archie, how come you pulled this guard duty while the rest of the boys are in raisin' hell tonight. *(He pushes the bite of eggs in Archie's mouth.)*

HENRY: Somebody has to.

OUTLAW: Yeah, but why you, cowboy? What happened last night?

HENRY: It's none of your business.

OUTLAW: Oh yes it is, too. I want to hear it. Archie will tell me, won't you boy? Eggs taste good, cowboy.

HENRY: *(To Archie.)* You do and I'll—

OUTLAW: *(Demanding.)* Archie!

ARCHIE: *(Beginning rather helplessly.)* It was just another stupid poker game. Corbin was cheating and I saw it. I told Henry and Henry drew on him That's all.

OUTLAW: If that was all, Archie, Mr. Corbin would be out here eatin' hay, not Henry.

HENRY: *(Before Archie can start.)* You shut your mouth, priss.

(The Outlaw plays with his gun, just to terrify Archie.)

ARCHIE: The gun is why Henry's out here. Not supposed to have guns in camp, that's all.

OUTLAW: *(Not satisfied.)* Go on.

ARCHIE: *(Compulsively.)* All right! When Henry drew his gun he dropped his cards and there's not supposed to be two ace of hearts either!

(The Outlaw laughs.)

ARCHIE: They woulda killed each other if Mr. White hadn't been here. They woulda both lost their jobs, too, if this wasn't twenty square miles of wheat to thresh next week. They were acting like some saloon characters from twenty years ago.

OUTLAW: Man's got to protect himself, Archie.

ARCHIE: Yeah, but he's supposed to use his brain, not his gun.

OUTLAW: Well, you want to use the quickest thing you got, whatever that is.

ARCHIE: You shouldn't cheat till you learn how to play, Henry.

HENRY: You started it all, Archie. I'd be spendin' his money right now if it wasn't for you and your big mouth. "Corbin's cheatin', Henry," like a damn idiot.

OUTLAW: Henry's right, Archie. You talk too much.

HENRY: There's a horse comin'.

OUTLAW: *(Quite calm, having heard it already.)* Uh-huh.

HENRY: *(Nodding in agreement.)* Sounds like a Morgan horse to me.

OUTLAW: *(Watching Archie, playing along.)* Black, with...white feet.

HENRY: Seven, eight years old maybe.

OUTLAW: *(Knows it isn't a horse by now.)* Still got all his teeth, though.

   (And they laugh and Archie was completely taken in.)

ARCHIE: It's the rest of your gang, I guess. *(Then quite dispirited, to Henry.)* He asked me while ago what time it was, Henry.

HENRY: Relax, Archie. It's just Mother comin' to collect you for prayer meeting.

ARCHIE: I hear it now. It doesn't sound like a horse at all. It sounds like an automobile!

   (They laugh.)

ARCHIE: It does!

HENRY: Archie, the closest road is five miles from here.

OUTLAW: *(Very amused by now.)* So if it is a car, it's a damn fool drivin' it.

ARCHIE: *(Feeling quite anxious.)* How did you get here? Where's your horse?

OUTLAW: 'Bout a mile back.

ARCHIE: I could get him for you.

OUTLAW: You could have her for breakfast.

ARCHIE: She's dead.

OUTLAW: I shot her.

ARCHIE: You saw the fire and walked to here.

OUTLAW: Oh there's no foolin' you, is there Archie?

ARCHIE: *(Staring out into the night.)* It sure is a car all right. Are they lost or what? Who'd come out here in a car?

   (Then as Henry and the Outlaw are both very anxious, and clearly not willing to speculate about who this might be, Archie goes on babbling.)

ARCHIE: Was she a good horse?

HENRY: Would you shoot a good horse, Archie? Yes, you would. Archie would shoot a good horse if Mother told him to.

ARCHIE: Good horses get sick.

HENRY: *(Testing the Outlaw.)* A man shoots his horse is shootin' off his pecker, Archie.

OUTLAW: Shut up, cowboy.

HENRY: I was saying not to ask about it. It ain't your business, Archie. It makes you feel bad to shoot your horse. As bad as *(Turning around to face the Outlaw.)* shootin' off your pecker so don't make jokes about it.

ARCHIE: I wasn't joking, I was asking.

OUTLAW: *(As the car stops.)* Archie don't use his pecker anyway, so he wouldn't know.

ARCHIE: I do too. Use it.

(Henry and the Outlaw laugh.)

ARCHIE: I water the garden.

(They laugh and he continues.)

ARCHIE: I put out fires.

(More laughter.)

ARCHIE: Cuts the dust right off a wagon wheel.

OUTLAW: *(Getting his gun out again.)* Go on.

ARCHIE: That's all.

OUTLAW: *(Covering his nervousness about who's coming.)* You just been doin' chores with it? You ain't had any fun with it?

ARCHIE: Leave me alone.

OUTLAW: Any girls took a peek at it?

HENRY: Hell, he doesn't even look at it.

ARCHIE: Whose side are you on, Henry?

(And now, from offstage, we hear a voice full of anticipation.)

LILY: Tom? Tom?

HENRY: What is this?

OUTLAW: Sounds like a lady came in a car.

ARCHIE: Tom? Is that your name, Tom?

(And Lily rushes onstage, wearing a Barney Oldfield-type duster over her long split riding skirt. It also looks very expensive, but is clearly western and meant for hard use.)

LILY: Tom!

OUTLAW: *(Reacting to the duster.)* What the hell?

LILY: *(Thrilled to see him, but stops herself from running to him once she sees Archie and Henry.)* You are! You're still alive!

OUTLAW: *(Concealing whatever he feels.)* Well I wouldn't write you to tell you I was dead!

LILY: But anybody could've written that letter. Your handwriting's not as—

OUTLAW: Take that thing off. Let me look at you.

LILY: *(Delighted to.)* Just a minute. I almost didn't find this place, you know. They cut down that cottonwood tree. Good thing the water hole's still here. *(The jacket is off now.)* Now!

OUTLAW: Oh that's much better. You haven't changed a bit.

LILY: *(Walking into his arms.)* It's going to work out just fine, isn't it? I'm getting old and you're going blind.

(And the Outlaw turns Lily around to them, not able to give her quite the greeting he wanted to, but still obviously desperate to touch her.)

ARCHIE: Did you really come all the way out here in a car?

LILY: Big black Buick. Go see for yourself!

(Archie starts off toward the car, but Henry stops him.)

OUTLAW: Lily, this is the Tucker Brothers. Archie and Cowboy.

ARCHIE: His name's Henry.

OUTLAW: Boys, meet Lily.

LILY: *(She nods to them, but talks to the Outlaw.)* What a ride! That's at least forty miles! And there's no road at all for the last five!

OUTLAW: *(Starting for the bench now.)* Well, here, why don't you sit down a minute and—

HENRY: *(Disgusted.)* Look, folks. This ain't exactly Main Street out here. Could you take your visit on down the road so we can get some sleep?

OUTLAW: *(Ignoring Henry and walking her to the bench.)* There's no road, remember?

LILY: Boy, we're in big trouble if we have a blowout out here, I guess I could have rented a horse, but oh, Tom, *(In a mock scolding.)* where have you been?

HENRY: *(Irritated? but beginning to be curious.)* How come he couldn't meet you in town? Been a helluva lot easier to find.

OUTLAW: *(Breaking away from Lily.)* Can you shut your mouth and do whatever I tell you to do? Can you get the lady a drink and not ask any stupid questions, cowboy?

(Henry doesn't move.)

OUTLAW: And I told you while ago I wanted some whiskey but I don't see it out here, now, do I? Move!

HENRY: One drink and you go?

OUTLAW: Get it.

(And Henry goes into the cookshack and the Outlaw turns back to Lily.)

OUTLAW: Why the hell did you buy an automobile?

LILY: For the horn. I like the horn. A little man brought it. I kept him too. He…works on it.

ARCHIE: That's where I saw you! Outside that fancy hotel in town.

LILY: Oh Tom, you wouldn't know the old place now. It's solid white paint, no wallpaper. There's actually trees growing in barrels all along that front hall. Oh and the dining room is this bright green and Roy Luther hooked me up a waterfall, inside the dining room. And I'm about ready to go order another automobile to pick up my guests at the train station. They come in hot and thirsty and see those trees and that waterfall and they feel like staying a *week*.

ARCHIE: I saw that car too. That's some car all right.

OUTLAW: You think she's pretty?

ARCHIE: She's pretty.

OUTLAW: You got any money?

ARCHIE: I worked hard for it, if I do, and I'm not handing it over, no sir.

OUTLAW: Money for the lady. How much you got?

ARCHIE: I'm not interested in that.

LILY: And the price has gone way up, mister.

OUTLAW: You squirmy little mole. Tell me how much money you got!

ARCHIE: Twenty-eight dollars.

OUTLAW: You could have this pretty lady, all day, all night for a solid month with that money. All to yourself, just you and her. You ever thought about that?

ARCHIE: No.

(Henry comes out with the whiskey.)

OUTLAW: Do you know what you're going to be when you grow up?

ARCHIE: No.

OUTLAW: Sorry, that's what.

(And the Outlaw and Henry have a good laugh about that.)

LILY: Do you know what year this is? I'm not a whore. It's not a whorehouse. It's a hotel now and I own it.

OUTLAW: *(Clearly annoyed.)* A little pride goes a long way, girl.

LILY: I told them you were still alive. I just knew it. Roy Luther said Bob Ford got you.

HENRY: Bob Ford got Jesse James.

LILY: Daisy said it was Frank Canton.

HENRY: *(More energy than we've seen from him all night.)* He got Nate Champion at the Johnson County War.

LILY: Gus figured it was the Pinkertons. Chase you down like Kid Curry.

HENRY: Kid Curry killed himself.

OUTLAW: And I bet you know where.

HENRY: I do, that's true. Parachute, Colorado.

ARCHIE: Henry believes in outlaws.

HENRY: Shut up, Archie.

LILY: *(Laughs.)* Roy Luther swore he saw it in the papers.

OUTLAW: He saw Bill and Fred. They got Bill and Fred.

HENRY: Bill Carver?

OUTLAW: Bill my brother. His boy Fred. Nice boy, big hands.

LILY: Guess he just saw the name then.

HENRY: What name?

OUTLAW: *(Ignoring Henry.)* Well, how do I look? Old?

HENRY: Hey, your eggs got cold before you finished them. How 'bout some more eggs.

OUTLAW: We aren't gonna be here long enough for that, cowboy.

HENRY: Sure you are. The lady's tired and you could use some more food, pops. It looks like it's been a while. You want anything, ma'am? Might be a corn stick left from supper.

LILY: No thank you.

HENRY: Well, you just let me know if you change your mind. And just take your time there. We're glad to have you. Gets awful lonely out here.

ARCHIE: *(Dumbfounded but pleased by this change in Henry.)* See how nice Henry can be when he wants to?

LILY: Have you seen Bub Meeks?

OUTLAW: Lost a leg in prison, last I heard.

HENRY: They shot him trying to escape. Climbing up the walls at Idaho Federal.

OUTLAW: Well you're a real Outlaw expert, aren't you cowboy?

HENRY: Want your eggs sunny-side up this time?

OUTLAW: *(Now eager to get rid of him.)* That sounds good.

HENRY: Comin' right up. *(He goes into the cookshack.)*

LILY: Anybody else?

OUTLAW: They're in Bolivia, you know. Butch is alive.

ARCHIE: That's in South America.

OUTLAW: Thank you.

ARCHIE: I go to school.

OUTLAW: Or dead. Bolivia or dead.

ARCHIE: I don't get it.

OUTLAW: I wasn't talking to you.

ARCHIE: Your folks, is that it?

OUTLAW: Yeah, boy. My folks all died.

ARCHIE: Or went to Bolivia.

OUTLAW: *(Ignoring Archie.)* I've got a new picture with me. I want you to take it to the Western Union and switch it. Burn that one from Telluride.

LILY: I always thought it was better of Butch than you.

OUTLAW: This is a much better picture.

LILY: I had my picture made for my birthday. Beside my Buick. In front of my hotel. Wearing my duster and goggles. Looks like I cut it out of a magazine but it's me all right.

ARCHIE: Are we talking about a wanted poster?

OUTLAW: *We* were.

LILY: Well actually, *he* was.

ARCHIE: You want them to catch you?

OUTLAW: No, I don't want them to catch me. But I do want them to know what I look like now. I got my pride. *(To Lily.)* You're prettier than you were.

LILY: It's the money. Are you going to Bolivia?

OUTLAW: It's a long trip, but I bet they'd make you the goddamn queen of Bolivia.

ARCHIE: Do you speak Spanish? They speak Spanish.

OUTLAW: *(Furious with him.)* If I want to go to Bolivia, I'll go to Bolivia. They have tin mines there. Did you learn that in school? I'll rob mine payrolls. And I'll eat those green bananas and I'll lay around with this lady and have our dinner cooked by some mountain kid about your age who knows not to say a goddamned thing like who are you or what do you want. Except he will say good morning and thank you, muchas gracias. And we'll have a wonderful time and we won't think about you or all the people like you back here building houses and running for mayor.

ARCHIE: This is the best country in the world! I could be president!

OUTLAW: That's why we're talking about Bolivia! What's the matter with you?

LILY: You can't go to Bolivia either. The trip alone would kill you. And how do you know you *like* bananas?

OUTLAW: Don't you want to see the lady's car, boy?

(And Archie gets out of there quickly, knowing they want to be alone.)

OUTLAW: Got a kiss for the old man?

(They kiss and we see him relax for just a moment.)

LILY: *(Tenderly.)* You look awfully tired, Tom. I heard you were working horses in Montana, but you look like you've been living in a cave.

OUTLAW: *(A sense of purpose now.)* I've been…seeing your face.

LILY: This face? Or the old one. The young one?

OUTLAW: I mean…I think about you.

LILY: I waited for you to come back, you know. I kept eggs in the house for two years for you.

OUTLAW: Well, here I am, girl.

LILY: *(She has a small laugh.)* So I see.

OUTLAW: *(Impatient as always.)* You know what I want. Yes or no?

LILY: Yes or no what? I've seen you one day in the last twenty years!

OUTLAW: Helluva day.

LILY: What do you want, Tom?

OUTLAW: *(Her directness backs him off.)* Well, like I said in my letter, I… *(The more he looks at her, the more he can't say what he's come all these miles to say.)* I had some business down this way.

LILY: What business? Twenty years is a long time. Things happen. Tell me what your business is. Tell me what you want me to say yes or no to. Then ask me. A girl needs to hear a man talk a little.

OUTLAW: About what?

LILY: No, don't say anything now. I'm rested enough, I think. Come back to town with me. You'll be safe enough. They all think you're dead anyway. And if anybody asks who you are, which they won't, I'll say you're my father. *(He backs off even further.)* I'll get you whatever you want to eat and you can stay as long as you like. You'll like the hotel, there's lots of fancy eastern folks coming through all the time and we're getting our telephone next month so—

OUTLAW: Whatever happened to your rancher friend?

LILY: You shot him.

OUTLAW: Oh that's right I did.

LILY: *(Trying to regain his attention.)* He died. Tom. Roy Luther is dying to see you. It'll be just like you remember. You'll get a bath and some sleep and you can tell me everything you've done for the last—

OUTLAW: You want to hear me *talk?*

LILY: I want to know if you're still the man I knew, that's all.

OUTLAW: Well, the girl I knew…

LILY: Is right here, Tom.

OUTLAW: Woulda brought me a horse.

(And the Outlaw stands up now, and Henry opens the cookshack door, and Archie returns from looking at the car.)

ARCHIE: *(Running up to Henry, a conspiratorial tone in his voice.)* He's an outlaw, Henry. They've got his picture at the Western Union.

HENRY: He's no outlaw, Archie. Just some old prospector lost track of the mother lode, huh, pops? You were pannin' for gold and you lost your pan. Well, we got plenty more inside. Take this one when you're through with the eggs.

ARCHIE: Henry, he's with Butch Cassidy in this picture. They're at Telluride in this picture.

HENRY: *(Appreciating the clue.)* Is that so? Well, Cassidy's in Bolivia, now, Archie, and if this guy was anybody he'd be down there with him, so maybe they were just in a bar together sometime or Cassidy sold him a horse.

LILY: Butch sold *you* a horse, oh that's funny.

HENRY: *(Very cagey.)* Yeah, Cassidy didn't know much about horses, did he ma'am. The real expert was that doctor's son in the gang. What did your old man do, mister?

ARCHIE: They're *going* to Bolivia, Henry. That's what he came to ask her.

HENRY: Only she won't go. Or I know, she won't go on a horse and he won't go in a car! Is that the holdup, pops?

ARCHIE: Don't give him any ideas, Henry.

(The Outlaw laughs.)

OUTLAW: Would you like to see a holdup, Archie?

LILY: Come on. Eat your eggs and let's get out of here.

HENRY: Relax, Archie. A holdup is quick. A holdup would be over by now. Unless of course, you forgot how to pull one.

ARCHIE: *(Trying to stay in Henry's good graces.)* Yeah, you're supposed to bust in here. No, first you ride up on your horse. You don't shoot your horse first. *(Expecting Henry to be pleased.)* You ride up on your horse, you slam open the doors, you say everybody does what I say and nobody gets hurt.

(The Outlaw laughs.)

ARCHIE: And then you say up against the wall.

HENRY: No wall, Archie.

ARCHIE: The cookshack and spread your arms.

OUTLAW: Situation like this, I'd say down on the ground, Archie.

ARCHIE: Then it's throw your money over here.

OUTLAW: *(Pointing the gun at them.)* All right. Down on the ground, boys.
    (They hesitate.)

OUTLAW: Now!

LILY: What are you doing?

ARCHIE: Her too?

OUTLAW: I rode a thousand miles to see her. I don't want her dirty.

LILY: If this is for my benefit, you can stop right now because I've seen it, out-
    law. Get up, you two. We're leaving right this minute.
    *(And as Lily starts to move, the Outlaw grabs her, rough, and pushes her back
    down on the bench. Archie sees this and ducks his head even further into the
    ground.)*

ARCHIE: Throw our money over to you?

HENRY: Why don't you just shut up, Archie.

OUTLAW: Yeah, let's have your money.

HENRY: Don't have mine on me.

ARCHIE: Mine's in my bedroll, inside.

OUTLAW: See, Archie? I knew that already.

ARCHIE: She could get it for you.

OUTLAW: I don't need your money.

HENRY: So what are we doin' with our face in the dirt?

OUTLAW: *(Laughs.)* Ask Archie. It was his idea.
    (Henry sits up, furious with Archie, and slaps him hard with his hat.)

ARCHIE: Can we sit up?

OUTLAW: Sure.

ARCHIE: *(Aware of Henry's rage.)* Could you just tell us what you want so we
    could give it to you so you could go on, wherever you're goin'?

OUTLAW: Who says I'm goin' anywhere? I'm gettin' what I want. A visit. Hear
    some stories, see some people. I haven't seen any people for a long time.

ARCHIE: Why not?

LILY: Because he acts like this, Archie.

ARCHIE: I mean, what is this? Who are you?

HENRY: You mind your own business.

ARCHIE: This feels like my business to me.

HENRY: It's his past, it's his business.

ARCHIE: I can ask the man.

HENRY: You can shut up!

ARCHIE: Why should I? So he won't know we're scared?

HENRY: I'm not scared. I'm sick to death of you.

ARCHIE: Me? What about him? He's the one ordered you around all night. He's got his gun in our face and you're sick to death of me? I don't get you, Henry.

HENRY: You never have. You don't know a thing about me.

ARCHIE: Oh I get it. If she won't go with him, you will, is that it? You'll just disappear to Bolivia like one of your books come to life and I'll have to tell Mr. White what happened in the morning? Let Dad sit around the rest of his life wondering whatever happened to Henry while I'm out doing your work on the ranch? Well, why don't you tell him how many shots it took you to nail that coyote in the barn last year.

HENRY: *(Slaps him hard.)* And why don't you just remember we're all alone out here. And I've had you hanging around my neck as long as I can remember and if I decide to cut you loose, Diddly, nobody's ever gonna know.

ARCHIE: What does that mean?

OUTLAW: It means he's not on your side, Archie. Nobody is really, when you get right down to it, out here.

LILY: *(Trying a different approach.)* Look, I'm sorry you two got in the middle of this. It's just two old friends getting together someplace safe, all right? We'll be on our way now.

HENRY: He can't go into town, girl. His draw's so shaky he wouldn't last two minutes.

OUTLAW: *(Drawing his gun as he turns.)* Shoot him first?

HENRY: *(Grabbing Archie like a shield.)* Him first!

OUTLAW: That's fine. Get you both with one shot.

HENRY: *(Jumping away from Archie.)* God that was fast! You've still got it all, don't you! Now. Let's see if the kid can dance!

LILY: Now you look here!

OUTLAW: *(Laughs.)* Shoot at his feet, you mean?

ARCHIE: Henry! You're not reading this in some book. What the hell are you doing?

HENRY: Something I should've done a long time ago. Looking out for myself. He needs somebody to ride with him and I'm it! We'll take two of the horses off this place and be on our way.

OUTLAW: *(Quickly throwing Henry a rope.)* You better tie him up so he don't follow us.

HENRY: *(Catches the rope and grabs Archie.)* Yeah boy!

LILY: Tom! Put that gun away! This is ridiculous!

(The Outlaw is just as surprised as Lily is that Henry is willing to tie Archie up, but he doesn't show Henry that.)

ARCHIE: What did I ever do to you?

HENRY: Are you kidding? My whole life I spent so you could go to school, so you could dream about airplanes, so you could go to church. I'm out there feedin' half-starved cattle and raisin' scrub crops, still workin' for Dad when I oughta be long gone all because you can't do nuthin' and never could. The most help you can ever be is just get out of my way, Archie. All you ever think about is where your next bath is comin' from and tell 'em, Archie, what are you saving your money for?

LILY: *(Furious.)* I'm leaving right this minute and Archie's coming with me. Get whatever you need and let's get out of here.

(Henry trips Archie to make him fall down and to make it clear that Archie's not going anywhere. Henry starts to tie Archie up, and he's real rough about it.)

ARCHIE: *(An appeal to Lily.)* I'm saving for a buggy. I already ordered the lap robe and harness. *(Then to Henry.)* You watch. You'll want to borrow it. Well don't even ask. I'm gonna be somebody.

HENRY: Somebody's aunt, that's what you'll be. Dad took Archie to the Hart Ranch. They brought in forty-eight hundred head of cattle, Dad picked the hundred he wanted, then they rode with the drivers bringing the cattle back to Clovis. Know what Archie had to say about the trip? The ranch house was dirty.

ARCHIE: Noisy. We slept in a room where a man was killed. There was a bullet hole in the door!

HENRY: *(To the Outlaw.)* See what I mean?

ARCHIE: You coulda gone on that trip except Dad knew you'd get drunk.

HENRY: You ain't goin' nowhere now, kid.

LILY: What kind of man ties up his brother? *(To the Outlaw.)* And you! You ask me to meet you out here in the middle of nowhere after twenty years and then you won't even talk to me. And they don't play this kind of game even in bars anymore. I see this, all right, but it's when the school lets out for recess. Or when we celebrate Frontier Day.

HENRY: There. Done and tight! That's what I felt like my whole life, Archie. How do you like it, huh? *(Kicks him.)*

(Henry is proud of his work. The Outlaw takes his time coming over to him.)

OUTLAW: Now, who are you?

HENRY: What?

OUTLAW: You heard me.

ARCHIE: Why don't you tie yourself up now, Henry.

HENRY: Who am I?

OUTLAW: Hard to say, huh?

HENRY: You mean how old am I?

OUTLAW: Start there, sure.

HENRY: Thirty.

OUTLAW: Go on.

HENRY: Not married. Live at the ranch.

ARCHIE: Lives at home.

OUTLAW: Big ranch?

HENRY: Pretty big.

OUTLAW: You ride?

HENRY: Ride. Good. Good rider, yeah. Rope. Shoot too.

OUTLAW: What.

HENRY: *Shoot* what?

OUTLAW: How's this for "talk," girl? This what you wanted to hear?

HENRY: I shot a Navy Colt before, but a Winchester's what's around most of the time. If you need somebody…if it's got a safe in it, I know Hercules powder and dynamite.

OUTLAW: Where'd you learn that?

ARCHIE: He didn't. He's lying. He reads *Police Gazette* in the barber shop.

HENRY: Shut up, Archie, or we'll gag you too.

OUTLAW: Well, you look strong enough all right.

HENRY: Would I be inside or outside? Lookout? Horse-holder?

OUTLAW: What are you like, cowboy?

HENRY: What do I like? Same as everybody. Money and a good time.

OUTLAW: No. Something you did once. Where you've been. How you are. How you'd…be.

HENRY: I don't understand.

ARCHIE: Something you did once, Henry. A story.

HENRY: Deaf Charley and Peep O'Day don't tell stories.

OUTLAW: They're dead.

ARCHIE: More outlaws, I guess.

HENRY: Outlaws, you bet. The Wild Bunch. O'Day was a horse-holder. *(Turning to the Outlaw.)* Wasn't he?

ARCHIE: All the outlaws are dead, Henry.

HENRY: *(Vicious.)* What do you know about it, Archie? Shut up!

LILY: Do you want a blanket, Archie? Something to drink? *(She comes over to Archie and moves him out of their way.)*

ARCHIE: Why don't you go on. This isn't gonna be a very good time here. I know Henry when he gets like this and there's no stopping him. They won't hurt me. I hate this place.

LILY: Tom, stop this. Come home with me. Wherever you've been, it's been hard, I know, but I want you with me now. We've got some catching up to do.

OUTLAW: *(Interrupting her.)* You gotta tell me something, cowboy.

HENRY: You know about Hole-in-the-Wall and I'm gonna tell you about egg hunts as a kid?

OUTLAW: You set traps for 'em? Trail 'em through the desert? Use your shotgun, what? I never been on a egg hunt.

ARCHIE: Tell him about breaking horses, tell him about threshing soybeans with a stick. Tell him about your life, Henry.

HENRY: I get thirsty. It's the same thing all the time.

ARCHIE: It has to last longer than that, Henry.

HENRY: Good story would be good company, I guess, at night. Hiding out.
(No response from the Outlaw.)

HENRY: Okay. I'll tell you about egg hunts and you tell me about Hole-in-the-Wall.

OUTLAW: Go.

HENRY: *(Not enjoying this at all. It feels like school.)* The week before Easter, Mother would give us each a dozen eggs, each of us boys, marked so we'd know whose was whose. We'd hide 'em around the farm, this was back in Oklahoma. Then all week we'd look for—

OUTLAW: Hunt.

HENRY: Yeah, hunt. Hunt for each other's eggs and when we found some we'd hide 'em again in a harder place where only we knew so that at the end of the week on Easter morning, the boy with the most eggs won. Now it's your turn.

OUTLAW: Won what?

HENRY: *(A sudden hostility.)* Just won. If you were smart, you buried your own eggs and ate the other ones you found.

ARCHIE: We knew you were doing that.

OUTLAW: You cheated at egg hunt?

HENRY: I won, didn't I? I wanted to win. *(Now brighter.)* You can start with Flat Nose Currie. Did a horse really kick him in the face?

OUTLAW: Never knew the man. Before my time.

HENRY: Well, when *was* your time?

OUTLAW: I forgot.

HENRY: We made a deal!

OUTLAW: So maybe I'll cheat. You have a Christmas tree?

HENRY: *(Disgusted.)* The man says he's an Outlaw and then he asks me about our Christmas tree.

ARCHIE: He's crazy, Henry. It doesn't matter who he is. He doesn't have any gang to take you into. He's just crazy. Tell him about Christmas.

HENRY: You're Tom McCarty, aren't you?

OUTLAW: McCarty is dead. Tell me why you never have any money. Tell me how you done nuthin' for so long, Henry. Tell me why you're still living at home.

HENRY: It's none of your goddamn business!

OUTLAW: Tell me why you tied up your brother. Nobody I know *ever* tied up his brother. Why'd you do that? I mean, we got rules out here for this sort of thing, or used to. Is this how people do now? 'Cause if it is, I don't want any part of it. I'm goin' right back where I been and I'm stayin' put this time. *(Now as much to Lily as Henry.)* I mean, you drop out of sight for a little while and look what we got for boys now. And you're drivin' a car and talkin' hard, girl.

HENRY: You tell me who you are!

OUTLAW: *(Grinning.)* Kilpatrick.

HENRY: Dead.

OUTLAW: Sundance.

HENRY: Bolivia.

OUTLAW: *(Laughing, mocking.)* Nope. Dead. I'm Billy the Kid. I'm Jesse James. *(Henry pulls his gun, insisting on an answer.)*

OUTLAW: Okay cowboy. Now we all saw your gun. Now put it away. *(Henry cocks the pistol.)*

ARCHIE: Please, mister… *(Then to Lily.)* Or you tell. Tell Henry who he is.

OUTLAW: *(Cooling down a little.)* I killed Tom McCarty. That help any?

HENRY: *(Uncocks the pistol.)* How?

ARCHIE: *(Thinks this is all ridiculous.)* Who is Tom McCarty?

HENRY: Tom McCarty taught Butch Cassidy to rob banks.

LILY: Handsome, funny.

HENRY: They got ten grand outta Telluride.

LILY: The best horse-handler in the business.

HENRY: Tom McCarty was smart!

LILY: Smelled like wild mint and wore a long leather coat, aspen gold.

HENRY: I don't believe you killed him!

LILY: I loved that coat. And a green scarf around his neck. Oh my.

HENRY: Who are you to kill Tom McCarty?

LILY: I figured somebody'd kill him for his money someday, he had so much of it. I should've married him.

ARCHIE: Did he want you to?

OUTLAW: He did.

LILY: Well why didn't he say something. I was crazy for him!

OUTLAW: He was scared.

LILY: You know what you have to do to forget a man like that? You have to buy an automobile, for God's sake.

HENRY: *(Finding the Outlaw's satchel now.)* How do I know you killed him?

OUTLAW: You don't. But…I got his watch. *(Pitches it to Henry to make him drop the satchel.)* Maybe I bought it. I got his spurs. Maybe he gave them to me. I got his satchel, there. Maybe I was his friend.

HENRY: This McCarty's?

LILY: Does it say Forget-me-not, LTK on the back?

HENRY: It does.

LILY: It's McCarty's. I gave it to him.

HENRY: How did you kill him? No. Tell us what happened to his money. She said he had a lot of money. What's in that suitcase?

OUTLAW: Whatever it is, it's mine.

ARCHIE: What a great idea, rob an old guy out in the wheat field.

LILY: There's no money in that case, Henry. It's old wanted pictures, newspaper articles, books about his friends, books with his name in them.

HENRY: He's no outlaw. Some whore sold him that watch. He's just some horse thief, some gone-crazy sheepherder. Just a copperhead, prissy-ass grandpa. He sneaked up on the smartest bank robber in the West and shot him in cold blood. A worm, unless I hear different.

ARCHIE: Shut up, Henry.

HENRY: You're gonna tell us how you killed Tom McCarty, *if* you killed Tom McCarty, and then we're gonna tie you up and turn you in. Get a hundred dollars! Outlaw Killer Killed.

OUTLAW: Look cowboy, relax. I apologize for playin' with you like this. I've just turned mean or something. Let's untie the kid here and—

HENRY: *(A serious threat.)* You touch him and you're dead, mister.

OUTLAW: *(Much more carefully.)* That is money in that case. You're absolutely right. I liked your eggs. I'll give you some.

HENRY: *(Fairly contemptuous.)* I'm gonna take it *all,* after you tell me your "story."

OUTLAW: It's not much of a story. McCarty didn't want to hide, and didn't want to run. He asked me to do it.

HENRY: Shoot him?

OUTLAW: Bury him.

ARCHIE: After you shot him.

OUTLAW: I buried him alive. Just outside of Delta, Colorado.

HENRY: *(Quietly, but firmly.)* I know who you are.

OUTLAW: *(Bitterly.)* It's pretty exciting, isn't it?

HENRY: *(His excitement building.)* Well, I think so. They're looking for you all over this country! Nobody knows what happened to you or where you are and you're sitting right here. What do you know about that! I'm taking you in!

OUTLAW: Come and get me then.

HENRY: You don't think I can.

OUTLAW: Listen, Henry, I've done this over and over for twenty years now. I know how it goes. Somebody wants to kill me so they pull a gun. They yell and scream or they sneak up from the back, it doesn't much matter. It never works. *I* live. They, you, end up dead. I swear it's the truth. It's only fair to tell you. Now, you tell me you heard what I said.

HENRY: Well I know what happened at Delta, Colorado. You were holding the horses behind the bank. You heard one shot and you ran. And you've been hiding ever since! Boy are the boys in town gonna be happy to see you at the end of a rope! Swing in the breeze, mister outlaw!

OUTLAW: I don't think I'd take too well to jail, Henry. Just shoot me. I'll get close enough so you don't miss and I'll put my gun in my hand so it looks fair and all.

HENRY: You never even went back to see they got buried, did you?

LILY: Stop this right now! Both of you!

OUTLAW: *(Very firm.)* You know what to do here, Lily. Get out of the way and stand still!

HENRY: Bill and Fred, remember, Archie? Your brother Bill. His boy, Fred. You left their horses for 'em and you ran.

OUTLAW: They'd have done the same thing if it was me in there! That's just how it worked!

HENRY: They shot a man in the bank so they broke through the back door, but you weren't there. So they got on their horses and Freddie boy lit out toward Third Street on that big roan.

OUTLAW: Gelding. Suzy.

HENRY: You *don't* know what happened, do you? Well, how could you if you've been hiding ever since. This is some story, Archie. Some guy Simpson shot Freddie boy right through his left ear, loaded his gun, got where he had a better aim at Bill and took the back of his head clean off. Scalped him!

OUTLAW: You shut up! You read about me while you got your hair cut.

HENRY: The shot blew Bill right out of the saddle, but Fred's body kept riding around till somebody plugged the horse in the belly. Damn strong horse though. Made it all the way to the post office hitching post where it finally fell down in a big mess of blood, squashed Fred's body underneath, flat as flat. And where were you?

OUTLAW: Shut up! You just shut up!

HENRY: You were riding as fast as you could. Took West Gulch to that little island in the Gunnison River, picked up your fresh horse and disappeared. Left two mighty good fresh horses behind. Did I leave anything out?

OUTLAW: You...off hoping me or somebody like me would come save you from being a nobody all your life just by sticking a gun in your face.

HENRY: You're a coward! The smartest one of the bunch is nuthin' but a miserable coward!

ARCHIE: Stop it, Henry!

HENRY: I just told him a little story. See, Archie, you don't know all the stories. *(Making a lunge at the Outlaw.)* Now, you're coming with me and—

OUTLAW: Don't touch me, cowboy!

(Henry cocks his gun again, aiming squarely at the Outlaw's back.)

HENRY: Coward! Coward!

OUTLAW: *(Turns around.)* Why does it have to be you? Why couldn't it be somebody I—

HENRY: What are you waiting for, coward?

OUTLAW: You're asking me to kill you, boy.

HENRY: I'm daring you. You think you can say you're an outlaw and that makes you an outlaw? You ran. Real outlaws, real outlaws...

OUTLAW: It went wrong for me once in my life, Henry. It ain't gone right once for you. All you got in your life is my story to tell.

HENRY: And everybody's gonna know it was me that found you.

OUTLAW: Yeah, that's right. You got one shot. Turn me in and get your name in the paper.

HENRY: And my *picture* with you propped up dead on the ground beside me. Change my whole life.

LILY: He's warned you, Henry. This isn't a game to him! He'll kill you!

HENRY: Yes sir. I've been waitin' for this my whole life. All my miserable hot life!

ARCHIE: Sit down, Henry! He won't shoot you if you sit down!

HENRY: He don't have to fight back. He can just stand there if he wants, but I'm taking all that money. I'm taking you in!

OUTLAW: My brother dies so you can read about it in the barbershop!

ARCHIE: Run, Henry!

HENRY: *(Taking a step toward the Outlaw.)* Nice and easy, now, pops. Throw your gun over there.

OUTLAW: *(Standing still, his hand on his gun.)* I can't do that, cowboy.

HENRY: Then I'm coming after it. You draw and you're dead, mister.

OUTLAW: That's fair.

(And instantly the Outlaw pulls his pistol, both men fire, and Henry falls dead. Lily screams.)

ARCHIE: Henry!

OUTLAW: *(Taking a step backward.)* He wasn't married, I hope.

ARCHIE: He was my brother!

OUTLAW: I'm sorry.

ARCHIE: You killed my brother!

OUTLAW: He did it himself, really. I'm sorry. You shouldn't draw if you can't shoot.

ARCHIE: *(Straining against the ropes.)* Henry!

(Lily walks over to the Outlaw.)

LILY: *(In a cold fury.)* Is this what you do now? Ride around daring people to kill you?

OUTLAW: It's not my fault he missed, girl. I stood still, didn't I?

LILY: You are disgusting.

OUTLAW: He didn't give me a chance, honey.

LILY: Give me the gun. Now your knife. Now…stay put. *(She walks over to Archie.)*

OUTLAW: I'm fine. Just a little…stiff from riding.

(Lily cuts the ropes tying Archie. Archie gets up quickly, runs to Henry and, crying, embraces him, as Lily turns to face the Outlaw.)

LILY: *(Hands the Outlaw's knife back to him.)* Want to start carving the notch now?

OUTLAW: It was a fair fight.

LILY: He never had a chance and you know it.

OUTLAW: I tried to tell him.

ARCHIE: I tried to tell him.

OUTLAW: Well, then. It was a fair fight.

ARCHIE: *(Standing up, nearly screaming.)* Fair? You told him he would die! That's not fair. Fair is when both guys got a chance. Fair is when nobody knows how it will come out! You pulled him right in, didn't you. You dared him! If he could kill you, then he could be somebody.

OUTLAW: Henry wanted to kill an outlaw. Can't kill Indians anymore. Kill an Outlaw instead. Everybody out here feels that way. Must be the water.

ARCHIE: What water? *(And he stoops to pick up the gun.)* What's the matter with this country? This isn't what people are supposed to do! He's not supposed to tie me up and you're not supposed to…He was my brother and he was no good, but now you've gone and killed him! How do you think that makes me feel!

OUTLAW: You have to believe me, Lily. I'm tired of killing these boys, but they won't leave me alone.

ARCHIE: Henry! Henry!

(Lunging across the stage, Archie attacks the Outlaw in a fury of ineffective but desperate punches and kicks, which the Outlaw absorbs fairly passively.)

OUTLAW: I'm sorry, boy. I said I was sorry. Jesus, kid, come on.

(Archie sinks to the ground.)

OUTLAW: It's okay. You're a baby. It's all right. It's all gonna be over in just a little bit.

ARCHIE: Why did you have to come here? Nobody asked you to come here.

OUTLAW: I came to see her.

ARCHIE: *(Not listening to him.)* You didn't have to say anything about being an outlaw.

OUTLAW: I didn't! You did! She did! He did!

ARCHIE: You didn't have to pull that gun and ask for eggs. We'd have given you the eggs. But no! You sit around playing outlaw and my brother ends up dead. You could've lied about the money. If Henry didn't know you had money in that case, he'd have never told that Delta story and he'd still be here! Jesus God. Mother. What am I gonna tell Mother?

OUTLAW: You say this old outlaw wandered into your camp, hungry. He had a sack full of money and Henry wanted it. They fought. Henry died. Simple.

ARCHIE: Simple? Who's gonna believe an old outlaw came here. All the outlaws died.

OUTLAW: I wish.

ARCHIE: Just tell me your name. I have to have something to tell. Just sit down and tell me your name and then you and her can ride off.

OUTLAW: I'm Tom McCarty.

ARCHIE: That's who you said you killed.

OUTLAW: That's right.

ARCHIE: You killed yourself?

OUTLAW: I buried me alive. They killed Bill and Fred and I was the only one left. I gave it up. Disappeared.

LILY: So why didn't you come to me then?

OUTLAW: Because you're exactly where they thought I'd go. I couldn't put you in that kind of danger and you know it! I had to hide and I did. And then it got harder and harder to show back up, that's all.

ARCHIE: Is there money in that case?

OUTLAW: Forty, fifty thousand. Hard to spend that kind of money out here without attracting attention.

ARCHIE: So give it back.

OUTLAW: I don't know whose it is.

ARCHIE: You know what bank you got it from.

OUTLAW: Banks. Trains. It's a problem.

ARCHIE: What were you doing stealing it if you didn't really want it? What did you think you were going to do with it? You are one sorry outlaw, mister.

OUTLAW: I need a place to sleep, Lily.

LILY: How does prison sound?

ARCHIE: Give me the money. I'll give it to Dad, for Henry.

OUTLAW: It won't help. His son is dead. (Now trying to be lighter.) But I gotta admit. "Henry's dead, here's forty thousand dollars," sounds a helluva lot better than just plain, "Henry's dead."
(They do not laugh.)

OUTLAW: I should've got it in the back. Gunned down on Main Street. But no. I was so smart. I got away.

ARCHIE: I don't want to hear it.

LILY: (To Archie.) What are you going to do about Henry? His body.

ARCHIE: We'll bury him. There's three barrels. We'll put him in the barrels and bury him.

LILY: But your mother. Won't she want a funeral? What about the family? Your father won't want to see you without Henry, I bet.

ARCHIE: Well, he's not out here, is he, so I'm making the decision. You want me to watch him be dead till morning? Then what do I do? Carry him home in a sack? It's three days. He'd smell. I'd have to tie him on the horse. He'd fall off. I'd get off, tie him back up, ride on a little bit, he'd fall off again. Three days? No. We'll bury him. *(To the Outlaw.)* But you're gonna dig this grave, "outlaw."

OUTLAW: *(Fiercely.)* I never dug a grave in my life! *(Sees Lily's commanding look.)* But I don't have to go just yet. I could help, I guess.

ARCHIE: You're not going to *help*. You're going to do it.

OUTLAW: *(Still looking at Lily.)* That's what I said.

LILY: That's what I thought you said.

OUTLAW: *(After a moment.)* Good. Ready. Good idea, kid. That's just what I'll do. Dig it as deep as you want, you just tell me. Yes sir. You got a shovel?

ARCHIE: *(Fairly disgusted now.)* Around back there.

OUTLAW: *(To Lily.)* You just watch and see, girl. Be the nicest grave you ever saw. Real comfortable. Be everything a man could want.

LILY: I'll make us some coffee.

OUTLAW: That's a good idea too. Everybody's just full of good ideas.
(They stand there.)

ARCHIE: I hate this place. Nobody acts right out here. *(And then aware that they are staring at him.)* Shut up, Archie.

OUTLAW: That's the spirit. *(Wanting to get on with it.)* Okay. One grave, comin' up.
(And the Outlaw heads around the side of the cookshack and Lily starts up the steps into the cookshack and the lights come down.)

END OF ACT I

ACT II

Lights come up as the Outlaw is shoveling the last dirt onto a low mound, which is Henry's grave. Archie sits back quite disturbed but not saying anything. The Outlaw seems invigorated by his physical labor.

OUTLAW: *(Resting on the shovel.)* There. All done. Rest in peace. *(To Archie.)* Want a cross or anything? Marker?
(No response.)
OUTLAW: I could make one outta—
LILY: Tell him what you want, Archie. Do you want a marker?
ARCHIE: No. Just be in the way. The boys, coming back in the morning, still drunk, they'd trip over it. *(His anger building.)* It's in the wrong place anyway. You dug the grave in the wrong place. This is right where we sit down to eat.
OUTLAW: Why didn't you say that before?
ARCHIE: I didn't want you to stop digging.
OUTLAW: I'll do another one if you want. Just getting used to the shovel, really. How about over there?
ARCHIE: I want a funeral.
LILY: You need a family and a preacher for a funeral. If you'd wanted a funeral, you should've taken him home.
OUTLAW: *(Still so cooperative.)* I'll dig him back up.
ARCHIE: *(To Lily.)* We're having a funeral. I'm the family. He's the preacher.
OUTLAW: I killed him. I can't preach over him too. Wouldn't be right.
ARCHIE: If we were doing what was right around here, you'd be locked up by now. You dug the grave and now you're gonna preach the funeral. And then you're gonna get the hell out of here and you're gonna take her with you.
OUTLAW: No sir.
LILY: You're preaching the funeral all right, but I'm not going with you when you're through.
OUTLAW: Yes you are too, girl. That's what I came for.
LILY: Why didn't you say that right off? We could be in my bed by now. Asleep, by now. We didn't need to see your Wild West Show.
OUTLAW: What did you think I wanted if I didn't want you?
LILY: I have my own life now, Tom. And if I had any thoughts about going with you, which I might have had, seeing you early on tonight, I've sure forgot

'em all now, after what you did. Now, you owe this boy a funeral and I'm staying just long enough to see that he gets it and then I'm getting in my car and going back to town and tell the sheriff you're out here, in case he's interested. You're dangerous. And, I might have been in love with you once, but now…I'm a good citizen.

OUTLAW: Well why did you come out here, then?

LILY: I didn't believe you were still alive.

OUTLAW: *(Furious and hurt.)* And that's the only reason you came all the way out here? You were curious? You just had to know if the old desert rat died or not. Well I sure hope you're satisfied, girl. Contrary to popular opinion and in spite of everything I've tried, I am still alive. *(Quickly to Archie.)* All right. What do I say?

ARCHIE: You're the preacher.

OUTLAW: *(His anger taking another direction.)* We had a good time together, in case you forgot.

LILY: I remember.

OUTLAW: I'm the only man man enough for you, girl. I'm exactly what you need.

LILY: I need…a whole night's sleep and a hot bath and a month's vacation some-place green and a glass of gin, a couple more bartenders and running water, but I don't need you. And I don't know who does. You were mighty enter-taining all those years ago, but we've got traveling comedians now and a circus once a year and I guess Pancho Villa could probably use a broken-down gunslinger, but other than that I just don't know. You even look bet-ter on the wall anymore.

OUTLAW: I took my time getting back here, I'll grant you that. But I've seen these new people. *(Looking directly at Archie.)* There's nothing to 'em. All talk.

ARCHIE: *(Has heard enough.)* We're having a goddamn funeral. Now will you get on with it! Preach!

LILY: Watch your language, Archie.

OUTLAW: I wish it was me there instead of him.

ARCHIE: That ain't what I had in mind.

OUTLAW: It's the truth.

ARCHIE: You start out, "Family and friends…"

OUTLAW: *(Stalling.)* If he'd killed me, would you make him preach over me?

ARCHIE: Henry? He'd have drug your body into town to have its picture took by now.

OUTLAW: Well, if you're gonna take a picture, it's good to do it quick.

ARCHIE: Will you get on with this! I'm managin' to stay calm right now, but I'm not sure how long it's gonna last.

OUTLAW: If you think you might get really mad, I'll wait.

ARCHIE: So you can kill me too? Uh-uh. Preach or go.

OUTLAW: *(Looking at Lily, hoping to see her change her mind as he preaches.)* I'll preach. *(To Lily.)* You sing.

(She starts to hum.)

OUTLAW: Friends and family. Here lies Henry... *(He looks to Archie.)* Middle name?

ARCHIE: Jackson.

OUTLAW: Tucker. Born?

ARCHIE: 1884, Thomas, Oklahoma.

OUTLAW: Moved to...

ARCHIE: Clovis when he was twelve. Lived there ever since.

OUTLAW: He just had a short time on this earth, but he spent it, well, to tell the truth, he pretty much wasted it.

ARCHIE: *(Objecting.)* Hey!

OUTLAW: But it was his time. And if he wanted to waste it, well that was his business. His business was... *(He looks to Archie.)* ranchin'?

(Archie nods yes.)

OUTLAW: And he was real good at the stuff you had to be a real sunuvabitch to do. Lie, cheat, steal.

ARCHIE: Go on. You're doing just fine.

OUTLAW: He was bored so he read outlaw books. And he hated himself, but he took it out on everybody else. Now he's dead. Leavin' behind a mother and father?

(Archie nods yes.)

OUTLAW: Some brothers and some other family, I guess and maybe some children, who knows? They might miss him, but I wouldn't know why. So, rest in peace, Henry Tucker. The rest of us sure will now that you're gone, so you might as well. You didn't have much love for this brother of yours, Archie, but he done more for you than you would have for him had I killed him instead of you and I want you to take note of that. *(Bitter, personal.)* You didn't have to die, I tried to tell you that, but you didn't listen. Well, you were gonna die anyway, we all are, someday. But you were lucky. You had help. Unlike me. Yes sir, Henry Tucker, things are pretty bad when you can't count on somebody else to kill you. Dyin' just ain't something you should have to do for yourself.

ARCHIE: You're gettin' off the track here.

OUTLAW: Okay. Heaven and hell. I've got some bad news for you, Henry. But you might as well hear it right now, 'cause you're gonna be findin' it out for yourself pretty soon. I've been thinking about heaven and hell a lot here lately, like how they decide where to put you, and I think what it is, is that they put you in a big room forever with people exactly like you, how you were in life, I mean. And that's what makes it heaven or hell. Now you, you hated yourself, like I said, so it's gonna be hell. You'll be in with a whole bunch of ranch hands that never amounted to nuthin' and died mad.

ARCHIE: I got something to say. I didn't...we didn't get along, you and me, Henry, but you're my brother and I respect that. Rest in peace. *(Goes on, knowing they expect more from him.)* Lotta times I thought I was ready to kill you, Henry, and I know you really did try to drown me at least twice, so no, I didn't care much for you, but I sure didn't like seein' you die. Tell you what, Henry, the story I'm gonna tell about how you died, it's gonna be some story when I get through with it. If you're ever listening, you're gonna be real proud. I think that's about all I can do for you now. *(To the Outlaw.)* Now, finish up.

OUTLAW: *(Wants this to be over.)* That's it. I didn't know him.

ARCHIE: We need something from the Bible.

LILY: "Man that is born of woman is of few days and full of trouble."

OUTLAW: God that's gloomy. Where'd you pick that up?

LILY: At my rancher's funeral. You've never read the Bible in your life. What do you know?

ARCHIE: "The Lord is my shepherd, I shall not want."

OUTLAW: Are we through now? I ain't prayin' to no sheepherder.

ARCHIE: "For yea, though I walk through the valley of the shadow of death I will fear no evil, for thou art with me. Thou preparest a table before me in the presence of mine enemies, my cup runneth over."

ARCHIE AND LILY: "Surely goodness and mercy shall follow me all the days of my life and I shall dwell in the house of the Lord forever."

OUTLAW: Dust to dust, an eye for a tooth.

LILY: *(Not pleased with the Outlaw's offering.)* Say you feel bad. Say you're sorry.

OUTLAW: I *am* sorry. I don't know anything to say. I'm lonelier than I thought.

ARCHIE: Pray.

OUTLAW: I don't know how.

ARCHIE: Well, what do you want said at your funeral? Say that.

OUTLAW: What do I want said at my funeral? How 'bout, "Okay boys, reload!"

LILY: I don't believe this! You're not a bit sorry about this. This is just one more dumb boy that missed. What did I ever see in you? This is not a joke, here. This is a dead boy in the ground. Oh I wasted so much time waiting for you. Well no more! This is the end. I am free of you for good and praise the Lord for it.

OUTLAW: I am sorry. *(Louder.)* I'm sorry, Henry. *(Genuine.)* I really am sorry. I never stayed this long at a killing. *(Getting crazed.)* I'm sorry. *(Reaching quickly into his pocket.)* Okay. I'll show you, Henry Tucker. *(Swallowing the stuff he took from his pocket.)* That's how sorry I am.

LILY: What was that?

OUTLAW: I sure am sorry. I'm also jealous. You got something I want, Henry, so I'm comin' after you. Archie figured out what to do with you and I trust him to figure out what to do with me. It's not in your honor, Henry, it's just that now that you're gone, it feels like family and a man should die at home. *(To Lily and Archie.)* There! How's that for sorry! That was morphine. I've killed myself!

ARCHIE: *(Contemptuous.)* Well, that really is sorry.

LILY: Anything for a little excitement, huh Tom?

ARCHIE: Yeah, how do we know it was morphine?

OUTLAW: You don't. Why don't you just wait and see. Sit down. Who is the sheriff now anyway?

LILY: Nobody you'd know. Kid from St. Louis. Don't worry about him. He thinks you're dead.

OUTLAW: I wasn't worried. What ever happened to Daisy?

LILY: *(Lunging at him.)* Throw it up! You're going to throw it up!
(He fights her as she's trying to get her finger down his throat.)

LILY: Go ahead, bite me! Vomit! You can't do this!

ARCHIE: So this is an outlaw. This is how outlaws die.

OUTLAW: *(Breaking away from Lily.)* Nobody knows how to die, boy.

LILY: How much did you take?

OUTLAW: *(Pacing, raging.)* Nobody knows how to shoot anymore either! You'd think just one of these lousy cowboys could… *(Then like a drunken comrade.)* See, Archie, the problem with hiding is there's nothing to do. *(Then back to Lily.)* God I loved you, woman.

LILY: It's a little late for that, Tom.

OUTLAW: After I go here, Archie, shoot me. Just once. Don't overdo it. And turn me in. There's gotta still be a reward out somewhere. Buy yourself…something…Buick, something. *(Getting angry now.)*

LILY: *(Pacing.)* How many times did I get asked to get married? Only once. And you heard about that and came chasing across the country to shoot him. Then did you ask me to marry you? Or come with you even? No! You take off and I don't see you for another ten years. That rancher was rich!

OUTLAW: You got rich on your own, girl.

LILY: *(Angry.)* Yes I did.

OUTLAW: See? Say thank you.

ARCHIE: I'd leave the two of you alone, but I can't see sitting out in the wheat all night. I've got no place to go.

OUTLAW: I know how you feel. Same here.

LILY: *(Beginning to believe it.)* Did you take enough to kill you? Goddamn you. You never even asked me to go to Bolivia with you. You just talked about it and then killed yourself!

(The Outlaw slumps a little.)

ARCHIE: Why didn't you take the morphine out in the desert? Big bravery this is. Take it where there's people to see you, cry over you. You make me sick!

OUTLAW: *(Trying to defend himself.)* I went back to Hole-in-the-Wall and I didn't know anybody and there were…fences, everywhere, and I couldn't do it. And I'm dying in front of Lily because I want her to have my money. Not like she needs it, of course, but well… *(A silly, drugged smile on his face.)* she's who I thought of first. It's time for it, that's all.

ARCHIE: I should've helped Henry shoot you. What kind of thing is this to do to her.

OUTLAW: *(Enjoying the physical sensation the drug has produced.)* If you'll just shut up, this will all be over. How am I supposed to sleep with you yelling at me?

ARCHIE: *(Irritated at the outlaw's pleasure.)* Putting on quite a show, aren't you? Well, I don't feel a bit sorry for you. Go ahead. Go to sleep. Things getting dark yet?

OUTLAW: Hey, this is pretty nice, here. Just about perfect way to die, seem to me. It don't hurt…there's no mess to clean up. My heart's on this side, here. Put it right here.

ARCHIE: *(Furious at the vanity.)* Keep your head clean for the picture?

OUTLAW: *(To Lily, much more quiet.)* The doctor gave it to me when I broke my leg last year. He said, *(An uncomfortable laugh.)* "You take this all at once, McCarty, it'll kill you, so go easy." I didn't take any of it. I thought I might get…the horse might fall on me sometime out where… *(Beginning to have trouble talking now.)* where I couldn't get to…nobody around to help me and might not want to…couldn't just wait for it…or if you didn't want me…weren't around…

(The Outlaw drifts off here for a moment, his speech getting very slurred. There is a sudden, awesome quiet and they both know he has really taken the morphine—something about the way his body looks leaning against the cookshack. Lily backs away and Archie seems hypnotized by the sight of him. Lily finally turns to Archie. There is no pleading, there is simply a decision to be made. Archie looks at her, then back at the Outlaw, and then to Henry's grave.)

ARCHIE: Salt water will do it. If we can get it down him. *(Starting for the Outlaw.)* Well go on! It's inside somewhere.

(Lily rushes for the cookshack. Archie grabs the Outlaw and jerks him up.)

ARCHIE: Get up you! Sit up!

OUTLAW: *(Jolted awake.)* You don't have to squeeze. I'm not going anywhere.

ARCHIE: What am I doing?

OUTLAW: I was about to ask you that.

ARCHIE: *(Yelling to Lily.)* He killed my brother. I can't save his life!

LILY: *(Yelling back.)* Where's the water?

ARCHIE: Oh, hell, it's out here.

LILY: *(Rushing out.)* Where?

ARCHIE: On the ground. All we had was in the barrels. Take too long to draw another bucket. Get some vinegar.

LILY: And salt? It'll kill him!

OUTLAW: Bring it on.

ARCHIE: Get it.

(Lily goes back inside.)

OUTLAW: Dark. Things are dark.

ARCHIE: It's night. Things are dark at night.

OUTLAW: My feet feel real heavy.

ARCHIE: Your boots are heavy. Your feet are in your boots. Your feet only feel heavy.

OUTLAW: That's what I said.

ARCHIE: *(Yelling in to Lily.)* What are you doing in there? Come on!

LILY: *(Coming out with the salt and a big unmarked can.)* It's dark in there. This is something sloshy, but I don't know what. Could be cherries or beans…Got an opener?

OUTLAW: If I wanted my life saved, I picked the wrong crew.

ARCHIE: On the wall over the stove.

LILY: I looked already. You go.

ARCHIE: *(Handing the Outlaw over to her.)* Jesus God! *(Rushing for the cookshack.)*

LILY: You cold?

OUTLAW: Yeah. You know what happened to my coat?

LILY: I loved that coat.

OUTLAW: Dirty little Navaho took it. Stole it. Stole my coat. Little boy…

LILY: *(To Archie.)* Hurry up in there!

ARCHIE: *(Running out, having opened the can.)* Coming. Hold his head back. Come on, Tom. Open up now, drink this.

LILY: What is it?

(The Outlaw swallows some, chokes immediately and throws it up.)

LILY: Ah…tomatoes.

ARCHIE: Once more, Tom. You did just fine.

(Archie forces more down the Outlaw's throat with the same result.)

ARCHIE: I just had a bath, too.

OUTLAW: Taste…mouth… *(As he tries to reach in his pocket.)* Get…

ARCHIE: I'll get it. What am I looking for?

OUTLAW: Mint.

ARCHIE: *(Looking at Lily.)* Women really like this mint smell, huh? *(Finding some, putting it in the Outlaw's mouth.)*

OUTLAW: *I like it. (Then he chokes again.)*

ARCHIE: We have to walk around. Keep him moving. We can't let him sit anymore. *(Puts the Outlaw over his shoulder.)* You're gonna talk, you. You're gonna tell me your whole life story. Now, where were you born? Got any children? What color hair did your mother have?

OUTLAW: I'm all right. Just…late…tired…

ARCHIE: *(Slaps him.)* You're dying. You're dead if you don't keep moving. Kick your leg. Here! *(Kicks it for him.)* Kick. Kick.

(Archie feet get tangled in the Outlaw's feet and they both fall.)

ARCHIE: Oh God. *(Trying to get a rise out of him.)* They'll write about this. You killing yourself. How's that going to sound? Last Outlaw Kills Self.

OUTLAW: Bad. Sound bad…Lily…

LILY: Look at me, Tom.

OUTLAW: Pretty.

LILY: We can save you if you'll help us. You threw some up but there's still plenty left in you. You have to keep moving. Stay awake.

ARCHIE: Do you want us to save you? We have to know right now.

OUTLAW: I don't want to die. Don't let me die...

ARCHIE: *(Again trying to force him to talk.)* Why not? Why shouldn't we let you die? You killed my brother and who knows who else? You've obviously been thinking about it. Yes or no? Die or not.

OUTLAW: Not. Not. Archie. Please. Lily...

ARCHIE: *(Pulling Lily away from him.)* Prove it. Stand up. Stand up and we'll save you. Why do you want to live? You didn't a few minutes ago, and things haven't changed all that much.

OUTLAW: *(Trying to talk.)* Pretty.

ARCHIE: Pretty! That's why you want to live? Because she's pretty?

OUTLAW: *(Making it, standing up.)* Up. Live. *(And immediately, he falls back into Archie's arms.)*

ARCHIE: She's a whole lot better than pretty. Walk. Walk.

LILY: Give me his other arm.

(They shoulder the Outlaw between them.)

ARCHIE: *(After a moment.)* You cold?

LILY: Freezing.

ARCHIE: I don't know what I can do. I'd get you a coat but...he'd fall.

(She nods.)

ARCHIE: I know. Take his coat.

LILY: Good. Cold might pick him up some.

(They struggle to take his jacket off as they continue to talk.)

ARCHIE: That'd be good. We save him and you die of pneumonia.

LILY: You're cold too.

ARCHIE: Yep. Sure am. And so is Henry. That makes four of us. All cold. *(And he has awkward boyish awareness that now the two of them have to talk for what might be hours.)*

LILY: Archie...I'm sorry about Henry.

ARCHIE: *(Not wanting to talk abut it, starts to walk the Outlaw around again.)* Henry used to make Mother so mad. We'd be in church and Henry and some of his buddies would sneak up to the wagons parked out front. There'd be babies or little kids sleeping in the wagons and they'd switch the babies. People got home and found they had the right blanket with the wrong baby in it.

LILY: Is that how you got in your family in the first place?

ARCHIE: *(Surprised that she guessed this.)* That's what Henry says. Dad too when he's mad at me. Which is always. I don't mind, really. You gotta have a mean streak like you gotta have a mule out here.

LILY: You don't have that mean streak, Archie.

ARCHIE: *(Doesn't want to talk about that either.)* Dad wanted an orchard like we had back in Oklahoma. But the ground was so hard, we had to put dynamite in each hole to shake the dirt loose so the roots could take hold. Dad made me haul water on a sled for two years to keep those peach trees alive.

LILY: Did they make it?

ARCHIE: No. He's mostly raising cattle now. He's got this fool idea that the government's gonna need mules for the war, so he's just bought fifteen wild mares to start breedin' 'em.

LILY: There could be money in that.

ARCHIE: Hell, the war's gonna be over before the mules are old enough to sell.

LILY: You're old enough to leave home, Archie, find a place that suits you better. What are you waiting for?

ARCHIE: I can't leave, Lily, I was born here. Did Tom really shoot your husband?

LILY: We're all at the church. Saloon's even closed for the event. Roy Luther, tending bar, said he wouldn't believe I'd get married unless he saw it himself. Tom came in late. Sat at the back. Nobody saw him.

ARCHIE: But when the preacher said, "Anybody got any reason why I shouldn't marry these two," Tom stepped out in the aisle, said "Draw mister," and shot him.

LILY: Actually no, the rancher shot first, but Tom is quick, you know.

ARCHIE: I know.

LILY: He came by later. Said he rode three straight days to get there. Said they'd be after him so he had to go.

ARCHIE: Got on his horse and rode off.

LILY: Well, not right away, no. And the town, they didn't send a posse, after all. People knew the rancher was about to buy a herd of sheep and it got to be a joke. Roy Luther said I really did know how to take care of a sheepherder, all right. The town painted my house for me, to say thanks. *(A pause.)* I thought Tom was dead. The man just disappears.

ARCHIE: But he wants people to know him.

LILY: Well, he doesn't want to be forgotten, that's true. But he doesn't want to be recognized and shot either.

ARCHIE: What he wants is you.

LILY: *(Quickly.)* He wants it to be like it was. Every sheriff in—
   (The Outlaw stirs at the word "sheriff." He stands on his own, ready to fight, then breaks away from them, charging around.)

OUTLAW: Sheriff! God, it's Hazen! I can smell him he's so close! *(Crouching as if in battle.)* Reload!

LILY: *(Sensing immediately what to do.)* There's no way out! There must be twenty!

OUTLAW: *(Now creeping around as if behind rocks.)* Keep firing…one at a time… slip through. Take Teapot north. *(Now slumping as quickly as he awoke before.)* Brakeman…shoulda killed the brakeman.

LILY: *(Slapping him.)* Tom! Tom! *(But he doesn't recover.)* That's how we have to do it! Who else is there? *(Then quickly, yelling at the Outlaw.)* Jim Averill! It's Cattle Kate! We got a mess comin', honey!

OUTLAW: *(Charging around again, firing his gun.)* The Regulators! Is it the Regulators?

ARCHIE: *(Wanting to help.)* It's the Regulators!

OUTLAW: You're not taking me, Robert Connor. I got you, Bothwell!
(The Outlaw grabs Archie as if to strangle him, then collapses and they both fall. Archie pulls the Outlaw up to sit on the ground in front of him, sits on the bench. Archie massages the Outlaw's face and neck, trying to think of some way to continue the conversation with Lily, as she is momentarily out of breath.)

ARCHIE: So. Were you really a whore or not?

LILY: *(Quite annoyed.)* What difference does it make? You wouldn't be helping me if I were?

ARCHIE: No, I just meant, well, you don't seem like, you know…

LILY: No, I don't know.

ARCHIE: If you were a whore, then…

LILY: You might be wrong about whores, huh? You might be in big trouble if you had the money?

ARCHIE: *(Eager to change the subject.)* Tom! Hey Tom! *(Then to Lily.)* Come on. All I know is Remember the Alamo.

LILY: Frank Canton!

OUTLAW: *(Jerking up instantly.)* Kill Frank Canton! Come out here, Frank Canton!

ARCHIE: *(Yelling.)* They got him, McCarty!

OUTLAW: Got who?

ARCHIE: I can't tell!

OUTLAW: *(Losing consciousness.)* Nate? They got Nate?

ARCHIE: *(Attempting to revive him.)* It was Nate all right!

OUTLAW: *(Reviving.)* Light those fires, Brown. Burn 'em to kingdom come!
(Then the Outlaw falls unconscious. Archie knows by now not to let him charge off by himself in these moments of being awake. As a result, Archie is dragged

around the stage, as the Outlaw relives his past. Archie and Lily put him between them and begin to walk again.)

ARCHIE: *(Trying to talk to Lily again, this time more carefully.)* Were you born out here?

LILY: I don't talk about my life. It sounds like one of those books.

ARCHIE: I got it. Your family came out here homesteading and they got wiped out in a drought and your mother died having a baby so your daddy left to join up with the Mexican army, leaving you in the house alone. Some preacher's wife took you in and raised you till they died in a fire at a barn raisin'. They left you everything they had, which was two oil lamps and a Bible, so you moved to the city and got...work.

LILY: *(Has to laugh.)* Very good. You've been reading the books.

(Archie is pleased.)

LILY: Your mother is...uh...a little fat lady who wears her hair in braids wrapped around her head and sits out on the stoop at night to wash her feet before she goes to bed.

ARCHIE: That's her all right. When I think about her, away from home like this, all I see is a big white apron. She pays me ten cents for every turkey nest I find. Turkeys hide their nests, you know.

LILY: *(Distracted.)* No. I didn't know. *(Yelling again.)* Hainer's gonna give himself up!

OUTLAW: *(Charging out of his unconsciousness.)* Claverly, you lay one hand on me...I'll kill you. I'll give you all six of these and then I'll bash your... *(Then collapsing again.)*

LILY: *(Defeated, worried.)* Why did he do this? How are we supposed to go on? I can't do this all night. I don't know any more names. Why, Tom?

ARCHIE: But where did you get the money for the hotel?

LILY: *(Suddenly depressed and bitter.)* It's none of your damn business.

ARCHIE: I know what you did! It was a big ranch. You sold it!

LILY: And everything on it! Kicked out the whores and turned the place into a hotel. That rancher was rich. I had money left. I built a school. I named it for the rancher. Least I could do, you know. *(Irritated again.)* Don't you even know one sheriff's name? One deputy?

ARCHIE: *(Stares at the Outlaw, then yells.)* Daniel Boone!

(The Outlaw slumps even more.)

ARCHIE: Sorry.

LILY: No. I'm sorry. Nobody knows those names anymore. Just as well, I guess. It wasn't as much fun as we said it was.

ARCHIE: I bet you didn't get too many proposals after what Tom did.

LILY: *(Very hostile.)* Can't we talk about something else?

ARCHIE: Look. I know you're scared. But he'll make it. You'll see. His pulse is stronger already. Don't you think?

LILY: I don't know how to take it.

ARCHIE: You just count. You remember if you're counting faster than you did when you counted before.

LILY: I didn't count before.

ARCHIE: *(Much too cheerful for Lily.)* So you'd count next time. I counted before. I think he just might make it.

LILY: And then what?

ARCHIE: And then what?

LILY: No, you don't say what I said. You say something new.

ARCHIE: I don't know what to say. I don't know what we're talking about.

LILY: So what *do* you know? Ever had a beer, Archie?

ARCHIE: No.

LILY: Ever seen a girl without any clothes on?

ARCHIE: Just my little sister.

LILY: It's not the same, you know.

ARCHIE: Yeah. It's different.

LILY: Real different. So what *have* you been doing?

ARCHIE: Don't make fun of me. You won't tell me anything, so I won't tell you anything either. And I know a lot of good stories. I could fill up this whole night telling you my life. How I learned to rope calves or the time Bill got his hand eat by a catfish. *(Gets tickled in spite of himself at this memory.)* But I'm not telling! It's private! What do you care anyway?

LILY: I have everything all set and then he just drops in and tries to kill himself. And we're trying to save him! And all you know is stories. Well, you'll get a good one out of this, won't you?

ARCHIE: Do you want him to live or not, because if you don't then I'm a damn fool carrying him around all night. He killed my brother!

LILY: *That's* what we're talking about. He's a killer.

ARCHIE: I'll drop him on the ground right now if you say to.

LILY: You would not either.

ARCHIE: Go sit then. See what happens.

LILY: We should turn him in.

ARCHIE: Let's save his life first.

LILY: No. Now. While he's asleep. Let's put him in my car and take him into town and turn him in.

ARCHIE: He'd die on the trip. If you want him to live, we have to keep walking.

LILY: That car is the only reason we even stayed here two minutes, isn't it? He wouldn't ride in my car! Outlaws don't ride in cars, I guess. Well how's he going to get around anymore? What is he going to do if we save him?

ARCHIE: What will you do if we don't?

LILY: I'll do just fine! You give me one good reason for saving his life! It's over anyway and he knows it. That's why he pulled this stunt.

ARCHIE: You were his last chance, Lily. He had to take it.

LILY: Yours is the life worth saving here. If you leave right now, you can hop that early train. When the crew comes back tomorrow, I'll explain everything and you'll be on your own.

ARCHIE: I couldn't just disappear, Lily.

LILY: There's nothing for you here except winding up like Henry.

ARCHIE: I'm nothing like Henry and you know it.

LILY: Not now you aren't, but you wait. You'll get his work now that he's gone, won't you? It was that work that killed him. You'll dry up, Archie, just like he did.

ARCHIE: I'll get his share of the ranch, too, if I do his work.

LILY: Is that what you want, Archie? Twice as much desert to blow away. Your mother can get along without you. What are you so afraid of?

ARCHIE: Was that story true, about Delta, Colorado?

LILY: Yeah. Roy Luther told me the same thing. He ran away. Fast as he could.

ARCHIE: But why?

LILY: To get away, Archie. To live. So he could hide. It's not fair. I hate it.

ARCHIE: There's no way you can *hide* out here. I stand in the middle of our land and I think the only way out is straight up. I can see for fifty miles in any direction. I mean, if I could be in two places at once, I could ride a horse for a whole day and see myself.

(Lily doesn't understand.)

ARCHIE: I could see where I started from where I got to after riding all day. The only thing that ever really gets out of where we live is the train.

OUTLAW *(Sudden, unprovoked.)* Bill! Fred! *(Then falling back into Lily's arms.)*

ARCHIE: Good! He woke up on his own that time!

LILY: *(Almost tenderly.)* Whenever they were planning to rob a bank, Tom would always work a local ranch for a few months first. Get to know the town, you know. I always thought some of those ranchers missed his working their horses more than they missed their money in the bank. I guess he thought I'd bring him some beautiful horse to ride back tonight. I just...didn't think about it. I...forgot.

ARCHIE: What was it like when you...the old days, with him?

LILY: He'd blow in like the breath of God, horse sleek and black, and all you'd see was his flyin' coat and this big hat, and he'd make everybody else I'd ever met look real tired. And he knew you wanted him, and you did. Soon as you saw him you had to have him. That's still true. That's what happened to Henry.

ARCHIE: He'll make it. We'll pull him out of this. And then all you have to do is take that new picture he's got for you and burn it. Henry was an expert and Henry wouldn't have recognized him if Tom hadn't said Delta, Colorado, Bill and Fred.

LILY: He would never let me do that, Archie. You saw how proud he was of that new picture.

ARCHIE: So burn it.

LILY: But then what do I do with him? Drug his coffee when he gets mean?

ARCHIE: He loves you. He's old and he needs you.

LILY: But what about me? I'm not as old as he is. I'm not through yet!

ARCHIE: I don't blame him for wanting to look at you again.

LILY: He could've just asked me to send him a picture.

ARCHIE: No, I mean it. Your skin looks so soft.

LILY: And I have all the softest parts covered up. You should see *them*. *(She means this to sound irritated, so she is just as surprised as Archie when it comes out so seductively.)*

ARCHIE: Now why did you say that?

LILY: Sounds good, huh?

ARCHIE: I just never heard it before, that's all.

LILY: You really are a virgin, huh? Saving yourself for some church girl could be a real mistake, Archie.

ARCHIE: Dad says not to worry about it. There's nothing to it.

LILY: Dad...is wrong.

ARCHIE: *(After a moment.)* Well, if you want to tell me something I should know, you know, just one or two little things just to get me started...

OUTLAW: *(Eyes opening, slowly gaining consciousness.)* Lily?

ARCHIE: He's alive!

LILY: *(Smiling at Archie.)* Right here, Tom.

OUTLAW: Archie?

ARCHIE: *(Really pleased.)* You bet.

OUTLAW: Henry?

ARCHIE: No Henry.

OUTLAW: Oh that's right. I'm sorry.

ARCHIE: We've been through that already.

LILY: Can you sit up?

ARCHIE: *(Reaching in the Outlaw's pocket.)* Got something for you, old man. Nice piece of mint. Gonna cut that bad taste in your mouth. Here, open up. *(Taking some for himself.)* Thanks. Don't mind if I do.

LILY: I never knew how he got that mint smell. I don't think it grows wild around here. He must have it planted somewhere.

ARCHIE: From what I feel in his pocket, he could have it planted in there.

(She laughs.)

ARCHIE: Tastes good. I see why he likes it.

OUTLAW: What happened?

LILY: You tried to kill yourself. You took the morphine.

ARCHIE: You threw some of it up. That's tomatoes there on your coat. And we walked the rest of it out of you.

OUTLAW: Why did you do that? It would be all over by now.

ARCHIE: You asked us to. You said don't let me die.

OUTLAW: Well, damn.

ARCHIE: We saved your life. You should say more than well, damn.

OUTLAW: You're some kid, Archie. You walked for me all night, and now you're gonna talk for me all day. What do you want me to say?

ARCHIE: Ask Lily to marry you.

OUTLAW: I can't. I don't have any money.

ARCHIE: You've got a suitcase full of money!

OUTLAW: No.

ARCHIE: There's forty–fifty thousand dollars in that case!

OUTLAW: I said no. Look for yourself.

(Archie goes over and opens the satchel. He bends over it, looks through several layers and closes the satchel without saying anything, but he is shocked by what he sees.)

OUTLAW: I'm so sleepy.

ARCHIE: *(Very sympathetic.)* We wore you out, I guess. Kicked you, punched you, slapped you. Fought the Pinkertons with you all night. You took a real beating all right. *(To Lily.)* Is it okay for him to sleep now?

LILY: I think so. I think it would be good. There's still a few hours left before morning.

ARCHIE: You were going to ask Lily to marry you.

OUTLAW: You saved my life. I owe you something. *(To Lily.)* Lily, I've always loved you. I'm not much anymore. Will you have me? Will you marry me?

LILY: *(A fairly serious look.)* What do you think, Archie? Should I marry this outlaw?

ARCHIE: *(Beaming.)* It was my idea!

LILY: I think you're right. Yes, Tom, I'll marry you. But it better be tomorrow or I don't ever want to see you again.

OUTLAW: I can't live in town.

LILY: I have a farm. There's a house. There are horses.

OUTLAW: Good horses?

LILY: Not yet.

ARCHIE: That's your part. You got work to do when you wake up.

OUTLAW: Farm. *(And he drifts off into what looks like normal sleep.)*

LILY: We should sleep too. I feel terrible.

ARCHIE: I feel great! I never saved anybody's life before. The way I feel, I could thresh this whole field myself before they get back.

LILY: *(Enjoying his thrill.)* I bet you could, Archie.

ARCHIE: We did it! We saved his life! We really did it! The fight was Henry's fault anyway, mostly. He got to telling that story and things just got all out of hand. Tom tried to tell Henry not to come after him. Why, as far as Tom's concerned, it was just about self-defense, don't you think?

LILY: I'm not thinking about it.

ARCHIE: Saving somebody's life! That's got to be the best feeling in the whole world.

LILY: It's in the top three anyway.

ARCHIE: Did you see, Tom even knew my name when he woke up. He'll have you, that farm, those horses. He'll have a whole new life. And you, you'll have him. You sure he's all right here?

LILY: He's out till morning, I'm sure. How old are you, Archie?

ARCHIE: Seventeen.

LILY: *(Standing up.)* That's old enough. I need a favor.

ARCHIE: Well you just name it! I done all I could for both of them and they neither one deserved it probably. So you just tell me what it is and I'll do it.

LILY: I want you to take me in the cookshack or wherever your bed is, someplace warm where—

ARCHIE: God, yes. You must be exhausted.

LILY: —we can lie down. I want you to take off all these hotel clothes I've got on and I want you to make love with me. And if you'd like to dance first, that's all right. Or if you want to have a drink of whiskey, that's fine too. The only thing you can't do is say no. Don't say anything.

ARCHIE: You don't have to thank me, if that's what you're trying to do. I couldn't just let him die here.

LILY: *(Very firm, and very fast.)* I said you couldn't say anything. You must learn to shut up, Archie, and you must never…ever…assume that you know why anybody is doing anything.

ARCHIE: *(Gets the message.)* I said I would do whatever you wanted and I meant that.

LILY: *(Now much more personal.)* I don't know what's going to happen in the morning. He could wake up mean and kill us both. Or he could take off for Bolivia or just disappear for another ten years. Then again, he might take you up on your offer and marry me. So, this is just a little waiting time before we know what is going to happen. It's free clear time. We might as well be all alone in the whole world. And whatever happens in the morn-ing, I won't be seeing you very often, and you are the first person I have genuinely liked in a long time. And if you start threshing wheat, I'll end up helping you, and it'll kill me. This way, unless I've forgotten what to do, which is possible, because it's been ten years I've spent waiting for that man, we're both going to feel a lot better. Now, take my head in your hands and kiss me.

(Her speech has affected a considerable change in Archie. He seems taller, more poised.)

ARCHIE: *(After the kiss.)* Dancing, or drinking first…would just waste our time, don't you think?

LILY: You're going to do just fine.

ARCHIE: You are the most beautiful woman I have ever seen.

LILY: You're catching on real fast, Archie. I knew you would.

ARCHIE: I even have one of Mother's quilts.

LILY: Sh-h-h.

(And Lily smiles and a single light remains on the sleeping Outlaw as Archie and Lily step into the cookshack. There is a change in the lighting as we go from night to dawn. Then morning light comes up as Archie and Lily walk out of the cookshack, Archie carrying a coffeepot, Lily a skillet and some eggs. Lily has a quilt around her shoulders.)

ARCHIE: I guess it would be an engineer. The railroad...I don't know, It's important to me. I could sit there all day, swap stories with the fireman, check my pressure gauge, watch the sky cloud up, look out back at where we've been, see our smoke...Chief engineer on the Overland Flyer. What a job. *(Pauses.)* Or the war could need me, I guess.

(They sit down near the fire.)

LILY: The war would've had you already if they'd elected that Teddy Roosevelt.

ARCHIE: My dad says President Wilson is just plain yellow. Wouldn't last two weeks as sheriff of Clovis.

LILY: I'd like to see New York.

ARCHIE: Me too. Know what they've got there? Crowds.

(She laughs.)

ARCHIE: I want to bump into things, people, cars...I don't even know what things. I don't know what I'm talking about. Do you believe there's airplanes?

LILY: *(Laughs.)* Oh, Archie. This is going to make you so mad. I've seen one!

ARCHIE: You have not! You saw a picture of one. I've seen a picture of one. I want to see one fly over my head. Would you ride in one?

LILY: Three years ago, I took the train to St. Louis. It's as far east as I've been. That Teddy Roosevelt was up in an airplane with somebody called the Wright Brothers Flying Team. We were all down there watching him. He was waving to us. We were waving at him. He got so excited waving he almost fell out of the plane! Oh, it was the best day. People were standing around saying things like takeoff and air pocket. *(Her excitement is unlike anything we've seen from her to this point.)*

ARCHIE: Why didn't you tell me this before?

LILY: It's the only story I know. I was saving it for you.

ARCHIE: It's the best story I ever heard.

LILY: There are plenty more out there. All you have to do is get on the train.

ARCHIE: *(Defensively.)* Things happen here. Things are changing here too. I want to be here when it happens. People like me have to stay here and make it happen.

LILY: When it happens here, Archie, it will be secondhand. But I'm not going to say any more about it. You know what I think. Now, tell me how your brother got his hand eaten by the catfish.

ARCHIE: No, you tell me what else you saw in St. Louis.

(Before Lily can answer, the Outlaw stirs and we see that he is awake. Lily and Archie exchange pleased looks.)

ARCHIE: *(Much too bright.)* Good morning!

OUTLAW: Hold it right there!

(The Outlaw is seriously disoriented, and at the sound of Archie's voice, he springs up, then dives back down beside the cookshack and holds the gun on them. Archie protects Lily by moving in front of her.)

ARCHIE: Easy, buddy. It's just us.

OUTLAW: Buddy?

LILY: It's all right, Tom.

OUTLAW: *(Very grumpy, stands up.)* The hell it is!

ARCHIE: How do you feel?

OUTLAW: Bad.

LILY: We've got the coffee all ready.

ARCHIE: How about some eggs?

OUTLAW: *(He grabs his satchel.)* I gotta get out of here.

LILY: We can have some coffee first. And I'm hungry.

OUTLAW: Good-bye, Lily. Boy.

ARCHIE: Now, you wait a minute. We walked you around for hours, just the two of us, and it was cold out here and you're heavy, mister. We saved your life last night.

OUTLAW: Yeah, and if I don't get going, that threshing crew will come back and you'll get another chance to save my life. You may not care if your brother is dead, but your crew boss is gonna care that he's a man short today. I already said good-bye. That's all you're gonna get! *(Turns to go.)*

ARCHIE: You're on foot, remember? *(A pause.)* Only way out of here's in that car of hers. *(Then having a little fun.)* If you act nice, though, she might let you drive.

LILY: How many eggs, Tom?

OUTLAW: Just two.

LILY: And bacon?

OUTLAW: I'd rather have peaches. Are there any peaches?

LILY: *(Getting up, starting for the cookshack.)* I'll look. Archie?

ARCHIE: I'm not hungry.

OUTLAW: You are too. You should have some eggs. You like peaches?

ARCHIE: *(Setting the frying pan on the fire.)* Okay. Same as him.

(Lily goes into the cookshack as the Outlaw sits down.)

ARCHIE: They won't be back before noon. Probably not till six. It's Sunday. Can't miss church.

(The Outlaw nods.)

ARCHIE: Do you remember what you said last night?

OUTLAW: I didn't say a thing.

ARCHIE: You asked Lily to marry you. She said yes.

OUTLAW: Out of my head, I guess.

ARCHIE: *(Angry now.)* And you asked me to look in your case, there.
(This disturbs the Outlaw.)

OUTLAW: *(Firm, hostile.)* Nobody looks in my case.
(Lily comes out with the can of peaches and some bowls, which she hands to Archie.)

LILY: *(Starting to cook the eggs.)* Now, it won't be but just a minute.

OUTLAW: *(Brightly.)* So, got away again, did I?

LILY: You had help.

OUTLAW: I guess I should thank you.

ARCHIE: *(Angry.)* I wondered when you'd get around to that.

OUTLAW: You didn't have to do it, so I don't have to thank you. You think you always know the right thing to do, boy, well you don't. Maybe I was ready for it. Maybe if you knew about anything besides egg hunts, you'd have let me die. I mean, what do you know about anything, Archie?

ARCHIE: It was Henry told you about the egg hunts. And Henry's dead. I know about that.

LILY: *(Insisting that they both calm down.)* We'll just eat out of the skillet, here.
(She hands them each a fork and we have a moment of peace.)

OUTLAW: *(As they begin to eat.)* I love eggs. Thing I don't understand is how something so good can come from a chicken. A chicken!

ARCHIE: *(Matter-of-fact.)* I like fried chicken.

OUTLAW: Me too. With biscuits and gravy.

LILY: There are chickens on the farm.

ARCHIE: Her farm. Remember about her farm? Where you're going to live with her?

OUTLAW: Can't stand 'em. Make me nervous. Dirty animals. Shouldn't even be called animals.

ARCHIE: They're not. They're birds.

OUTLAW: They're ugly. They can't even fly.

ARCHIE: They lay eggs for you. They die to make your fried chicken.

OUTLAW: I couldn't live with chickens and that's the end of it.

ARCHIE: Cattle?

OUTLAW: Cattle are dumb.

ARCHIE: Crops?

OUTLAW: Work.

LILY: Just horses then. The horses on the farm are—

OUTLAW: Have to be young to work horses.

LILY: There are young people for hire.

OUTLAW: I don't like young people either. Jumpy. I don't like any of it. I only like eggs.

LILY: No chickens. I promise.

OUTLAW: No. No nuthin'. No marriage. No farm. No nuthin'.

(And there is a terrible pause, while everybody understands what has just been said.)

ARCHIE: You are so dumb. Nobody cares about outlaws anymore. You should've killed me, instead of Henry. He was your last real admirer and you shot him.

LILY: *(Trying to be calm.)* How are we going to wash these dishes?

ARCHIE: *(Bitter, hostile.)* Leave 'em. They'll figure it out! A new grave and dirty dishes. Somebody came in here, killed Henry and ate breakfast.

OUTLAW: They're gonna think you killed him! How about that! After we leave, there's gonna be one gun with one shot fired and one dead man with one bullet in him...and you. Dammit all, you're gonna get the credit for my good shot.

ARCHIE: You killed my brother and I saved your life!

OUTLAW: And I wouldn't tell anybody if I were you.

ARCHIE: *(Defensive.)* They'll understand. It was the exact right thing to do.

OUTLAW: It's as wrong as it can be, boy. It's one of your new ideas and it's nothin' but trouble. You wait and see.

ARCHIE: That's ridiculous.

OUTLAW: If you had an inch of guts you'd kill me back, and that's what they're all gonna say, the crew, your dad, all of 'em! Aren't they. I can hear 'em now. "So what'd you do, Archie?" "You did what, Archie?" That's exactly what they'll say. Isn't it!

ARCHIE: I don't know what they'll say.

OUTLAW: You do too. It's exactly what they'll say!

ARCHIE: What if it is? That doesn't make it right. It only means they're as backward as you and Henry.

OUTLAW: No, boy. You should've shot me. You have to kill 'em while you got the chance, or else you'll just have to fight 'em again some other day.

ARCHIE: Well I don't believe that.

OUTLAW: Well I'm glad I'm not gonna be there for the future then. This ain't something Jesse James made up, boy. This is how things are...here.

ARCHIE: *(Very strong.)* Were...here.

OUTLAW: *(Stronger still.)* Are! Everywhere!

ARCHIE: No! Not anymore. Not everywhere! No! Just out here in this damn scrub country. We're so far away from everything, everybody acts like there's no rules at all and anybody can just do whatever they like—well they can't. Or if they can, I don't have to sit here and watch them, not anymore. I've got my own ideas about how people should live and this ain't it. No sir.

OUTLAW: I shot the wrong boy all right. You're scared.

ARCHIE: *(Rejecting both ideas out of hand, suddenly seems very alert, self-possessed, proud.)* I am not. I've got a better idea. *(Picks up the Outlaw's satchel.)*

OUTLAW: That's mine.

ARCHIE: *(Triumphant, taking charge.)* I'm going to burn them!

OUTLAW: You Will not! You put that down! They're all I've got!

ARCHIE: She's all you've got but you don't know it. Once they're gone, you'll have a chance of finding that out.

OUTLAW: *(Pulls his gun.)* You give them to me!

(Archie pulls a wanted poster out of the satchel and crumples it up.)

ARCHIE: You'll have to kill me for them. I don't think you will. Wouldn't be fair. Actually I like that about you. That and the mint. *(Throwing the poster in the fire.)*

OUTLAW: *(Archie is right, puts the gun away.)* It won't make any difference. They'll still know who I am.

ARCHIE: Good then. I have your permission.

(Archie upends the satchel, dumping all the newspaper articles, wanted posters and other bits of evidence of the Outlaw's exploits on the fire.)

ARCHIE: *(Very formal.)* All the outlaws are dead. McCarty was an outlaw. McCarty must be dead.

LILY: And the only picture we have of him is twenty years old, so who is this old-timer we got here?

ARCHIE: *(Now much more personal.)* You can't just keep riding around. She loves you. You can forget everything that's happened and start all over.

OUTLAW: If I forget everything that's happened, then what do I have that she would want, boy?

ARCHIE: How should I know? But she said she would marry you so there must be something.

OUTLAW: *(To Lily.)* Look, I was pretty groggy last night. I don't remember any of this.

LILY: That's what I said all right.

OUTLAW: Boy I sure don't know why.

ARCHIE: Maybe she likes your talk. *(Pauses a moment.)* Come on. Do you ever know why anybody does anything?

LILY: I also said it better be today or I never want to see you again.

(And there is another pause, but this one is much more pleasant. This one has some acceptance in it.)

OUTLAW: *(Looking at Lily, but talking to Archie.)* Go ahead. Burn the satchel too, why don't you?

ARCHIE: *(Holding it out to him.)* That'd be wasteful. Nice case.

OUTLAW: *(Looks at Lily, then at Archie.)* Keep it.

ARCHIE: *(Dusting it off; looking at it.)* Thanks. I will. I'm gonna need something like this. *(To Lily.)* Do me a favor.

LILY: I owe you one.

ARCHIE: Write to my mother. It's Olivia Tucker, Clovis. Tell her to take care of herself. Tell her—

LILY: —You did what you could. You'll write when you can.

ARCHIE: Yeah. Thanks.

OUTLAW: Running away, huh, Archie? They'll know you did it for sure now. Gonna go east? Where they do things civilized?

ARCHIE: I don't know where I'm going. I'm just getting on the train. There's just got to be some town that makes some sense.

OUTLAW: Go east. You'll fit right in.

ARCHIE: Prissy little boy like me.

OUTLAW: Exactly.

(And Archie heads for the cookshack to gather up his things.)

ARCHIE: *(As he steps up into the cookshack.)* He needs a bath.

OUTLAW: The hell I do!

LILY: I'll see that he gets it.

(As Archie is inside the cookshack, she and the Outlaw try to talk again.)

LILY: It was the car, wasn't it. If I had come on a horse, none of this would have happened. You just didn't want to ride away in an automobile.

OUTLAW: Just seemed awful fancy, that's all.

LILY: That didn't used to be a problem for you.

OUTLAW: I liked a fancy girl, all right. I sure did.

LILY: Well, then…

OUTLAW: I'm gonna need a new coat. Long, gold color.

LILY: I think we can handle that.

(And he stands there a moment, just looking at her.)

OUTLAW: Now just how, exactly, are you gonna "see" that I get my bath?

LILY: Oh I'll draw the water, hand you the brush, get myself a beer, pull up a chair and watch. You remember.

OUTLAW: Yeah, it's all comin' back to me now.

LILY: But we'll have to call you something else in town. Tom McCarty is dead.

OUTLAW: It won't work. Roy Luther will know it's me.

LILY: He'll call you whatever you want. He'll call you Clara Mae if you buy him a beer.

OUTLAW: I could be Doc. How about Doc. I was courtin' a Doc's daughter so they called me Doc. It's a joke.

LILY: Doc is good.

OUTLAW: Doc it is.

(And now Archie comes out of the cookshack carrying his things, one of which must be his mother's quilt all rolled up.)

LILY: *(Walking over to him, kissing him.)* Good-bye, Archie.

ARCHIE: I'll send you picture postcards, so don't sell the hotel or move or anything.

LILY: Send me one from France.

ARCHIE: From the war if I get there.

LILY: From France. From New York. From France.

ARCHIE: *(As the Outlaw takes her arm.)* You bet I will. Good-bye, Lily.

OUTLAW: Come on, girl. *(Practically dragging her now.)* A war is just what you need, runt.

ARCHIE: The name's Archie.

OUTLAW: That's a runt name, for sure. Come *on,* girl. *(Walks offstage.)*

LILY: *(Backing away toward the Outlaw.)* Goodness and mercy.

ARCHIE: Huh?

LILY: *(A blessing.)* ...follow you all the days of your life.

ARCHIE: *(Affectionately.)* Oh yeah. What do you think the chances of that are?

LILY: I don't know. Fair.

ARCHIE: Good-bye, Lily.

LILY: *(As she turns to join the Outlaw.)* Let's get out of here. They could be back anytime. It's almost noon.

(Archie watches her go, then walks up to Henry's grave and takes a look around the camp area. Finally, he seems ready to go.)

ARCHIE: Jesus God in heaven, it's Archie Tucker from Clovis, New Mexico. And I know you can see me, so you must've seen everything that went on down here tonight and listen, I want to know… *(Very flip and irritated.)* Was this all your idea? *(Pauses.)* Because if it was…go work on somebody else for a while. I've got things to do. *(Starts to walk off, then stops when he hears Lily's voice.)*

LILY'S VOICE: Well, what are you waiting for? Get in. The handle's right there on the door.

OUTLAW'S VOICE: Just getting the feel of her, that's all. Real smooth, isn't she.

LILY'S VOICE: Real shiny too. Wait till it's light. You'll see.

(And as we hear the car doors slam, Archie has something else to say to God.)

ARCHIE: Well, okay. I do appreciate what you did for me with that coyote back on the road there, so I'm grateful. Thank you. I mean, I do want to stay in touch.

(Archie pauses, knowing he won't be in touch as often as he has been in the past, but excited about what lies ahead for him. We hear the cars engine start, then drive off.)

ARCHIE: Tell you what. First time I get up in one of those airplanes. You keep your eye on ol' Archie Tucker. I'll… *(Raises his hand in a fond salute and smiles.)* wave to you.

(The lights, which by now are down to a single light on Archie's face, black out, as the sound of a train whistle and the faint strains of some World War I song end the play.)

THE END

Traveler in the Dark

Traveler in the Dark was originally produced by the American Repertory Theatre, Cambridge, Massachusetts, Robert Brustein, Artistic Director, in February 1984 in a production directed by Tom Moore. The cast was as follows:

Stephen . . . . Damion Scheller
Sam . . . . Sam Waterston
Glory . . . . Phyllis Somerville
Everett . . . . Hume Cronyn

The following year, *Traveler in the Dark* premiered on the West Coast at Center Theatre Group of Los Angeles at the Mark Taper Forum, Gordon Davidson, Artistic Director, in a production directed by Mr. Davidson. The cast was as follows:

Stephen . . . . Scott Grimes
Sam . . . . Len Cariou
Glory . . . . Deborah May
Everett . . . . Claude Akins

INTRODUCTION

I wrote this play because I was very confused about the relationship between me and my mind. I had always thought being smart was some kind of protection. But it isn't, really, and I had just learned, or rather, just accepted that. What I felt as I sat down to write was that all my mind did on most days, was make things worse.

And indeed, according to the critics, what my mind did here was make up my worst play yet.

I mean, critics usually hate the play you write after you win the Pulitzer, but they really hated this one. Jack Kroll called me the "crisis laureate." And an LA critic's review was so vicious as to make me decide to stop writing for four years. Why did they hate it? I don't know. Maybe because it's the kind of philosophical writing that's only supposed to be done by Brits, or maybe because it talks about faith, and faith is something we don't talk about in the theatre, or maybe because the main character is a smart rich doctor who isn't happy, and critics don't care about that, or maybe they hated it because it doesn't work, or hasn't yet. (I heard there was a great production in Canada.) Maybe it's actually very good and is just waiting for the right production, or the right actor.

It's all very mysterious, that is, not given to us to know.

All I in fact know, is that my great friend Susan Kingsley died three days before the play opened. And all the writing and thinking I had done about death in this play did not help at all.

CHARACTERS

STEPHEN: a pale twelve-year-old boy, the son of Glory and Sam. He is a smart boy who speaks quietly and hasn't watched much television or played with many other children. He has an alert, questioning manner, a fierce respect for his father, and a more childlike love for his mother.

SAM: a world-famous surgeon. He is a brilliant loner, a man who has found his problems not quite worthy of his skills in solving them. He can seem preoccupied, impatient, and condescending. But he can also be counted on to handle any situation. His sense of humor is what makes you put up with his infuriating personal security.

GLORY: a lovely woman, who takes her responsibilities as a wife and mother quite seriously. She speaks quickly and laughs easily. She is blessed with a rare grace, an elegance of spirit, and nobody understands how on earth she has stayed married to Sam for all these years.

EVERETT: a country preacher, Sam's father. He is a one-time fire-breathing evangelist who now spends his time burying the same people he worked so hard to save. Everett has gotten old, but Sam, in particular, has not noticed this. He is a great favorite with the ladies, has a wizard's command of the language, and a direct, personal relationship to God and the heavenly hosts.

Traveler in the Dark

ACT I

The play takes place in the overgrown garden of a country preacher's house.
There are stone animals, including one large goose, stone benches, a crumbling
stone wall and a small pond. Various objects are imbedded in the wall—toys,
mainly, but also such household objects as cups and saucers. It is not important
that these objects be seen by the audience. In fact, the less impressive this gar-
den appears, the better. It is Sam's connection to the garden that is important,
not ours.

    Sam comes out the back door onto the porch, then walks down the steps
and into the garden. He smiles and nods, happy to see it again. As he walks
through the leaves, he kicks a hidden toy, bends over, picks it up, and recognizes
it as an old toy car of his. He brushes the leaves out of it, then races it up his
arm. Then he puts the car back in the wall and walks to the other side of the
garden, where he discovers a geode. He picks it up, looks at the upstairs win-
dow of the house, then puts the geode back where it was. Now, Sam sees that a
section of the wall is completely gone, and with it, apparently, the stone goose.
He begins to lift the rock back into place. Glory opens the back door and calls out.

GLORY: Sam?

SAM: I'm out here. Come. Look.

GLORY: Don't tell me now. Let me guess. *(She looks around.)* It's the backyard.

SAM: It's Mother's garden.

GLORY: I'm sorry. *(She walks into the garden.)*

SAM: There are all kinds of stone animals, rabbits and things down there, somewhere, and watch where you step. One of those piles of leaves is a pond.
(Now he sees the stone goose buried under a pile of rock.) Wait a minute. *(He*
lifts the goose up and puts her in her rightful place on the wall.) There she is.
Mother.

GLORY: *(Shakes her head.)* Sam…

SAM: This place is a mess. Dad never did like this garden. He said Mother
should save her knees for church.

GLORY: Sam, I'm worried about Stephen. He doesn't understand.

224

SAM: *(Going to the old tool chest near the porch.)* What's there to understand? Mavis is dead.

GLORY: Sam, she was more than your head nurse. Mavis carried a puzzle for Stephen in every purse she owned. She was his friend. He doesn't believe it.

SAM: *(As he sweeps the top of the wall with a whisk broom.)* He will. He'll be fine. Nobody ever died on him before, that's all. He'll get the hang of it, you'll see.

GLORY: He's upstairs right now going through all your old books.

SAM: That's all right, too. They can't hurt him now. Here, hold this a minute. *(He hands her a stone rabbit, while he cleans out the space in the wall where it belongs.)*

GLORY: Stephen needs you to explain this to him, Sam. I try to get him to talk about it, but he won't. You've got to tell him something that will make him feel better.

SAM: Like what?

GLORY: If I knew like what, I'd tell him myself.

SAM: What did you say to make *you* feel better?

GLORY: I don't feel better.

SAM: See what I mean?

GLORY: *(Irritated with him.)* But I want to feel better, and so does Stephen.

SAM: There isn't anything to say. Mavis waited too long to have herself checked. I did the operation. She died. Stephen knows all of that already.

GLORY: But he doesn't know what it means.

SAM: It doesn't mean anything. It's just…bad luck. *(He takes the stone rabbit from her and replaces it in the wall.)*

SAM: There. Doesn't that look better?

GLORY: *(Giving up for now.)* I called your dad. He had another funeral to preach this morning. He'll be here as soon as he can.

SAM: There's no reason for him to come home. We can just meet him at the church.

GLORY: He wants to see you, Sam, and the funeral's not 'til two o'clock. *(Sam resumes his work on the wall.)*

SAM: Is everybody coming back here or what after the funeral? I know Mavis didn't have any family left here.

GLORY: We're all going to Josie Barnett's.

SAM: Josie Barnett is a joke.

GLORY: Mavis loved her.

SAM: Mavis loved Dad.

GLORY: You don't want them all coming here, do you?

SAM: God, no.

GLORY: Well, then…

SAM: Is Josie Barnett…going to…try to…sing…at the funeral?

(She doesn't answer, so he knows the answer must be yes.)

SAM: Christ.

GLORY: Sam.

SAM: It's just an awful lot to pay for a free meal.

(Still she doesn't answer.)

SAM: Couldn't we just go to a restaurant?

GLORY: I don't believe you. Can't you let up on these people for one day? One day? Mavis was one of these people, you know, and your dad is one of these people, and I am one of these people. *(She pauses.)* And so are you.

SAM: Okay, okay.

STEPHEN: *(Calling from inside the house.)* Dad?

SAM: Out here, Stephen.

GLORY: *(To Sam.)* Will you try? Will you try to get him to talk about it?

SAM: If he wants to talk, I'll listen. *(Pause.)* If that's what you mean.

GLORY: You know what I mean.

(By now, Stephen is walking up to them, carrying a stack of old nursery rhymes and fairy tales.)

STEPHEN: What a great house! Why didn't we ever come here before?

SAM: It's just easier for Grandpa to visit us, Stephen.

STEPHEN: This garden is terrific! Did you put all these things in the wall?

SAM: No, Stephen, Mother did. *(Smiling at Glory.)* It was her way of teaching me not to leave my toys outside.

STEPHEN: I found a whole room of books, Dad, way at the top of the house. Like a forest of books growing up out of the floor. Just books and a rocking chair. I've never seen a room like that.

SAM: Those were Mother's books, Stephen.

STEPHEN: The ones I saw were all kids' books. *(Pause.)* But where did you sit? Is it your rocking chair or hers?

SAM: Hers.

STEPHEN: They're strange books, Dad. I didn't see a single one I'd ever seen before.

SAM: I know. Your books…make sense.

GLORY: I'm sure Grandpa would let you take some of them home if you wanted to.

SAM: Stephen's way too old for those books, aren't you?

GLORY: This is a beautiful *Mother Goose.* I can just see her holding you on her lap and reading this to you. *(And she reads.)*
Humpty Dumpty sat on a wall.
Humpty Dumpty had a great fall.
All the King's horses and all the King's men,
Couldn't put Humpty together again.

STEPHEN: I don't get it.

SAM: *(Laughs.)* Good boy.

GLORY: *(Carefully.)* Stephen, it just means, there are some things that once they happen they can't be fixed.

STEPHEN: But how did he get on the wall in the first place? Eggs can't climb.

SAM: *(Breaking the bad news.)* His…mother…laid him there.

GLORY: Sam.

STEPHEN: Then how did he fall? Eggs can't walk either.

SAM: She told him he was a man. See? She dressed him up in a little man's suit. He didn't know he could fall. He didn't know he could break. He didn't know he was an egg.

STEPHEN: So what happened to him? Did he run all over the sidewalk and people slipped on him or did he dry up in the sun or what?
(Sam tests a big stone and finds it loose.)

SAM: Something like that.

GLORY: *(Not pleased with Sam's answer.)* I'm sure somebody cleaned it up, Stephen.

STEPHEN: But who?

GLORY: Who do you think? *(Pause.)* Mom.

SAM: No. I think Mom fell off the wall the day before.
(Glory is irritated with Sam, but she does her best not to show it. Sam puts the big stone where it belongs, as Glory turns her attention to Stephen.)

GLORY: Now Stephen, the funeral is at two o'clock. But Grandpa's coming home first, and then we'll all go to the church together. He was sorry he couldn't be here to meet us when we got here, but he had another funeral to preach this morning.

STEPHEN: Okay.

GLORY: We'll have to be very careful what we say to Grandpa. Mavis called him every Friday night, you know, told him everything that had gone on at the hospital all week. He loved Mavis more than any of us did, I think. *(Pause.)* I know…he was disappointed when your dad fell in love with me instead of Mavis. There's nothing he likes better in this world than Mavis and your dad.

STEPHEN: Liked.

GLORY: What?

STEPHEN: Liked better. Nothing he liked better than Mavis and Dad.

GLORY: You don't stop liking people just because they die, Stephen.

SAM: Sometimes you like them better. Harry Truman, for example.

(Glory picks up another book and starts to look through it.)

STEPHEN: Can we go fishing while we're here? Mavis told me that's what you do in the country. You fish till you're hungry, eat till you're sleepy, then sleep till it's time to wake up and go fishing.

GLORY: I don't know why not.

SAM: We're not going to be here that long, Stephen.

GLORY: Do you want us to tell you what's going to happen at the funeral?

STEPHEN: Am I going to sit by myself?

GLORY: No, you'll sit with us.

STEPHEN: Then no. If I need to stand up or anything, you can just grab me.

(Sam gives Glory a "let-him-alone" look, and Glory returns his look, as if to say "this is what I was talking about.")

SAM: Stephen, is there anything you want to ask me about any of this?

STEPHEN: Do I have to say anything at the funeral?

SAM: No. And you don't have to listen, either.

(Glory doesn't think this is helping Stephen a bit. She tries to interest him in the book she has.)

GLORY: Now here's one I like, "The Princess and The Frog." See, Stephen? The princess kisses the frog and he turns into a prince.

(Sam makes some move that indicates he has understood her irritation.)

STEPHEN: You've got the frog colored in, Dad, but you made him all brown.

SAM: That's what color frogs are, Stephen.

STEPHEN: Now how could a frog turn into a prince?

GLORY: It was magic, Stephen. Magic always works.

SAM: *(A direct communication to Glory.)* Magic had nothing to do with it. The frog *believed* that the beauty could turn him into a prince. One kiss from her and he would be handsome, and play tennis, and mix martinis, and tell jokes at parties, just like all her other boyfriends. *(Pause.)* But years later, the prince started to turn, slowly at first, but finally and irreversibly, back into the frog he always was.

STEPHEN: It doesn't say that in this book.

SAM: *(Scraping the dirt off some of the toys that have fallen out of the wall.)* It doesn't have to. You are born a frog and that is it. It's not so bad, but it is *it*. Frogs should know better, but they don't.

STEPHEN: Then they're not as smart as they think they are.

SAM: Smart isn't magic, Stephen. It's just smart.

GLORY: That is not how the story ends.

SAM: *(Quite intense.)* It is how the story ends. The princess got old and the frog croaked.

(As Glory stares at him.)

SAM: Get another book, Stephen.

STEPHEN: *(Getting what he thinks Sam means.)* Go away, Stephen.

SAM: No. Come back. But no more fairy tales. There *are* some good books up there. *Call of the Wild. Lord of the Flies.* Read about Donner Pass.

(Stephen jumps down off the wall and goes into the house. There is a moment of silence.)

GLORY: *(After Stephen has gone.)* Is that your idea of help?

SAM: What?

GLORY: You, the frog, married me, the princess, and Humpty Dumpty was a hit-and-run.

SAM: He's old enough to know what happens.

GLORY: Nobody's old enough to know what you think happens.

SAM: I refuse to lie to him. He could live a long time *hoping* it will all work out.

GLORY: He could live a long time *having* it all work out, unless you convince him it's impossible and he doesn't even try.

SAM: What do you want me to say?

GLORY: Life is good.

SAM: When?

GLORY: All the time!

SAM: Like today, for example.

GLORY: No, not like today. People don't die every day.

SAM: Oh Glory, I'm afraid they do.

GLORY: Not people you know.

SAM: Oh, I see. It doesn't count if we don't know them.

GLORY: It doesn't hurt if we don't know them.

SAM: It doesn't matter, you mean.

GLORY: No, I don't mean that.

SAM: What *do* you mean?

GLORY: You tell him the wrong things.

SAM: I tell him the truth.

GLORY: And he believes you!

SAM: Well, I can't help that.

GLORY: He's a child!

SAM: I want a divorce.

GLORY: I want this day to be over.

SAM: *(After a moment.)* I do want a divorce. I want to leave here in the morning and take Stephen with me.

GLORY: You can go for the weekend, Sam, but Stephen has school on Monday.

SAM: Since we're having one funeral anyway, we might as well have the other one and be done with it. When we all wake up, this will *all* be over.

GLORY: What is the matter with you?

(Stephen opens the porch door, but they don't hear him. He starts to come down the steps, but then realizes what this conversation is about. He goes back up the steps, climbs quietly over the railing and sits, out of sight, behind a tree.)

SAM: I just never stopped to think about it, I guess. It doesn't make sense, this marriage. It never has. Ask your mother.

GLORY: It works well enough, Sam. It calms you down, and it keeps me from getting too comfortable. And no, we don't always agree on things…

SAM: We don't ever agree on things.

GLORY: But it's good for Stephen to hear both sides.

SAM: No. It confuses him. I'll tell Dad tonight, and in the morning I'll go over and tell your mother and then I'll get Stephen and go. I'll send you as much money as you need and you can have everything we own. All the houses, all the cars, everything.

GLORY: That's ridiculous.

SAM: Okay. I'll keep the cars.

(There is a long silence.)

GLORY: *(Finally.)* You're serious!

SAM: Always have been. *(Then overly cheerful.)* I thought you knew that.

GLORY: You're upset.

SAM: True.

GLORY: I mean you're upset about Mavis. You don't think you can work without Mavis. Well, leaving me isn't going to bring Mavis back to you.

SAM: Mavis has nothing to do with this.

GLORY: Nice work, doctor. Quick and clean. You find the tumor and you cut it out. You don't even need your fancy table or your hotshot team for this surgery, do you? You're so good, you can do it in the backyard.

SAM: Wherever.

GLORY: Look. Let's just get through the funeral, okay? And then if you still feel this way we'll talk about it when we get home.

SAM: I don't want to talk about it. I want to quit. I want to go somewhere else. I want to start over.

GLORY: Life doesn't start over. It starts, it goes on for a while, then it stops.

SAM: God that's gloomy.

GLORY: I sound like you!

SAM: No you don't. I would never say *that*. Mavis didn't have to die. There was a time she could have done something about it. This is that time for Stephen and me.

GLORY: You can't leave me.

SAM: You'll be okay. Move back here if you want. I know your mother has room out there.

GLORY: Of course I'll be okay. I'm talking about you. Do you have any idea what it takes to live your life?

SAM: I can probably figure it out.

GLORY: I know you can't take care of Stephen.

SAM: Stephen is old enough to take care of himself.

GLORY: Stephen would end up taking care of you. And you're important, so somebody should do all the things that allow you to work, but it shouldn't be Stephen.

SAM: We'll share it. I'll help him. He'll help me.

GLORY: I think we better wait till we get home to talk about this.

SAM: I think we're talking about it already.

GLORY: The answer is no.

SAM: Yes, well, it wasn't really a question, Glory.

GLORY: I'm going inside.

SAM: I'm not.

GLORY: Fine.

SAM: *(Staring at the goose.)* There once was a woman called Nothing-At-All
Who rejoiced in a dwelling exceedingly small.
A man stretched his mouth to its utmost extent
And down in a gulp both house and woman went.
(Stephen appears from behind the tree. He is holding a framed photo and another fairy-tale book.)

STEPHEN: *(Pointing to the photo.)* Is this you, Dad?

SAM: *(Startled by his presence.)* Stephen!

STEPHEN: Is this you in this picture?

SAM: *(Staring at the photo.)* Yes.

STEPHEN: Who is this with you?

SAM: That's Mother...and that's...Mavis.

STEPHEN: And it's Halloween I hope.

SAM: Yes.

STEPHEN: What were you? I can't tell.

SAM: Elves.

STEPHEN: Did Mavis tell you I lost her cat?

SAM: I gave her that cat.

STEPHEN: I know. I'm sorry, Dad.

SAM: When was this?

STEPHEN: Last Saturday. After the movies we went back to her apartment, and I asked Mavis if I could let Peaches out, only Mavis didn't hear me because she went in the bedroom to rest a little bit. But Peaches kept crying and scratching at the back door. So I opened it and she got away. When Mavis woke up, we looked and looked, but we couldn't find her anywhere. *(Pause.)* I guess Mavis didn't tell you because she didn't want you to be mad at me.

SAM: It's all right, Stephen. Cats just...go like that.

STEPHEN: Maybe Peaches knew something was wrong.

SAM: Maybe she did. *(Pause.)* Stephen, your mother and I were just talking—

STEPHEN: *(Quietly.)* I guess your birthday's going to be pretty lonely this year.

SAM: *(Pause.)* Yes. I guess it will be.

STEPHEN: I wouldn't like it if I had the same birthday as somebody. I mean, I know there are plenty of people born on the same day as me, but—

SAM: People used to ask Mavis where she met me, you know, and she'd say, "Oh, at the hospital. In the nursery." And then she'd say, "I hadn't been alive two hours when in came Sam Carter screaming at me already." *(Pause.)* That's a picture I'd like to see, all right. Dad and Mavis's dad staring through the glass window looking at the two of us side by side in our little beds. One howling boy for the preacher, and one rosy-faced dumpling for the custodian at the church.

STEPHEN: Mavis wasn't fat, Dad.

SAM: No. But I did have the idea that she put on her uniform in the morning, and then stepped on an air pump to puff herself up for the day.

STEPHEN: I'm not going to like Saturday much either.

SAM: She loved you so much, Stephen. You were the only little boy she had. You were so good to her, you gave her so much.

STEPHEN: All we ever talked about was you, Dad.

SAM: Yeah, well, she just loved to talk, Stephen. And I didn't leave her time to learn anything else. *(Pause.)* It never occurred to me that she would die, Stephen. It just didn't seem like something she'd do. I'm sorry I didn't warn you, I should have known it, my mother died, didn't she? I guess I just forgot.

STEPHEN: Yeah.

SAM: Well…

STEPHEN: Why do people read these books?

SAM: What?

STEPHEN: I know you told me not to read any more, but I was taking it back upstairs and I didn't get this one either.

SAM: Which one?

STEPHEN: I think Sleeping Beauty's father was a fool.

SAM: All right. But don't just say he was a fool. Prove it to me. Build your case.

STEPHEN: He gives a party for his daughter and he invites twelve of the thirteen fairies in the land. Twelve good fairies he invites. He does not invite the thirteenth fairy.

SAM: Because she's a bad fairy, that's right.

STEPHEN: But the bad fairy comes anyway, and now she acts even worse because she wasn't invited. "I have a gift for the little princess," she says. "When she is eighteen, she will prick her finger on a spinning wheel and die."

SAM: That's how it goes, all right.

STEPHEN: It's ridiculous. If you know you have a thirteenth fairy living in your country, and you know what she can do, then how, exactly, can you forget to invite her to a party?

SAM: Well…

STEPHEN: How did anybody that dumb get to be king?

SAM: He wasn't dumb. He just forgot.

STEPHEN: He forgets there's a bad fairy living there and look what happens. Everybody sleeps for a hundred years, till he wakes up with his kingdom turned into a jungle and some prince upstairs kissing his daughter.

SAM: *(Strangely affected by this story.)* He forgot because he didn't want to remember! He didn't want her to come to the party! The *last* person you want at that party is that thirteenth fairy. So you just hope she doesn't show up because you know if she does show up, there isn't a damn thing you can do about it.

STEPHEN: *(Reacting to his fathers anger.)* It's just a story, Dad.

SAM: Yeah, I know. That's why I never let you read them.

STEPHEN: But you read them.

SAM: *(Disclaiming all responsibility.)* Mother read them to me. *(Almost a confession.)* And then, when I learned how, yes, I would read them to her. *(Pause.)* Every day when I came home from school, here she'd be, with a glass of milk for me and a pile of things she'd found in the ground that day, like dragons' teeth, witches' fingers, and fallen stars. *(Then remembering so clearly.)* I would sit, there, where you are, and she would work. And we would sing. Her favorite Mother Goose was page twenty.

(He sings as Stephen is looking for it.)

SAM: We're all in the dumps
For diamonds are trumps,
The kittens have gone to St. Paul's.
The babies are bit,
The moon's in a fit
And the houses are built without walls.

STEPHEN: The houses are built without walls?

SAM: Yes.

STEPHEN: How could they stand up?

SAM: *(Suddenly very distant.)* She died before I could ask her that, Stephen.

STEPHEN: What was she like?

SAM: She was the gingerbread lady. Curly red hair and shiny round eyes and a big checked apron. Fat, pink fingers, a sweet vanilla smell, and all the time in the world. Sing to you, dance with you, write your name on the top of a cake.

STEPHEN: Did she die all of a sudden like Mavis?

SAM: Mother was sick for a long time, Stephen, but sick or not, everybody dies all of a sudden.

STEPHEN: I guess that was pretty hard, too, huh?

SAM: It was awful. I took it, well, like it happened to me instead of to her. I wouldn't eat. I broke things. But now, well, if she hadn't died, I'd be the biggest momma's boy you ever saw.

(Everett enters from the side of the house. He walks with some difficulty, but he's keeping his spirits up with an extraordinary act of will.)

EVERETT: Samuel!

SAM: Hello, Dad.

(They embrace, but it is difficult for them.)

SAM: *(A bit awkward.)* I'm sorry I couldn't save her.

EVERETT: *(Pulling away.)* You did your best, didn't you?

SAM: Yes.

EVERETT: Well, that's all anybody expects, Sam. *(Shifting his attention to Stephen.)* Hello, Stephen. Remember me?

STEPHEN: It's only been a year, Grandpa. *(Stephen gives him a small hug.)*

EVERETT: Where's your mother?

STEPHEN: Inside. Want me to go get her?

EVERETT: I'm glad she's here.

SAM: You knew she would come, Dad. *(He helps Everett.)* Here. Sit down.

EVERETT: I'm fine. I'm fine. Are you all right?

SAM: I'm fine.

EVERETT: You look tired, Sam.

SAM: I'm not tired, Dad. I'm just grown up.

EVERETT: I miss seeing you, son.

SAM: I'm sorry, Dad. They keep me pretty busy these days.

EVERETT: Oh I know. Mavis told me. *(His fatherly pride showing.)* She said you could do things nobody else even thought of. She said there were dead people standing in line at the water fountain because of you. She sent me all the clippings. I liked that one about the governor. That was a good picture of you.

(No response from Sam.)

EVERETT: Oh how she loved you, son. "Well," she'd say, "we had another miracle today."

(Another long silence.)

SAM: How was your other funeral? Who was it?

EVERETT: *(Glad to have something else to talk about.)* Connie Richards. I told her to come see you when she first got sick, but she wouldn't hear of it. She said you were too famous. You were too far away.

(Sam does not answer.)

EVERETT: She felt the same way about God. But I guess she figured she didn't have to get on the bus to go see Him.

(Everett reaches down to pat Sam, but he moves away, and Everett goes over to pat Stephen. He just needs to pat somebody, and Stephen is too polite to resist.)

STEPHEN: Where did you tell them she went, at the funeral?

SAM: Stephen, Grandpa's sermons are his business. He says what he has to say.

EVERETT: I told them she went to heaven.

STEPHEN: Why did you have to say that?

EVERETT: *(Ignoring Sam's silencing look.)* Because that's where she went.

STEPHEN: *(Doesn't believe this for a minute.)* And that's where she is right now, singing and flying around? It sounds like fairy tales to me.

EVERETT: Oh no, God's heard enough of her singing already. He'll have her light the candles or something.

STEPHEN: *(A conspiratorial look at Sam.)* They have candles in heaven? Isn't it too windy for candles?

EVERETT: If God wants a candle to stay lit, it stays lit. What they don't have in heaven is matches. But then, angels don't need matches. They just put their pointer finger up to it, like so, and poof, it's lit.

STEPHEN: *(Much simpler, actually childlike.)* How do they do that?

EVERETT: *(Sounding more like the wizard he is.)* It's because they're pure spirit now, Stephen. The life in them is like sparks, like fireworks. Oh, they could really light up the sky if they felt like it, but they don't want to show off, you know. They don't want people dying down here just to get in on the fun. But now, shooting stars…

STEPHEN: Meteors, you mean.

EVERETT: Right. That's somebody new up there. Somebody hasn't quite figured out how to control themselves. *(Suddenly flinging his arms out wide.)* Pow!

STEPHEN: Great!

SAM: *(Quietly, but firmly.)* Stephen, go find your mother. Tell her Grandpa's here.

(Stephen leaves.)

SAM: *(After a moment.)* That's enough, Dad.

EVERETT: Don't be mad at me, boy. I can't help talking about angels. I just know so many of them, now.

SAM: *(Being careful not to get angry.)* I don't want you telling Stephen there's a heaven and a hell, because if you do, I'll have to tell him who it is who assigns the rooms.

EVERETT: You do want him on the right waiting list, don't you?

SAM: I don't want him thinking about it at all. *(Then more calm.)* Let's just say, if there is a hell, if Stephen does go to hell, I'd like for it to be a surprise.

EVERETT: No grandson of mine is going to hell.

SAM: No grandson of anybody's is going to hell. There is no hell. There is no heaven. Life is summer camp and death is lights out. It's all just over, Dad. Time's up. The end. You lose.

EVERETT: Is that what you tell their families at the hospital?

SAM: What is there to say?

EVERETT: There's comfort.

SAM: There's all your friends waiting for you? There's your Heavenly Father with His arms open wide? No, no. I've been straight with them all along, so I'm not about to get to the end and lie. I do what I can and then we both just quit.

EVERETT: Mavis would never quit.

SAM: Mavis quit before I did. I briefed the team, I opened her up, but what did I find? Her bags were packed. She was checking out. She was going, as you say, home. No, I keep them out of God's hands as long as possible, so you just keep your sermons to yourself.

EVERETT: *(Carefully.)* Was Mavis in any pain?

SAM: No.

EVERETT: Did she...know it was happening?

SAM: No.

EVERETT: So she couldn't give you any...message for me.

SAM: No. *(Then trying to concentrate on something else.)* But she just bought a new car. I know she'd want you to have it. It has power steering and everything. We drove it down here for you. That's it... *(Motioning in that direction.)* out in the driveway.

EVERETT: I appreciate the thought, son, but I don't think I could... *(Pause.)* No. You were right to bring it.

SAM: Glory packed up all her clothes and put them in the trunk. We thought there might be people around here who could use them. Everything else, furniture and everything, was rented. Except her TV, and I took that in for the nurses' lounge. So, it's all done, I think.

EVERETT: That part's done, anyway. *(He notices the picture Stephen brought out before.)* Anything I have—of hers, you know—you can have it if you want it. I'd like to keep her letters, but after I die, they'll be yours too, of course, like everything else I have. Do you want this picture?

SAM: Stephen found it.

EVERETT: I always liked this one. *(Hoping Sam will say no.)* You don't want it, do you?

SAM: No.

EVERETT: Yes, I guess you have plenty of pictures of the two of you. They're probably all up and down the halls at the hospital.

SAM: Can we talk about something else?

EVERETT: I'm sorry, son. Just all those years of her hanging around you, I think of her as part of the family. Probably thought she'd be part of the family someday.

SAM: She loved you, Dad, not me.

EVERETT: Oh, she loved you, all right. If it hadn't been for you, she'd be right here, working at County General.

SAM: She was too good for your little hospital.

EVERETT: But not good enough for you.

SAM: We don't have to have this argument anymore, Dad. Mavis is not yours and she's not mine. She's dead.

(Stephen enters with a book of illustrated Bible stories.)

STEPHEN: Hey, I like this one about the whale. What does it mean? This guy, Jonah, gets swallowed by a whale and then the whale throws him up.

EVERETT: It means you can't run away from God, Stephen.

SAM: *(Annoyed that Everett is talking religion again.)* No, Stephen, it means you shouldn't go to sea in too small a boat.

(Glory comes out, wearing an apron and drying her hands on a dish towel.)

GLORY: Hello, Everett.

(They embrace.)

EVERETT: Glory Butler, you are still the prettiest girl in ten counties.

GLORY: Are you doing all right, Everett?

EVERETT: Yes I am, thank you.

GLORY: *(Remembering how distant this man can be.)* I hope you don't have this too often, two funerals in one day.

EVERETT: *(Making an effort to talk to her.)* Your mother was at the one this morning.

GLORY: How'd she look?

EVERETT: Rich.

GLORY: She does like to show it off, doesn't she?

EVERETT: All she could talk about were her two new fillies—both jumpers, she said. And she's got a new exercise boy. He was…there with her today.

GLORY: *(A knowing smile.)* Was he all dressed up, or was he just driving the car?

EVERETT: *(Confirming her worst fears.)* All dressed up.

GLORY: She's so funny. When Daddy died, she walked me up to the casket, held my hand and said, "Glory, I'm never going to be lonely again."

(Glory laughs and Everett smiles.)

EVERETT: I told her you were coming down for Mavis's funeral, but she said she wouldn't bother you here. *(A pause.)* Our house always was a little plain for her.

GLORY: I made us some sandwiches. They're on the counter if you want one.

EVERETT: I should eat something I guess. Don't you want one, Sam?

(No response from Sam.)

GLORY: We'll be there in a minute. *(Pause.)* I straightened up your kitchen a little. I hope you don't mind.

EVERETT: No. Just so you put it back the way it was before you leave.

GLORY: Everett, I was just trying to help. I'm sorry.

EVERETT: *(Walking toward Stephen.)* I know Stephen's hungry, aren't you?

STEPHEN: Grandpa?

EVERETT: What, son?

STEPHEN: If the people in heaven are all spirit, if they don't have any flesh anymore, how does God know who's who?

EVERETT: *(Putting his arm around Stephen, and walking him out of the garden.)* Spirit's how God tells us apart anyway, Stephen. When we get to heaven, why as far as He's concerned, we haven't changed a bit.

(Glory is left alone with Sam. Sam has a pair of snippers from the tool chest and is cutting the weeds that have grown up around the wall.)

GLORY: I'm beginning to see the garden now, Sam.

SAM: I don't know why I'm doing this. He'll just let it go again.

GLORY: Did you and Mavis play out here when you were kids?

SAM: *(Putting the snippers down.)* Maybe I've done enough.

GLORY: Where did your mother find these animals?

SAM: I don't know.

GLORY: *(As she picks one up.)* Was she strong enough to carry them? They're very heavy.

SAM: Please. *(Taking it away from her.)* Just leave them alone, okay?

GLORY: He won't let me touch anything in the house, and you won't let me touch anything out here. It's just me, I guess, I mean, your mother was... allowed to work here, wasn't she? Or maybe it's a museum, or a shrine.

SAM: What's the matter with *you?*

GLORY: *(Has to laugh.)* What's the matter with me.

SAM: Did you call your mother?

GLORY: I did, in fact. I told her you were leaving in the morning and taking Stephen with you.

SAM: And what did she say?

GLORY: She said she would see you at the funeral and tell you good-bye.

SAM: So we'll have something to talk about anyway.

GLORY: She said it was another woman. She said you and Mavis were...

SAM: ...having an affair? No.

GLORY: Someone else, then. Do you want to leave me for another woman?

SAM: I don't want another woman. I want you to be the woman I want.

GLORY: Can I have a straight answer please.

SAM: We've both had affairs. Haven't we.

GLORY: Well, that's it, I guess.

SAM: It what?

GLORY: The truth.

SAM: That is not the truth. That is just a fact. The truth is what the facts mean.

GLORY: I am so tired of your mind. You would've been so much better off without it.

SAM: I would have been nothing without it! With the exception of a mother who died and left me with the preacher, my mind is all I ever had. *(He stops.)* Except Stephen.

GLORY: *(She shakes her head.)* And your mother and Mavis and me.

SAM: Yes.

GLORY: Did you forget us for a moment?

SAM: No, I didn't forget you. But it *is* getting easier. There's only one of you left.

GLORY: What a lovely thing to say. What a great time we're having here. Such a good reason to come home and such a spirit of love and understanding. Just relax, Glory. This will all blow over in just a little while. He's always like this, but he's not always so much like this.

SAM: I'm not always like this.

GLORY: No. When you're sick, it's worse. When you're tired, it's worse. But the rest of the time you are exactly like this. You just don't notice it, because this is how you always are. Like I said.

SAM: Then why have you stayed with me.

GLORY: I don't know, it's not over yet. Something like that.

SAM: It is over.

GLORY: *(Picking up the Sleeping Beauty book.)* No, this is just the part where I sleep for a hundred years. Then the prince comes and I wake up.

SAM: Jesus Christ.

GLORY: I'm still here for two reasons. One is that you need me. And I have no idea why you need me but you do. I can feel it. I see it all the time. I don't understand at all, but I have no doubt whatsoever.

SAM: And what is the other reason?

GLORY: The other reason is my business. And I'm not about to tell you when you're threatening to leave me.

SAM: Well, I know it can't be that you're having a good time. You should've married that baseball player.

GLORY: If I had married Jerry Pine, I would've spent half my life at Yankee Stadium, wishing he wouldn't chew tobacco, and hoping he won't spit on national TV. *(A pause.)* Maybe I would have a better time without you. I could laugh and travel and give away Mother's money, but you...well... This is not a job that just anybody could do, you know, putting up with you.

SAM: So this is your chance. I'm offering you a way out.

GLORY: I want a way in, Sam.

SAM: There isn't any way in. There never was. You never had a chance. I married you to spite my father. *(Pause.)* There. Can you hate me now? Can I leave now?

GLORY: I know you loved me.

SAM: Do you?

GLORY: I know you love me now.

(He turns to go.)

GLORY: Where you going?

SAM: *(After a moment.)* I have to find Stephen before Dad turns him into a Christian.

GLORY: Let them alone. You can't change your father and you can't protect Stephen from the entire world. It's one thing to take away the television and give him *Scientific American* instead of *Mother Goose,* but Everett is his grandfather. Let them talk. Stephen can see what there is and decide for himself.

(Before Sam can answer, Everett comes back outside alone.)

EVERETT: Maybe you two been gone so long you forgot this, but we have a thing out here called respect for the dead.

GLORY: What?

EVERETT: And Glory, if you're going to your mother's, I wish you'd go on and go so we could have our funeral in peace.

GLORY: Everett, I don't know what you're—

EVERETT: Don't you realize what you're doing to that little boy?

GLORY: What did he tell you, Everett?

EVERETT: That he's leaving tomorrow with Sam and you're moving in with your mother. Is that right?

GLORY: He hears everything we say, Sam, I've told you that over and over again. Jesus Christ.

SAM: Why shouldn't he know? I'm just sorry I didn't tell him before he heard it through the wall, like that. He wasn't surprised, I'm sure. Divorce is not exactly unknown in the world. Now that he knows the truth, he'll feel better.

GLORY: *(To Everett.)* What did you say?

EVERETT: I didn't know what to say. I said, "Maybe Mom is just lonesome for the country. She'll get tired of it soon enough and be right back home, quick as quick."

(Very strong, as Sam shakes his head.)

EVERETT: I said that to make him feel better. I wanted him to feel better.

SAM: And he believed you?

EVERETT: I *saw* him feel a little better, yes.

GLORY: Thank you, Everett. You did the right thing.

SAM: Cover it up, that's right. Put a little Band-Aid on it. It worked with me, didn't it? I have spent my life straightening out the lies people have told him. No, Stephen, there is no Santa Claus. No, Stephen, when you die, you do not go to heaven. No, Stephen, people won't like you better because you're smart, they'll be afraid of you because you're smart. No, Stephen, love is not forever, and God is not good. And tomorrow is not another day. Tomorrow is this day all over again.

EVERETT: Well, wasn't he lucky to have you around.

GLORY: I'd better go find him.

EVERETT: I think that's a good idea.

(Glory goes into the house and Everett and Sam are left alone.)

SAM: I don't want to hear what you have to say about this, Dad. You don't know what you're talking about, and you're not going to change my mind.

EVERETT: That's as good a confession as I ever heard.

SAM: You never liked Glory in the first place. You should be happy I'm leaving her.

EVERETT: She's a good girl, and she's been a good mother to Stephen. Whatever is the matter between Glory and you…is probably you.

SAM: I see.

EVERETT: But it's your boy who'll end up paying for this, Sam.

SAM: Doesn't seem fair, does it? Well, I'm sorry, Stephen, that's just how God is. Suffer the little children to come unto me, for theirs is the wages of sin.

EVERETT: When somebody dies it makes everything hard, Sam, but what we all do is try not to make anything worse.

SAM: When somebody dies, you try to make it make a difference, make it mean something.

EVERETT: Sam, I never thought this marriage would work, you know that. But we're having a funeral today. Can't you take one day of your life to think about Mavis? God knows, you took everything else she had for your own use, but now you're even taking her funeral. *(Pause.)* I'm sure she's happy for you to have it, that's just how she was, but it makes me mad, Sam. You make too much noise, son. You always did. Relax. Grieve.

SAM: No. This marriage was never right, and I want it straight now.

EVERETT: After the funeral, just leave Stephen with me for a few days, and you and Glory go down to Green River, work this thing out.

SAM: I don't want to work it out. What could we work it out to? Back to where it was at the beginning? In the beginning was the word, and the word was *pretend.*

EVERETT: I saw that beginning, same as you, and there wasn't any pretend about it. You were hopeless. You drooled around here for years until Glory called you with that math problem. Here was poor Mavis practically polishing your shoes to get your attention. But no, all you wanted was the pretty little rich girl, swimming in her own private lake out there. But how was she ever going to notice the preacher's kid? So you took up cross-country, didn't you? And pretty soon, you could run the ten miles out to her farm, and still have the breath to stand there and smile.

SAM: Why don't you say what you mean. Divorce is a sin.

EVERETT: Sam, your mother used to say your marriage was like your favorite shirt. You could wear it day after day, and you could try to keep it clean, but sooner or later it was going to have to go in the wash. But as soon as it was clean, you could press it fresh, and put it back on, looking good as new.

SAM: I don't have a favorite shirt. And I don't need advice from you.

EVERETT: What does she say? Does she say "Whatever you want, Sam"?

SAM: She will. Glory will do what Stephen wants. Stephen wants to be with me.

EVERETT: Stephen will be ready to go home tomorrow morning. Glory may not have all the answers to his questions, like you do, but she's home when he gets there.

SAM: That's not enough.

EVERETT: If you leave her, you'll lose him.

SAM: Stephen is mine. He always has been.

EVERETT: And you're supposed to be so smart. *(No response.)* Maybe you ought to make a list of the things you don't know, just for your own protection, see. *(A pause.)* Put this at the top.

SAM: This...what?

EVERETT: Boys and their mothers.

SAM: Whatever you say, Dad.

EVERETT: This is…a subject I took a few lessons in myself, Sam.

(Glory comes out onto the porch carrying a cup of coffee for Everett.)

GLORY: Sam? Don't you want a sandwich? We should leave in twenty minutes.

SAM: No thanks. I don't want to spoil my dinner.

(Stephen runs past her and down the steps.)

GLORY: Don't get dirty now, Stephen. Watch where you sit.

(Stephen is carrying a Bible he has found inside. Glory follows him into the garden.)

STEPHEN: Dad, I found your Bible!

SAM: *(Alarmed.)* Glory, where—

STEPHEN: *(Still very excited.)* I thought it was Grandpa's, but it's yours!

GLORY: *(To Sam.)* In your old bedroom, I think.

STEPHEN: *(Showing it to him.)* See? It says Samuel Carter.

SAM: The church gives them away, Stephen.

STEPHEN: No, look, Dad! On the next page, it says—

SAM: *(To Everett.)* Did you give this to him?

(Everett shakes his head no.)

STEPHEN: See, it's right here. It says August 27, 1949, Jesus came into my heart.

SAM: Well—

STEPHEN: Only you've got it spelled H-E-R-A-T. Jesus came into your heart before you could even spell it!

(Glory hands the coffee to Everett.)

SAM: I didn't have any choice, Stephen. Night after night you sit there in the revival and every head is bowed and every eye is closed, and Dad is down there at the altar calling "Oh sinner, come home." And people all around you are saying "Bless me Jesus, save me Lord."

And the first night eight people go down and the second night twenty people go down, and the third night everybody in the whole third grade goes down, and those are the big kids, so I'm impressed. And you look up at Dad and he's looking straight at you, saying "God see my boy, see my own dear child, speak to him, Lord," and I heard it, all right. I couldn't go home if I didn't.

So before I could stop myself, I walked down the aisle, shaking and crying, saying "Here I am, Daddy." I knelt down at the altar, and he put his hand on my head and said "Praise the Lord," and I was saved. And he…was relieved. What kind of a preacher are you if you can't save your own child?

EVERETT: I didn't save you. He did.

SAM: Then after the service, we all waited for him in the front pew where he gave us all brand-new Bibles and had us turn to the front page and write down August 27, 1949—

SAM AND STEPHEN: —Jesus came into my heart.

STEPHEN: Did you read this?

EVERETT: He read it straight through before school even started that year.

SAM: I was too young to read, Dad. I just looked at the pictures, Stephen.

EVERETT: He knew hundreds of verses by heart. I'd be reading a verse in a sermon, and I'd look down at him in the front row, and he'd be mouthing the words right along with me.

SAM: Take it easy, Dad.

EVERETT: But I was so proud of you, son!

SAM: I know, but—

EVERETT: Stephen, we had Junior Church one Sunday a month, you know, where only the kids would come, and your dad started preaching there when he was only nine years old. By the time he was twelve, people all over the state had heard about him.

STEPHEN: You never told me you were a preacher, Dad.

EVERETT: That summer, at the revival, I announced in the newspaper that your dad was going to preach the sermon one night, and so many people came that there wasn't enough room for them all in the tent, so we had to open up the sides so people could sit on the grass and see him. He talked about Abraham that night. Abraham and Isaac.

STEPHEN: *(Finding the picture in the Bible.)* Here's Abraham right here. *(Walking toward Sam.)* But he's killing his little boy.

SAM: That's him all right. God says to Abraham, "If you really love me, you will sacrifice your son. You will build a fire, tie him to the top of it, slit his throat, say a prayer, and burn him up."

STEPHEN: Why?

EVERETT: The Lord was testing Abraham, Stephen.

SAM: The Lord was bored, Stephen. He was just looking for something to do.

EVERETT: Oh no. God had big plans for Abraham. And He had to make sure Abraham was the right man for the job.

STEPHEN: Is this God, here, in the clouds?

SAM: There's a much better picture of Him on page fifty-eight. That's Him in the burning bush.

STEPHEN: And He isn't burned up?

EVERETT: He *is* the fire.

STEPHEN: He is?

EVERETT: God really knows how to get your attention, all right.

SAM: He's lonely, Stephen. He sits and waits for somebody to notice Him, and then, when they don't, or when they don't notice Him enough, well, He plays His little tricks, He gives His little tests.

EVERETT: He has His reasons for His tests.

SAM: That's what you said when Mother died. God is testing us, son. God has His reasons, only we can't know what they are.

EVERETT: God didn't kill her.

SAM: He just let her die. He took her back. He was only kidding. She wasn't mine. She was His.

GLORY: Stephen, why don't you take the Bible inside. We don't want it to get—

SAM: She died when I was about your age, Stephen. About a month after my preaching triumph. But we didn't call it dying, did we, Dad? We just said God was missing her something awful and she went on back where she belonged, didn't we?

EVERETT: Yes, we did. And I don't know how He got along without her for as long as He did.

STEPHEN: I don't understand. Could God have saved Granny if He wanted to?

EVERETT: Yes, Stephen.

STEPHEN: Then why didn't He?

EVERETT: We do not understand everything that happens, but if we believe He loves us, we don't need to understand. Understanding is His work, not ours.

SAM: That's right. He sets it up, we live through it, and He writes it down. What we think of as life, Stephen, is just God gathering material for another book.

STEPHEN: Was God missing Mavis too?

SAM: Stephen—

EVERETT: *(Quickly.)* I don't know, Stephen. But I do know He has His mysterious ways of working things out. Your daddy is a doctor today because his mother died when he was so young.

SAM: Jesus Christ.

EVERETT: They worked puzzles on her bed right up to the day she died. I'd come in to check on her, and she'd be asleep, but your dad would be reading *Mother Goose* to her like she could hear every word. He worked real hard but he couldn't save her. He was just a boy.

SAM: Jesus God.

EVERETT: But now, every time he goes into that operating room, God gives him another chance. How many people are alive today because of him! Hundreds! Thousands maybe. Praise be to the power and the wisdom of the Almighty God.

SAM: You are a hopeless old fool!

GLORY: Sam, you apologize to your father!

SAM: God is not in control.

GLORY: Please, Sam, remember what we're doing here.

SAM: I will not have Stephen walk into that funeral believing God has some reason for this! *(He turns to Stephen.)* He's lying to you, Stephen. He lied to me and now he's lying to you and I won't have it! God had nothing to do with Mavis dying. It just happened. It was a goddamn rotten thing to happen, but God didn't do it. No. God is not in control and hasn't been in control for some time. *(He pauses and shifts into the master storyteller he can be.)* He lost it...over Job. God made a bet with the Devil and lost it all. *(Glory shakes her head and wanders off a bit. Sam relaxes a little, now that he has won.)*

SAM: The Devil said, "Sure Job loves you. Why shouldn't he? He's the richest man on earth. But you take all that away, and he won't pray to you then, no sir."

Well, God just had to find out. So in one afternoon, He killed all his sheep, all his camels, all his oxes and his asses and his daughters and his sons. And Job still prayed. So the next afternoon, God set a fire that burned up his house and everything in it, turned all his friends against him, sat Job down in the ashes and gave him leprosy.

And even then, Job prayed. Job suffered more than any man had ever suffered. As much, in fact, as God had ever suffered. And when God realized that Job could suffer just as well as He could, everything changed. For God saw that He had sinned, but Job loved Him still. And in that moment, God found God, and it was man.

And ever since that time, God has been up there believing in us with all His heart, believing we can do whatever we want, and wondering why, exactly, we do what we do. We must have our reasons, but He can't, for the life of Him, figure out what they are.

So He watches, but He can't help us. So He weeps. All God can do now is cry. The oceans, Stephen, are the tears God has cried since Job.

GLORY: *(Coming back.)* We need to go, Sam.

SAM: *(Continuing.)* God is not in control. We are. There is no heaven, there is no hell. There is this life, created, in your case, by your mother and me. Life on earth, which we can make better through careful thought and hard work. But *we* make the progress, and *we* make the mistakes. Not God. God has nothing to do with this, so there is no point in believing in Him. He's just another fairy-tale king, as far as I'm concerned. If you want to believe, believe in yourself. In your power, in your mind, in your life. This life. Because that's all there is.

(Everett looks at his watch, then straightens his tie.)

GLORY: *(Coming quickly to be near Stephen.)* That's all your father thinks there is, Stephen. But he really doesn't know. Other people… *(Her anger is making it hard for her to talk.)* find other things. Other people believe other things. And it makes them feel…different. Better.

SAM: Well, what can I say after that.

EVERETT: *(Standing up.)* Maybe you can tell me what to say at this funeral.

SAM: No thanks.

EVERETT: I'll say it was an accident, how's that? I'll say it was a stupid mistake that somebody made. And we won't pray, of course, but we will sing. Something like "Moon River," you know, whatever we feel like. It doesn't matter what we do, does it, Sam? It doesn't mean a thing.

SAM: I don't know, Dad. It's your show.

EVERETT: This is no show!

SAM: It is a show and you know it.

EVERETT: Well I'll tell you one thing, boy. My show works.

SAM: Oh, you think so, do you?

EVERETT: Yes I do. My show works. It works so well that you—yes, even you—have come home to see it. Haven't you?

SAM: *(Brushing off his pants.)* We need to take two cars.

GLORY: No we don't.

SAM: I'm not going to the supper. I don't want anybody coming up to me with coleslaw on their plate. I don't have anything to say about it.

GLORY: Stephen, go with your father, then, and I'll take Grandpa.

STEPHEN: Am I going with Dad forever, or just to the funeral?

SAM: I want you to do both those things, Stephen. I want you with me. Some new town, some other place. I'm sorry I didn't tell you myself, but I wanted to—

GLORY: Stephen, do you remember what I told you inside?

STEPHEN: Yes.

GLORY: All right, then.

EVERETT: Let's go, Glory.

GLORY: I'm ready. *(To Sam.)* You are coming.

SAM: Yes. We're coming.

(After Everett and Glory have left, Sam puts on his suit jacket.)

SAM: What did she tell you inside?

STEPHEN: She said I shouldn't worry about it. She said you were just upset. She said everything would be all right.

SAM: Did she say how it would get that way?

STEPHEN: No.

SAM: She just believes it will.

STEPHEN: That's what she said.

SAM: Funny, huh?

STEPHEN: I don't know.

SAM: *(Straightening Stephen's hair.)* Well, we can talk about it some more tonight. You're a real smart boy, and you'll just think your way through it. Just like any other problem. And you'll make your decision.

STEPHEN: Do I look all right?

SAM: You look good.

STEPHEN: So do you.

SAM: Thanks. Okay. *(Looking at Stephen.)* Do we have a handkerchief?

STEPHEN: *(Pats his pocket.)* Mom gave me some Kleenex.

SAM: Okay, then. Here we go. *(Then quietly.)* God help us.

(They walk offstage.)

END OF ACT I

ACT II

The lights come up, but they are not bright. It is sometime after midnight. Sam wanders into the garden and looks up at the house. There is only one light on, in that little room at the top of the house. Sam whistles the little tune he sang for Stephen in the first act and the light goes out. He sits down on the wall. Stephen opens the back door and walks out. Stephen is wearing his pajamas and a big sweater.

SAM: *(As Stephen sits beside him.)* Hello, Stephen.

STEPHEN: I waited up for you.

SAM: Yeah. I saw. What time did you get home?

STEPHEN: I don't know. Eight-thirty, something like that.

SAM: Is everybody asleep?

STEPHEN: I don't know. They probably think I'm asleep and I'm not, so I probably think they're asleep and they're not. Grandpa was pretty tired. He might be asleep.

SAM: Did you see Granny Butler at the supper?

STEPHEN: She told me I needed a haircut.

SAM: What do *you* think?

STEPHEN: I told her she smelled like bug candles.

SAM: And what did she say to that?

STEPHEN: She said she liked it. She said it kept the bugs away.

SAM: So. What time did you get home? *(Then remembering.)* Oh, I'm sorry. You already told me that. Let's see. Did you talk to anybody else?

STEPHEN: Not really. This one lady asked me if I ever met Mavis. I said yes and she asked me if I wanted a coke. *(Pause.)* But *everybody* was talking to Grandpa, like Mavis was almost his daughter or something.

SAM: She was, in a way. *(Pause.)* You know what he did for her? *(Then realizing what he is about to tell.)* If I tell you this, you've got to promise me not to let him know you know. I mean, you can't ask him for it.

STEPHEN: What is it?

SAM: Well, Mavis's father was the custodian at the church, and her mother worked late, so when she was little, Mavis was always hanging around the church after school. And Dad didn't want her to feel she was any less than me, you know, so… *(An odd pause.)* Dad sent off for the books, and learned some magic tricks for Mavis. Not big tricks, but…making a salt shaker disappear, things like that. And it was their secret, but I found out, of course. Mavis told me. So I went right in and asked him to do it for me, but he said, "What are you talking about? I can't do any magic tricks." But I badgered him for a solid week until one night at supper, he gave in, picked up the salt shaker and said, "Watch close now."

STEPHEN: Terrific!

SAM: No. Not so terrific. I watched too close, I guess. I saw how it worked and ran around the table to his jacket pocket, reached in and pulled out the salt shaker. I said, "Don't put it in your pocket, Dad. Make it disappear."

STEPHEN: You spoiled it.

SAM: Yes. *(Pause.)* Well. What were you reading upstairs?

STEPHEN: Donner Pass.

SAM: *(Laughs a little.)* Oh yes. The Family Picnic.

STEPHEN: Come on, Dad. Did they really eat each other? Got caught in a blizzard and ate each other?

SAM: That's all they had, Stephen. They had to eat.

STEPHEN: But they died anyway, the Donner Pass people. They ate each other up and it didn't save them.

SAM: They did what they thought they had to do. They didn't know it wouldn't save them. *(Pause.)* But the whole trip was like that. Day after day, they'd left things behind, thrown out beds and chests and tools and toys…to make the wagons lighter, so they could travel faster…so they could get to Donner Pass.

STEPHEN: If they threw everything out, what did they think they would live on once they got there?

SAM: They thought it was enough just to get there. They thought they were smart enough to figure it out, whatever it was, up the road. It's a pretty standard American idea. All you need is your brain. Then if all you have is your brain, well…you can eat it.

STEPHEN: Can we go there sometime? I bet there's a marker, isn't there? Donner Pass Memorial Park or something.

SAM: Sure, Stephen. *(As if reading it.)* In memory of the families who died by the side of the road, because the things that would have saved them were too heavy to carry such a long way.

STEPHEN: Didn't anybody tell them what could happen?

SAM: Yeah, probably. But they didn't listen. Other people get caught in blizzards and have to eat their families, not me. I'm smart.

STEPHEN: Not smart enough, huh.

SAM: Nobody is smart *enough*.

STEPHEN: Somebody out there might be. Some spaceman.

SAM: I don't think so, Stephen.

STEPHEN: *(A bit disappointed.)* Why not?

SAM: See that cloud? Straight across the sky, there?

STEPHEN: Yeah.

SAM: It's not a cloud. It's us. It's the Milky Way. You can't see it in the city, but out here, you can. *(Pause.)* The earth spins around the sun, while the sun spins around the center of the Milky Way, while the Milky Way chases Andromeda going like a billion miles an hour. *We're* the spacemen, Stephen.

STEPHEN: *(After a moment.)* Is there a center of everything?

SAM: The Big Bang Theory says there *was* one, but it blew up.

STEPHEN: Grandpa would say God did it, God lit the fuse.

SAM: Yes. He would.

STEPHEN: Did He?

(Sam doesn't answer.)

STEPHEN: Is there a God, Dad?

SAM: *(Taking Stephen in his arms.)* When I am out here, on this wall, in this garden, looking up at the sky, I think, yes, there is something out there. I actually want there to be something out there. I want there to be a God, and I don't want it to be me.

STEPHEN: Are you feeling better, Dad?

SAM: I'm sorry about all this, Stephen. But once we get going…First thing in the morning, we'll put all our things in Mavis's car and take off. Dad doesn't want it he said. So we might as well take it, don't you think, like she left us a getaway car. When we stop for the night, you can call your mother if you want, and just see if she can guess where we are.

STEPHEN: I don't want to move, Dad.

SAM: You want to stay with your mother, you mean.

STEPHEN: I don't want you to leave us.

SAM: We'll go someplace wonderful. Northern California, maybe, with the ocean out the front door, and the redwoods out the back. And we could get a horse if you want. I always wanted a horse.

STEPHEN: I can't leave, Dad. Mom needs me. She doesn't have anybody.

SAM: Stephen, your mother has more friends than the Red Cross.

STEPHEN: *(Getting up off the wall now.)* It's not the same thing. She needs *me*.

SAM: No, you're right. That's true. She does. I need you too, but…she said it first, huh?

STEPHEN: Don't you love Mom anymore?

SAM: I guess not.

STEPHEN: What did she do?

SAM: Nothing.

STEPHEN: Did you love her when you married her?

SAM: Yes.

STEPHEN: Did she change?

SAM: No.

STEPHEN: Did you change?

SAM: No, not really.

STEPHEN: So what happened to it?

SAM: Stephen, there will be days when it doesn't matter that you're smart. When it won't help. When your extraordinary mind is of no use whatsoever. When all it will do is tell you how bad things are.

STEPHEN: But you told me to think about it.

SAM: Yes, but… *(Struggling here.)* You can't think about this the way you would any other problem. You can't just add up the numbers and read the result, because it doesn't work that way. It's like you wanted to open a bottle of beer, but all you had to use was your calculator. It wouldn't work. You need to use something else.

STEPHEN: I would sell the calculator and buy a bottle opener.

(No response from Sam.)

STEPHEN: I would go next door and borrow a bottle opener.

SAM: I would call upstairs and ask your mother where she hid the bottle opener.

STEPHEN: She didn't hide it. You just didn't look. You never look. You're out of the house for eight hours and you act like we've taken all the stuff out of the cabinets and hidden it away like a treasure hunt. *(Imitating Sam's call.)* Glory, where's the peanut butter?

SAM: *(Defending himself.)* I just got home. I'm tired. I don't want to go looking. I want the peanut butter.

STEPHEN: *(Very angry.)* It's in the basement. It's in a box marked Dad's Old Shoes.

SAM: What does she do? Hold little indoctrination sessions with you?

STEPHEN: I don't want to move, Dad.

SAM: We don't even have to stay in this country, you know. We could go to South America and become river rats. Or how about Africa. Spend the whole day outside.

STEPHEN: So what would I do? Wait outside the hut all day for you to come home?

SAM: You'd go to school.

STEPHEN: I already go to school. And I already sit and wait for you to come home and I already don't like it. I wouldn't like it any better in Africa.

SAM: I'll come home.

STEPHEN: No you won't.

SAM: We'll go fishing.

STEPHEN: No we won't, Dad.

SAM: I love you, Stephen.

STEPHEN: If you could stop loving Mom, you could stop loving me.

SAM: No, Stephen. Your children are not the same as your wife or your husband.

STEPHEN: Your children are an accident.

SAM: Stephen!

STEPHEN: You didn't want any children at all. I wouldn't even be here if it weren't for Mom.

SAM: Did she tell you that?

STEPHEN: No, but it's true, isn't it. Isn't it!

SAM: Yes. But I didn't know I would get you. If I had known it was you, I'd have wanted you.

(No response from Stephen.)

SAM: I know I've been gone too much and never taken any time off, but I want to change all that. I want to be with you now.

STEPHEN: You don't want to do anything but work and you can't even do that right. What kind of doctor are you if you can't save your own nurse?

(Suddenly the back-porch light comes on and Everett steps out.)

EVERETT: Stephen? Are you out there?

SAM: *(More quiet, but more intense.)* Stephen, I didn't kill Mavis. You don't understand.

EVERETT: *(Calling again.)* Stephen!

STEPHEN: *(To Sam.)* What's there to understand? She's dead.

EVERETT: *(To Glory, who is in the kitchen.)* They're outside, Glory.

SAM: Stephen, medicine doesn't always work.

STEPHEN: Then it might as well be magic, Dad.

SAM: Stephen, people die all the time. People have to die sometime.

(Everett walks out into the garden.)

STEPHEN: *(Louder than necessary.)* And it's no big deal, huh.

EVERETT: *(Hearing him.)* There you are. We thought we lost you.

SAM: *(Sees his father, but keeps talking.)* It's sad, Stephen, but no, it's not any big deal.

STEPHEN: *(Standing up.)* Well, if it's not any big deal when people die, then it's not any big deal when they live, or where they live, so I'm living with Mom.

(Everett sits down, making Sam even more uncomfortable.)

SAM: Stephen, I tried to save her—

STEPHEN: *(Jumping up now.)* I'm living with Mom.

SAM: Ask him! He'll tell you. I did everything—

STEPHEN: *(Screaming.)* I'm living with Mom.

SAM: Are you listening to me?

STEPHEN: Don't call us! Don't come see us!

SAM: Stephen!

STEPHEN: *(Moving toward the house.)* Don't come get your things!

SAM: What do you want me to say?

STEPHEN: Buy new things! *(Stephen runs out of the garden and up the steps into the house.)*

(Sam just stands there a minute, then turns to Everett, who is still sitting by the wall.)

SAM: If you're looking for Stephen, he went inside.

EVERETT: *(After a moment.)* That's good. It's cold out here.

SAM: *(Very controlled.)* Then why don't *you* go inside.

EVERETT: And do what?

SAM: And talk to somebody else!

(No response from Everett.)

SAM: God, for example.

EVERETT: I *did* talk to God.

SAM: I'm sure you did.

EVERETT: He told me to come out here and sit with you, and He'd get back to me in the morning.

SAM: Did He tell you what to say to me?

EVERETT: No. God's not much good on detail.

SAM: But you have some ideas, I guess.

EVERETT: Are you mad at God or me?

SAM: I'm not sure. I get you confused.

EVERETT: What did I do?

SAM: You let Mother's garden go to hell.

EVERETT: Sam, I'm an old man.

SAM: You didn't deserve her.

EVERETT: Of course I didn't. She was a gift. Like Glory is a gift. Like Stephen is a gift.

SAM: She was nothing to you. Nothing at all. You never paid any attention to her. You spent all your time tending the flock.

EVERETT: I did love your mother, Sam.

SAM: You loved God more.

EVERETT: Of course I did. And she knew I loved God more. She knew I loved *you* more.

SAM: You didn't love me, you loved Mavis. Yes! You even loved Mavis more than Mother. First God, then Mavis, then the ladies in the choir, then the congregation, then the shut-ins, then the sick, then the starving Chinese and the heathen, wherever they are, then me, then Mother.

EVERETT: I'm sorry if it seemed that way.

SAM: It *was* that way!

EVERETT: All right. It *was* that way. She was last on my list. All right. But there was a power in me, like there's a power in you, and I couldn't let anything get in its way.

SAM: Why couldn't you let anything get in its way? What good did it do? I mean, it didn't work, Dad.

EVERETT: I was called to it, Sam. Same as you. And you know your Glory understands what your work means to you. Your mother was exactly that way for me. Of course, I never saved lives the way *you* do, but I was—

SAM: We can't save lives. God couldn't save Mother. Medicine couldn't save Mavis. Lives are lost from the start. All you do is promise them another one, and all I do is make this one last longer. But it's *our* victory, not theirs. My work saves *my* life. Or used to. Oh boy. Day after day I've been real proud of myself 'cause I won one more round. Right? Wrong. Death wins. Death always wins.

EVERETT: Not in my book.

SAM: No, not in your book. But I don't believe in your book. I don't, in fact, believe in anything. It has taken me my whole life, Dad, but I have finally arrived. I am free of faith. Glory be. Praise the Lord.

EVERETT: *(Almost laughing.)* Oh, He's really after you this time, isn't He?

SAM: And He has to shake me to make me listen, doesn't He?

EVERETT: Well, I probably believed that in the old days, but God's not as physical as He used to be.

SAM: That is *not* what you "probably believed" in the old days. That is *exactly*

what you said from the pulpit the Sunday after Mother died. You pointed
to me, sitting there on the front row of the choir, where everybody in the
whole congregation could see me, and you told them the story. "There was
my little boy, Samuel, sitting on his dear mother's bed, and he didn't know
she was dead, he was just sitting there, reading as loud as he could, as fast
as he could, but he was shaking like a young tree in a driving rain. And I
walked in and saw that she was dead and put my hands on his shoulders
and made him stop shaking and made him stop reading and listen. And I
said, 'Son, your mother has gone to her reward.' And he heard me."

Now by this time, they're all crying, the whole church is crying, but
you weren't through, were you? You walked over to me and pulled me up
out of my seat in the choir and grabbed my hand and held it to your heart
and you said to your congregation, "That's what God has to do, sometimes. He has to shake us to make us listen."

EVERETT: *(Quite shaken himself.)* I didn't mean to talk about it, Sam. Not that
Sunday, anyway. I just lost my place in my sermon, somehow. And everything got all blurry, all of a sudden, and all I knew was, I had to keep talking and…that was the best I could do, son.

SAM: Yeah, well, do you want to know what God said to me? What I heard
when I quit shaking?

EVERETT: Sam, Sam…

SAM: I heard God say, and He was almost laughing when He said it—God said,
"Sam, Sam, how could you have been so dumb."

EVERETT: I don't know what to say to you, son.

SAM: I don't want you to say anything to me. I want you to leave me alone.

EVERETT: Where am I supposed to go, Sam? This is my house.

SAM: This is Mother's house. Yours is the one with the steeple on the top.

EVERETT: No. That's God's house.

SAM: Then where do you live, Daddy? I mean, when you go home, who opens
the door?

EVERETT: Oh, son. *(Pause.)* You do.

SAM: *(Very cold.)* Well I'm awful sorry about that, Dad, but you don't get the
boy you want, you get the boy you get.

EVERETT: This hurts me too much now, Sam. You're the only one who…Look,
maybe you shouldn't come down here anymore. I'm happy here. My whole
life is peaceful here. And I can still pray for you and keep up with you, but
well, I'll just see you in the newspapers from now on, okay? Maybe you'll

send Stephen to visit me now and then, but I won't come there, and you don't come here, all right?

(Sam is suddenly still, and there is a long silence.)

SAM: Will Stephen forgive me?

(Everett takes a long time here.)

EVERETT: *(Quietly.)* I don't know. Do you forgive me?

SAM: *(Much more quiet.)* I don't know.

EVERETT: Well then, it's hard to say. Some of these things are inherited, I think.

(Glory comes out of the house.)

GLORY: Everett? Sam? What are you two doing out here?

EVERETT: Oh, you know. Reminiscing.

GLORY: Look Sam. Look what I found. I thought you gave me all your letter sweaters, but you didn't. You kept one for yourself, didn't you.

EVERETT: He couldn't get in the sports banquet without it.

GLORY: I remember that banquet. You were the only member of the cross-country team.

EVERETT: I remember they served cauliflower. Bless your mother's heart, you were the only athlete who ate it.

GLORY: Everett, you need to put on something warmer if you're going to stay out here.

EVERETT: *(Standing.)* Did Stephen go to bed?

GLORY: I made him some warm milk.

EVERETT: I didn't think I had any milk.

GLORY: I made a glass for you, too.

EVERETT: I'll go sit with him, then.

GLORY: Don't you like milk?

EVERETT: I don't know. I'll see. *(He goes into the house.)*

GLORY: *(Turning to Sam.)* Come on, Sam. Put this sweater on.

(Sam takes the sweater finally, and puts it on as he talks.)

SAM: I liked that run before school every morning. Out of the house...down the street...Everybody asleep but me and the milkman. I got to feeling real useful, you know, like I was supposed to check out the town before everybody got up. Mile after mile, so far, so good, I'd think. No fires, no stray dogs, and no lights on, so nobody's sick. We did okay. We made it through another night.

GLORY: You were right not to come to the supper, Sam.

SAM: Did they wonder where I was?

GLORY: They're used to your being gone, I think.

SAM: Like you.

GLORY: No. I'm not used to it. But I don't take it personally anymore.

SAM: Like they do.

GLORY: Maybe they do. I don't know.

SAM: They think…that I think…that I'm better than they are.

GLORY: You do!

SAM: I know. They're right.

GLORY: And that's why you don't go. You can't stand for them to be right.

SAM: That's right.

GLORY: *(After a moment.)* Well…you missed some great stories about Mavis.

SAM: I'm sure I did.

GLORY: Your dad told one about you and Mavis, and Timmy somebody—he didn't remember the name—coming back from church camp down at Green River. And you were speeding down the road in that old Volkswagen of hers. And suddenly you saw a policeman coming up behind you and you realized not only were you all three drunk, but you didn't have your driver's license, and you knew you'd never get into medical school with that on your record, so Mavis said, "I'll drive." And you said, "What?" And she said, "Change places with me. I'll drive." And you said, "Mavis, we're going seventy miles an hour." And she said, "Move over."

SAM: *(Realizing she doesn't know the end of the story.)* Is that all he told of it?

GLORY: Is there more?

SAM: We climbed over each other and she got behind the wheel. I told her to slow down, but she told me to shut up. When the police car pulled up beside us, she rolled down the window and yelled to the officer that the accelerator was stuck, and he took one look at the car, and believed her. He made some motions with his hands like she should downshift or kick the accelerator, which she did, then she hit the brake, smiled at him, pulled off the road, got out of the car, and threw up.

GLORY: So she wasn't drunk anymore.

SAM: Right.

GLORY: Smart.

SAM: *(With great, unprotected joy.)* Yeah. Mavis was as smart as they come. *(Pause.)*

GLORY: Sam, I've been thinking about all of this.

SAM: Yes. It's that kind of night, isn't it.

GLORY: I think you're right. I think I'll go to Mother's for a while. A month maybe. You take Stephen and go, Sam. Back to the city or on a trip, whatever you think is best. I don't want to fight with you now. I'd just like a month to think.

SAM: I see.

GLORY: I didn't bring the right clothes to suit Mother, but she'll take me shopping, I guess. And she's giving a big party next week. People I haven't seen in years. Maybe some of them will have learned something in the meantime.

SAM: Don't count on it.

GLORY: My riding clothes are still out there, so that's good. I'll be able to check out this exercise boy of hers.

SAM: Uh-huh.

GLORY: And I thought maybe Everett might need me. We can go through Mavis's clothes, and I'll help him sort her letters and look at the pictures with him and hear the rest of the stories again. (Pause.) I'm all packed.

SAM: Glory...

GLORY: I just came out here to—

SAM: Will you not leave...just yet? Will you sit with me awhile?

GLORY: I will.

SAM: (This is hard for him at first.) When you went to the supper, I drove over to Mavis's house. Where they lived when we were kids, I mean. I don't even know who lives there now. I just parked out front for a while. I always liked that house. Those lilac bushes are still there, remember?

GLORY: Sure I do. All over the place.

SAM: And for one moment, I was sixteen and I had it all to do over again. And I could forget your hair, and forget your mouth and your smell, and love Mavis. Marry her. Somebody exactly like me. Somebody who believed in hard work, who couldn't wait to be an adult. Somebody who never read "Sleeping Beauty" and never said a prayer except, "God let me stay awake long enough to get everything finished."

GLORY: You were two of a kind all right.

SAM: And in the next moment, the moment after I was sixteen and could forget your hair, I was sixteen and I wanted your hair in my mouth, in my eyes, all over me. I wanted to catch you swimming naked in your pond. I knew you did it. You told me you did it.

GLORY: (Confessing.) Of course I did. I wanted you to catch me.

SAM: I never had a chance. I hopped over to that pond like every frog in every fairy tale my mother ever read me, and you kissed me, and I believed. I remember that kiss, I can still taste the butterscotch sucker I took out of your mouth to have that kiss, and I'm still dizzy and hot all of a sudden, and I remember loving you. *(Pause.)* And I guess that kiss...was the last I ever saw of Mavis.

GLORY: Bless her heart, she worshipped you. I knew it, everybody knew it.

SAM: So, once I was in love with you, she had to go to nursing school, didn't she? But she never married, just in case you got hit by a truck or something.

(Glory laughs but knows it's true.)

SAM: Right. Nursing school was her last chance to get my attention, but it didn't work. I didn't look at her in high school and I haven't looked at her since. Why should I look? I knew she'd be there.

GLORY: Sam...

SAM: Mavis was two feet away from me, across the table from me, her whole life, and what did she get from this life with me? Nothing. Invitations to dinner from you. Tennis on Saturday with you. The four of us at the movies, me sound asleep and Mavis holding the popcorn between you and Stephen. Nothing.

GLORY: Mavis got as much from you as you would let her have. That's all she wanted. You're a genius. People make exceptions. They settle.

SAM: You have done more than settle. You have bet your lives on me. It was worse for Mavis, but it's the same for all of you. None of you had any right to count on me, but you did, and I let you, and now, instead of saving any of you—

GLORY: Is that what you think you're doing in our lives, saving us?

SAM: I want to help you.

GLORY: We're all right down here. We think our little thoughts and we have our silly troubles and we fight our losing battles as bravely as we can. The last thing we need is for you to come in and solve our problems for us. Our problems, Sam, are how we fill up our days.

SAM: It's easier for you in the winter, I guess. Your days are shorter.

GLORY: *(A flash of anger.)* I don't need you to save me! *(Then recovering.)* I just need you to...be on my side whenever you can. *(When he doesn't respond, she continues.)* See me...hear me...give me some room, and save me some time. That's all.

(Still no response from Sam.)

GLORY: I've already got a God, Sam. And I see Him all the time, everywhere I go. And He may seem limited and primitive to you, but the dances are fun and the songs are sweet, and every day is a holy day.

SAM: So what is your God doing tonight?

GLORY: I don't know. Maybe He's just…watering the grass.

SAM: Okay. I can't save you. But neither do I have the right to destroy you all.

GLORY: I am not destroyed! I'm mad at you because you're acting like this, but I am not destroyed. And if you think you destroyed Mavis…if you're out here feeling sorry for Mavis…Mavis had you all day, Sam. Mavis had the best of you! I never had the conversations she had with you. I never sweated with you for twelve hours to work one of your miracles. We—you and I—never held our breath till the dead man sat up, Sam.
(And he doesn't respond.)

GLORY: No, Sam. Don't feel sorry for Mavis. And don't be mad at me. I have been—Stephen and I have been—happy, all these years, to have what was left over when Mavis finished with you.

SAM: So you're happy she's gone.

GLORY: *(Horrified.)* How can you say that?

SAM: You sounded jealous, that's all.

GLORY: I was jealous. You loved her. But that doesn't—

SAM: No, Glory. I didn't love her. I had every opportunity to, but I didn't.

GLORY: Well…I loved her. And I think she loved me. And right now, I'm feeling real lost without her.

SAM: She was jealous of you.

GLORY: What on earth for?

SAM: You've got it all.

GLORY: I've got you, you mean.

SAM: You're a great-looking woman and Stephen adores you, and you float through everything like you're on a…like you were born wearing a life jacket. *(Pause.)* Mavis had to work hard for everything she ever had, while you…well, you…just enjoy yourself.

GLORY: Listen, Sam. It's not as easy as it looks.

SAM: Yeah, well, you've had a lot of practice.

GLORY: *(In a rage.)* I did not agree to sit here and take the blame for this. It's not my fault! *(She starts for the house.)*

SAM: I didn't love her, I used her. And then…when she really needed me…She was counting on me to see it, Glory, only I wasn't looking. And I wasn't looking because I didn't want to see it. Other people die, Glory—not me, not my family, not my friend!

GLORY: None of us were looking, Sam. Three weeks ago, I knew she looked awful. I told her to get a haircut.

SAM: It's the thirteenth fairy, see. You don't invite her to the party because you don't want her to come, but she comes anyway, because she lives there, just like you do. But you forgot, didn't you?

GLORY: Sam…

SAM: I forgot Mavis was alive and she died.

GLORY: You were trying to save her!

SAM: I was showing off! I could fix it. I could pull her through. I could make it disappear. She could have lived for months. A year maybe, but no, I have to go in and save her.

GLORY: Even if it was a mistake…

SAM: I believed I could save her.

GLORY: Well you couldn't.

SAM: So now I just turn around and believe I couldn't?

GLORY: Yes!

SAM: No! It was the belief that was the problem in the first place! I believed in everything. I even believed in you—or love, I guess. Didn't I? Yes. And in God, and fairy tales, and medicine and the power of my own mind and none of it works!

GLORY: Sam…please…

SAM: But I want to believe! Stephen wants to believe! He does! I see it! After everything I've told him, he still wants to believe. But how can I let him believe when I know what happens, when there is no good reason for what happens, when there is no reason to believe.

GLORY: *(Trying another tack.)* Sam, you've got this all mixed up. You married me because I'm good for you, and you operated on Mavis because you were the best one to do it, because she wanted you to do it, because you wanted to do it.

SAM: No! *(In his own private hell now.)* I believed, once again, I believed I might be able to do something and… *(Very distant, suddenly.)* Mavis believed I could save her and all the faith in the world wouldn't save her. Won't save any of us. Won't do a thing except make fools of us. Give us tests we cannot pass. Bring us to our knees, but not in prayer—in absolute submission to accident, to the arbitrary assignment of unbearable pain, and the everyday occurrence of meaningless death. Only then can we believe…that dreams, like deadly whirlpools, drown us in their frenzy…that love blazes across a black sky like a comet but never returns…and that time, like a desert wind, blows while I sleep, and erases the path I walked to here, and erases the path that leads on.

(Sam's anger has been so raw and so violent that he now simply stands, but we are certain he will not speak for quite a while.)

GLORY: *(Without looking up.)* Oh, Sam…Oh, sweet baby…*(Now standing up, but not looking at Sam.)* I went in to see her, you know Tuesday morning, and she'd already had her shot, so she was pretty dopey, but she said, well, she said a lot of things. "Well," she said, "it looks like Sam's gonna get his hands on me after all."

(She looks to Sam for a response but there is none. As Glory continues, Sam walks slowly downstage and sits on a rock and buries his head in his hands.)

GLORY: Anyway, then she said, "Glory…Sam might not be able to fix this, you know. I might not be there for him, this time, when he needs me…I might not be as helpful as I have been. I'll be asleep, see, that's my excuse. Anyway, if I don't make it…I want him to know what I loved…why I loved him. It was only one thing he did, really. We were ten years old, and Everett had this magic trick and Sam knew how it worked, and he showed me how it worked. He knew it wasn't magic, and he knew it didn't always work, and he wasn't afraid to know. Tell him that's why I loved him. He wasn't afraid to know." Then she said, "I've caught it from him, I guess. I'm not afraid either."

(As Glory and Sam remain seated, spent, on the ground, the back door opens and Stephen comes out.)

STEPHEN: Mom?

GLORY: You need to be in bed, honey.

STEPHEN: Are you going to sleep out here?

GLORY: I don't know.

STEPHEN: Want me to get you a blanket?

GLORY: No thanks, sweetie. I'm going to stand up, just…any minute now.

STEPHEN: What's the matter with Dad?

GLORY: It's just late, honey. He's real tired.

STEPHEN: Why doesn't he say anything?

GLORY: He just needs to be quiet now, Stephen.

STEPHEN: *(Walking toward Sam.)* Dad?

GLORY: Come over here if you want to. Keep me warm.

(Stephen comes to sit down with Glory and they hug.)

STEPHEN: Maybe we should eat again.

GLORY: Anything sound good to you?

STEPHEN: No.

GLORY: Did you and Grandpa have a nice talk?

STEPHEN: He was going to teach me how to play Chinese checkers, but, well…
he lost his marbles.

GLORY: *(Laughing.)* Did you say that or did he?

STEPHEN: I did. He said…he couldn't find them. But I thought…you could use
a joke.

GLORY: Boy, is that the truth. I'd give you a dollar for it…

STEPHEN: …if you had a dollar.

GLORY: You got it.

STEPHEN: I'll put it on your bill.

GLORY: Done.

STEPHEN: Maybe he's asleep.

GLORY: Who?

STEPHEN: Dad.

GLORY: He might be asleep. But I wouldn't say anything you don't want him to
hear.

STEPHEN: *(Picking up the geode.)* What's this?

GLORY: I don't know. A rock.

STEPHEN: It's round. Rocks aren't round.

GLORY: I don't know, Stephen. Ask your father.

STEPHEN: You ask him.

GLORY: You're the one who wants to know.

STEPHEN: Maybe it goes in the wall.

*(Stephen gets up and walks around the garden looking for a place the geode
might go. At one point he gets close to Sam, but Glory motions for Stephen to
go around him.)*

STEPHEN: A rock this big ought to be heavier.

(Glory doesn't know how to answer him, so she just smiles and watches.)

STEPHEN: How did it get so round?

GLORY: I don't know, Stephen.

*(Everett comes out of the house and takes a couple of steps. He is very reluctant
to interrupt this, whatever it is.)*

EVERETT: I'll say good night, I guess.

GLORY: Good night, Everett.

EVERETT: You can come inside now, if you want. I'm going to bed…and there's
chairs in here.

GLORY: We're all right, Everett.

EVERETT: Well, then…

(He looks at Sam, then at Glory, who shakes her head and motions for Everett not to say anything.)

STEPHEN: Grandpa, do you know what this rock is?

EVERETT: No, Stephen.

STEPHEN: I found it out here in the garden.

EVERETT: I found a whole drawer full of them upstairs. I brought that one out here to look at one day.

STEPHEN: But whose are they? Where did they come from?

EVERETT: They're Mary's.

STEPHEN: Who's Mary?

EVERETT: Your grandmother. Sam's mother.

GLORY: I saw those dancing pictures upstairs, Everett. If she danced as great as she looked, she was a real catch.

EVERETT: *(Pleased to be invited to come talk.)* She sure was. And nobody could understand why she married the preacher except she was having a better time than anybody else and she had to find some way to pay for it.

GLORY: She sounds like me.

EVERETT: If she were alive today, she'd bake you a batch of chocolate chips and eat them every one while they were still hot. Then she'd send you the wax paper she baked them on and write you a note, telling you to let her know the minute you went off your diet.

STEPHEN: And she liked these rocks?

EVERETT: Well, I don't know. I guess so. I didn't even know she had them till she died. I was looking for a list she made, who she wanted to have her piano, things like that, and I found them. I found a lot of things. I found the world she lived in, a world I knew very little about. I know she loved me, but I don't know why. She must have loved those rocks, but I don't know what they are. *(Now he looks at Sam.)* I guess you can be a real big part of somebody else's world without ever understanding the first thing about it. Somebody can give you their life and you'll never know why. Never know what they wanted from you, or if they ever got it. Then when they die, well, knowing so little about these people makes it real hard to lose them. *(Pause.)* I kept meaning to ask Sam about those rocks. I know she'd want him to have them.

SAM: *(Finally.)* It's not a rock. It's a geode.

STEPHEN: *(Running down to him.)* You mean with the crystals inside?

SAM: Yes.

STEPHEN: Well, let's open it up and see it! Where's the hammer?

SAM: *(Sudden alarm.)* No! *(Then more quietly.)* Once you crack them...She didn't like to crack them.

STEPHEN: Then how do you know what's in there?

SAM: You don't. She said...it was better for it to be safe than for you to know what it was, exactly.

STEPHEN: Dad?

SAM: I'm here, Stephen. *(He sits, but still holds the geode.)* I thought I could save Mavis. *(To Stephen.)* I thought I could protect you. I can't do any of those things. I don't know what I *can* do. I don't know what to say. I have nothing for you.

STEPHEN: *(Pointing to the geode.)* I'll take that.

SAM: The geode?

STEPHEN: Yeah.

SAM: It's not mine.

EVERETT: Yes it is.

SAM: It's nothing.

STEPHEN: It's okay. I like it.

SAM: I like it too. When Mother died I gathered them up and put them in that drawer. Yes, you can have it. It's...your mystery now.

STEPHEN: *(Taking the geode.)* Thanks.

(There is silence all around.)

STEPHEN: Dad?

SAM: Yes.

STEPHEN: Where did she go, Dad?

SAM: Where did Mavis go?

STEPHEN: Yes.

(And there is more silence.)

SAM: I don't know, Stephen.

STEPHEN: I saw her in the coffin, but it wasn't her.

GLORY: *(Gently.)* It was her, Stephen.

STEPHEN: I mean, she wasn't there anymore.

SAM: No.

STEPHEN: *(Carefully.)* Did you see it go, Dad?

SAM: What?

STEPHEN: *(Still very careful.)* In the operating room? Did you cut her open and it got out?

(And Sam doesn't answer for a moment. His heart is broken, his anger turned to grief and longing. Glory, Everett and Stephen are silent and perfectly still.)

SAM: Yes. *(Pause.)* I cut her open and it got out. I was standing there over her and…

STEPHEN: *(Quietly.)* What was it like? *(Now very slowly.)* Could you feel it or see it or hear it? Was it cold or white or like air maybe or what?
(And Sam stands there a moment, searching for the answer, searching for the memory, trying to see it again. Finally, he shakes his head. The words are coming, but he has no idea what they are.)

SAM: It was… *(And suddenly, the words come from him the way "it" came from Mavis in that moment.)* It was forgiveness.
(Sam stands there quietly a moment, as a kind of peace seems to come over him, and then over Everett, and then Glory. Stephen, however, doesn't quite understand.)

STEPHEN: *(Finally.)* For what, Dad?

SAM: I don't know, Stephen. For whatever I did. For all those years.

STEPHEN: Did she forgive me for losing her cat?

SAM: *(Not directly to Stephen, and not quickly.)* Yes, Stephen.

EVERETT: *(Quietly.)* I wondered what happened to that cat. Every week, on the phone, I had to say hello to that damn cat.

STEPHEN: *(To Everett.)* I didn't mean to lose Peaches, she just—

GLORY: *(Interrupting him, to soothe him.)* It's all right, Stephen. I owed Mavis money.

SAM: You? What for?

GLORY: *(A bit embarrassed as the story begins.)* I had my eyes done. Last March when I told you I came to see Mother, I flew to Chicago and had my eyes done. I didn't want you to know it, so I borrowed the money from Mavis.

SAM: And I never noticed it.

GLORY: No.

SAM: *(Inspecting her eyes now.)* Nice work. *(Then inspecting more carefully.)* Great work.

GLORY: She said we had to preserve your illusions.

SAM: I like it.

GLORY: That's good. It was a lot of money.

EVERETT: It was four thousand dollars.

SAM: I didn't know Mavis had any money.

EVERETT: It was my money.

GLORY: I didn't know that.

EVERETT: I didn't know it was for you.

SAM: *(To Everett.)* I'll pay you back.

EVERETT: Good.

GLORY: Thank you anyway, Everett.

EVERETT: *(After a moment.)* I owe you an apology, Glory.

GLORY: What on earth?

EVERETT: I told Mavis your marriage wouldn't last. That your mother was stingy with her money and your looks wouldn't last forever. I told her if she'd just wait, she could have Sam all to herself.

STEPHEN: Why did you do that?

EVERETT: It was…an old dream of mine.

SAM: You were wrong.

EVERETT: I know.

GLORY: Well, not completely. Mother *is* cheap.

EVERETT: I'm sorry, Glory.

GLORY: It's all right, Everett. You didn't know.

SAM: *(After a moment.)* I'm the one who needs to apologize to you, Glory.

GLORY: It's all right, Sam.

SAM: I only wanted to leave because—

GLORY: You don't have to tell me that, Sam.

SAM: I don't know why I wanted to leave you. I can't leave you. But maybe I didn't want to hurt you like I…maybe I was afraid I would lose you, too.

GLORY: Sam, it's been a sad, sad day. We're all so lonely for her, we've all…said things.

SAM: Yeah, I know, but I said mine on purpose.

GLORY: You were mad.

SAM: That doesn't make it right. I need you. I love you.

GLORY: I know, Sam. I tried to tell you that this afternoon.

SAM: I guess I wasn't listening.

GLORY: *(Carefully.)* No, I didn't think you were.

SAM: *(Takes his time before he begins.)* Glory, if you could…hold on a little longer, I want to be a better man.

GLORY: I can do that, Sam.

(He shakes his head, first out of relief; and then in confusion.)

GLORY: You don't understand, do you.

(He shakes his head no.)

GLORY: I'd explain it to you if I could, or maybe you'll explain it to me in a week or so, or maybe we'll just love each other anyway and never know.

SAM: Please…forgive me.

(And Glory extends her arms to Sam, and they embrace. And when they break the embrace he sees his father.)

SAM: And Dad…I'm sorry, Dad.

EVERETT: I'm all right, son.

SAM: No, Dad. I want you to know that I—

EVERETT: I said it's all right, son.

SAM: I love you, Dad.

EVERETT: Yes. I know.

STEPHEN: *(After a moment.)* I'm cold. Is anybody else cold? It's cold out here.
(And Sam knows they are all waiting for him to speak, to say whether he is finished here.)

SAM: Well, maybe…we could…go in the house. I didn't think I wanted to go in the house, but now—

EVERETT: I haven't changed a thing, Sam.

SAM: Yes, well, *(Smiling at Everett and himself.)* that's what I was afraid of.
(Glory squeezes his hand or laughs a little at him, and Everett shakes his head, but they are all still waiting for Sam to make the next move.)

SAM: Dad, if it's all right with Stephen and Glory, we'd like to stay here a few days, if it isn't too much trouble.

STEPHEN: Hey! Great!

EVERETT: What do you mean? You *have* to stay here. You haven't finished cleaning up this garden. And Stephen hasn't read all my books and I know I can't eat all that food we brought home from the supper.

GLORY: *(Gathering up something she has brought outside.)* You can't eat all that food because Josie Barnett can't cook. I thought people in the country could cook.

EVERETT: *(Now moving toward the house.)* What Josie Barnett can't do is sing. None of these girls can sing a lick. I keep praying I'll go deaf, but then… *(Looking to heaven, but aware that he's making a joke.)* I ask Him for so much.
(Stephen follows Everett's eyes to the heavens and finds the stars.)

STEPHEN: *(As though they were in the middle of a conversation about stars.)* But Dad, what holds the stars up there? Why don't they fall?
(And there is a pause, while Sam doesn't explain it.)

EVERETT: Sam, what was that other verse, do you remember, that other verse of "Twinkle, Twinkle."

GLORY: I didn't know there was another verse.

EVERETT: Well, maybe it wasn't a real verse, but Sam's mother sure said it all the time.

SAM: No, it was a real verse. I remember reading it. I just don't remember...

EVERETT: *(Getting it now.)* As your bright and tiny spark

SAM: *(Remembering.)* Yes, yes. *(Then repeating.)*

Guides the traveler in the dark

Though I know not what you are

Twinkle, twinkle little star.

(He continues to look at the stars.)

EVERETT: Right. That's it, exactly.

THE END

Sarah and Abraham

Sarah and Abraham was originally commissioned by Actors Theatre of Louisville. It was first presented as a workshop production at Actors Theatre of Louisville in the 1988 Humana Festival of New American Plays. It was directed by Jon Jory with the following cast:

Abraham	Michael Zaslow
Tom	Edward James Hyland
Jack	William Verderber
Sarah	Beth Dixon
Hagar	Valarie Pettiford
Virginia	Alma Cuervo
Isaac	Jonathan Davidson
Voice of the Narrator	Frederic Major

Originally produced by the George Street Playhouse in 1992. This production was directed by Jack Hofsiss. The cast was as follows:

Abraham	William Katt
Tom	John Hickok
Jack	Steven Keats
Sarah	Tovah Feldshuh
Hagar	Christine Andreas
Virginia	Lee Chamberlin
Isaac	Carlo Alban

INTRODUCTION

When I was in high school, I won a state writing competition with an essay which I titled, "Why Do Good Men Suffer." Someday, some scholar will say that that was the real title of every play I ever wrote. And that will be right.

This particular bit of suffering was something I wondered about for years, as I sat at church five times a week, reading the Bible because it was there. I couldn't figure it out. How, or why, or how *exactly* did Sarah give her maid to her husband?

I don't claim to have found the answer in this play. But I looked for it anyway.

CHARACTERS

SARAH: the leading actress of an improvisational theatre company.

ABRAHAM: Sarah's husband, an actor in the company.

HAGAR: a younger actress, formerly a member of this company, now a movie star.

JACK: the artistic director of this company.

WILLIAM: a young actor.

VIRGINIA: a Bible scholar turned playwright.

TOM: the stage manager.

THE ACTION

Takes place during the six-week rehearsal of a small improvisational theatre company.

THE SET

A shabby rehearsal hall, seemingly empty except for beat-up rehearsal furniture and tables for the stage manager, and director. In the corners of the room, however, stand dusty costume trunks or wardrobes, frayed upholstered chairs and chaises, old carpets, worn cushions, and tattered banners—which the actors will use to create the Bronze Age desert kingdom of Sarah and Abraham as they work.

Nothing in the way of set dressing should be brought onstage between scenes until the play reaches the technical rehearsal. Until that time, the stage manager and the actors should manage the props and set pieces themselves.

Sarah, Abraham, Hagar, and Isaac are the actors' character names, but I have used them throughout the script to indicate both the actor, and the character the actor is playing.

As the written script evolves from the improvisations, it is indicated by quotation marks. Direct quotes from the Bible are indicated by dashes.

Sarah and Abraham

ACT I

SCENE I

Tom, the stage manager, wearing jeans, boots and a down vest, is putting down some strips of masking tape on the floor. He works in silence, as Abraham enters. He is quite handsome and fit. You would not for one moment, think that this man was anything on earth but an actor.

ABRAHAM: Hey there.

TOM: Cold enough for you?

ABRAHAM: Tell me about it. Anything I can do there?

TOM: I'm fine. Where's Kitty?

(Abraham takes off his coat and muffler.)

ABRAHAM: Giving an interview at the *Journal*. I think. Or maybe it's one of the TV stations. Why?

TOM: *People* magazine called.

ABRAHAM: That's fantastic.

TOM: They want to do a whole story on her! One of their stringers saw the show in previews, told them Kitty was the next Meryl Streep and they should get their ass out here.

ABRAHAM: That's fabulous. When are they coming?

TOM: Friday. This could really be it for her, you know. Would you go with her, if she got a job?

ABRAHAM: Of course I would. But Kitty's not going anywhere. She loves this town, and she practically founded this theatre. What does she need New York for? *(A moment.)* And I don't totally hate it here. I mean, I like going out to the lake in the summer. And I love Kitty, and believe in what she's doing. And Jack keeps using me, you know, *(A gesture.)* Hamlet's valet's friend, Romeo's florist. So, what the hell. I'll be famous in my next life.

(And Jack enters coughing.)

JACK: Cliff. Great. You're here. I wanted to talk to you. Where's Kitty?

ABRAHAM: Doing an interview.

(Jack greets the stage manager.)

JACK: Tomashevsky. *(And notices the lights are dim.)* What? We couldn't pay the light bill?

(And as Tom turns the lights up, the house lights go down, and we are aware the play has begun.)

ABRAHAM: Now is this true about Monica Mars coming back for this show?

JACK: Sure is. She flew in from L.A. last night.

ABRAHAM: What did you say to her, "Hey, Monica, why don't you give up your fabulous film deal and come back to your old company and work for nothing?"

JACK: Just about. She doesn't start shooting again til summer. Why shouldn't she come?

ABRAHAM: Is she getting top billing or Kitty?

JACK: Kitty will, of course, but that's what I… *(Sees that Tom is listening.)* wanted to talk to you about.

ABRAHAM: Me?

JACK: *(He draws him aside somewhat.)* I mean, I think your work has been real interesting lately. And I feel like we've kind of gotten into a rut here, you know, show after show, Kitty Wells was brilliant, Kitty Wells was profound…

ABRAHAM: She *is* profound.

JACK: I know. So yes, Kitty's going to get the billing, and Monica's gonna help us sell some tickets, but *(A moment.)* this is going to be *your* show, Cliff. You're the real star. Or you will be when it's over. I want *you* to play Abraham.

ABRAHAM: You're kidding.

JACK: I wouldn't be asking if I didn't think you could do it, Cliff. But you're gonna have to do whatever I say, O.K.?

ABRAHAM: Oh, man. And Kitty's playing Sarah?

JACK: That's right. And Monica will play your mistress, but you'll be the one we're watching. I mean, who do we remember from this story. Sarah? No. Hagar? No. Abraham. Yes. Abraham the Patriarch. That's you, guy. And I'm sure I don't have to tell you what a role like this could do for your career.

ABRAHAM: No. You don't.

JACK: So are you in?

ABRAHAM: I can't believe it. This is great. Does Kitty know about this?

JACK: Not yet.

(And now the others enter.)

JACK: But she's about to. *(Brightly.)* Good morning.

(Sarah enters, stamping the snow off her boots. She is a handsome midwestern woman in her mid to late thirties.)

SARAH: Hi guys. Jesus, it's cold.

TOM: Kitty, *People* magazine called. They're sending a photographer on Friday.

SARAH: What time?

(Tom is stunned by her lack of excitement. He looks at Abraham, who has an I-told-you-so look.)

TOM: Ten.

SARAH: Thanks, Tom.

(Abraham goes to her, gives her a kiss and takes her bag.)

ABRAHAM: How'd the interview go, hon?

SARAH: O.K., I guess. You know, how do I prepare for a role, what's it like working with the same people all the time, things like that. But I got the feeling that all she really wanted to know was why was it *me* on the stage instead of her.

ABRAHAM: Because you're prettier, that's why.

SARAH: You didn't even see her.

ABRAHAM: I didn't have to.

SARAH: *(Kissing him.)* Thanks, hon. I'm sorry about that coffee this morning. I must have lost count while I was measuring.

ABRAHAM: I thought it was great, actually. A real stand up cup of Joe.

(Sarah turns to Jack.)

SARAH: So, Jack. Why are we doing a Bible story? People hate the Bible.

JACK: Not if you're in it, they won't.

SARAH: Who am I playing?

JACK: Sarah, of course, and Cliff is your Abraham,

(Kitty looks at Cliff, but before she can say anything, Monica enters.)

JACK: —and our own Monica Mars is the pagan princess from Hell. *(He goes to her.)* Good morning, darling lost one.

(Hagar wears layers and layers of thin cottons. She is exotic and sexy in a completely unselfconscious way, and looks like the movie star she is now. Her hair is out of control, her body is perfect. There is a chorus of Hellos, etc. Hagar has changed from being in Hollywood, but she tries to put them all at ease and get back into the life she used to know here.)

HAGAR: *(Looking around.)* Oh man, I've been so busy missing this *(She goes to hug Abraham.)* I forgot what a dump it is. Hi Cliff. *(She hugs Sarah.)* Sarah. That was a great review you got this morning.

SARAH: I'm sleeping with them is how I do it.

HAGAR: Whatever works, hon.

(Jack looks up as Virginia enters. She is a little nervous, and doesn't seem to know where she is. But she has a natural competence and grace that helps her cover it.)

JACK: There you are. *(He goes to her and takes her arm.)* And now, I'd like all of you to meet Virginia Mason, world famous Bible scholar and soon-to-be playwright from the University of Wisconsin.

(The others are all somewhat surprised by this. If they didn't know it before, they know now. Jack is up to something. There is another chorus of Hellos.)

JACK: This is Cliff and Kitty, and Monica Mars, of course, and Tom, over there is our stage manager. *(He sees they are waiting for an explanation.)* I thought since none of us know jack shit about the Bible, we should have Virginia do the writing on this one. *(A moment.)* And I heard her speak a few weeks ago and couldn't get her out of my mind...so, here she is.

(Clearly, Jack has more than a professional interest in Virginia.)

VIRGINIA: I'm so happy to be here. I've been a big fan of this company for so long. But I don't really know very much about the theatre.

JACK: It's easy. You'll see. We pick a subject, then we improvise until we get to know the characters and how the story goes. Then you pull the whole thing together and write the scenes. So... *(Taking her over to it.)* this is our table...

(Sarah sees Abraham staring at Hagar.)

ABRAHAM: *(Taking Sarah's arm.)* Our little Monica looks pretty good, doesn't she?

SARAH: She certainly does.

HAGAR: It's the money.

JACK: *(Holding Virginia's chair.)* And until the costume designer gets here, we just pull our rehearsal clothes out of wardrobe, you know, sandals, black hair.

(Sarah wants Jack's attention now. She comes up to him.)

SARAH: Jack, maybe it would be fun if I played the maid this time, and Monica played Sarah.

JACK: You're perfect for Sarah. You're just exactly who she must have been. Or so Virginia tells me. And if you hate being Sarah, well, then, *(A moment.)* we'll know she hated it too.

(Hagar comes to the table.)

SARAH: But Jack...

JACK: *(Friendly but a little weary.)* Oh for Christ's sake, Kitty? What do you want? It's the lead.

SARAH: It's the wife. I'm always the wife.

HAGAR: And I'm always the one with no clothes on.

JACK: So can we we get started here?

(Sarah watches as Abraham holds Hagar's chair for her.)

SARAH: *(Turning to Virginia.)* O.K. Virginia. Tell me quick. Do I die?

VIRGINIA: Night after night.

JACK: *(Handing out some papers.)* Ladies and Gentlemen, welcome to our humble hall. Where some night in the early spring we will pounce upon the unwitting audience with the opening of Who was Sarah, Who was Abraham, and *(Kissing Virginia on the forehead.)* What the Hell Happened to Them.

(And the lights dim or change to indicate a change of scene.)

SCENE II

As the lights come back up, Virginia opens a large map and spreads it out in front of them on the table.

VIRGINIA: *(Finishing her sentence.)* …so Abraham came down to Iraq to marry Sarah, but he took her home to Turkey to live.

ABRAHAM: Abraham was an Arab?

VIRGINIA: Think of Omar Sharif.

(Abraham leaves the table, and wanders over toward the trunks and discarded furniture.)

SARAH: And what did Sarah do all day?

VIRGINIA: *(Looks at Jack, then answers.)* She was a High Priest.

HAGAR: A High Priest of what?

JACK: Let's just call it the old Mesopotamian Moon Worship.

(Abraham has found a couple of old blankets, which he has draped over an upholstered chair, to create a mound that looks like a hillside knoll.)

SARAH: I didn't know that. How do we know this? Does everybody know this?

VIRGINIA: Just academics, mainly, but word is leaking out. There's a whole canon of Sarah stories, and hundreds of thousands of coins from the time with her picture on them, and several huge statues found in the temple at…

JACK: *(Shaking his head.)* Kitty, who Sarah *really* was is not part of our story here. It's the Bible version we're after. How marriage used to be. You loved this man. *(Indicating Cliff.)* You stood behind him, all the way. When God told him to move, you started packing.

(Sarah nods but doesn't answer.)

ABRAHAM: *(Climbing up his hillside.)* Now when God talks to me, particularly the first time, who do I think it is?

(Jack takes some pieces of paper from Virginia.)

SARAH: *(Amused.)* What are you doing?

ABRAHAM: *(Enjoying himself.)* Watching my sheep.

JACK: Tom, can we get some copies of this?

(Jack walks out into the playing area, looking for something to use as a prop.)

ABRAHAM: And how old is Abraham now?

JACK: Virginia?

ABRAHAM: *(Stretching out.)* Have I had my lunch?

VIRGINIA: In Bible years?

ABRAHAM: I'm eating some figs, I think. But where did I get them? Does my robe have pockets?

SARAH: Just rest, Cliff. It's the first time you've been in the shade all day.

(Jack sees what he was looking for, a piece of driftwood, which he hands to Abraham for use as a shepherd's crook.)

JACK: Here you go.

HAGAR: Jack, I have a little costume fitting at four.

SARAH: How little?

JACK: Hey. It's hot in the desert, O.K.? *(Then to Hagar.)* Thanks, Monica. We'll see you tomorrow.

(Hagar gathers up her things and leaves.)

ABRAHAM: *(To Jack.)* And what's going on between Abraham and Sarah right now?

JACK: What do you mean?

ABRAHAM: Well don't you think they're having some money trouble? Or maybe things have gotten real routine in the bed or something.

JACK: Sure. That sounds right. *(Backs away.)* O.K., Tom, you read God. And Abraham, you're not written yet, so just see how it feels to hear it.

(Sarah and Virginia are whispering about something, and studying the map.)

ABRAHAM: No problem.

TOM: *(Reading.)* "Abraham."

ABRAHAM: *(As though answering roll call.)* Here.

TOM: *(Reading.)* "Get thee out of thy country,…away from thy kindred…and unto a land that I will show you."

ABRAHAM: Who is this?

TOM: "Where I will make of you a great nation. Where I will bless you and make your name great. Where I will bless those who bless you, and curse those who curse you. For in your name, Abraham, will all families of the earth be blessed."

ABRAHAM: *(Startled at the impact of it.)* Wow.

JACK: Good. You got it. He matters for a change.

ABRAHAM: I know. So is he really going to tell his wife, that some *voice* told him to move to…California? I mean, if it was me…

JACK: It *is* you.

ABRAHAM: I'd just say I was tired of being broke and how about if we go to the coast for pilot season and see how we make out. You know, give her a business reason.

JACK: O.K. Now Sarah, darling. There he is. The love of your life.

(She nods and approaches him.)

SARAH: Abraham.

ABRAHAM: *(Gestures.)* Come on up.

(Sarah, not really in character yet, walks up to his hillside, stops, then sweeps her hair off her neck in a very contemporary gesture of exhaustion.)

SARAH: God it's hot out here.

(Abraham wipes his forehead with his shirtsleeve.)

ABRAHAM: Yeah. It is. *(A grin.)* Let's move.

JACK: *(A burst of laughter.)* I love it.

ABRAHAM: Thanks.

SARAH: Tom, can you get me a skirt? I can't do this in pants.

JACK: *(Walks up to them.)* Now they don't talk very often, these two. Abraham probably doesn't even sleep up there most nights. And Sarah's gone a lot. Sacrificing things, working with the virgins, whatever. So it's a fairly formal relationship. *(A moment.)* Tom, what can we use for some shade?

TOM: I'll see what I can do.

(Jack and Tom search for some kind of shade as Sarah and Abraham talk.)

SARAH: *(Playing with the formality.)* Greetings, husband. How are your sheep?

ABRAHAM: Not ba-a-ad.

(Sarah has to laugh and punches him affectionately.)

JACK: *(To Abraham.)* Now this is a really old marriage. Maybe twenty years.

VIRGINIA: Forty.

JACK: And everything is in her name. So Abraham owes this lady.

SARAH: *(Getting a cup from the table.)* Oh God, don't tell him *that*.

JACK: Why not?

SARAH: Then he'll really hate me.

JACK: He doesn't hate you.

SARAH: If he owes me, he hates me.

JACK: O.K. now. One more time. Only let's have it the end of the day, so Abraham's had time to think about what to say.

(Jack walks over to the table and sits down with Virginia, leaving Sarah and Abraham alone in the playing area.)

SARAH: *(The first hint of the Sarah voice.)* Good evening, husband.

(Abraham jumps down from his rock.)

ABRAHAM: I can't do it. The guy may be a jerk, but he's not stupid. A voice? Come on. He's not going to tell her…

SARAH: *(Calmly.)* Maybe Abraham doesn't have to tell her. Maybe she knows he's been thinking about something.

ABRAHAM: Good.

SARAH: It could only be two or three things.

ABRAHAM: Right. He's just got to get out of there.

SARAH: That's what she thought.

ABRAHAM: Well what choice does he have? I mean, if Abraham doesn't make his move pretty quick, he might be stuck out here forever, middle of *nowhere*, trading what… *(He looks at Virginia.)* his sheep for their sheep? But if he goes to the coast, he can get rich.

SARAH: Rich enough to buy another wife? A wife that won't be so routine in the bed?

ABRAHAM: I'll buy you some slaves.

SARAH: I don't want any slaves.

ABRAHAM: Anything you want then. I always wanted to buy you things, it's just I didn't…

SARAH: I want our life to stay the way it is.

ABRAHAM: It's already changed. As soon as I started wanting something else, it was over, wasn't it?

SARAH: No. It's not over til you leave me.

ABRAHAM: I'm not leaving you. All Abraham wants to do is move to the coast.

SARAH: Where everybody leaves everybody and nobody gives a shit.

JACK: Wonderful! Right on the money. God, I had no idea this was so rich. Five minutes everybody. Virginia, are you getting all this, or should we start taping everything? Nice work, Sarah. Really hot.

(Abraham follows Jack out the door to the hallway.)

ABRAHAM: What do you think? Will they see why God picked me?

(Sarah takes a deep breath and walks over to Virginia.)

SARAH: What did Sarah look like?

(Virginia opens a book on the table.)

VIRGINIA: There. Six feet tall and drop-dead gorgeous.

SARAH: What's that?

VIRGINIA: A divine cloud over her tent. One of the Sarah stories says it was there all the time, like a sign, and her doors were always open, and a light, not a candle, but a mysterious light shone day and night.

SARAH: So, how much does Sarah know about this coast Abraham wants to go to?

VIRGINIA: She's heard of it, I'm sure, from the traders. But probably the only thing she knows for sure is that they're heathen. They're sun-worshippers.

SARAH: Then why would she go with him?

VIRGINIA: Mission work, maybe. Priests like Sarah were always traveling around setting up new centers of moon worship.

SARAH: Actually, I can see worshipping the moon.

VIRGINIA: I know. I can too. Fertility, crops…

SARAH: Mystery, romance…

(And the lights dim to indicate end of scene.)

SCENE III

The actors now have xeroxed pages in their hands. Sarah ties on a rehearsal skirt as Tom sets up a tent-frame to one side, and drapes it with sheets of frayed canvas. Hagar stands at a wardrobe, putting on eye makeup.

JACK: All right, now. Virginia has finished a new scene for us, so we'll just read through it. Real easy. Just like we did yesterday. Scene One is Abraham hears from God. Scene Two is a trader comes into the camp and describes this terrible famine creeping toward them, giving Abraham just the business reason he was looking for, and this is Scene Three. Abraham talks to Sarah. *(He motions toward the set.)* O.K. Now, Sarah's tent will be here on a hill. *(Indicating the poles now in the set.)* Looking something like this. Poles or something. And it's one of those long desert twilights. Plain. Campfires glowing,

SARAH: Children playing after supper…

ABRAHAM: Camels and goats tied up for the night…

JACK: It's your standard desert tribe getting ready for bed. Abraham has finished his rounds, and he climbs the hill to find Sarah.

ABRAHAM: And what is she doing?

JACK: Looking out at the tents.

ABRAHAM: To see if I arranged them right?

SARAH: She likes the way they look.

JACK: Tom, cue Sarah's music. It's your line, Abraham.

(Tom punches a tape recorder on his desk, which plays a sacred Mesopotamian melody on a primitive stringed instrument.)

ABRAHAM: *(Reading from the script.)* "Sarah, my love. I have had some disturbing news from the south. A famine lies upon the land of Canaan."

SARAH: "I too have heard this news."

(Jack leans over to Virginia and whispers something we can't hear. Virginia makes a note in her book.)

ABRAHAM: "We must leave this place. If the famine sweeps north, it could destroy us."

SARAH: "There is no need to move, Abraham. Our God is pleased with us. Our wells are full. Our prayers will keep them full."

ABRAHAM: "I would take all who dwell with us, and travel south toward the coastal trading center of... *(He checks the pronunciation.)* Byblos? Byblos?

VIRGINIA: *(Saying it correctly.)* Byblos.

ABRAHAM: "For by entering into trade we will not have to depend on our crops and herds to feed us."

SARAH: "You would leave this land of peace and prosperity, where our storehouses are full, where we have served our God's purpose, and wander into the land of the Philistines?"

ABRAHAM: "I would stand and greet the Pharaohs when they float their barges to my shore."

SARAH: "I have seen your thoughts in my dreams, Abraham. You would grow rich in the service of false gods."

ABRAHAM: "I was born to the desert. But I would end my life in sight of the great sea."

JACK: O.K. Good.

ABRAHAM: This is great, Virginia. "In sight of the great sea."

JACK: Let's go on.

ABRAHAM: O.K., but can I paraphrase some of this, Virginia? It feels a little stilted.

JACK: It is a little stiff, love.

SARAH: I like it stiff.

ABRAHAM: You would.

SARAH: What's that supposed to mean?

ABRAHAM: I'm sorry. I didn't mean "you." That's what Abraham is feeling. Sarah's a prude. This is *her* town and he knows it. That's why he wants to get away. They worship her here.

SARAH: He knew that when he married her.

ABRAHAM: Well, maybe he didn't know how tired he'd get, walking up the hill to talk to her.

SARAH: She'll meet him wherever he says. It's not her fault she's a priestess. But they're depending on her now. The whole tribe.

ABRAHAM: If she doesn't want to be a Priestess, why doesn't she quit?

SARAH: Would that make him happy?

ABRAHAM: She's not interested in making him happy.

SARAH: Yes, she is too.

ABRAHAM: They why won't she go with him to the coast?

SARAH: She does go with him to the coast, didn't you read what Virginia gave us?

ABRAHAM: No, not yet. I wanted to...

SARAH: They run smack into this famine, just like Sarah said they would. But when they get to the border, there's a problem. The Pharaoh needs a priest, they say, and he likes them pretty. So I have to hide in a basket. Then when they find me in the basket, I have to say I'm not your wife, I'm your sister, so they won't kill you.

ABRAHAM: O.K. Thanks.

SARAH: Only now that I'm your sister, they tie me up, set me on a camel and I spend the next month in the harem.

JACK: The Bible doesn't say a month.

SARAH: A night, a month, what difference does it make? *(To Abraham.)* So I ask my Gods and they make it rain. But when the Pharaoh finally finds out I *am* your wife, not your sister, he's so mad at what his Gods will do to him for taking me, that he gives me back to you as fast as he can, and heaps all these presents on you and gives me one of his daughters for a maid.

HAGAR: Yes, Ma'am?

SARAH: Only by then, you're so mad at me, for being right about we never should have come here, that you fuck this maid, and you keep fucking this maid til she gets pregnant.

HAGAR: And whose fault is that?

(Sarah is so upset, she runs out of the room.)

SARAH: It's not mine, I can tell you that.

JACK: *(Calling after her.)* Sarah, wait. Where are you going?

SARAH: I don't know. *(She slams out the door.)*

(Jack follows her as fast as he can, as Abraham turns to Hagar and shrugs.)

ABRAHAM: What did I say?

HAGAR: *(Taking off her sweater.)* Is that how the story goes, really?

ABRAHAM: I don't think so. I mean… *(Enjoying this look at her body.)* That's not why I sleep with you, because I'm mad at her.

HAGAR: I don't care if it is. She never talks to me anyway. She never did. What does she think, it's some kind of sin to go work in the movies?

ABRAHAM: Maybe she does.

HAGAR: It's not just her, either. Everybody around here feels that way. As far as I can tell, you're the only one who's looking at me and seeing a real person.

ABRAHAM: You're a beautiful woman.

HAGAR: So if it's comfort you're offering me, Abraham, I'm not going to turn you down.

ABRAHAM: I had no idea you were so unhappy.

HAGAR: In Hollywood, we believe in treating people nice.

ABRAHAM: Even men?

HAGAR: Especially men.

(Abraham, slightly uncomfortable, turns to Virginia.)

ABRAHAM: What's going on? Is Jack coming back?

VIRGINIA: I don't know.

ABRAHAM: Well, look, it's almost five o'clock, anyway. I'm leaving.

HAGAR: Yeah. Me too. *(To Abraham.)* Can you drop me off at the Oyster?

ABRAHAM: Sure.

(Hagar and Abraham put on their coats and prepare to leave as the lights dim.)

HAGAR: Did you ever think about doing a movie?

ABRAHAM: Well, sure I thought about it.

HAGAR: You'd be great.

ABRAHAM: I'd love to do a movie.

(They go out the door. Jack enters from another door.)

JACK: Where'd everybody go?

VIRGINIA: They went to the Oyster. They said rehearsal was over.

JACK: Goddamn him.

VIRGINIA: Who, Cliff?

JACK: Do *you* find him attractive? *(Then quickly.)* No. Don't answer that.

VIRGINIA: Of course he's attractive. Isn't that why you cast him?

JACK: Let's get you back to the hotel, what do you say?

(Lights change or dim for the end of the scene.)

SCENE IV
Sarah and Jack are alone in the room.

SARAH: Are you mad at me?

JACK: Of course not. Why should I be mad at you?

SARAH: I thought we were doing something last night.

JACK: Jesus. I'm sorry. I got talking with Virginia and...

SARAH: I just feel so...I mean, when the only time I see you is in rehearsal, I...I miss you.

JACK: I'm sorry, sweetheart. Can we do it tonight? We'll drive out to Harry's and drink them all under the bar, what do you think?

SARAH: I think they're probably all still under the bar from the last time we were at Harry's.

JACK: Damn right they are.

SARAH: It's all right. I think I'll just go home tonight. I've been really beat lately. But what I wanted to say was...I feel like you're not on my side. You're making Sarah this imperious bitch who lords it over everybody.

JACK: No, you're just feeling like an imperious bitch because that's who Sarah was.

SARAH: She was not. Everything she did was for somebody else.

JACK: I'm sorry about our date. Can we do it tonight?

SARAH: No, that's all right. I don't know what's the matter with me. Maybe it's Monica.
(Virginia enters.)

JACK: It always was Monica, as I remember. *(He kisses her.)* Virginia, Kitty thinks we're making Sarah too pushy.

SARAH: What if we had a scene between Sarah and the Pharaoh in the harem? Where Sarah gets to dance or something.

JACK: The audience doesn't care about the Pharaoh. And she didn't sleep with him. Right, Virginia?

VIRGINIA: No, all they did was perform the Sacred Marriage.

SARAH: And that's not sleeping with him?

VIRGINIA: No, that's him sleeping with your virgins while you watch.

SARAH: For what?

VIRGINIA: Rain.

JACK: She was celibate, O.K.? Priests could have households and husbands, but no sex.

SARAH: She was in the harem for a month, Jack. Who knows what happened?

Are you afraid the audience won't like me if I've had a lover? I mean, I *know* Abraham didn't want her. But the Pharaoh was a different kind of man. He wasn't afraid of her power. Maybe he even got off on it. Sarah would've liked that.

JACK: I'm sure she would.

SARAH: So what if she risked herself for once? Would that be so terrible? Sarah spends an evening with an elegant stranger? Someone with some charm? Talking about something other than sheep? Lifting a glass, forgetting who she was, sinking backward, her robe slipping off her shoulders? *(Turns to Virginia.)* Would it?

VIRGINIA: No.

JACK: No, what?

VIRGINIA: That wouldn't be so bad.

JACK: It would be horrible. How could we believe in her after that? What is the problem here?

SARAH: My problem is, Abraham falls in love with that little whore and it's not fair.

JACK: Go on.

SARAH: This girl's not like all the others. Couldn't Sarah just have one happy scene before she loses her husband to this Hagar?

JACK: All what others?

SARAH: Darling director, my husband has had every virgin in the valley.

JACK: Physically. Yes. He has wives and children in the village. But that doesn't mean Abraham loved these women. He probably just didn't want to hurt their feelings.

SARAH: Keep up the morale, you mean.

JACK: It's you he loves. You and you alone.

SARAH: It's O.K., Jack.

JACK: It's *not* O.K. You're a beautiful woman. The most beautiful woman he's ever seen. From the first moment he saw you…

SARAH: Please.

JACK: …when you interpreted his dream, he has known that he was not free, that his passion for you was …

SARAH: *(Amused.)* All right. We get the idea.

JACK: It's more than an idea. He loves who you are and what you can do. There's not a woman in the world who could compare to you.

SARAH: He has said that.

JACK: All he wants is to spend the rest of his life with you. Protect you, care for you, give you everything you need.

SARAH: O.K. Yes. I mean, he does still live with me, so that's something.

JACK: He is yours, Kitty. Yours alone.

SARAH: *(Carefully.)* I think he's already sleeping with her.

JACK: Absolutely not. I would know it if he was.

(Abraham and Hagar walk in laughing.)

HAGAR: Well, it seemed kind of silly to ask them to close the set for the nude scene, when everybody who sees the movie's gonna see me nude anyway.

SARAH: All right. But he wants to.

JACK: *(To Abraham.)* Where's my sandwich?

ABRAHAM: Right here. Tomatoes and lettuce.

JACK: He hasn't slept with her. He hasn't even seen her. She's your property. You made rain, and the Pharaoh gave you his little girl to say thanks. *(He takes the sandwich.)* O.K.? *(He takes a bite.)* And Abraham got some gifts too, some camels, some…*(Struggling to think of them.)* camel blankets, some camel saddles, some drivers, some food for the camels, a couple of camels' hair coats, and the weight of twelve big camels in solid gold bars. *(Jack looks around at the group.)* All right?

SARAH: He gets the money, and I get the maid.

JACK: And then…

SARAH: And then he gets the maid.

ABRAHAM: *(Taking off his coat.)* You said you didn't want a maid.

(And the lights change to indicate a change of scene.)

SCENE V

Lights come up on Hagar, humming a melody we haven't heard before, brushing Sarah's hair. The actors carry their scripts, but don't read from them. Sarah is in a foul mood.

JACK: Any time, Sarah.

SARAH: She's hurting me.

HAGAR: She is not.

SARAH: And why can't I talk to her? The audience isn't going to know we didn't speak the same language.

JACK: What would you say?

SARAH: It wouldn't matter what I said. It would just give us some way to…

HAGAR: Get to know each other? Borrow each other's clothes?

SARAH: It doesn't have to be so ugly.

HAGAR: It's not ugly. I'm a slave, for God's sake. Let me be one.

JACK: Tom, read the narrator again, please.

SARAH: Are we actually having a narrator or not?

JACK: Maybe. Go Tom.

(As Tom reads, Abraham walks into the playing area, wearing a calf-length robe, tying a rope around his waist.)

TOM: *(Reading from the Bible.)* —And when the famine had ended, Abraham took his wife Sarah and the slave girl and all who had been with him in Egypt, and his nephew Lot, and dwelt in Bethel, in Canaan.—

(Abraham comes to stand beside Tom.)

TOM: —And Abraham walked with Lot to the top of a hill from which they beheld the plain of Jordan.—

ABRAHAM: "Choose which lands thou wouldst have, for thy family."

TOM: —And Lot saw *(Tom notices Abraham's coat.)* Nice coat.

ABRAHAM: Thanks.

TOM: —And Lot saw that the plain of Jordan was well supplied with water and so chose him that part, setting his tents toward Sodom.—

(Tom keeps reading, but goes back to his table and sits down.)

TOM: —And when Lot had departed, the Lord spoke to Abraham saying—

ABRAHAM: —Lift up your eyes, to the north, the south, to the east and the west. For all the land that you can see I give to you and to your seed forever.—

(Sarah stops Hagar from brushing and speaks to Abraham. He turns around, as though he had been relating this incident to her.)

SARAH: "And who was this God, my husband? By what name did he call himself?"

ABRAHAM: *(Quoting the Lord.)* —I am the Lord that brought thee out of Ur of the Chaldees, to give thee this land to inherit it.—

SARAH: *(Indicates to Hagar to kneel back down.)* "And how did he appear unto you?"

ABRAHAM: "As a smoking furnace with a burning lamp passing through it." *(Abraham is transfixed by Hagar.)* "He said he would make me a covenant." *(Hagar blushes.)*

ABRAHAM: "'Unto thy seed,' he said, 'have I given this land, from the river of Egypt to the river Euphrates.'"

SARAH: "Go on, my husband."

ABRAHAM: "He said he would give me as many descendants as there were stars in the sky."

SARAH: "And what response did you make to this God."

ABRAHAM: "I said, 'Behold, my Lord, to me thou has given no seed.'"

(Sarah opens a trunk, making a loud noise, gets something out and closes the trunk.)

SARAH: *(Very strong.)* "Seed your Lord has given you in abundance, Abraham. But yet no *heirs.*"

JACK: You can't help it, Abraham. You have to ask who this chick is.

ABRAHAM: "Sarah. Good wife, this chick is new to your household."

SARAH: "She is called Hagar, my husband. The daughter of the Pharaoh, whom he has given me as a servant. But she speaks not our language."

ABRAHAM: "I see that she is lonely."

SARAH: "She has been trained only in art of giving pleasure. But she is young yet. We will find other occupations for her."

(Tom rings a soft gong, a signal to Sarah. But something is stopping her from speaking.)

JACK: You have another line, Sarah.

SARAH: "Remain here for a moment, husband. I have sent for my scribe, and would take counsel with her."

(Sarah walks away, leaving Abraham and Hagar alone.)

JACK: Thanks.

SARAH: Would I really leave them alone?

JACK: You're not afraid of a slave girl. And even if you are, you're certainly not going to show it, O.K.?

(The melody Hagar was humming before, now returns played on a flute or other primitive stringed instrument. Sarah stands near Virginia just outside of the playing area, her arms wrapped tightly around her chest.)

SARAH: It's all over, isn't it. From the first moment he sees her.

VIRGINIA: Pretty much.

(Sarah watches intently as Jack talks Hagar and Abraham through their blocking.)

JACK: All right, Hagar. Back up, then bow, then kneel. And that's still not enough, and so prostrate yourself. Now Abraham. Show us you're tickled by this bowing and scraping, but don't move toward her yet. Now. Bend slightly, from the waist.

ABRAHAM: "Oh poor child, does your mistress never speak to you?"

(Hagar runs across the space and clings to his feet.)

HAGAR: "Master! You speak as one of my own family."

ABRAHAM: *(Has to laugh.)* "Yes, Princess. I learned your language from the traders. *(Helping her up.)* It is a beautiful tongue, and pleasing easy in my mouth. But I am afraid I yet know only the words for buying and selling."
(She sinks back to her knees and rests her head against his thigh.)

HAGAR: "Say those words then, Master, that I may love thee for speaking them."

ABRAHAM: *(Lifting her up again.)* "Your price is too high, sir. I will offer you half."

HAGAR: "Kind sir, I would accept half from such a man as you."

ABRAHAM: "But I would pay four times."
(She stops and he catches her in his arms.)

HAGAR: "Then what is it I may sell you, my Lord?"
(Abraham laughs easily, and sweeps her up in his arms.)

ABRAHAM: "Wonderful girl. Wonderful."

JACK: That's great, Virginia. Perfect. Only I think we can do without her tongue and his mouth, or whatever that…

VIRGINIA: *(Has to laugh.)* Right.
(Suddenly, Hagar bursts into a mocking improv of the scene, pulling Abraham down to the floor with her.)

HAGAR: Take me master, Kill me. Take as long as you like!

ABRAHAM: But what would my wife say?

HAGAR: Nothing I could understand, my darling.
(Abraham sweeps Hagar up lightly now, and before he realizes what he is doing, he kisses her happily and comfortably, with what everybody recognizes immediately as easy intimacy.)

ABRAHAM: Wild about you.

HAGAR: *(Embarrassed.)* Why didn't anybody warn me about these Turks?
(But it's no good to try and hide it. She and Cliff are lovers. And Sarah knows it.)

JACK: *(Nervously.)* O.K. Let's go back to…

SARAH: No. Let's go on.

JACK: Let's take a break, sweetheart.

SARAH: I have sent for my scribe and would take counsel with her. *(Looks around.)* Come on, Virginia.

VIRGINIA: I can't.

SARAH: Yes, you can.

JACK: *(Realizes the seriousness.)* Try it, Virginia. Tom, you take notes. Abraham and Hagar, off to the side please.
(Virginia walks uneasily into the playing area, feeling completely out of place. She is not an actor and that is apparent, at the beginning.)

VIRGINIA: *(Nervously.)* Yes, my Lord.

SARAH: They're lovers.

VIRGINIA: Not yet, Your Highness.

SARAH: Oh for Christ's sake, Virginia.

VIRGINIA: I'm sorry, Mistress.

SARAH: *(Furious, her thoughts running together.)* She cries a few fake tears about being lonely and he's takes her right to bed. Does everybody know about this?

VIRGINIA: This is the first I've heard, Madam.

SARAH: *(Has to laugh.)* I like "my Lord" better.

VIRGINIA: I do too.

SARAH: O.K. *(To Jack.)* Get ready, you guys. I'm going straight to the giveaway if I can. Let's go back, Virginia.

(Sarah and Virginia take their original positions.)

VIRGINIA: Yes, my Lord. You sent for me.

SARAH: My husband, Abraham, would take the Egyptian girl, Hagar to his bed.

VIRGINIA: *(Looks up from her writing.)* Send her away, my Lord. She is not respectful of our ways.

SARAH: I cannot. I fear that Abraham would follow her.

VIRGINIA: Then you must let him go.

SARAH: *(Pacing, working hard to find this.)* I cannot. He has served me well.

VIRGINIA: *(Disagrees.)* He has lived well for serving you.

SARAH: He has not had a wife as other men.

VIRGINIA: He has children in the valley. And women to serve him.

SARAH: He would have his own child in his own house.

VIRGINIA: And where is it written that a man shall have his own child in his own house?

SARAH: *(Holds up her hand for Virginia to stop.)* Such a law does not have to be written.

VIRGINIA: But as a High Priest, you cannot bear his child.

SARAH: No. But I could take their child as my own, could I not?

VIRGINIA: Yes, that is your right.

SARAH: *(Carefully.)* Then that is what I will do.

VIRGINIA: Why, my Lord?

(Sarah struggles to find the answer, looking at Abraham, who has turned his back on her, pretending not to pay attention.)

SARAH: *(Finally.)* My Abraham is a comfort to me.

JACK: Great. And…wait a beat and…Hagar. Scream.

(Hagar screams, but it is hard to tell whether it is extreme pain or pleasure.)
JACK: O.K., Sarah. Go get the little bitch. Just remember, neither of you understands a word the other says.
(Sarah stalks over to Hagar, who screams again at the sight of her.)
HAGAR: No, Lady! God save me. Help me! She's going to kill me!
SARAH: *(Pulls Hagar up from the floor.)* Get up, you.
HAGAR: Where are you taking me? Please! Abraham!
JACK: Abraham, get into Sarah's tent!
ABRAHAM: Uh-uh. I don't go in there unless she invites me.
JACK: She sent for you.
ABRAHAM: *(Actually worried.)* O.K. O.K.
(Sarah jerks Hagar to her feet outside the tent.)
HAGAR: You're hurting me!
(Sarah holds the girl firmly.)
SARAH: You are the daughter of the Pharaoh.
HAGAR: *(Pleading.)* What did I do?
SARAH: *(Rearranging Hagar's dress.)* Stand up straight.
HAGAR: Please, Mistress...
SARAH: And don't beg.
JACK: Fabulous. Right on in, now. And your cheating ass when they get there.
(Sarah and Hagar walk in upright and regal, both of them, and stop about six feet from Abraham. He bows.)
SARAH: Feed it to me, Virginia. Right from the Bible.
VIRGINIA: *(Quietly.)* Behold Abraham, my God has restrained me from bearing. I pray thee...—
SARAH: O.K. I know the rest of it. *(To the still bowed Abraham.)* Behold, Abraham.
(Abraham eases himself up, but he is not at all comfortable with the two of them standing in front of him.)
SARAH: My God has restrained me from bearing.
(He nods.)
SARAH: I pray thee...— *(Sarah picks up Hagar's hand and looks straight at Abraham.)* Go in unto my maid.—
(Abraham backs up. Sarah takes one step toward him, with Hagar.)
SARAH: For it may be that I obtain children by her.—
(Hagar looks at Sarah, but Sarah will not return her glance, but instead keeps her eyes focused on Abraham. Jack picks the Bible off the table and reads.)
JACK: And Abraham hearkened to the voice of Sarah.

ABRAHAM: I am yours to command.

JACK: *(Continuing to read.)* —And in the tenth year that Abraham had dwelt in the land of Canaan, Sarah, Abraham's wife, took Hagar her maid, the Egyptian...

(Sarah lifts Hagar's hand to Abraham. He hesitates, Sarah takes another step toward him, and places the girl's hand in his, and steps back.)

JACK: ...and gave to her husband Abraham to be his wife—

(Hagar kneels before Abraham and kisses the hem of his robe. Abraham bows to Sarah, then straightens up and tries to compose himself, as Hagar strokes his feet. Sarah nods to him to get Hagar up. He reaches his hand down to the girl and lifts her to her feet.)

SARAH: *(Quietly.)* So be it.

(There is silence onstage. Abraham looks up at Sarah. Then Jack can't help himself.)

JACK: Jesus Christ. When you held out your hand like that, my heart was...

SARAH: Thanks.

JACK: There's not another actress in this whole country with that kind of power, Kitty.

(Hagar brushes by Sarah and gives her a good-natured hug.)

HAGAR: *I'm* impressed.

ABRAHAM: *(Finally come up to Sarah.)* I'm sorry. I can't just stand here and not grab you.

SARAH: *(Seems especially moved.)* Thanks, sweetheart. I love you too.

JACK: O.K. team. Everybody that's not involved in that hug, can go home. But Abraham...

(Abraham breaks out of the embrace with Sarah.)

JACK: Could I see you for a minute?

(Abraham looks quickly over to Hagar.)

ABRAHAM: Can't do it now, Jack.

(Abraham realizes everybody is looking at him. Sarah has seen this glance at Hagar, and so has Jack.)

ABRAHAM: I promised Paul I'd go with him to pick up the tents.

(But they all know this is a lie.)

JACK: How about after the show tonight?

ABRAHAM: Can't do that either. How about Friday before rehearsal?

JACK: Good. Ten-thirty, then. Coupla things I want to talk to you about.

(Lights dim or change for end of scene.)

SCENE VI
Jack is pacing. Cliff is waiting. Virginia sits quietly.

JACK: Old Sarah's a smart girl.

ABRAHAM: No kidding.

JACK: So what does she see in *you?*

ABRAHAM: I never thought about it.

JACK: She should dump you so fast.

ABRAHAM: Because of Hagar, you mean.

JACK: You're not even trying to hide it!

ABRAHAM: This is not like other marriages, Jack. It's more like a little corporation. We're business partners, Sarah and me. What I do on my time is my business.

JACK: I see that, I do, it's just this problem with the audience.

ABRAHAM: What do you mean?

JACK: They're going to hate you.

ABRAHAM: Hate me?

JACK: Yeah. It looks like you used Sarah's influence to get rich, and then you dumped her for a piece of Egyptian tail.

ABRAHAM: Not on purpose I didn't. It's in the script.

JACK: I give up.

ABRAHAM: What? If it's about my work, just tell me. Maybe you'd like a little more nobility.

JACK: What I'd like is a little more respect for your wife.

ABRAHAM: *(Getting out his notebook.)* O.K.

JACK: I mean, Sarah *is* funny and smart, so you wouldn't be making it *all* up, right?

ABRAHAM: Abraham loves Sarah, Jack. He always has. It's just time for her to lose one.

JACK: It's more than one she's losing.

ABRAHAM: O.K. She's losing the whole thing. But nobody gets to stay on top forever.

JACK: That's as wrong as it can be. Abraham does not have *attitude,* Cliff. Now please. The audience wants to love you. All we have to do is stay out of their way.

ABRAHAM: *(Taking a note.)* No attitude.

VIRGINIA: I need to make a call.

(He nods to her and she leaves.)

JACK: Good. Now. Let's go on to Hagar. What do you want from *her?*

ABRAHAM: Sex.

JACK: Just sex?

ABRAHAM: No it's not just sex. It's sex the way I like it. Right?

JACK: No. That's not enough.

ABRAHAM: O.K., then. How about how much money I could make in Egypt as Hagar's husband?

JACK: Can't you have some passion for the girl?

ABRAHAM: Passion.

JACK: I want you obsessed with her. You can't think of anything else. Night and day, you smell her perfume, you hear her sigh, you feel her fresh young limbs wrapped around you.

ABRAHAM: *(Making a note.)* Sure.

JACK: Because the audience see, the audience can forgive you passion.

ABRAHAM: Yeah, this is great.

JACK: And Abraham is a passionate man. He loves his God and follows his orders, and he loves these two women, one a priest, and the other a slave. Now that's a story we can sell.

ABRAHAM: You're doing a helluva job on this. Does that about take care of it?

JACK: Unless you have some idea what this *God* sees in you.

ABRAHAM: I do what he says, that's what it is. God's going to make me the father of millions, and I'm going to give him all the credit.

JACK: O.K., then. Be nice to Sarah.

ABRAHAM: I miss talking to her.

JACK: What a great idea.

ABRAHAM: Thanks.

JACK: Try to find a moment to show us that. Where are you off to?

ABRAHAM: Monica gave me this agent's name to call. You ever thought about films?

JACK: From time to time.

(Abraham goes out the door, as Sarah is coming in.)

ABRAHAM: Hi.

SARAH: Cliff, could you come out to the house sometime and…nevermind.

ABRAHAM: O.K.

(Cliff leaves and Kitty walks on into the room.)

JACK: What was all that about?

SARAH: Cliff has moved out. I guess. He hasn't been home for a week.

JACK: Is that so bad?

SARAH: I don't know. Maybe it is, maybe it isn't.

JACK: What do you mean?

SARAH: I'm pregnant.

(Jack is stunned. But he knows enough to be enthusiastic.)

JACK: Kitty. That's wonderful. A baby!

SARAH: I know. It's the strangest feeling.

JACK: Uh. Have you and Cliff…

SARAH: Do I know whether it's his baby or yours? No. I don't.

JACK: Kitty, we only had that one… *(He stops.)* And that's all it takes. Jesus. *(He stops.)* What are you going to do?

SARAH: Well, I think we can pretty much tell what your response is.

JACK: Kitty, please…

(Virginia walks back in with Hagar. Tom approaches from backstage.)

HAGAR: Virginia. Great scarf.

VIRGINIA: Thanks.

TOM: Jack, do you want me to schedule those auditions for this afternoon?

JACK: So, what do you think, folks? Should we cast somebody as God and have him walk around like he was really there, or what?

SARAH: What do we need God for if we've got you?

(And as Virginia laughs, the lights change for the end of the scene.)

SCENE VII

Abraham and Sarah are pacing, going over their lines. Hagar is standing in the center of the playing area, as Tom helps her adjust the pregnant padding under her sweater. She is cranky and uncooperative.

TOM: How's that?

HAGAR: God, I forgot how repulsive this pregnant get-up was.

ABRAHAM: *(With a wink in his voice.)* There are some of us who find it *very* attractive.

JACK: *(Furious at him.)* Oh for God's sake, Abraham. Can we just do the scene?

SARAH: The scene is well underway, it seems to me.

(Hagar, kneels down in the center of the playing area, picks up her script from the floor.)

HAGAR: The scene is bullshit.

JACK: Some time has gone by. Hagar is pregnant, but one night, Sarah yelled at her, and she freaked out and ran away from camp. So this is what happens when the men bring her back. Abraham, you start.

(Abraham clears his throat, then goes to stand by the kneeling Hagar.)

ABRAHAM: *(Reading.)* "Hagar begs your forgiveness, my love, for running away, and for cursing you in public. She asks that you punish her in front of the entire household, so they may learn from the error of her ways."

(Sarah comes a step closer.)

SARAH: "And she promises to behave toward me with respect?"

ABRAHAM: "She does."

SARAH: "I would hear this promise from her lips."

ABRAHAM: "Say to the lady,"

HAGAR: *(Standing up.)* Didn't anybody hear me before? This scene is bullshit! I am not some whining little slut who'd run off into the desert just because Sarah yelled at me.

JACK: Actually, darling, I'm afraid you are right now. But by the end of the play…

HAGAR: And Virginia hasn't got a clue how hard it is to be a slut.

VIRGINIA: That's true.

HAGAR: How can Sarah be mad at me for getting pregnant? Isn't that why she gave me to him?

SARAH: I'm doing everything I can to make you comfortable.

HAGAR: I'm pregnant, darling. I'm not going to *be* comfortable.

SARAH: I've even given you your own tent.

HAGAR: With a fucking guard outside it night and day.

SARAH: In case you need anything.

HAGAR: Great. Tell him to bring me three weeks worth of food and water and a camel.

JACK: Virginia, can Sarah let Hagar go?

VIRGINIA: No, she can't. It would be a major diplomatic embarrassment to the Pharaoh.

SARAH: And you can't go out in the desert, because you might lose the baby.

HAGAR: And once I have the baby, there'll be some other reason I can't leave, won't there? Like the slave traders will swoop down on me and steal him.

SARAH: Isn't this what the script says, you despise me?

HAGAR: I'm a prisoner here! You're using me to hold onto your husband.

SARAH: If you would make an effort to learn our language, you might have something to do other than wait for my husband's visits.

HAGAR: Abraham is eighty-six years old. Do you think we have a good time in my tent?

SARAH: Well, you should've thought of that before you went after him.

HAGAR: I'm sorry, Ma'am. But your husband didn't take going after, he only took holding still for.

SARAH: Of all the goddamn...

ABRAHAM: *(To Hagar.)* Please, darling, maybe you should...

JACK: Don't call her darling!

ABRAHAM: *(Turning to Jack.)* Maybe we should start again from the top.

JACK: Hagar.

HAGAR: My name is Monica.

JACK: Abraham loves you. But you can't leave the camp before the baby is born.

HAGAR: Why not?

JACK: Because if Sarah doesn't adopt the boy, then he won't be legitimate.

HAGAR: I don't care whether he's legitimate or not!

JACK: Well, Abraham does. *This* is the baby the voice told him he would have. This baby will grow up to be Ishmael, the ancestor of Mohammed, the founder of Islam.

HAGAR: I don't care who he grows up to be. I can't say these lines.

ABRAHAM: Are there particular lines you're...

JACK: Abraham, shut up.

HAGAR: Don't you know what's going to happen to this baby when I have it? Sarah is going to take him away! Here she stands, everybody treating her like some kind of goddess, and all the time, she's planning to steal my child. *(Tearing off her pregnant padding.)* Now when in this goddamn play do *I* get *anything* except screwed?

SARAH: *(Wearily.)* Would you rather I just kill you?

HAGAR: Why don't you just do this play without me.

JACK: We can't.

SARAH: If you won't say the lines, we'll have to. This is the theatre.

HAGAR: *(And she turns to leave.)* This is *your* theatre, Sarah. And every show is *your* show. Well, I say, the hell with you.

JACK: No! Monica!

HAGAR: What!

SARAH: Jack...

JACK: Monica, I've got an idea.

HAGAR: *(Getting her coat from the piles.)* Tell it to my manager. I'm leaving.

JACK: *(An offering.)* How about a new scene where...

(She stops.)

JACK: ...if you'll go back and apologize to Sarah, God will give you whatever you want.

SARAH: I thought we weren't having a God.

JACK: Virginia, can Abraham...

VIRGINIA: *(Thinking quickly.)* Yes, he could. The Bible says an angel of God came to see Hagar in the desert.

JACK: Great. Abraham will come find you.

HAGAR: And say what?

JACK: And say whatever you want.

HAGAR: I want to go home.

JACK: I know we can work this out.

SARAH: But why should we? Is she the last whore in the world?

ABRAHAM: She's the last one whose father is King of Egypt.

SARAH: What does that mean?

ABRAHAM: It means she's good for business.

(Sarah turns away in contempt.)

ABRAHAM: You remember business.

JACK: Virginia. What does Hagar want?

VIRGINIA: It's something for Ishmael.

HAGAR: What for Ishmael?

VIRGINIA: You want a promise that Ishmael won't have to worship the moon.

HAGAR: Yeah. It's weird to worship the moon.

VIRGINIA: You want him to follow your religion, not Sarah's.

HAGAR: Keep talking.

VIRGINIA: When Abraham learns you ran away, he goes out into the desert and finds you, and promises you that Ishmael can worship the sun instead of the moon. And to prove it, he promises to have the boy circumcised, like your brothers and your father in Egypt.

HAGAR: And what else.

VIRGINIA: And himself too. Abraham has to circumcise himself too.

HAGAR: And what else.

VIRGINIA: *(Can't think of anything else.)* And all the men in the tribe.

HAGAR: Okay. That's good. It means I stand for something.

ABRAHAM: It's great. It's exactly what we were missing.

JACK: And you'll come back?

VIRGINIA: *(Quietly.)* Amazing.

HAGAR: I'll come back.

VIRGINIA: I bet that's exactly the way it happened.

JACK: O.K., then. That's what we'll do.

HAGAR: *(Putting her coat back on the hook.)* And I can apologize real good to Sarah. Wash her feet or something.

SARAH: *(Frosty.)* That won't be necessary.

(There is complete silence. Sarah puts on her coat.)

JACK: O.K., everybody. I guess that's all, until Virginia gets this written.

VIRGINIA: Jack, how is Abraham going to explain this circumcision business?

JACK: I don't know.

SARAH: It's easy. Abraham just climbs up to my tent one day and says, "I'm living with Hagar now and she's got this thing about my dick." *(And with that, she heads for the door.)*

(Jack motions behind her back for Hagar to say something to Sarah.)

HAGAR: *(Walks over to Sarah.)* Look, I'm sorry I made such a scene. My real problem is…you're so damn good. It's why I left the company in the first place. I mean, you're a real actor. I'm just an entertainer. You've got all this wisdom and power, and all I've got is good legs.

SARAH: *(Seems disoriented.)* It's just a difference in the way we work. I'm real technical, and you're…

HAGAR: Hollywood trash.

SARAH: No, that's not what I was going to say. You're O.K. You're better than you know. You're what everybody wants. Even me. I would give just about anything for a little entertainment right now. *(To Jack.)* You're through with me for today, right?

JACK: Sure.

SARAH: See you at half-hour.

(And there is a half-hearted chorus of Yeah, Bye, etc., and Sarah leaves the room.)

HAGAR: *(To Virginia.)* I hope I didn't hurt your feelings.

VIRGINIA: You had to. I hadn't been paying much attention to you.

HAGAR: To Hagar, you mean.

VIRGINIA: Hagar is the only woman in the Bible that God ever talked to directly, you know.

HAGAR: Well, maybe you'll put that in somewhere.

(Jack jerks Abraham aside.)

JACK: Are you a complete fool? Don't you see what you've done?

ABRAHAM: What?

JACK: You treated Sarah like shit. So she treated Hagar like shit, and now we all have to get circumcised. *(A moment.)* You promised me you would be nice to Sarah.

ABRAHAM: Well, I guess it didn't work for me.

JACK: It didn't work for you? All right, Cliff. Fine.

(Abraham takes Hagar's arm, completely unruffled by his conversation with Jack.)

ABRAHAM: Ready, love?

HAGAR: *(Taking his arm.)* Yes, sir.

VIRGINIA: *(Trying to help.)* Jack. How about some lunch?

JACK: What?

VIRGINIA: You know. What God did in the middle of the day.

JACK: Sure.

(After Abraham and Hagar leave, Jack turns to Virginia.)

JACK: Do you see what's happening? He's forgotten who gave him this fucking part. He thinks it's all him, he thinks this whole thing is working because of him. *(Slowly and bitterly.)* Well, I know how to fix that.

(Virginia says nothing and the lights go to black.)

END OF ACT I

ACT II

SCENE VIII

A single light comes up on Abraham. Sarah sits at the table. Jack calls out from the shadows.

JACK: Cliff, have you got anything to eat?

ABRAHAM: There's a ham sandwich in my bag. I ordered meatloaf, they gave me ham.

JACK: You don't want it?

ABRAHAM: I hate ham. It's bad for you. There oughta be a law against it.

(Jack gets the sandwich from Abraham's bag.)

JACK: Thanks. O.K., guys. Scene Eight.

(Abraham looks at Sarah, then speaks to Jack.)

ABRAHAM: I talk to you outside a minute?

JACK: What about?

ABRAHAM: Kitty, do you mind? Jack and I need to...

JACK: What?

ABRAHAM: You want to talk about it with her here?

JACK: Talk about what?

(Abraham looks at them, then can't restrain himself.)

ABRAHAM: My wife is pregnant, right?

JACK: Yes, she is.

ABRAHAM: Then why doesn't she say anything to me about it?

(Jack takes a moment to have a drink of his coffee, and purposefully puts his response in Bible terms.)

JACK: It's God who tells Abraham about the baby. He comes up to your tent one day...

ABRAHAM: Yeah, I know, I looked it up. I made him some lunch and he told me Sarah was going to have a baby.

JACK: Yes.

ABRAHAM: But don't you think she would say something to me about this? My wife is having a baby. I'm her husband and she's having a baby.

JACK: Yes, I do. I think you should talk about it.

ABRAHAM: Thank you.

JACK: Would you like her to start?

ABRAHAM: Yes, I would. Abraham, I'm having a...

SARAH: Abraham, I'm having a baby.

ABRAHAM: O.K.

SARAH: Fine.

ABRAHAM: So who is the father of this baby? And don't say it's me, because Abraham is a hundred years old.

SARAH: It's God.

ABRAHAM: It is not. God can't have any children. He's in heaven.

SARAH: God does what he feels like, Abraham. One day he's with you, the next day he's not. Unless, of course, you believe that he's with you all the time only you don't get *how*.

(Abraham can't stay in the story.)

ABRAHAM: Is it my baby?

SARAH: I don't know, Abraham. Maybe it is. Maybe it isn't. You're living with a slave girl anyway. What do you care?

ABRAHAM: You're my wife!

SARAH: Oh please. After all the women you've had over the years, where do you get off telling me I can't have an affair and have a baby.

ABRAHAM: All right.

SARAH: *(Thinks that's the end of it.)* O.K., then.

ABRAHAM: So whose baby is it?

JACK: —And the Lord visited Sarah as he had said, and the Lord did unto Sarah as he had spoken, and Sarah conceived.—

(Tom enters. Abraham goes back to talking in Bible terms.)

ABRAHAM: No. God is my friend. Now what about that Abimelech character? That's the father of this baby. He's one of those kings Sarah goes around performing all these religious rituals with. Only now we find out there's nothing religious about it. She's just fucking them.

JACK: Cliff...

ABRAHAM: Only this time she got caught. Didn't she.

SARAH: No, that wasn't it at all.

ABRAHAM: *(But he can't stay in Bible terms.)* Goddamn you. And I trusted you too. I thought you loved me.

SARAH: I do love you.

JACK: She raises this child as your son.

ABRAHAM: You don't want a child.

SARAH: I always wanted a child.

ABRAHAM: Then why didn't you say that?

SARAH: I wanted to tell you, but you weren't home.

(Virginia enters. Abraham goes back to speaking in Bible terms.)

ABRAHAM: So what am I supposed to do now? Go back and live with Sarah and raise God's child?

JACK: Maybe you are. I don't know.

ABRAHAM: Does Sarah want a divorce?

SARAH: No. She doesn't.

ABRAHAM: Because God can't marry her, I guess.

JACK: No. She can't marry God.

SARAH: She doesn't want to.

VIRGINIA: She'd never see him.

JACK: We have to get started. Where's Monica?

HAGAR: *(As she enters.)* Waiting in the hall.

JACK: All right, then. Abraham and Hagar center stage for Scene Eight. God tells Abraham that Sarah is having a child. Read please, Tom.

(Abraham meets Hagar at the center of the stage and puts his arm around her.)

TOM: And Hagar bore Abraham a son, and Abraham called his son's name, Ishmael. And when Ishmael was thirteen years old...

(Abraham addresses Sarah directly. And this time, he doesn't care who hears what.)

ABRAHAM: This is a joke, right? You're not really pregnant.

SARAH: Cliff, it is perfectly obvious that you are capable of meeting somebody and changing your life. I can do the same damn thing. *(Pause.)* Or did you think I was blind. Or too old. Did you think I would just reach for a Kleenex and watch you leave me?

(Jack tries to get them back to the story.)

JACK: Sarah will be the mother of nations.

ABRAHAM: *(Turning to Jack.)* No, no. God said *Hagar* would be the mother of nations.

JACK: He changed his mind. Maybe he didn't like how Ishmael turned out. Hear the word of the Lord. *(He opens a Bible.)* —Sarah shall bear thee a son. And I will establish my covenant with him and with his seed after him.—

HAGAR: Ask him, Abraham. What about *my* son.

JACK: What's his name again?

ABRAHAM: Ishmael.

JACK: *(Looking at the Bible.)* I will multiply him exceedingly.

ABRAHAM: *(To Jack.)* You're mad at me.

JACK: Am I?

ABRAHAM: God is mad at me because I waited so long to do those circumcisions.

JACK: Could be.

ABRAHAM: O.K., O.K. I'll get all the men together and *do* it. I'll say we're all getting infected, living out here in the desert, never taking a bath. I'll give a feast.

JACK: Sure, Abraham. Have a feast if you want.

ABRAHAM: I want to know when we're having something written down for this act. Are we doing Sodom and Gomorrah?

JACK: I don't think so.

ABRAHAM: But those are big scenes for me. Walking around with God, looking for ten good men, saving my brother's life?

JACK: We're not doing Sodom and Gomorrah because it doesn't have Sarah in it. Sodom and Gomorrah is just you and Lot and a bunch of whores and drunks.

ABRAHAM: So?

JACK: You can do Sodom when you do the movie.

ABRAHAM: I don't get it.

JACK: *(Turning to Sarah.)* What shall we name the boy? Isaac?

SARAH: It's a beautiful name.

ABRAHAM: What about your work?

SARAH: What about it?

ABRAHAM: You'd never let anything interfere with your work.

SARAH: *(Very silly.)* I heard a voice, Abraham. A voice told me to have a child.

HAGAR: She's jealous.

ABRAHAM: Of what?

HAGAR: Of the whole thing. Of you and me. She did this to get even.

SARAH: She did this…

VIRGINIA: *God* did this, Abraham.

ABRAHAM: God got my hundred year old wife pregnant?

JACK: I love this. I absolutely love it. *(Pause.)* Virginia, this is exactly how we start the second act.

SCENE IX

Sarah appears to be alone onstage. She wears a loose linen dress, padded to appear in the late weeks of pregnancy. She mutters to herself, as she works on her attitude for the scene. As she works, she experiments with the feel of the costume, seeing what it will do.

SARAH: Laughter. Sarah laughs. *(Pause.)* The Lord has brought me laughter. Let all who will laugh, laugh with me.—Ha Ha.

(Tom emerges from the shadows to dress her bed, which is made from one of the tables we used earlier. He adds pillows, spreads, and bedclothes for a new baby.)

TOM: You look wonderful. You look so happy.

SARAH: I am happy. Finally, I'm doing something that has to do with me.

TOM: I'm putting your slippers right down here.

SARAH: I went over to Mom's last night and asked her how... *(Patting her stomach.)* Isaac would know I was his mother. She said he'd recognize my voice.

TOM: How long do you think you'll keep working?

SARAH: I'm not working after he's born, I can tell you that.

(Jack enters.)

JACK: Kitty, darling. You look fabulous. You feel so human here.

SARAH: I like this lady. Whenever she has a choice to make, she does the right thing.

JACK: I'll say. Your childbed, Madam. Here, let me...

(As Tom exits, Jack helps Sarah up into her bed.)

JACK: I adore you.

SARAH: *(Dreamily.)* If you'd have told me five years ago that I'd be having a baby...

JACK: No, I know. When you first told me about it, I...

SARAH: You freaked out.

JACK: I just hadn't ever thought about it, you know. But now that I see how happy it makes you...

SARAH: It's a miracle. I know.

JACK: I only wish everyone were doing as well. I'm afraid we're going to have to replace Cliff.

SARAH: Replace him? It's only a week til previews.

JACK: Not for here. For New York.

SARAH: For New York?

JACK: Yes, New York. Those people who saw the run-through yesterday are from the summer series at the Joyce. And they loved it, of course, and they want it for the first show of their season. They're sending me a contract today. We're going to New York, my love.

SARAH: Jack. Have you talked to Cliff about this? *(She leans back on the bed.)*

JACK: Not yet. I really thought he was right when I cast him, but he's really resisting me now.

SARAH: No, I know.

JACK: So all you have to do is tell me who you want your Abraham to be. Somebody like Bill Hurt would be great. Wouldn't hurt to have a star.

SARAH: Bill Hurt would be wonderful.

JACK: We can go a long, long way with this show, Kitty. No more of this regional life for us, sweetheart. We're going to the big time. You and me. *(He takes her face in his hands.)* God, I love you. *(Then leaves.)* Gotta go.

(Sarah lies back on her bed and arranges her covers, as Tom comes on again, and Virginia enters, dressed as a handmaiden, or in this case a midwife.)

VIRGINIA: My Lord, your midwife is ready.

SARAH: Virginia! Are you really going to play this?

VIRGINIA: I am. I'm taking a leave of absence. My assistants can handle the classes and I...want to see this through.

SARAH: *(Reaching out for her hand.)* Good, I'm glad. I'm going to need you.

VIRGINIA: Do you think Hagar should come to Isaac's birth or not? Historically, she would *be* there, as a member of your household, but we don't have to have her if you don't...

SARAH: No. *(Appearing more uncomfortable.)* No Hagar.

VIRGINIA: Just the nurses then. We'll keep Hagar outside with the rest of the tribe.

(Abraham stalks up to the edge of the stage.)

ABRAHAM: Jack, I think I should be in this scene.

(Jack responds from his side of the stage.)

JACK: I'm not surprised.

ABRAHAM: She's my wife.

JACK: Well, then. Send a card, why don't you. Or some flowers.

ABRAHAM: Watch it.

JACK: I'm hoping to, Abraham, if we can ever get to work here.

ABRAHAM: So talk to me.

JACK: All right. Now. God called you up last night, with some bad news. He likes Sarah's boy much better than Hagar's boy. Much more his type. You know, obedient. All that. So he's cutting your Egyptian brat out of his will, and giving everything to Isaac. O.K.?

ABRAHAM: I want to be there.

JACK: At the birth? No. *(Comes round the stage and calls to the stage manager.)* Tomashevsky. It's showtime. The birth of Isaac. Go Sarah.

SARAH: *(Breathing heavily, in labor.)* "Call for Lord Abraham. My time is near."

ABRAHAM: I'm right here.

VIRGINIA: *(In character.)* "He cannot be found, my Lord."

SARAH: *(More insistent.)* "Find Lord Abraham."

JACK: Louder, Sarah.

SARAH: "Find Lord Abraham."

ABRAHAM: If she's really giving birth, I could hear her all over the camp. I'd be there in a second.

SARAH: *(Not screaming.)* "The child is coming!"

VIRGINIA: "Yes, my Lord."

ABRAHAM: Why can't I go to her?

JACK: You're working.

(Sarah sits up on the bed, as Virginia comforts her.)

SARAH: "Where is he?"

VIRGINIA: "I don't know, my Lord."

SARAH: "If I die…"

VIRGINIA: "You will not die, my Lord."

(Sarah grabs Virginia to hold onto her, but there is no attempt to imitate a birth here. Rather than pain, Sarah conveys something like surprise, or shock that this is actually happening.)

SARAH: "The child is coming! Help me. Help me. Abraham!"

JACK: And…blackout!

(Jack signals for the blackout, but there is none.)

JACK: *(With a real gleam in his voice.)* And…who's got the baby?

TOM: *(Pitching it onstage to Virginia.)* Right here.

JACK: O.K. Abraham. Go see the pretty baby.

(Sarah composes herself in the bed now, attended by Virginia, as Abraham enters. He is furious with Jack, and determined, somehow, to take control here.)

VIRGINIA: And Abraham called the name of his son that was born unto him, whom Sarah bare to him, Isaac.—

SARAH: *(Brightly, happily.)* "How do you like this child, husband?"

ABRAHAM: "I know not what to say to a child. Perhaps when he is…"

(Abraham actually sees the baby now, and the effect on him is immediate. He extends his arms and Sarah gives him the child to hold. He clasps the child to him, overcome with emotion.)

ABRAHAM: "He is a beautiful boy." *(Abraham takes a moment, then speaks, his voice filled with love.)* "My Lord has said to me that this boy Isaac that, *my son, Isaac,* will be a king of my people, that my Lord's everlasting covenant shall be with him, not with me. That all that I have done and dreamed shall be for Isaac. That God's purpose shall be accomplished not in my life, but in his." (*Now, reverent and very happy, he puts the baby back in Sarah's arms and kisses her.*)

SARAH: "When he is weaned, we will give a feast, to prove to all who would doubt that such a thing could happen, that this child of our old age lives and loves us."

JACK: O.K. Virginia. Take the baby away now. It's time for his nap.

(*Virginia carries the swaddled bundle offstage, as directed.*)

JACK: Isaac?

(*Isaac enters, wearing jeans and a T-shirt.*)

ISAAC: Right here.

JACK: Well, come on in here Isaac. What are you, three now?

(*Jack pushes the boy down and he duckwalks over to Sarah.*)

SARAH: You don't have to do that, honeybun. Just stand there and love your sweet Mom.

JACK: Ready?

(*Sarah strokes Isaac's hair.*)

SARAH: "Hagar."

HAGAR: (*Comes up to Sarah.*) "Yes, Mistress."

SARAH: "I'm giving a feast for my son."

HAGAR: "Yes, Mistress."

SARAH: "I would enjoy it if you would come and dance for us."

HAGAR: "I would be happy to, Mistress."

SARAH: (*Proceeding.*) "But Hagar. Your son, Ishmael, though he is not required to attend this feast, must not interfere with it in any way. For this is my son's first feast and I would not have him confused by foreign beliefs."

HAGAR: Yes, Mistress.

JACK: Kitty, do you have that welcome speech?

SARAH: Brothers of Nanna?

TOM: Do you want this with the music, Jack?

JACK: If you've got it. Let's just run through this little feast and see what happens.

(*There is a blast of a ram's horn and Sarah steps up on a platform, in full ceremonial attitude.*)

SARAH: (*Joyous and ceremonial.*) "Brothers of Nanna, Sisters of Nikkal, the Lord has given to us a child, born these three years ago, whose name is Isaac, whose weaning feast I now proclaim for two weeks hence, when all shall cease their travail and shall eat and drink from the fullness of the land, and shall make offerings to the Gods on high for holy be their name. Amen."

(Abraham steps up onto the playing area, as if into the center of the feast.)

ABRAHAM: "Good wife. I don't see the boy, Ishmael."

SARAH: "I have forbidden him to attend, husband. He is preaching the religion of Egypt and committing idolatry in the camp."

ABRAHAM: "I was not aware of this. I will speak with the boy."

SARAH: "I have spoken with him, husband. He will not listen. Hagar herself cannot control him."

ABRAHAM: "She has neither the skill, nor an interest in controlling other people."
(Sarah walks away from him and up to the position from which she will view the dance. And now the music begins, and Hagar steps out of her dress, and is wearing only a slip, but it must look like something a maid might have danced in thousands of years ago. This is eroticism at its easiest and best. She picks up a tambourine and begins to dance. They are all amazed. It is directly pagan, in that everybody understands it immediately. At some point in the dance, Sarah cannot watch any longer. She turns away, as Hagar makes it perfectly clear what Abraham sees in her. When the dance is over, Abraham lifts Hagar to her feet.)

SARAH: "Husband."

ABRAHAM: "I will speak with the boy, Ishmael. And if he does not obey my orders, then I will send him away with the herdsmen where he…"

SARAH: "…where he will corrupt their minds and harden their hearts as well. No, husband. The boy must go."

ABRAHAM: "But his mother could never remain in the camp without him. She is…devoted to him."

SARAH: "Then she must go."

ABRAHAM: "But Ishmael is my son, too."

SARAH: "Hagar."

HAGAR: "Yes, Mistress."

SARAH: "I can no longer abide the presence of your son in my camp. For your faithful service to me and my house, I grant you your freedom and that of the boy."

HAGAR: "Thank you, mistress."

ABRAHAM: "I will send five of my men with her to…"

SARAH: "No. They must go alone."

ABRAHAM: "Sarah. If you send them alone into the desert, they will die."

SARAH: *(Ignoring him.)* "You will take your clothes, and the presents others have given you, and leave the camp at once."

HAGAR: "Yes, Mistress."

ABRAHAM: *(Stepping out of character.)* So she's sending me away too. Is that it?

JACK: She *is* making you choose, but that's fair.

SARAH: "Stay with me, Abraham. The boy is our enemy."

ABRAHAM: I don't know that.

JACK: Big mistake.

(Abraham looks over at Jack.)

ABRAHAM: Passion, right?

(And Abraham walks over to Hagar, takes her face in his hands, and kisses her, with the most convincing display of passion we have ever seen, puts his arm around her and walks her offstage. The music ends and Sarah picks up the skirt of her dress so it will be easier for her to move.)

SARAH: And my husband leaves with his whore and for all I know, I never see him again.

VIRGINIA: Yes.

SARAH: But I have Isaac, is that it?

JACK: That's the idea. Make you a big star. Mother of the Father of the Jews.

SARAH: But is the audience going to understand why I did this?

JACK: Sure they will. Religious purity. All that.

(Sarah, Jack, and Virginia leave the stage and then downstage, in a dark corner, our attention is drawn to Abraham and Hagar embracing. She holds a large limp doll in one hand. Her dance music returns, slower, and sadder. The shadows of trees are projected behind them, so that it seems like an outdoor night scene.)

ABRAHAM: "I cannot bear to lose you."

HAGAR: "Please let me go. She will kill me if she finds we are still here."

ABRAHAM: "Take this loaf of bread and this jug of water and go to Beersheba. The wells there are mine, and I join you as soon as I can." *(He gathers her up in his arms again.)* "And take this ring, *(And he hands her a ring.)* that anyone who questions you will know you are my wife. Don't ride the camel, but walk beside him. In the shade. *(A moment.)* And remember there are wild dogs in the night *(He can't go on.)* Hagar. Hagar."

(The music swells as she breaks away from him and wanders toward an upstage area which is empty except for a large rock. Abraham goes offstage, as a brilliant light comes up on Hagar, and some kind of rattle starts to shake.)

VIRGINIA: *(Reading offstage.)* —But when Hagar arrived in Beersheba, she found no well from which to drink, for the servants of Abimelech had taken it violently away.—

(Hagar slumps down against a rock, and cradles the doll in her arms.)

VIRGINIA: *(Continuing.)* —And as the water was spent in her bottle, Hagar laid down her child, Ishmael, under one of the shrubs, and said,—

HAGAR: Lord, let me not see the death of my child.

VIRGINIA: *(Continuing to read.)* And Hagar lifted up her voice and wept.—

HAGAR: *(Calling out.)* "Abraham!"

(Abraham strides across the stage, looking even more wealthy than before, and sees Hagar.)

VIRGINIA: "And the angel of the God called to Hagar and said…"

ABRAHAM: "Fear not, Hagar, for I have come. I have driven our enemies from the well. Come drink."

(Abraham crosses over to Hagar, lifts her up, then gives her water from his pouch.)

VIRGINIA: —And the lad grew and dwelt in the wilderness and became an archer. And Hagar took him a wife out of the land of Egypt. And Abraham sojourned there, in the land of the Philistines, for many years.—

(There is a moment of silence, and then Abraham takes a step toward Jack, still holding Hagar's hand.)

ABRAHAM: Doing what? What am I doing with the Philistines for many years.

JACK: Getting rich. Isn't that what you wanted?

ABRAHAM: Yes, I did, but…

JACK: You made your choice. What are you so upset about?

ABRAHAM: I didn't have any choice and you know it. Hagar would've died out there.

JACK: You don't get it, do you?

ABRAHAM: *(To Hagar.)* Excuse me, darling. *(He drops to his knees.)* Could I speak to God, please.

JACK: *(Laughing.)* Very funny.

(But Abraham is serious.)

ABRAHAM: Lord who spoke to me in the wilderness, hear me now.

(Jack walks over to Sarah, who has been watching with interest.)

JACK: Are you hungry?

SARAH: I'm always hungry.

JACK: Then let's go get something to eat.

(Abraham jumps up.)

ABRAHAM: You took my wife, you threw me out of the camp, and now you try to kill the only family I've got left. What the fuck do you want from me?

JACK: Don't forget everybody. We move into the theatre tomorrow.

(Jack leaves and Abraham is left sitting downstage with Hagar. Virginia walks through.)

ABRAHAM: I need some help, Virginia.

VIRGINIA: O.K.

(Hagar kisses Abraham lightly and leaves.)

ABRAHAM: Does the Bible say what Abraham did when he was confused?

VIRGINIA: No, it doesn't.

JACK: I mean, once I see what this God's up to, how can I still love him?

VIRGINIA: Well. I think…what Abraham does right now, is solve the problems he, Abraham, can solve, and not try too hard to understand what God is doing. He makes his own decisions, I mean. He protects the ones he loves and keeps working to provide for his people. *(A moment.)* Abraham has the courage to let God…be weird or cruel or do whatever He feels like doing for a while, and simply trusts that God will wake up, which God has been known to do, and reward his faith and his patience.

(Abraham thinks a moment.)

VIRGINIA: Can you do that?

ABRAHAM: I think so. That helps a lot. *(He kisses her.)* Thanks.

VIRGINIA: You're welcome.

(Lights dim to indicate the change of scene.)

SCENE X

Sarah is in full costume. Jack holds a clipboard.

JACK: I talked to the casting agent this morning. Bill Hurt is doing a movie. Dustin Hoffman might be available, but has to have an offer before he'll read it…

SARAH: I think you should take Cliff. I think there should be somebody in the show that knows where it came from.

JACK: And you don't?

SARAH: I don't want to go, Jack. I want to stay here and have my baby. I'm sure you can find…

JACK: But the baby isn't coming til November.

SARAH: I know, but I want to get ready. Buy a crib, hang some wallpaper, you know. Make a nest.

JACK: Fuck the nest. This show could transfer and run for a solid year.

SARAH: I don't want to wake up in New York Hospital the morning after the baby's born and wonder who I can get to take care of him so I can work. I don't want to work. I want to take care of the baby.

JACK: Kitty, you are a world-class actress. I can't let you sacrifice your one shot at the big time.

SARAH: Who says this is my one shot at the big time? Who says I can't go to New York later if I need to. If this is my one shot at anything it's being a mother, and I'm going to take it.

JACK: There's lots of mothers. Millions of mothers.

SARAH: And I bet they all feel just like I do.

JACK: Which is why nobody wants to hire them.

SARAH: I can't believe you said that.

JACK: I want you *with* me.

SARAH: I can't.

JACK: But you've got so much to do in the world, so much to give.

SARAH: Well, maybe I want to keep some of it.

JACK: *(Turning away.)* Great.

SARAH: They're going to love you. You'll be the talk of the town, you and Cliff.

JACK: You bet your ass we will.

SARAH: And I will be right here cheering for you.

JACK: You will be nowhere, Sarah. I can't believe you're doing this to me.

SARAH: And what about what you did to me?

JACK: You were who I wanted, not some baby. And you were supposed to love me. Not some baby.

SARAH: And you weren't supposed to make me choose between you and "some" baby, Jack.

JACK: It's a goddamn hormone is what it is. I'm fucked by a hormone.

SARAH: It's a baby!

JACK: Don't you want to be a star?

SARAH: Cliff wants to be the star. He'll do whatever you say.

JACK: You're damn right he will, and I'll make him the biggest star anybody ever saw, and you'll have your baby.

SARAH: Yes.

JACK: And the baby will grow up and leave you. And resent all the sacrifices you made for him.

SARAH: I know that.

JACK: So what is the point?

SARAH: The point is that everybody leaves me anyway, Jack. So I want to be with the baby while I can.

JACK: You'll be sorry about this. This really pisses me off. *(He turns around to walk out.)*
(Abraham enters.)
ABRAHAM: Oh hi there. I was just looking for you.
JACK: Do you want this fucking part or not?
ABRAHAM: Yes, I do.
JACK: Then I don't want any more bullshit. Either you play this thing today or I'm going to find somebody who can. You got that?
ABRAHAM: O.K. *(Watches Jack leave then turns to Sarah.)* I need to come by the house sometime and pick up some things.
SARAH: Not the cat.
ABRAHAM: Ten years together and all you want is the cat?
JACK'S VOICE: Abraham!
SARAH: Do you want the cat?
ABRAHAM: I never did like that cat.
SARAH: O.K., then.
(Abraham turns and leaves.)

SCENE XI

Hagar and Abraham stand with their backs to us, facing the sunset, his arms around her waist. Flute music plays in the background. This is a technical rehearsal on the actual stage, so we have full lights, costumes, and props. Abraham's costume is positively regal.

JACK'S VOICE: Can we brighten up the sunset a little?
VOICE FROM THE BOOTH: Like that?
JACK: Thanks. O.K. Whenever you're ready.
VIRGINIA'S VOICE ON TAPE: "And the lad grew and dwelt in the wilderness and became an archer. And his mother took him a wife out of the land of Egypt. And Abraham sojourned there, in the land of the Philistines for many years."
ABRAHAM: "May the pleasure of these days never end."
(Hagar strokes Abraham's face.)
ABRAHAM: "May you live many years after I am dead, blessed by the joy you have given me."
VIRGINIA'S VOICE: —But it came to pass that after these things, God appeared unto Abraham and said—

(Jack steps onstage, dressed in a dark business suit, looking very much like a banker. There is something new in his manner. Something dark and insistent.)

JACK: "Behold, Abraham. Here I am."

(Abraham turns around, kneels, and bows his head.)

ABRAHAM: *(Whispers reverently.)* "Yes, Lord. I am your humble servant. What would you have of me?"

JACK: *(Daring him.)* Take now thy son, Isaac, and get thee into the land of Moriah, and offer him there for a burnt offering upon one of the mountains which I will show to thee.—

(Abraham looks stunned. As Jack walks to the edge of the stage and puts on a headset, Hagar turns to Abraham.)

HAGAR: "What troubles you, husband?"

ABRAHAM: "My Lord has commanded me to go to Mount Moriah and sacrifice Sarah's son Isaac."

HAGAR: "He means for you to kill the boy?"

JACK: *(Quietly over his headset.)* I can't see Hagar's face, Bill.

(The light on her face changes.)

JACK: That's better. Go back, Hagar.

HAGAR: "He means for you to kill the boy?"

ABRAHAM: "I know not what he means by this, but only what he asks."

HAGAR: "But husband, surely you cannot..."

ABRAHAM: "My God has commanded me thus. I cannot refuse."

HAGAR: "And if he asked you to kill *our* son, would you refuse him?"

(Abraham looks offstage.)

ABRAHAM: Jack?

JACK: I warned you Abraham.

ABRAHAM: *(To Hagar.)* Would you go back please, darling?

HAGAR: "And if your God asked you to sacrifice *our* son, would you do it?"

(Abraham answers quickly now.)

ABRAHAM: "Yes."

HAGAR: *(Bitterly.)* "This is a jealous God."

ABRAHAM: "I must go. This time I must obey Him with haste. But when I return in three days, I will tell thee all I know of this God who has blessed me so richly."

(Hagar turns and walks downstage. Abraham looks after her, takes a step as if to follow her, then stops.)

ABRAHAM: "Yes, Lord. I am ready."

JACK: That's better, Abraham. Much better. *(Giving light cues.)* And on three to black,

(Lights dim to near black.)

JACK: Then on six for the desert at dawn.

(And the lights gradually pull back up into dawn as Virginia enters dressed as a scribe.)

VIRGINIA: And Abraham rose up early in the morning to prepare for his journey, taking two of his young men with him.—

(Abraham walks to meet Sarah, who appears from the other side of the stage, Abraham is very much the noble lord.)

SARAH: "Abraham."

ABRAHAM: "Good evening, Sarah. I trust you are well."

JACK: More blue, Bill. Go on Sarah.

SARAH: "I am, thank you, husband. And I can see that your God has blessed you exceedingly."

ABRAHAM: "He has granted me wisdom in matters of trade and counseled me so that I may conduct myself in a seemly manner among foreigners."

SARAH: "I have seen you often in my dreams."

ABRAHAM: "Good wife, I have come to see the boy Isaac."

SARAH: "I am glad. He too, has missed you."

ABRAHAM: "I am journeying to Moriah, and thought to take him with me. It will benefit him greatly to see how a man can survive in such a harsh land."

SARAH: "But what is the purpose of your journey, my husband?"

(Abraham takes a moment.)

ABRAHAM: "A small village there produces saddlebags and bridles of exceptional quality. They have agreed that I shall sell their wares at the market in Byblos." *(Then altering his tone.)* "Perhaps you would agree to accept a new saddle as a gift from me."

HAGAR: Is Sarah really going to fall for that?

JACK: Quiet!

(But something about that warning has affected Sarah.)

SARAH: "And go you also to give thanks to your God for the riches he has bestowed upon you?"

ABRAHAM: "As in all things, I will heed his word. If he bids me build an altar, I will do so."

HAGAR: Don't listen to him, Sarah.

JACK: We're not improvising any more, darling. We've got to get through this tech, now please...

HAGAR: She's smarter than this. And she loves her boy. Can't she see he's lying?

JACK: Her boy needs a father and she knows it. Go on, Sarah.

(Sarah looks over at Hagar.)

SARAH: "Take the boy, then, for I would have him see his father in the exercise of his trade. But see that he worships not at this altar, for your faith is not his."

ABRAHAM: "This I will do."

(Sarah holds out her arm to Isaac, who enters now, carrying a sheepskin pouch over his shoulder.)

SARAH: "Isaac, my sweet child." *(She takes his hand, but turns to Jack.)* I think Hagar is right. Shouldn't I have a moment of doubt here?

JACK: No.

SARAH: What if he doesn't bring him back?

JACK: Say the line.

SARAH: "Go with your father."

ISAAC: "Yes, mother."

(Isaac gives Sarah a kiss, then Abraham takes his hand and leads him off a little way.)

VIRGINIA: "And Abraham rose up and went unto the place of which God had told him."

SARAH: *(To Hagar.)* Thanks.

HAGAR: I tried.

(Jack comes onstage, carrying a knife and some rope.)

JACK: It just hit me what's the matter with this scene. Abraham.

SARAH: What's that for?

JACK: You really hate that little rat, don't you.

ABRAHAM: Whatever you say.

JACK: *(To the light booth.)* We have to hold for a minute, Bill. I want to change some of this blocking...

SARAH: To what?

JACK: Something else.

(As Jack rearranges Abraham and Isaac, Sarah walks over to stand with Virginia.)

SARAH: Do you know what this is about?

VIRGINIA: No.

JACK: O.K. Virginia. Where were we?

VIRGINIA: —Then on the third day, Abraham lifted up his eyes and saw the place afar off, and said to his young men...—

(Jack watches as Isaac stands beside Abraham.)

ABRAHAM: —Abide ye here below while the lad and I go yonder and worship.—

JACK: Give Isaac the knife.

(Abraham picks up the wood and gives Isaac the knife.)

VIRGINIA: —And Abraham took the wood of the burnt offering, and the fire in his hand, and a knife and they went both of them together.—

ABRAHAM: Can I have a real knife?

SARAH: Not if Isaac is carrying it.

JACK: Tomorrow, Abraham. *(Taking off his headset.)* Now just stand there. I want to move this altar a little… *(Calling to the stage manager.)* Tom?

(Tom enters and helps Jack push the stone altar into place.)

SARAH: *(Approaching Jack as he works.)* What are you doing?

JACK: My job, darling. Say your lines, Isaac.

ISAAC: *(Looking up at Abraham.)* "Father?"

ABRAHAM: "Yes, my son."

ISAAC: "I see the fire and the wood, but where is the lamb for a burnt offering?"

ABRAHAM: "God will provide a lamb, my son."

JACK: Now, Abraham. Grab the kid.

SARAH: No. You'll scare him!

(Isaac yelps as Abraham sets him on the altar.)

JACK: Now tie his wrists.

(Abraham pins the boy down and ties his wrists.)

SARAH: We don't need that!

ISAAC: "Father!"

ABRAHAM: "Quiet, son."

SARAH: *(To Jack.)* Jack, stop this.

ISAAC: *(Really scared.)* "But father…"

SARAH: The scene was good.

JACK: It wasn't scary. *(Moving around toward the altar.)* Pull his hood back. I want to see that neck.

SARAH: No!

JACK: Get your knife, Abraham.

ABRAHAM: *(Raising it over his head.)* Like this?

SARAH: Willie, this is just acting. Are you all right?

JACK: *(To Abraham.)* That's good.

SARAH: Cliff…

ABRAHAM: What *is* it with you? Can't I have *one* scene in this play?

SARAH: He's a child. You're not mad at him.

JACK: Hold him, Abraham.

SARAH: You're mad at me.

ABRAHAM: Get *her* out of here.

JACK: Higher, Abraham.

SARAH: No!

JACK: Now kill him!

(Sarah sees the vengeance in their eyes and runs offstage screaming. And as Abraham plunges the cardboard knife down, as if to kill the boy, Virginia screams, runs up and catches Abraham's arm.)

VIRGINIA: Abraham! Stop! Jack! You can't kill the boy! That's not what happens.

JACK: We didn't kill him!

ABRAHAM: I could though.

JACK: Thanks. That's all I wanted to know. Great work.

HAGAR: This is sick. *(Leaves the stage.)*

VIRGINIA: *(To the boy.)* Are you all right?

ISAAC: Yeah. *(Gets down from the altar and takes the bindings off his hands.)*

VIRGINIA: You've gone way too far here.

JACK: I have not. This is exactly what it would have felt like.

VIRGINIA: What it looks like is ritual murder. Is that what you want?

JACK: We didn't kill him. Now back off.

VIRGINIA: Where's Sarah?

JACK: *(Most condescending.)* Try the bathroom.

VIRGINIA: *(Running offstage.)* Kitty!

JACK: *(Disgusted.)* O.K. Play the tape, Tom.

VIRGINIA'S VOICE: —Then Abraham beheld behind him a ram caught in a thicket by his horns: And Abraham went and took the ram, and offered him up for a burnt offering in the stead of his son.—

(Abraham looks out toward Jack.)

ABRAHAM: Better?

VIRGINIA'S VOICE: And the Lord said unto Abraham—

(Abraham, turns slowly, kneels, facing upstage and listens to the voice of the Lord.)

JACK'S VOICE ON TAPE: —because thou has done this thing, and hast not withheld thy son, thine only son, I will bless thee. I will multiply thy seed as the stars of the heaven, and as the sand which is upon the sea shore; and in thy seed shall all the nations of the earth be blessed; because thou hast obeyed my voice.—

(Abraham stands, as Jack rushes onstage to hug him.)

JACK: All right. Finally.

(*Abraham sits down on the altar. The feeling of camaraderie with Jack is so strong, he is reluctant to speak, but the weight of what has just happened is too much for him.*)

ABRAHAM: But when I get back to Beersheba, Hagar has left me.

JACK: Yes. That's right.

ABRAHAM: And Sarah is dead?

JACK: Sarah is dead. Right. She saw it. In a dream or something. She didn't know you let the boy go. She thought you killed him.

ABRAHAM: And she died.

JACK: And she died.

(*Abraham nods, but in spite of himself, a desperate cry escapes him.*)

ABRAHAM: "Sarah!"

JACK: Perfect. One perfect little moment of regret. I knew you could do this.

ABRAHAM: Thanks, Jack.

(*Jack looks up to the booth.*)

JACK: Any problems up there?

VOICE FROM THE BOOTH: Done and done.

JACK: O.K., then, let's lock the board til after the preview. (*Turning to Abraham.*) Cliff, the press people in New York want some photos of you on the set. Can you give Tom a few minutes?

ABRAHAM: Sure.

(*Tom enters, replacing some props. He speaks on his headset.*)

TOM: Thanks, folks. Half-hour is at seven-thirty. And Hagar, I've got those tickets for your agent.

ABRAHAM: How does the house look, Tom?

TOM: Sold out. Oh, and the *Journal* wants to talk with you after the show.

ABRAHAM: What about?

TOM: I'll find out who it is, if you want me to.

ABRAHAM: No, that's O.K.

TOM: And your agent called.

(*Hagar enters.*)

ABRAHAM: He's my agent now? I've never met the man.

TOM: He said he was bringing two guys from Tri-Star and he'd meet you before the show.

ABRAHAM: (*Puts his arm around Hagar.*) O.K. You hungry?

(*Tom hauls out his camera gear now.*)

TOM: Jack said I have to get these photos, Cliff. It won't take a minute.

ABRAHAM: Oh right. Sure. Where do you want me?

HAGAR: I'll just meet you at Sammy's, how's that?

ABRAHAM: *(Kissing her.)* That's fine.

TOM: *(Taking a photo.)* That's good. Could you kiss her again, please. *(Abraham laughs, as though this is a silly request. And then complies.)*

ABRAHAM: Here it comes.

HAGAR: I'm ready.

(They kiss and Tom snaps a few more shots, as they improvise a few more poses. And then Hagar leaves.)

HAGAR: O.K. See you later.

(Abraham continues to stand, as Tom takes his pictures. And it seems to us, that with each picture Tom takes, Abraham grows more noble, more memorable, more grand.)

ABRAHAM: What do you think they'll ask me? The reporter, I mean.

TOM: Oh, you know, how you prepare for a role, what it's like, working with a company this way. *(A moment.)* What you're doing next. *(A moment.)* What do the Tri-Star guys want?

ABRAHAM: I forget what he said on the phone. Something with Glenn Close, I think.

TOM: *(Finished now.)* Well, that should do it. I'll get you the contacts so you can pick the ones you want them to use. *(Tom exits.)*

(Sarah walks through to pick up something she has left on the stage. She makes no attempt to contact him visually.)

ABRAHAM: You're really not going with us to New York?

SARAH: No. I'm not.

ABRAHAM: Why not?

SARAH: Because Jack is a tyrannical bastard and you are his blind slave, and…I don't want to work right now.

ABRAHAM: But this is the best show we ever did.

SARAH: I know that.

ABRAHAM: You *have* to come with us, Kitty. It's what we worked our whole lives for in this rat hole, to take some show to New York!

SARAH: I worked my whole life in this rat hole because I loved it, because I loved you, because we were making something out of all that work, but no. You had to go and…

ABRAHAM: Me? You're the one having the baby.

SARAH: Oh, are *you* the victim now? You the wounded one? You the one with the broken heart?

ABRAHAM: You're leaving me for some baby you don't even know!

SARAH: Yes I am. As fast as I can.

ABRAHAM: You'll be sorry.

SARAH: Why does everybody keep saying that to me? Is that supposed to scare me, "I'm going to be sorry?" Because if it is you can save your breath. I'm going to be sorry either way, more or less, every day about something so it might as well be that you thought you were free to hurt me. You thought I would always be there. I am sorry. But you were wrong.

ABRAHAM: Why didn't you tell me?

SARAH: Tell you not to hurt me? I thought you knew it. I thought people knew it. I thought it was basic human knowledge. Don't hurt me.
(A moment.)

ABRAHAM: I don't know how this happened.

SARAH: What did you *think* would happen?

ABRAHAM: I thought we would get through it.

SARAH: Like all the other times?

ABRAHAM: Yes, like all the other times. What's so special about this time?

SARAH: Nothing, really. Except, I guess that if you really don't want something to break, you have to force yourself to stop dropping it.

ABRAHAM: But I miss you so much. I miss talking to you. I miss going home with you. I miss talking about the show.

SARAH: I liked that too.

ABRAHAM: *(Demanding.)* What do you want me to say? Whatever you want me to say I'll say it. *(He puts his hands on her shoulders, now, trying to get through to her.)*

SARAH: *(She throws his hands off.)* You're going to be a big star.

ABRAHAM: Yes, I am.

SARAH: Say thank you. *(And she turns angrily and storms offstage.)*
(Lights dim to indicate change of scene.)

SCENE XII

Onstage, lights come up on The Tomb. This is the real performance. A throne is in place far upstage. A strange blue light shines on the altar, which has become Sarah's bier.

VIRGINIA'S VOICE ON TAPE: —And Sarah died in Hebron, in the land of Canaan.

And Abraham laid aside his labors in Beersheba, and came to mourn for Sarah and to weep for her.—

(Abraham walks onstage, looks at the tomb, then turns upstage.)

SARAH: "Abraham."

(At the sound of her voice, Abraham whirls around.)

ABRAHAM: "Sarah. I did not think to hear your voice again."

SARAH: "My spirit is permitted this moment."

ABRAHAM: "I have chosen a tomb for you. It is the cave of Machpelah, which the children of Heth have sold me for a burying place."

SARAH: "It is good. I would remain in this land. And when you die, husband, where shall you rest?"

ABRAHAM: "I do not know."

SARAH: "I would welcome your company at Machpelah if there is room enough."

ABRAHAM: "You would have me with you?"

SARAH: "Should I wake, my husband, it would comfort me greatly to have your company on my journey."

(He goes to her and takes her hand.)

ABRAHAM: "I have not loved you as you deserved."

SARAH: "Nor was I made to love a husband, but rather my people and my God."

ABRAHAM: "Still I have loved you."

(Sarah nods, unable to speak.)

ABRAHAM: "Your son Isaac is well. When it is time for him to marry, I will send one of my servants to that land from whence we came, to take him a wife from our family there."

SARAH: "That would please me."

ABRAHAM: "It is my God who has commanded me thus."

SARAH: "Then farewell. And grace be unto you, husband, and to your son Isaac. I can speak no more."

(She sinks into his arms, and he lays her gently back on the stone slab.)

ABRAHAM: Sarah.

VIRGINIA'S VOICE: —And Sarah was an hundred and seven and twenty years old; and these were the years of the life of Sarah.—

(Abraham stands and looks away a moment.)

VIRGINIA'S VOICE: —Then again Abraham took a wife, and her name was Keturah. And she bare him Zimran, and Jokshan and Medan and Midian and Ishbak and Shuah.—

(Abraham takes off his beautiful robe and lays it over Sarah's body.)

VIRGINIA'S VOICE: —But Abraham gave all that he had unto Isaac.—
(Abraham leads Isaac onstage, who kneels and kisses Sarah.)
VIRGINIA'S VOICE: —And when Abraham died, his sons Isaac and Ishmael
buried him in the cave of Machpelah with his wife, Sarah.—
*(Abraham makes his way back to the throne and sits down on it and closes his
eyes. Isaac then drapes a robe over him.)*
VIRGINIA'S VOICE: —And these are the days of the years of Abraham's life which
he lived, an hundred and three score and fifteen years.—
*(Virginia enters, wearing white robes, kneels briefly before Abraham, then kiss-
es Sarah's forehead and strokes her hair, then takes Isaac's hand and moves to
center stage.)*
VIRGINIA: —And it came to pass after the burial of Abraham, that God blessed
his son Isaac; and said, "Go not down into Egypt; but dwell in the land
which I shall tell thee of; and I will bless thee; for unto thee and unto thy
seed will I give all these countries, and I will perform the oath which I
sware unto Abraham thy father. I will make thy seed to multiply as the stars
of heaven, and in thy seed shall all the nations of the earth be blessed
because Abraham heard my voice and obeyed.—
*(Virginia kneels with Isaac and we hear the sound of the audience clapping.
And the lights dim to indicate a change of scene.)*

SCENE XIII
*Lights come up as we hear the sound of applause and Sarah sits up from her
bier. Neither of them has any idea what to say after playing that scene. They
begin taking off parts of their costumes. Tom enters immediately.*

TOM: Good show, everybody. Half-hour tomorrow night is seven-thirty.
SARAH: Thanks.
(Now Isaac comes in in street clothes and kisses Sarah.)
SARAH: Willie, sweetheart. You were great. You want to go get a hamburger?
ISAAC: I can't. My parents are here.
SARAH: O.K. I'll see you tomorrow.
(Isaac kisses her, then waves to Abraham.)
ISAAC: Goodnight, Cliff.
ABRAHAM: Take it easy.
(Hagar comes on in her street clothes.)
HAGAR: Good work out there, Sarah.

SARAH: Thanks.

HAGAR: *(To Cliff, though somewhat indirectly.)* I'll be at the Oyster, if anybody needs me.

ABRAHAM: How about if I just bring the Tri-Star guys over?

HAGAR: I like Tri-Star.

(Hagar exits and Virginia enters from another dressing room.)

VIRGINIA: Good night, everybody.

ABRAHAM: You ought to be real proud of yourself, Virginia. How does it feel?

VIRGINIA: I'm scared about the critics.

ABRAHAM: *(He hugs her.)* Don't worry. They'll love your work, I know they will. You think you'll do this again?

VIRGINIA: Maybe.

ABRAHAM: *(He kisses her.)* You have to. There's not a lot of good writers around. O.K. Gotta get dressed.

(Abraham ducks behind a screen to get dressed.

SARAH: So what do you think, Virginia? Are the conservatives at the seminaries going to freak out over this?

VIRGINIA: I don't think so. I mean, it is what happened. If anybody says anything to you, get their name and I'll send them some books. (*Virginia kisses her.)*

SARAH: Are you hungry?

VIRGINIA: I could use a burger. See you at Timmy's?

(Sarah gives her a hug now. A real moment of solidarity. Jack enters, and Virginia exits without saying anything to him.)

JACK: Cliff, what kind of housing do you want in New York? Hotel or apartment.

ABRAHAM: *(From behind the screen.)* Hotel. Near the park if they can swing it. So I can run.

JACK: Will do. And we made an offer to that…actress we talked about the other day. And it looks like it's a done deal.

(Cliff, looking very elegant in his jeans and gold-rimmed glasses, comes out from behind the screen, putting on his watch and rings.)

ABRAHAM: Great.

(Jack's cellular phone rings.)

JACK: Yeah. *(He listens.)* O.K. guys. It's my spy at the *Journal.* *(He listens.)* Fabulous. Read it to me. *(He listens, then quotes.)* "Cliff Well's transformation from tribal househusband to noble patriarch is nothing short of miraculous. Before our very eyes, the pagan age of mystery and moon worship ends, and the sun rises on the world as we know it." *(To the caller.)* Thanks, Marge. *(He turns off his phone.)* We did it. You did it, Cliff. You got them. I knew you could.

ABRAHAM: *(Coming out from behind the screen.)* It was you, Jack. All you. Did they say anything about you?

JACK: About the director? They don't have a clue what we do. Thanks, though. *(He turns to Kitty.)* Well, well. What do you know.

SARAH: It worked.

JACK: You better believe it worked. Cliff, you coming?

ABRAHAM: Yeah. Give me a minute.

(Jack exits.)

SARAH: Congratulations.

ABRAHAM: Thanks. *(A moment.)* Are you going to be all right here?

SARAH: I'm not dying, Cliff. I'm just…

ABRAHAM: I know. You're just…

SARAH: Staying home.

ABRAHAM: O.K. Well. I've got to go. *(He leans over to kiss the top of her head. He is as tender as he knows how, trying to say everything he doesn't know how to say.)* Thanks. *(He leaves.)*

(A single light holds on Sarah, as she watches him go. She turns, her face composed, a slight smile…)

SARAH: That's all right. It's O.K.

THE END

Loving Daniel Boone

This play was commissioned by and premiered at Actors Theatre of Louisville at the 1992 Humana Festival of New American Plays, March 1992, under the direction of Gloria Muzio. The cast was as follows:

Daniel Boone . . . . Gladden Schrock

Russell . . . . Rod McLachlan

Flo . . . . Catherine Christianson

Hilly . . . . Dave Florek

Blackfish . . . . Chekorah Mishenack

Indian . . . . Steve Willis

Mr. Wilson . . . . Mark Shannon

Rick . . . . Skipp Sudduth

Jemima Boone . . . . Kathryn Velvel

Squire Boone . . . . Eddie Levi Lee

INTRODUCTION

When the Kentucky Historical Commission asked me to write a play celebrating Kentucky history, I sat down and made a list of the things I loved best about Kentucky. It was a silly list including things like Mammoth Cave, Shaker Lemon pie, spoonbread, country ham, the Paris Pike, and the whole town of Harrodsburg. But the most remarkable thing on the list was something known to all Kentucky schoolchildren as The Boone Tree, a simple tree stump on which was carved a simple message—D. BOONE KILL A BAR, 1803. ZOIS.

Now Daniel Boone would not have carved his name in a tree. Never. But a lot of other people have, over the years, for the simple reason that they had Boone fever, a Kentucky disease which has two forms. The Boone believers, like me, make regular pilgrimages to Boonesboro, buy tiny buckskins and toy long rifles for our children, and fanatasize about meeting a modern man who is Boone's equal. The others, the Boone bashers, do things like sneak into public parks and wrap the Boone statues up in toilet paper. Fie on them, I say. And yet, it must be very hard to be a hero today, without heroic paths to walk, or heroic battles to fight.

So. This play is about heroes, dead and alive. And about how a lover from the past can still be very much in the picture.

CHARACTERS

(In order of appearance.)
DANIEL BOONE: the frontier hero.
RUSSELL: a settler.
FLO: a cleaning woman in a history museum.
HILLY: the new night cleaning man.
BLACKFISH: Chief of the Shawnee.
MR. WILSON: a curator at the museum.
RICK: a mechanic.
JEMIMA: Boone's daughter
SQUIRE BOONE: Boone's brother
(Other Indians and Settlers may be used, but are not essential.)

THE ACTION

The play takes place both in the museum where Flo has been working, and in the frontier Kentucky of 1778 to which she has gained access. Care should be taken so the set does not suggest we are doing an outdoor drama. Representations of the frontier life should rather be bold and mysterious, helping to indicate that this is the world that Flo prefers. Further, there will be no barriers to Flo's movement between the worlds. Frontier costumes should be vivid and sensuous. Present-day costumes should be as simple as possible.

All actors will speak with a Kentucky accent, but should be careful not to lower the perceived intelligence of Kentuckians by doing so.

Loving Daniel Boone

ACT I

IN THE FOREST

In dim light, we see two men in buckskins holding long rifles, one leaning comfortably against a tree, the other squatting nervously beside him. Owls hoot in the darkness. Or it could be Indians signaling each other. Russell, the nervous one, drinks from his canteen.

RUSSELL: You got any opinion about this?

BOONE: No. I don't.

RUSSELL: But you *are* thinkin' about it, right?

BOONE: No. I don't think I am.

RUSSELL: Why not?

BOONE: It don't concern me, Russell.

RUSSELL: It does too concern you, and you know it.

BOONE: All right, maybe it does. That still don't mean I have to think about it.

RUSSELL: You know damn well what you think about this. You just don't want to say it.

BOONE: Well. Maybe I don't.

RUSSELL: So *why* don't you want to say it?

BOONE: Do you want to say what *you* think?

RUSSELL: Yes, I do. I think they're gonna kill us.

BOONE: Well, maybe they will. I'd just relax, if I were you.

RUSSELL: How do you think they'll kill us, exactly?

BOONE: Rush in, knife us. Hide in the bushes and shoot us. It's hard to say.

RUSSELL: Both at the same time, or me first?

BOONE: You first.

RUSSELL: Be just my luck, they'll kill me first, and then you'll talk your way out of it.

BOONE: I'd have to try, Russell.

RUSSELL: 'Fore you know it, the whole gang of 'em would be walkin' you back to their camp. "Hey, Blackfish, look what we got here. It's Daniel Boone."

BOONE: Yeah. I could see somethin' like that.

RUSSELL: Course you'd eventually escape.

BOONE: Maybe I would.

RUSSELL: Of course you would. Get home, get paraded around the fort. Get elected to the legislature, for God's sake.

BOONE: No, I know.

RUSSELL: Well why not? I'd vote for you. If I were still alive, I mean.

BOONE: If you want to try sneakin' out of here right now, let's go.

RUSSELL: You think we could get past 'em?

BOONE: Probably not.

RUSSELL: But if we head back to the salt lick, they'll just get the whole party.

BOONE: I was thinkin' if the Shawnee had all of us for the winter, they might not attack Boonesborough til the spring.

RUSSELL: I think about 'em sometimes, back at the fort, dryin' tobacco, diggin' wells. Wonderin' where the hell we are.

BOONE: Course now…

RUSSELL: Yeah.

BOONE: They could all be dead.

RUSSELL: I know.

(Daniel hears something, smiles, and comes up to a squatting position.)

BOONE: Well, Russell. Maybe our red brothers are gonna forget about us for the night.

RUSSELL: *(A deep sigh of relief.)* Oh Lord. Really?

BOONE: Nope. Here they come.

(And to the sound of a loud war cry, shrieking Indians come onstage in the darkness and attack them. A furious struggle begins. Boone and Russell are outnumbered, outfought, and finally, dragged offstage.)

IN THE MUSEUM

And then, an overhead light switches on, and we find we are not in the forest at all, but rather, in a museum, with painted backdrops of pioneer struggles, large cases of rifles and household equipment, huge stuffed birds and animal skins, etc. In the center of the room is a tree stump, on which is carved D. Boone Kill A Bar. 1803. ZOIS.

The person who turned on the lights is Flo, the night cleaning woman. She is in her mid 30s, and almost pretty, with long dark hair. She wears a long skirt and moccasins. Following her is Hilly, a young man wearing faded jeans and a black T-shirt. Flo pushes the cleaning cart into the room. Hilly carries the mop and pail and the feather duster.

FLO: So. In this room, you start with the birds. Cause if you do the floor first and then do the birds, the dust from the birds will fall on the floor and you'll have to do the floor all over again.

HILLY: Whatever you say, Flo.

FLO: I guess starting tomorrow night you can do it however you want. But tonight, you do it like I say, so I can know it's done right.

HILLY: O.K.

FLO: What's your name again?

HILLY: Hilly.

FLO: And you be real careful around this tree stump. Daniel Boone himself carved his name right there. D. BOONE KILL A BAR. 1803.

HILLY: O.K.

FLO: Now on these cases, you have to use Windex and a cloth. Not a paper towel. Not ever. It makes a streak. *(She gets a cloth.)* Like this.

HILLY: *(Beginning to get exasperated.)* Anybody can clean things.

FLO: Not Daniel Boone's things, they can't.

HILLY: What about inside the cases?

FLO: You try and steal anything out of these cases and they'll have you in jail, mister.

HILLY: Who said anything about stealin'?

FLO: You've probably been in jail anyway.

HILLY: Do I look like I've been in jail?

FLO: You do. Actually.

HILLY: Well, what if I was?

FLO: What did you do?

HILLY: You know that statue of Daniel Boone in Cherokee park?

(Her face pales as she remembers what happened to that statue.)

FLO: That was you?

HILLY: It was.

FLO: And they actually gave you this job after you did that?

HILLY: It was the judge's idea. Somethin' about my debt to society.

(Flo throws down her broom, and heads for the door.)

FLO: I'm going to get Mr. Wilson down here right now. I will not have a known vandal all by himself in this museum all night, I will not.

(He grabs her arm.)

HILLY: He already knows what I did. The judge told him all about it.

FLO: Well I don't trust you. You'll mess it up! You'll bring in your spray paint or your whatever it is, you'll pee on it.

HILLY: I will not. What I did to Daniel Boone I did for personal reasons. And I'm not gonna do it again, because…because I'm not. *(Changing tone.)* I'll do this right. You watch. I'll do it so good, they'll think you did it. O.K.? *(And suddenly, her attention is drawn away from him.)*

IN A TEEPEE

Daniel Boone is pushed into the room by a young Indian brave, who ties him to a totem pole, then leaves.

IN THE MUSEUM

FLO: O.K.

IN THE TEEPEE

Chief Blackfish enters and walks up to Boone. Then all around him, studying him. Boone is badly beaten up.

BLACKFISH: So this is the famous Daniel Boone.

BOONE: Pleased to meet you, Blackfish. Where are all the others?

BLACKFISH: You speak our language.

BOONE: I speak your language. I walk your land. I kill your bear.

BLACKFISH: Are you scared?

BOONE: Yes, sir.

BLACKFISH: Good. *(Chief Blackfish leaves.)*

IN THE MUSEUM

HILLY: How long you been doin' this?

FLO: Start with the birds.

HILLY: Yes, ma'am.

(Flo sits down in the guard chair, and wraps a shawl around her shoulders. Hilly begins to dust the birds.)

IN THE TEEPEE
Russell is thrown into the teepee, more or less at Boone's feet.

BOONE: Russell.

RUSSELL: They made you run the gauntlet. Why did you have to run it and not us?

BOONE: All part of the deal I made.

(Flo gets up from her chair.)

RUSSELL: What else did you promise them? How come we're not dead?

BOONE: I said when spring came, I'd lead the war party back to the Boonesborough, and they could capture everybody else too. Sell *all* our scalps to the British if they felt like it.

RUSSELL: What did you do that for?

BOONE: Just tryin' to get 'em to relax, Russell.

RUSSELL: But you're not really gonna do that, are you?

BOONE: Not unless I have to.

(Flo takes a piece of jerky out of her pocket, walks over to the teepee and hands it to Russell. Russell takes a bite, then looks at Daniel.)

RUSSELL: Where's yours?

BOONE: I ate already.

(Russell notices the look Flo is giving Boone.)

RUSSELL: I don't believe it. This Indian woman's in love with you.

BOONE: She doesn't look like an Indian somehow. She looks like a white woman.

RUSSELL: She looks damn hostile to me.

BOONE: I've heard of this. Some lost white woman wanderin' around out here.

RUSSELL: Does every damn thing you hear interest you?

BOONE: Don't it you?

RUSSELL: No, it don't.

BOONE: I think this girl knows more about this country than any man we know. Look at how she moves. If we weren't watchin', we wouldn't even know she was here.

RUSSELL: If we weren't watching, we wouldn't know we was here.

(Flo turns to leave the teepee.)

BOONE: *(To Flo.)* Hey. You don't have to leave. Where are you goin'?

FLO: To get you some blankets. *(She leaves.)*

RUSSELL: What did she say?

BOONE: She'll be back.

RUSSELL: Did you know this girl was in this camp?

BOONE: I reckon I did.

IN THE MUSEUM

Flo walks back to the guard chair and sits down. She pours herself a cup of coffee from a thermos.

FLO: Why'd you do that to Daniel Boone?

HILLY: Because he pisses me off.

FLO: He's the best man who ever lived in Kentucky.

HILLY: See what I mean?

FLO: He came through the Cumberland Gap and found Kentucky. He saved the fort at Boonesborough.

HILLY: And then named it for himself.

FLO: The other settlers named it for him because they'd have all died if he hadn't been there.

HILLY: Come on, Flo. This was a guy went around writin' his name on the trees.

FLO: He wrote his name on the trees because he just killed a bear and he had to stay awake all night watchin' it.

HILLY: Is that what you do when you can't sleep? Carve up your furniture?

FLO: I watch TV.

HILLY: O.K.

FLO: O.K. what? He didn't have a TV.

HILLY: He wanted to be a star.

FLO: He did not. He saved his daughter from the Indians.

HILLY: There's not a man alive who wouldn't go save his daughter from the Indians.

FLO: What Indians?

HILLY: It's not my fault there aren't any Indians to save my daughter from. Daniel Boone chased them all away.

FLO: He did not. He liked Indians.

HILLY: Then where are they, huh? *(He points to his work.)* How's that look?

IN THE TEEPEE
Chief Blackfish re-enters.

BLACKFISH: How many white people are in the fort?

BOONE: Twenty, thirty, maybe.

RUSSELL: The Chief speaks English now?

BOONE: He does if he wants you to understand what he's saying.

BLACKFISH: Do they have water?

RUSSELL: They have water.

BOONE: Not enough. But killin' those people won't stop the rest of 'em you know. There's too many of 'em. Just over the mountain. It's like the mountain is a big dam holdin' them back.

BLACKFISH: So is that why they have sent you, to find a way through the mountain?

BOONE: They *didn't* send me. I'm just…tryin' to get out of their way.

BLACKFISH: They don't belong here. This is Shawnee hunting ground.

BOONE: No, I know. But the way white people see it, a place don't belong to somebody unless they bought it. Just keepin' it sacred, like you done, that don't count. So as soon as this revolution is over they're gonna come in here, chase you off this land, divide it up, and buy it.

BLACKFISH: From whom?

BOONE: From you if you'll sell it to 'em. The best way to let white people know somethin' is yours is to tell them what you want for it.

BLACKFISH: What would I do with the money?

BOONE: I don't know. Isn't there something you want?

BLACKFISH: I want the white man to get back.

BOONE: Then sell him the land for his guns.

BLACKFISH: *(In disbelief.)* They wouldn't do that.

BOONE: Try it.

IN THE MUSEUM
Flo laughs outloud. Hilly turns around to see what she's laughing at.

FLO: Sorry.

(And he turns back to his work.)

IN THE TEEPEE

BLACKFISH: I think you could be very useful to us.

BOONE: Could be. Can you untie Russell here, and the rest of the men, or do they have to stay tied up?

RUSSELL: Whose side are you on, here?

BLACKFISH: Do I have your word that they won't attack our women?

BOONE: What do you say, Russell, can you keep yourself in line, here?

RUSSELL: They took my gun, didn't they?

BOONE: *(To Blackfish.)* They'll be O.K. for a while.

BLACKFISH: Then we will untie them. But if they escape, we will kill you.

BOONE: That's fair enough.

> *(Blackfish leaves.)*

RUSSELL: So I can't run off or they'll kill you?

BOONE: You can go whenever you want.

RUSSELL: And they won't kill you?

BOONE: Maybe they will. I don't know.

RUSSELL: Do you just not care if they kill you?

BOONE: It's not the worst thing that could happen.

IN THE MUSEUM

FLO: Where are you from, Hilly?

HILLY: Hart County.

FLO: I know Hart County. Mammoth Cave is just about my favorite place in the whole state.

HILLY: Is that what you're gonna do next? Go get a job cleanin' Mammoth Cave?

FLO: I'm going to Boonesborough, if it's any of your business.

HILLY: Did you used to go to Mammoth Cave with your boyfriend and smooch while they turned the lights out?

FLO: When they turned the lights out, I looked back the way I came and saw the silhouette of Martha Washington on the wall.

HILLY: You really looked at that?

FLO: I think you better get back to work.

HILLY: I have to admit, though, I liked that Echo River. I always felt like you could step out of your boat, follow some dark passage with your torch, and come right up on John Hunt Morgan makin' gunpowder under a ledge.

(Flo doesn't answer immediately. But this is exactly what she wanted to do.)

FLO: You went in your own boat?

HILLY: Lot of times. What did you do? Pay to go with a guide? How many times did you do that?

FLO: If you went in your own boat, you *could* get off. How did you get in? Is there another entrance to the cave?

HILLY: Well sure there is. I'll take you there if you want, but I wouldn't count on seein' John Hunt Morgan, if I was you. He's dead.

FLO: So what if he's dead? Everybody I see *here* is dead. Dead people walkin' the streets. Dead people askin' me how I am. If I have to spend my life with dead people, I'd rather be back there, where the dead people did things.

HILLY: I'm not dead. How long you had this idea we was all dead?

FLO: Then you tell me one livin' thing you've done. You think wrappin' Daniel Boone up like a mummy makes you a livin' human being?

HILLY: Are your folks all dead? Your Mom and Dad? How about your girl-friends? You got anybody living in your building or anything?

(She doesn't answer.)

HILLY: You've just been goin' around, haven't you, workin' in all the state historical things, lookin' for a way in, haven't you. A way back into history, I mean.

FLO: They do it in the movies.

HILLY: Maybe you should go work in the movies.

(Flo wishes she hadn't said any of this now.)

FLO: Me?

HILLY: Why not? I'd go see you. What time do you have?

FLO: Eight-thirty.

HILLY: Is it O.K. if I go call Linda? She's about ready for bed by now.

FLO: It's time for your break anyway.

HILLY: Thanks. *(Hilly leaves.)*

(Flo opens one of the cases and gets out a gun.)

IN THE TEEPEE

RUSSELL: So what's the worst thing?

BOONE: I don't know what you mean.

RUSSELL: You said gettin' killed wasn't the worst thing.

BOONE: No.

RUSSELL: So what is?

BOONE: Oh, I don't know. Gettin' marched back to North Carolina, I guess. Stayin' there my whole life. Bein' buried in my cornfield.

RUSSELL: Well, I'm goin' back.

BOONE: But what are you goin' back *for*, Russell. Nothin's gonna happen til the spring. And at least bein' here, we're eatin' up the Shawnee's food instead of what little they got left at the fort.

RUSSELL: What about Rebecca? Don't you think she'd like to know you're not dead?

BOONE: What she'd like to know is if I'm *not* dead, how come I've been gone so long.

RUSSELL: Come on. Go with me. You could leave again as soon as you wanted. Surveyin', scoutin'. Anything. There's always somebody wantin' to hire you.

BOONE: I'm not hirin' out ever again, Russell. Every trail I blaze is gonna mean a thousand people followin' me stompin' it down. Every fire I build out here's gonna have a homestead around it in five years.

RUSSELL: People tellin' their children, right here is where Daniel Boone made his first camp in this county.

BOONE: But I can't quit leadin' any more than they can quit followin', so right now, it's just a flat out relief to be right here, where I can't go no further. *(A moment.)* Only thing that would make me happier is if I was tied up. *(Boone looks up as Flo enters the teepee. She is very glad to see him, but her affection is laced with some aggravation. She is carrying some blankets and a gun. She gives him the blankets.)*

RUSSELL: Well, look at that.

FLO: I got your gun back for you.

BOONE: Thanks.

(Flo hands Boone the gun. He looks at it carefully.)

BOONE: This isn't my gun.

FLO: It has your initials on it.

BOONE: No, I know. Russell here, goes around the whole world carvin' my initials on things.

FLO: Where do you want to go? Do you want me to take you back home?

BOONE: Not right away. I was thinkin' I'd let 'em…get the crops in first.

FLO: So what did you do? Get yourself captured so we could go fishin'?

BOONE: Maybe I did. What's runnin'?

FLO: Looks to me like you are.

BOONE: Right into your arms, Flo. I sure am.

(*She leaves.*)

RUSSELL: What was that all about?

BOONE: She said she'd lead you out if you want.

RUSSELL: I am not draggin' some Indian woman back to Boonesborough.

BOONE: Well, that's the difference between you and me, Russell. I never could say for certain what I wasn't gonna do.

(*Blackfish enters with Flo.*)

BLACKFISH: Shel-ta-we.

BOONE: My father.

BLACKFISH: It is a wise leader that persuades his men to live peacefully with their enemy.

BOONE: And it is a wise chief who treats his captives with respect.

RUSSELL: What's going on? I told you she was trouble.

BLACKFISH: As a token of my friendship, I give you this woman for your wife.

RUSSELL: Your wife. What kind of pagan practice is that?

BOONE: I can't refuse him, Russell, you know that.

RUSSELL: You don't want to.

BOONE: No. That's true. Unless she objects.

BLACKFISH: I have spoken with her. She will abide by my wishes.

IN THE MUSEUM

Hilly comes back into the room, and Flo reappears from behind one of the cases.

FLO: Is Linda your wife?

HILLY: My daughter. You oughta have a child, Flo, before it's too late. You'd like it. Make you forget every damn thing except how to do right by her.

FLO: I'm not married.

HILLY: Well, get married then, if that's all that's stopping you.

FLO: No thanks.

HILLY: You got somethin' against marriage? Daniel Boone was married.

FLO: You lay off me and Daniel Boone.

HILLY: I can't do it, Flo. I can't see a nice girl like you throwin' yourself away on a dead guy. (*A beat.*) Didn't you ever meet anybody you liked?

FLO: Why are you askin' me all this?

HILLY: I want to know what you want in a man.

FLO: Why?

HILLY: So I can see if I've got it.

FLO: You?

HILLY: Why not? You want me to put on one of those buckskins?

FLO: What I want, is to get through this night and never see you again.

HILLY: Flo. You never know when you're gonna meet the right person. You can't count somebody out just because they're available.

FLO: I am not attracted to you in the slightest. You have no interest in history, and no sense of responsibility to the present.

HILLY: How do you know that?

FLO: You think women are so desperate to find a man that they'll take anybody who's even half-way nice to them.

HILLY: I'd go a lot further than half-way if you'd let me.

FLO: I'm sure you would. But if there was any other woman in this building, you wouldn't look at me at all.

HILLY: Not so. I saw women all day today. And you're the first one I wanted to talk to.

FLO: You're playing with me and I don't like it.

HILLY: Yeah, well, you're ignoring me and I don't like that either.

FLO: I have responded to every single thing you've said.

HILLY: You have not. You think I'm a bum.

FLO: I do not.

HILLY: O.K. A criminal.

FLO: I think you talk too much.

HILLY: It takes a lot of talk to get through to you, Flo. I don't like that name. What's the whole thing, Florence?

FLO: I have to go to the ladies.

HILLY: I'll be here.

IN THE TEEPEE

Russell is preparing to leave. Boone is now dressed like an Indian, and from all the evidence, is being treated very well.

BOONE: So what's your idea here?

RUSSELL: Simple. Go back. Let everybody know you're alive. See what's goin' on. Come back and get you.

BOONE: Why don't you just stay put if you get there. Give Rebecca a hand. File my claims, too, if you think of it. You know. Get the fort ready.

RUSSELL: When do you think they'll attack?

BOONE: Not as long as I'm here. But if somethin' should happen to me here...

RUSSELL: That's it, see. I don't trust 'em.

BOONE: Russell, we've been here two months and all they've done is traipse around, showin' us off to their friends. Why don't you wait til the braves are all out huntin' next month. Go then.

RUSSELL: Cause you'll probably go hunt *with* 'em.

BOONE: Gotta earn my keep somehow.

RUSSELL: I'm leaving. I'll find a couple good men, maybe Squire would like to come. We'll march right back here and...

BOONE: Russell. They'll bring me back themselves as soon as they decide what to trade me for. You're one of the few fighting men we've got. If you get to Boonesborough, promise me you'll...

RUSSELL: Shouldn't be more than a month at the most.

BOONE: If you're so concerned for my well-being, then why don't you just stay here with me?

RUSSELL: Cause I'm tired of watchin' you and these Indians, if you want the truth of it, fixin' their rifles, gettin' yourself adopted, marryin' this girl. It ain't right.

BOONE: We've seen a lot of things, you and me.

RUSSELL: And we'll see a lot more, once we get you out of this.

BOONE: It isn't me we're worried about.

RUSSELL: I'll be O.K.

BOONE: Just stay off the trail, then. You hear me? And if they catch you, don't fight 'em. Just take your whippin' and come on back here.

RUSSELL: Yes, sir.

BOONE: So I'll see you in a couple of hours.

RUSSELL: No you won't either.

BOONE: Well I hope not. I had enough of arguin' with you to last me at least a month.

(But from the look on Boone's face, we know Russell has very little chance here.)

IN THE MUSEUM

Hilly is now working on the glass in the cases. Flo looks up as Mr. Wilson, a rather academic, but not unappealing man dressed in a shirt and tie enters, carrying a Polaroid camera. She seems nervous, but very happy to see him. At first, Mr. Wilson cannot see Hilly.

FLO: Mr. Wilson!

MR. WILSON: Oh hi, Flo. I'm sorry to bother you. I meant to take care of this this afternoon, but the Board of Directors met until almost six, and…

FLO: What did they say? Are they going to let you write your book on Sycamore Grove?

MR. WILSON: Uh. No. They said maybe next year. *(A moment.)* Well, who knows. Maybe they meant it.

FLO: But you're ready now…

MR. WILSON: Yes. And by next year, who knows what it'll be like. I mean there's only that one sycamore left as it is.

FLO: But you've applied to some other sources, haven't you? Maybe…
   (Hilly appears. And at the mere sight of him, Mr. Wilson's demeanor changes radically. It's as if Flo disappeared.)

MR. WILSON: Well, well. Who's this?
   (Flo feels like she's been dropped out a window.)

FLO: This is Hilly, the new man. Hilly, this is Mr. Wilson.

MR. WILSON: Jeff, Jeff. I forgot this was your first night. Hilly, is it? *(Now clearly flirting.)* I see you haven't done any big damage yet.

HILLY: Florence is watchin' me pretty close.

MR. WILSON: That would certainly be my approach.
   (Flo has to get out of there.)

FLO: Do you need me to do anything before I…

MR. WILSON: No, no. I just have to have a photograph of the Boone knife for the Quarterly. But Hilly can help me. *(He gets the knife out of the case.)*

FLO: I'll be back in a minute, then. *(She leaves as quickly as possible.)*
   (Suddenly alone with this handsome man, Mr. Wilson is very nervous.)

MR. WILSON: *(To Hilly.)* So. Do you mind?
   (Mr. Wilson hands Hilly the knife, and proceeds to lay out a mat on which to photograph it.)

IN THE TEEPEE
   Boone is whittling. Flo rushes in.

FLO: How could you let them leave.

BOONE: Did they get him?

FLO: You let them walk right down the trail like they were invisible.

BOONE: Did they get them both?

FLO: No. Just the other one. Russell got away.

BOONE: That's something anyway.

FLO: But I told you I would help! I could've at least gotten them to the river. Goin' by themselves, they made so much noise, I could hear them halfway across the village. They might as well have been singing.

BOONE: They probably *were* singing.

FLO: You have no business bringing these people out here. That other one just got himself killed trying to show you how brave he was.

BOONE: I know that.

FLO: They don't listen. They think they're you.

BOONE: I know.

FLO: Or what's worse, they think because they're *with* you, they're safe. They think you know where you're goin'.

BOONE: I have never said that. Never.

FLO: You don't have to say it. How could Daniel Boone not know where he's going?

BOONE: I have *never* known where I was going. That's the whole point. Settin' off for someplace I've never been. How *can* I know where I'm goin'?

(Suddenly, she is overcome with love for him.)

FLO: No, I know. And how can they watch you go and not want to go with you.

BOONE: Come here.

(Flo goes to him and he opens his arms and holds her for a moment.)

BOONE: What's all that drummin' about? Are they gonna roast him?

FLO: They don't care about him. They're waiting for you to come out there to avenge him.

BOONE: So they're gonna roast me.

FLO: There's some of 'em sure would like to. If you can manage to stay put til dark, I'll come show you where they put him and we can bury him.

BOONE: That'd be good. Seein' as I already dug the grave, the least I can do is put the man in it.

FLO: When did you do that?

BOONE: Little while ago. Didn't you hear me?

FLO: The Shawnee say you don't touch the ground when you walk.

BOONE: *(Stroking her hair.)* Try not to. It's quieter that way.

IN THE MUSEUM

Mr. Wilson begins taking pictures, Hilly holding the knife with its point piercing the piece of paper. Mr. Wilson is making a valiant attempt to resist the attraction he feels for Hilly.

HILLY: Did Daniel Boone really carve his name on that tree?

MR. WILSON: Oh, please.

HILLY: He didn't?

MR. WILSON: *(Referring to the knife.)* Now lay it down flat. Good. *(Then back to the subject.)* No, he didn't. The date is way off. Daniel Boone was in Missouri in 1803.

HILLY: Possible he didn't know what year it was, I guess.

MR. WILSON: It isn't just that. The tree says, D. Boone Kill A Bar. Now if Boone used the past tense correctly in letters, why wouldn't he use it on a tree?

HILLY: So somebody else carved it? But why would they do that?

MR. WILSON: So they could sell it, to somebody. *(Mr. Wilson waits for a photo to come out of the camera.)*
(Hilly looks at the knife a moment, then holds the knife high over his head, like the statue of Boone.)

HILLY: Guess who?

MR. WILSON: *(Laughs.)* That's good. *(He snaps a picture.)*

HILLY: What about the hunting shirt? Was that his?

MR. WILSON: Heavens, no. Boone was big. That shirt would be snug on *(He looks at Hilly.)* either one of us.
(Hilly puts the knife down. Mr. Wilson waits for the pictures to develop.)

HILLY: So what do you have that really belonged to Daniel Boone?

MR. WILSON: That depends on who you talk to.

HILLY: I'm talking to you.

MR. WILSON: Nothing.

HILLY: You're kidding.

MR. WILSON: Boone was captured so many times, the Indians ended up with all his stuff. All we've got, really, is a cast of his skull upstairs in the vault.

HILLY: What, did the Indians tie him to a post and slap some plaster on his head?

MR. WILSON: The impression was taken after his death, I believe.

HILLY: Jesus.
(Mr. Wilson laughs a little. in spite of himself.)

MR. WILSON: But we do have a number of authentic Boone documents, land claims, things like that. And one ember carrier that, in all probability, came from the Boone household.

HILLY: I had an ember carrier once, but I forgot where I put it.

MR. WILSON: You are wondering why we have all these things on display if we know them to be fake.

HILLY: I am. You're right.

MR. WILSON: It's for the simple reason that even false views of historical personages are nevertheless, interesting to historians.

(Hilly's real feelings begin to emerge now.)

HILLY: But people believe this stuff. They come here to see it. Florence for example, thinks every single arrowhead is something Boone found.

MR. WILSON: No she doesn't. Oh, maybe when she first came here she did.

HILLY: But you straightened her out.

MR. WILSON: I did.

IN THE TEEPEE

Boone and Flo come in the teepee from burying the man who tried to escape with Russell.

FLO: Did you know him, that man we just buried?

BOONE: No, I didn't. Why?

FLO: I just wondered if he had any family.

BOONE: Probably does.

FLO: Will you have to find them and tell them something when you get back?

BOONE: Like I'm sorry, you mean? I could, I guess But I probably won't. For all I know, he might be better off.

FLO: Better off dead?

BOONE: I had a dream about dyin' once.

FLO: You were dying, or you were dead?

BOONE: Dead.

FLO: How was it?

BOONE: It was O.K. I knew a lot of people there. Nobody was after me for anything. *(He looks at her.)* You were there too.

FLO: I was?

BOONE: And heaven was a great big lake, early in the morning. The water was real still and kind of a gray blue. We were all just sittin' there fishin', two, three people to a boat, drinkin' our coffee and watchin' the sun come up.

FLO: It's gonna frost tonight.
BOONE: That'd be okay too.

IN THE MUSEUM

HILLY: What's the trouble?
MR. WILSON: Hilly, Was any other staff member in here tonight?
HILLY: No. Why?
MR. WILSON: There's a gun missing from this case, that's all, but I'm sure someone's borrowed it and just forgotten to sign it out. Would you ask Flo to come see me when she comes back? I'm in my office.
HILLY: Sure.
MR. WILSON: Or you could come tell me she's down here and I'll...
HILLY: I'll send her up.
MR. WILSON: That's O.K. I'll come back down in a few minutes.
HILLY: We'll be here.

IN THE TEEPEE
Flo and Boone are more relaxed now.

FLO: Where are you going to go when you leave here?
BOONE: I'd like to just keep goin', I guess. See the rest of Kentucky and keep goin', right on into places don't even have names yet. *(A moment.)* Name them all after you. Look real good on a map someday. Here's Virginia, here's Carolina, and everything west of here is Flo.
FLO: I'd like to see that too. Whatever's out there. It wouldn't even matter if I liked it. I know I'd like seein' it. Maybe I'll come with you.
BOONE: I'd like that. Probably wouldn't be any way of gettin' back, though. Couldn't keep goin' if we kept turnin' back.
FLO: That's O.K.
BOONE: *(Patting her.)* That's what we'll do then. You and me. As soon as it's warm.
FLO: What about your family?
BOONE: Well, you've got the right idea about family, Flo. It's better to really be gone. Better than sittin' there with 'em wishin' you were gone.
(Flo picks up the gun and stands up.)
FLO: I'll go get us a smoke.

IN THE MUSEUM

Hilly is working on the cases as Flo comes back in carrying the Boone gun.

HILLY: I'm tryin' this little treatment I use on our tile at home. Seems to be working pretty good.

FLO: Looks good.

HILLY: *(Noticing the gun she carries.)* The boss says there's a gun missing from one of the cases.

FLO: I know. I just found it back there. Somebody probably forgot to sign it out. They do that all the time. What happened to your wife?

HILLY: My wife?

FLO: Yeah. How come your daughter is living with you instead of with her? I mean, I assume you're divorced.

HILLY: She's dead. She was killed. We were nearly all killed.

FLO: Killed? In an accident, you mean?

HILLY: I don't know. Maybe it was, maybe it wasn't.

FLO: I know you for two hours and you're just now telling me your wife is dead?

HILLY: A lot of people are dead, Florence. It's not your recommended way of starting a conversation, telling you everybody I know who's dead.

FLO: Did you cry?

HILLY: Maybe I did. I don't remember. I was too busy tryin' to explain it all to Linda.

FLO: What did you say?

HILLY: Everything I could think of. Her spirit is free. You'll see her again some day. We only put her in a coffin so she won't get wet when it rains. You know. *(A moment.)* Lie. Lie. Lie.

FLO: And did she believe you? Does she still want to talk about it?

HILLY: So, we finally found something more interesting to you than Daniel Boone. My dead wife.

FLO: You didn't kill her, did you?

(A moment.)

HILLY: I thought about it.

FLO: What does that mean?

HILLY: It made me really mad, Florence, that she would do that to us.

(Flo feels she can't ask anything else. But Hilly relents and tells the story.)

HILLY: We both saw the truck coming. I told her she didn't have room to pass. She said she did. That's all. *(A pause.)* It was pretty much of a mess. And it was a long time before anybody came along.

FLO: Were you drinking?

HILLY: Would you get off this subject? You have no right asking me any of this. And I have no desire to tell you any of it. You think the dead are still alive. Well, I'm here to tell you they aren't. O.K.? *(A moment.)* "Were we drinking." What do you think this is, T.V.?

FLO: I don't know what to ask. Who watches Linda while you're at work?

HILLY: Why don't you ask how you think you're ever going to get work if you keep stealing things from the museum. Even on your last night. For God's sake, Florence. They probably fired you. Is that what happened?

(Mr. Wilson enters.)

MR. WILSON: There you are, Flo.

FLO: *(Holding up the rifle.)* I found this in the back. Miss Carter sent it out to be polished. It just hadn't been put in the case yet.

(Mr. Wilson takes the rifle and hands Flo one of the two pieces of paper in his hands.)

MR. WILSON: Can you do me a favor and decipher these lines for me? *(To Hilly.)* Flo's our resident expert on Boone's handwriting. Takes the rest of us two hours with a magnifying glass. All she has to do is look at it. *(He points to a word.)* This one.

(Flo looks at the piece of paper.)

FLO: "Necessary."

MR. WILSON: To what?

FLO: *(Looking again.)* "Necessary to notice political events."

MR. WILSON: *(Handing her another document.)* And this one?

FLO: "I am Well in health, but Deep in Bankruptcy."

HILLY: So Boone was broke?

FLO: He was. But he didn't write that last one. This looks to me like that Corbin woman again.

MR. WILSON: Good. Thanks. That's what I thought.

(Mr. Wilson looks at Hilly, then at Flo. Then speaks to Hilly, or rather, dismisses him.)

MR. WILSON: Would you excuse us for a moment.

HILLY: Sure. What do you need? A half-hour, ten minutes?

MR. WILSON: Five should do it.

(Hilly leaves. Mr. Wilson returns the gun to the case and locks it.)

MR. WILSON: I'm going to miss seeing you when I have to work late like this. I had hoped to get a little party together for you, so everybody could say good-bye. But...

FLO: You were the only one I ever talked to really.

MR. WILSON: I mean, I really appreciate the care you've taken with everything here. Do you think you could… *(He pauses.)* …have dinner with me sometime?

FLO: Have dinner with you?

MR. WILSON: I mean, I've wanted to ask you for quite a while now, but I wasn't sure it was a good idea while we were still working together.

FLO: I thought you were living with someone.

MR. WILSON: He left.

FLO: I'm sorry.

MR. WILSON: It was my decision, really. I'm trying to… *(He stops.)* I want to meet somebody. A girl. I want to get married. I think.

FLO: You think.

MR. WILSON: And my therapist says if I really want to meet women, then the first thing I have to do is start really seeing the women I already know.

FLO: And you picked me.

MR. WILSON: Yes, I did. I know you like me. We care about the same things. *(Flo is suddenly very angry. She tries not to explode.)*

FLO: And I seem like the kind of person who would…

MR. WILSON: I know it might be hard at first, but…

FLO: I probably wouldn't even care if we ever had sex. I probably don't even like it. I'd just be so flattered that somebody from upstairs noticed me…

MR. WILSON: I'm sorry. This was a mistake.

FLO: Yes, It was.

MR. WILSON: I hope I haven't offended you.

FLO: Why don't you just…

MR. WILSON: Go upstairs and drink.

FLO: No. Go home. Why don't you just go home.

MR. WILSON: I don't want to go home.

FLO: He's still there, isn't he.

MR. WILSON: How can I ask him to leave before I know whether I can do this or not?

FLO: I don't know.

MR. WILSON: Flo. Please. I don't know anybody else. Could I just ask you one…

FLO: What.

MR. WILSON: I don't know what women want. I have a good income. And I'm a decent, responsible man. I just want to know if that will be enough.

FLO: In short?

MR. WILSON: *(Gets the message.)* Ah.

    (Hilly returns.)

HILLY: All done in here?

MR. WILSON: *(Very upset now.)* Yes, of course. We were just chatting. *(Mr. Wilson turns to Flo one last time.)* I could give you a ride home later if you wanted.

FLO: I have my car. Thanks.

MR. WILSON: All right. Good night, then. *(Mr. Wilson leaves.)*

    (And Flo's anger gets away from her. She speaks as though Mr. Wilson were still in the room.)

FLO: My same car I've parked in the same spot beside your car every day for the last two years.

HILLY: Did he fire you?

FLO: No, he didn't. He asked me out to dinner.

HILLY: He's gay.

FLO: I know that.

HILLY: So.

FLO: So what?

HILLY: So give him a break.

FLO: You mean go out with him?

HILLY: You know what I mean.

FLO: No, I know.

    (He sees her regret and her isolation, and likes her for them.)

HILLY: You're all right, Florence.

FLO: I'm just so mad all the time. Why am I so mad?

HILLY: It's O.K. I used to feel like that myself.

FLO: And what did you do about it?

HILLY: After I quit drinking, you mean? Well, I thought about what was making me mad, and one night, I went over to Cherokee park and...

FLO: ...wrapped Daniel Boone up like a mummy.

HILLY: *(He grins.)* You got it. Made me feel great.

    (Flo nods, then continues, as though it's part of the same subject.)

FLO: Did the truck turn over? Did the truck driver die too?

HILLY: Are you serious?

FLO: I want to know. Was there a fire?

HILLY: All right, Florence. What's it worth to you?

FLO: Never mind. I'll just sit here and you can go work.

HILLY: No, I'll tell you what. Eat supper with me. Don't go have your supper in the lounge or something. Sit here and have supper with me, and I'll tell you the whole gory thing.

FLO: I didn't bring anything to eat. I usually just...

HILLY: You eat what's left in the refrigerator, don't you.

FLO: I do. Actually. There's always something...nobody wants.

HILLY: Then I'll share mine with you. But I have to warn you that Linda made it, so I hope you like cream cheese. Is it a deal?

(Flo thinks about it a minute.)

FLO: Are you hungry now?

IN THE TEEPEE

Blackfish walks in. Boone wakes up.

BLACKFISH: Shel-ta-we.

(Boone stands.)

IN THE MUSEUM

HILLY: I am, actually. Do we have to do anything before we eat?

FLO: No, Just...get the food, I guess.

HILLY: *(Checking his pocket for change.)* What kind of soda do you want?

FLO: Root beer.

HILLY: You got it.

FLO: Thanks.

(Hilly leaves.)

IN THE TEEPEE

Chief Blackfish walks into the teepee.

BLACKFISH: Governor Hamilton has offered us twenty ponies, and one hundred pounds sterling for you.

BOONE: Take it.

BLACKFISH: I think they will offer more.

BOONE: Maybe they will.

(Flo walks into the teepee to stand beside Blackfish. Blackfish takes Flo's hand, then speaks to Boone.)

BLACKFISH: I think you have brought us great good fortune these few months. I think we will keep you a little longer. *(Blackfish leaves.)*

BOONE: What's this good fortune I've brought them? That doesn't sound right.

FLO: No, it isn't. It's finally occurred to the Shawnee, and to the British, that since you're sittin' here, givin' no sign of tryin' to escape, this would be an ideal time to attack Boonesborough.

BOONE: Does that mean we have to go back?

FLO: You know it does.

BOONE: O.K. then. We'll leave as soon as it's dark.

FLO: You'd get there faster without me.

BOONE: Maybe. And maybe I wouldn't get there at all without you keepin' me headed in the right direction.

(She picks up her bedroll.)

FLO: Who is it you don't want to see?

BOONE: It's *what* I don't want to see, Flo. Like all my friends gettin' killed in this fight.

FLO: If you *don't* go, they'll be killed for sure. What have you been doin', sittin' here hopin' the settlers will give you up for dead and abandon the fort?

BOONE: I guess. Only what they've *been* doin' is sittin' there, tryin' to hold out til I get there. *(He kisses her lightly.)* O.K. Now. You'll need somethin' warmer to wear. *(He picks up his jacket.)* Put this on. You go get us somethin' to eat and I'll go steal us a coupla ponies and we'll go.

(Flo takes off her shawl, and puts on his jacket, leaving her shawl on the floor of the teepee. Flo leaves the teepee.)

IN THE MUSEUM

Hilly returns with his bag of lunch.

HILLY: Florence? Florence? *(He walks back to the teepee, finds it empty. He notices Flo's shawl on the floor. He stoops and picks it up.)*

(She enters through another door, wearing the Boone jacket.)

HILLY: I found your shawl.

(Flo covers her alarm. Hilly notices the jacket.)

FLO: Thanks.

HILLY: It was in the teepee. Nice jacket.

FLO: Thanks.

HILLY: Well. Let's see what we've got for supper, what do you say.

FLO: Were you hurt at all, in the crash?

HILLY: I was laid up for a few weeks. Yeah. But I didn't have a job then, so it wasn't like I had somewhere to go.

FLO: So your wife was mad at you for not getting a job. Is that what the fight was about?

HILLY: Jesus, Florence. I got laid off.

FLO: Why?

HILLY: They don't tell you why they're layin' you off. They just do it.

FLO: What kind of work was it?

HILLY: It's nice to have somebody to talk to, isn't it, Florence.

FLO: It's not my fault I don't know how to talk. Who have I got to talk to?
    (He hands her a sandwich.)

HILLY: Here.

FLO: Thanks.

HILLY: I got Linda started eating these cream cheese and banana sandwiches. You know. Had to be better than hot dogs. Right? What do you do when a kid won't eat? I thought everybody liked to eat. The books tell you don't make them eat, or they'll have eating problems the rest of their lives. But if you don't make them eat, they're not gonna *have* the rest of their lives, are they. I don't know why they write those books.

FLO: *(Chewing a bite of the sandwich.)* It's very good.

HILLY: Same thing with sleeping. They tell you, "Just let the kid cry." What they don't tell you is what the hell you're supposed to do while the kid is in there crying. *(He takes the bread off his sandwich.)*

FLO: I feel bad eating up your supper.

HILLY: She's getting better about making the sandwiches, though. *(He picks out a big chunk.)* That's almost what you'd call a slice. Isn't it.
    (And now from offstage, they both hear a voice.)

VOICE: Flo! Where are you! I know you're here somewhere.

FLO: Oh, no.

HILLY: Who's that?

FLO: My boyfriend.

HILLY: Your boyfriend? If you've got a boyfriend I want my sandwich back.
    (She hands him the sandwich.)

FLO: I have to get out of here.

HILLY: What do you want me to tell him?

(Flo dashes into the teepee. A large man wearing shorts over a sweatsuit, appears, an envelope in his hand.)

RICK: Where's Flo? Who are you?

HILLY: Name's Hilly.

RICK: Where's Flo?

HILLY: In the teepee.

(Rick charges over to the Teepee.)

RICK: The hell she is. *(He tears open the front flap of the Teepee. Not finding Flo there, he turns back to Hilly.)* All right, wise guy. Where is she?

HILLY: How should I know?

RICK: Flo! You come out here right now or I'll tear this place apart.

HILLY: Can I give her a message?

RICK: I tell my wife I want a divorce, and then I get this letter from Flo saying she's leaving.

HILLY: You're married?

RICK: What did she tell you about me?

HILLY: Did Florence *know* you were married?

RICK: That's what I came here to tell her. After I told my wife about Flo, then I was gonna tell Flo about my wife. I love Flo. She knows I love her. *(A moment.)* Why don't women ever believe what you tell them?

HILLY: Beats me.

RICK: And now she's gone.

HILLY: She's not gone, she's just…You looked in the teepee?

(And with that, the men leave by different doors calling for Flo.)

RICK: Flo?

HILLY: Florence. It's O.K. He's getting a divorce.

IN THE FOREST

Daniel Boone and Flo appear.

BOONE: How long do you think it will be before they know we're gone?

FLO: They know it already.

BOONE: Then why'd they let us go?

FLO: Because they wouldn't have any fun at all burnin' up Boonesborough if you weren't there tryin' to stop 'em.

BOONE: That's true.

FLO: So how come I don't see you shakin' with fear?

BOONE: I shake so fast, nobody's ever seen it.

(She laughs and sits down. He opens a canteen and gives her a drink. Then he sits down behind her, and she leans back against him. He begins to stroke her hair. She turns around, as though she's heard something.)

FLO: Was that a bear?

BOONE: Brown. I think.

FLO: I'm afraid of bears.

BOONE: You should be. *(He puts his arms around her, and kisses the side of her face.)*

IN THE MUSEUM

Rick returns, more angry than ever.

RICK: She's not here. I searched the whole place.

HILLY: No, I know. What else did she say, in her letter?

RICK: That she didn't want to see me anymore. That she was in love with somebody else, and she was going off to be with him.

HILLY: Did she ever say anything like this before?

RICK: Last couple of weeks, all the time. I told her she was crazy.

HILLY: She *is* a little crazy, I think. Nothin' serious, though. I like her.

RICK: Are you and Flo havin' some kind of…

HILLY: No sir.

(But Rick is enraged. He grabs Hilly by the shirt and pulls him up off the bench.)

RICK: You are! She's leavin' me to run off with you.

HILLY: I just met her tonight. I swear it.

RICK: Then how do you know she's crazy?

HILLY: She's in love with Daniel Boone.

RICK: Very funny.

(Rick puts Hilly down as Mr. Wilson enters.)

MR. WILSON: Flo?

HILLY AND RICK: She's not here.

RICK: He knows but he's not telling.

MR. WILSON: She went home?

HILLY: She's with Daniel Boone.

RICK: *(To Mr. Wilson.)* Who *is* this guy?

MR. WILSON: You were our Santa at the Christmas Party.

RICK: Rick. Right.

MR. WILSON: Right. *(To Hilly.)* What do you mean, she's with Daniel Boone?

HILLY: I mean, she's found some kind of way of, I don't know, she goes into the teepee and she's gone. And she comes back with things, guns and things, wearing old leather jackets and smellin' like a wood fire.

RICK: She always smells like a wood fire.

HILLY: And does she have a fireplace at her house?

RICK: No.

(Mr. Wilson goes back to look at the teepee.)

HILLY: Well, there sure as hell isn't one in here. Flo heard your voice and high-tailed it to Boonesborough.

MR. WILSON: You looked in the ladies, I guess.

RICK: I did.

MR. WILSON: All right. *(To Rick.)* I'll check the parking lot. You check the upstairs bathrooms. And you… *(To Hilly.)* check the log cabin room and stay there. She likes you.

RICK: And what if we don't find her?

MR. WILSON: I don't know.

HILLY: What do you mean, you don't know? We have to go get her.

AT BOONESBOROUGH

Flo and Boone stand, inside a cabin. Boone's Indian clothes show the effects of the journey.

FLO: Where is everybody?

(A young woman enters. It is Boone's daughter, Jemima Boone.)

JEMIMA: Dad!

(Boone embraces her.)

BOONE: Hello, Jemima. Where's your mother?

JEMIMA: They left. They went back to North Carolina. Everybody left. They thought you were dead. *(She looks at Flo.)* We all thought you were dead. What have you been doing all this time?

BOONE: Jemima, this is Flo. I found her out there, just wanderin' around lost and half-starved. The Shawnee killed her man and child.

JEMIMA: I'm sorry.

FLO: Thanks.

BOONE: Did Russell make it back?

JEMIMA: He came back a long time ago. He's telling everybody that you could've escaped when he did, but …
(Squire Boone, Daniel's brother, enters.)
SQUIRE: Daniel. How did you get through?
BOONE: Hello, Squire.
SQUIRE: Our scout just came back sayin' there's four hundred Indians out there armed with British rifles.
BOONE: He's right. I just talked to 'em.
SQUIRE: Talked to 'em? What did they say?
BOONE: Oh, you know. Give us the fort. Things like that. *(A moment.)* They've got this letter to us from Lt. Governor Hamilton. It says if we abandon the fort, and promise not to come back onto Indian land, the Shawnee will hand us over to the British and nobody will get hurt.
SQUIRE: And if we stand and fight?
BOONE: Well, then, I reckon we'll all be killed.
SQUIRE: We'll be lucky if we aren't the only ones left in the fort by sundown, Daniel. You have to tell our people something.
BOONE: Something like what, I'll stay and die if they will?
SQUIRE: That'd be enough, comin' from you.
BOONE: O.K., then. Let's go tell 'em that.
SQUIRE: *(Feeling much safer suddenly.)* How've you been?
(Boone claps his arm around Squire and laughs.)
BOONE: Not bad. *(Then turning back to Jemima.)* Jemima, get Flo somethin' to eat.
(They walk out of the cabin.)

IN THE MUSEUM

Mr. Wilson enters a room we haven't seen before, in which stands a log cabin, to find Hilly dressing himself in the frontier clothes that were hanging on the wall.

MR. WILSON: What are you doing?
HILLY: Going to Boonesborough. Did you find Flo's car?
MR. WILSON: It's in the parking lot, all right. But maybe she's taking a walk.
HILLY: She's gone and you know it.
MR. WILSON: Was it something I said?
HILLY: More like everything everybody ever said.
MR. WILSON: Including me. *(Watching Hilly dress.)* You're serious about this.

HILLY: You bet I am. I want her back. And if I have to steal her away from Daniel Boone then that's what I'll do.

MR. WILSON: I'm going with you.

IN BOONESBOROUGH

Boone and Squire stand at the front gate of the fort.

BOONE: Just see if you can keep everybody makin' bullets, while I go out and tell Blackfish the decision.

SQUIRE: I think I should come out with you. All the Indians have to do is kill you, and everybody else will just give up.

BOONE: Squire, the Indians don't want to kill any of us. I'll be all right. Just tell your man in the blockhouse that if he sees me light out for the gate, don't wait for some kinda signal, just open fire.

IN THE MUSEUM

Rick enters. Hilly sits down to put on the frontier boots.

MR. WILSON: You didn't find her either, I guess.

RICK: Nope. I called her house. She's not there. I called her mother's house. She's not there. And I called the police.

HILLY: What did the police say?

RICK: Nothing. I got a machine.

HILLY: The police department has a machine?

(Mr. Wilson reaches into the cabinet for a jacket and begins to put it on.)

RICK: Yeah, you know, tell us your name and what happened and we'll get back to you. What are you guys doing?

MR. WILSON: *(To Rick.)* Hilly and I can take care of this. Why don't you leave us your number and if we find out something, we'll give you a call.

RICK: O.K. Sure. I have to go over to the garage and change my ball joints anyway. Maybe I'll stop back when I'm done. *(Rick leaves.)*

MR. WILSON: Flo was dating a mechanic?

HILLY: Get dressed if you're coming. And you can leave that attitude here, O.K.?

MR. WILSON: You actually think we can step inside the cabin, wearing these clothes and be in Boonesborough?

HILLY: I just hope she didn't change her mind and go somewhere else.

MR. WILSON: No, that's where she was going, all right. It's in her file upstairs. Reason for ceasing employment: going to Boonesborough.

HILLY: And that didn't seem strange to you?

MR. WILSON: Well, sure, but she wasn't herself lately. *(Mr. Wilson opens the case.)* But I haven't been myself either. The man I've been seeing…

HILLY: I don't want to hear about it. Why didn't you just ask her? "Hey, Flo. When you *get* to Boonesborough, what year's it gonna be?" *(Hilly reaches into the case and gets knives, guns, and powder horns for both of them.)*

MR. WILSON: You're right. I should've asked.

HILLY: Damn right you should have. She was counting on you, and him, whatever his name is, Rick, to hear what she was saying and stop her. Catch on. That's what she was hoping for, for somebody, somewhere, to catch on. But nobody did.

MR. WILSON: She seemed happy enough.

HILLY: Oh yeah? What *is* happy enough? She hasn't killed herself yet? The way I see it, you were her last hope, til I came along.

MR. WILSON: Then why didn't she say so?

HILLY: If you have to *tell* your last hope that they're your last hope, then it's way worse than you thought. *(Mr. Wilson grabs a hat and puts it on. And then begins to get dressed.)*

MR. WILSON: Okay, Okay. What part of Boonesborough do you think we're going to? When they first built it, or all those little wars in 1777, or…

HILLY: What's the worst it could be?

MR. WILSON: The Siege.

HILLY: That's probably it, then. Is there anything I ought to know?

MR. WILSON: It's September, 1778. There are about thirty men, maybe twenty boys and a couple of women and some children inside the fort. Their powder supply is very low. For ammunition, they're digging bullets out of the wall and melting them down. They have no bread, and only root vegetables and a little meat. They have a well, they dug that in 1777, but…

HILLY: Just the highlights, O.K.?

MR. WILSON: O.K. It's hopeless. *(A moment.)* Boone has no chance. None.

HILLY: Good. *(Hilly opens the door to the cabin, peers in, then holds it open for Mr. Wilson. Mr. Wilson looks in.)*

MR. WILSON: What if we can't get back?

HILLY: Florence gets back.

MR. WILSON: Not this time she didn't.

HILLY: Well this time…isn't over yet. After you.

> (*Mr. Wilson steps into the cabin, and Hilly follows him.*)

END OF ACT I

ACT II

In the darkness, drums and Indian flutes are heard. Seated on a blanket down-stage, Blackfish picks up a burning twig from the fire and lights a long pipe. As he passes it to Boone, a circle of dim light comes up on them.

BLACKFISH: In two days, the moon will be full. By that time, you must take your people and leave this fort, my son.

BOONE: *(A moment.)* Yes, I know. That's what you said yesterday.

BLACKFISH: Will you go?

BOONE: Look. To tell you the truth, even if we wanted to go, I don't know if we could get everything packed in two days. You know, there's all the venison we salted down, and all those candles we made...

BLACKFISH: You can leave the meat for us.

BOONE: Well, why don't I send some out for your supper tonight. That way you can...

BLACKFISH: If it was up to me, of course, I'd let you stay here.

BOONE: Of course you would. And if it was up to me, I'd just head west, but the fact of the matter is, I have to go along with the rest of my people in there and they've decided to stay and fight.

BLACKFISH: *(Very angry.)* But you will all die if you stay here.

BOONE: No, I know. That's what I told them.

BLACKFISH: Tell them what Dragging Canoe has said, "that a dark cloud hangs over this land." That no Indians have lived here for many years because of this cloud. That the bones of the ancient men rise up in the night and kill him who sets his lodge poles in this place.

(Boone takes a moment, and then is struck by a great idea.)

BOONE: I know. How about... *(A pause.)* if you go away instead of us?

BLACKFISH: How about...if we both go away?

BOONE: Good. O.K.

BLACKFISH: And the British can have the fort.

BOONE: No. They can't.

BLACKFISH: So we're back to killing you.

BOONE: I guess so.

BLACKFISH: In two days then.

BOONE: Well. How about if we talk about it again tomorrow?

BLACKFISH: I will see you tomorrow, my son. Perhaps after my belly is full of your meat, I will have some better ideas.

BOONE: Maybe you will.

(The light goes out on them, they exit, and the light comes up on…)

BOONESBOROUGH

And the whole stage now suggests frontier Boonesborough, complete with palisade, cookpots, and all the other trappings of frontier life. Flo and Jemima are seated near the cabin door, pouring melted lead into molds to make bullets. Behind them, a young man walks, as though patrolling the palisade, wearing a tall hat and carrying a rifle.

FLO: You pour and I'll hold the mold. Easy now.

JEMIMA: I don't think we're going to…

FLO: *(Interrupting.)* Watch what you're doing.

JEMIMA: We're not going to fool the Shawnee having these boys walk around the palisade all day. They know how many of us there are.

FLO: No they don't either. They've got so many white people lying to 'em about so many things, they don't know what to think.

(Russell and Squire walk through arguing.)

RUSSELL: If we keep pourin' our water on the roof, what are we going to drink?

SQUIRE: Just because Daniel doesn't know how much water's down there, doesn't mean there isn't enough. We're gonna soak the roof now, or watch it burn later, and those are his exact words.

JEMIMA: Daddy's putting all our water on the roof?

SQUIRE: There's a regiment of Virginia militia on their way, Russell. All we have to do is hold the fort til they get here.

RUSSELL: And what are they gonna see, huh? A big battle goin' on? No. Everybody slaughtered? No. All they're gonna find is four hundred Indians standin' around scratchin' their heads, wonderin' why all the white men died of thirst.

(Squire and Russell exit.)

FLO: *(Seeing Jemima's worry.)* There's plenty of water, Jemima. There's a river under this whole part of the country.

JEMIMA: How do you know that? Have you been down there? You think Dad knows everything. You'd do whatever he said.

FLO: Yes, I would. And everybody else better too or won't any of us get out of this.

JEMIMA: We're not going to get out of this. I should've gone home with Mother. We're going to die here.

(Russell is seen sneaking a long drink from his canteen. Boone comes up to him.)

BOONE: There you are.

RUSSELL: I know that.

BOONE: Did you check that powder supply?

RUSSELL: Not more than two days worth, I'd say.

BOONE: That'll have to do, then.

RUSSELL: I could try makin' a run for Fort Logan, if you wanted me to. Maybe they've got some they could spare us.

BOONE: No. We need you more than we need the powder.

RUSSELL: But what if the fight lasts longer than two days?

BOONE: I don't see how it can, Russell. I mean, once we run out of powder, it'll end pretty quick. *(Boone grabs the canteen away.)* What've you got here? *(Boone opens it.)*

RUSSELL: What do you think it is. Whiskey.

BOONE: I knew it.

(And to Russell's surprise, Boone takes a swig.)

BOONE: Thanks.

(Squire enters.)

SQUIRE: Blackfish is signaling he's ready to talk, Daniel.

BOONE: O.K. I'm comin'.

(Flo sets one mold aside and picks up another one.)

JEMIMA: How old was your child?

(Flo hesitates, trying to remember the lie she and Boone worked out.)

FLO: Four.

JEMIMA: And your husband?

(Flo is not a practiced liar.)

FLO: Forty—…Forty, I think.

JEMIMA: Did the Indians scalp them or knife them or torture them or what?

FLO: No, they just…dragged them off I guess. Maybe it wasn't even Indians. They'd just gone down to the river to get water and when they didn't come back, I went looking for them, only all that was left was…

JEMIMA: Was what?

FLO: *(Has no idea what to say.)* Their hats.

JEMIMA: And that's where Dad found you?

FLO: I guess my mind must've gone blank or something. Because the next thing I knew, your Dad was giving me a drink of water and asking me who I was.

JEMIMA: Where are the hats now?

(Flo cannot for the life of her think of an answer to this. A look of pain comes across her face.)

FLO: *(Quoting Hilly.)* You don't have any right asking me any of this. And I have no desire to tell you any of it. "Where are the hats?" What do you think this is, a story I made up?

JEMIMA: I'm sorry.

(They hear the sound of drumming.)

JEMIMA: *(Seeing her father at some distance.)* Daddy is opening the gate!

FLO: He's showing them he's not afraid.

(Russell enters with a pan of bullets.)

RUSSELL: He is not. He's daring them to shoot him so he can die first. *(Then picking up some bullets from Flo.)* Are these ready?

JEMIMA: What do he and Daddy talk about when he goes out there?

FLO: They're trying to work out a treaty, I think.

JEMIMA: What kind of a treaty? I thought we all voted to get killed.

RUSSELL: Is this all you done? Lord God. I'll get you some help over here.

(Russell exits.)

FLO: Thanks.

JEMIMA: Then is Daddy a traitor? Colonel Calloway says…

FLO: Don't you believe what anybody says, Jemima. Your father is the bravest man that ever lived in this country.

JEMIMA: He is not. He's afraid of Mother. He's afraid of Colonel Calloway. He's afraid of the British. He's afraid of the whole state of North Carolina. And most of all, he's afraid of honest work.

FLO: Is that what your mother says?

JEMIMA: Well she ought to know.

FLO: I'm sure she worries about him, when he's gone.

JEMIMA: She doesn't even sleep. Not one minute. How would you feel if you had six children and your husband was…

(Squire enters and interrupts.)

SQUIRE: Jemima. Your Dad says come out to the gate right now.

JEMIMA: What for?

SQUIRE: The Indians want to see you. Some of them are the same ones that stole you away that time, and they want to see you.

JEMIMA: I won't go.

(Flo grabs her by the arm and takes her over to Squire.)

FLO: Yes, you will go, young lady. Your father wouldn't ask you to come out there if it was dangerous so…there. Now go.

JEMIMA: Squire, please, don't make me go. I don't want to go out there.

(And as she continues to protest, Squire leads her away. And then, as Flo returns to her work, the cabin door opens slightly. And then opens further, and Hilly steps out.)

HILLY: *(Whispering.)* Florence. Hey Florence.

(Flo turns and sees Hilly.)

FLO: Hilly?

(He looks both ways, as though he's crossing the most dangerous street in America. And then steps out.)

HILLY: Well I'll be damned.

FLO: What are you doing here?

HILLY: I came to get you. *(He walks on over to her.)*

FLO: Why?

HILLY: Why do you think? To take you back.

FLO: I don't want to go back. And even if I did, why would I go back with you?

HILLY: You must've wanted me to come, Florence, or you wouldn't have told me where you were going.

(Mr. Wilson pokes his head out of the cabin now.)

FLO: Mr. Wilson!

HILLY: And once he knew I was coming, he came along to pick up some stuff for the museum.

(Mr. Wilson is holding an ember carrier.)

FLO: You can't stay here. I won't let you.

(She sees Mr. Wilson pick up something.)

FLO: Put that down.

HILLY: From the looks of things, I'd say Mr. Boone could use two more men. *(To Mr. Wilson.)* Too bad we didn't bring some real guns, huh, Wilson?

FLO: You two go right back in that cabin and go right back to the museum right now.

(Boone enters.)

BOONE: Flo, we need those bullets as soon as they're done. And you two, *(He points to Hilly and Mr. Wilson.)* we just lost a man from the blockhouse, so one of you get up there and take his place.

FLO: They can't. They just came in from...

BOONE: I don't care where they came from. What's your name?

MR. WILSON: Wilson.

BOONE: Get up there in the blockhouse, and see if you can keep from gettin' shot in the head. And you... *(He points to Hilly.)* Come with me. *(Boone leaves.)*

MR. WILSON: *(Looking around.)* Let's see. The blockhouse. The blockhouse.

HILLY: *(Points.)* Up there.

(Mr. Wilson leaves.)

FLO: Please, Hilly. I appreciate you bein' worried about me, but...

HILLY: I can't talk right now, Florence. But you look real good, and I'm glad I found you. So I'll see you later. O.K.?

FLO: I don't want you here.

HILLY: Then it's a good thing you're not in charge. *(Calling after Boone.)* Daniel Boone. Wait up. *(Hilly rushes off.)*

(Flo sits down, weary and very disturbed. And Rick comes out of the cabin.)

RICK: Son of a bitch.

(Flo turns around.)

FLO: Not you too.

RICK: What did you think, I'd be to scared to come? I'd just stand there and watch those two jokers come to the rescue?

(She shakes her head.)

RICK: I just didn't want to come with *them*, that's all.

FLO: But you could get killed here.

RICK: I had some stuff I wanted to talk to you about.

FLO: The way my day is going, you're probably married.

RICK: I should've told you right off. But I was afraid you wouldn't keep seein' me.

FLO: Well, you were right there.

RICK: I'm sorry. I just told my wife I want a divorce. Will you marry me, Flo?

FLO: I don't think so. Thanks, though.

RICK: Why not? You said you wanted to have a child. Well I want to have a child too.

FLO: *Now* you want to get married. *Now* you want to have a child. *Now* you'll say anything I want won't you?

RICK: I had no idea you were serious about this.

FLO: I only told you a hundred times.

RICK: And I was supposed to believe that? Believe you wanted to live at Boonesborough? Believe you were in love with Daniel Boone?

FLO: You didn't even think I was crazy for saying it. You didn't even say I should go see a doctor. You have no idea how hard it was for me to tell you those things. And all you did was laugh.

RICK: *(Deliberately.)* I won't ever do that again.

FLO: Not to me, you won't. At least Hilly believed me.

RICK: That hayseed. He'd believe anything.

FLO: You still don't believe it. Even standing here inside the fort, you don't believe it.

(An arrow whizzes by him, nearly missing his head.)

RICK: All right. I believe it. But it's crazy. I think you should see a doctor.

(Russell appears.)

RUSSELL: *(To Rick.)* You. Don't I know you from…

FLO: He's just leaving.

RUSSELL: No he's not, either. Boone wants a party to go out and kill a buffalo, and *(Pointing to Rick.)* he's it.

RICK: *(Quietly, to Flo.)* I'm the buffalo?

RUSSELL: *(Very irritated.)* Why the hell is Boone feeding those savages?

FLO: He's just trying to prove to them that we have food.

RUSSELL: So we're supposed to starve in here?

FLO: We are if it keeps them from attacking.

RUSSELL: *(To Rick.)* Get goin' you. One of the boys just spotted a buffalo down by the spring. Unless the Indians got it already. And don't get yourself scalped out there or you'll be sorry. *(Russell leaves.)*

RICK: I can't kill a buffalo.

(She hands him the gun lying on the ground beside her.)

FLO: You'll be all right. They're very slow.

RICK: Will you feel better about me if I come back with one?

FLO: No.

RICK: Yes you will, too. *(And with that, he tromps off toward the gate.)*

AT THE FRONT GATE

Boone offers Hilly a bucket of water.

BOONE: Want a drink?

HILLY: Sure. Why not?

BOONE: Spill as much as you can while you're drinkin' it. I want Blackfish's boys to get really thirsty just watchin' you.

HILLY: Why haven't they attacked already?

BOONE: Could be a lot of things. *(Boone throws the whole bucket of water on the ground.)* Maybe one of the other Chiefs isn't here yet. Maybe the medicine man says it isn't the right time. Maybe Blackfish is waitin' for us to offer him more money than the British.

HILLY: And maybe he knows if they start fightin', one of his braves might kill you. And then he couldn't capture you any more.

(Flo and Squire come up to them. Boone has a growing appreciation of Hilly.)

BOONE: Where'd you say you were from?

HILLY: Up north.

BOONE: You want to walk out and sit a spell with us?

HILLY: Sure.

BOONE: Florence is gonna come translate, in case we run into anything complicated.

FLO: *(To Boone.)* There's somethin' you need to know about him. He's...

BOONE: He's part Indian, I can tell you that much. *(To Hilly.)* Let's go. *(Boone gives Squire his rifle to hold.)*

FLO: *(To Hilly.)* Is that true?

HILLY: Yes, Ma'am.

(Boone puts his arm around Hilly and they leave Squire behind.)

BOONE: *(To Hilly.)* So how's it goin' up north?

HILLY: Pretty quiet. Everybody's workin' so hard, nobody much feels like they're doin' anything.

BOONE: Work is like that.

HILLY: Feels like all the excitement is somewhere else. You know. Like how're you supposed to amount to anything if you've got all this crap you have to do.

BOONE: Got to do it though, or else you'll wind up like me, always wonderin' where everything went. Didn't I have some land around here somewhere? Anybody seen my wife?

IN THE BLOCKHOUSE

Mr. Wilson is standing guard, pointing his rifle out the hole in the wall. Russell pokes his head up into the blockhouse to talk.

RUSSELL: Boone said there was a new man up here.

(Mr. Wilson adopts a new way of speaking, what he imagines to be a frontier dialect.)

MR. WILSON: Wilson. Yeah. What's goin' on out front?

RUSSELL: Nothin'. I want to know where you stand, Wilson.

MR. WILSON: Right here, sir. As long as you say.

RUSSELL: Where you stand on Daniel Boone, mister.

MR. WILSON: What do you mean.

RUSSELL: The man hides out with the Indians for the winter and then shows up here lookin like a redskin himself. Spends all his time out there talkin' with that savage like he was his old friend. I say let's chain Daniel Boone to the gate and get the hell outta here, every man for himself.

MR. WILSON: What about the women and boys?

RUSSELL: What about 'em?

(Mr. Wilson summons his courage and hopes his dialect will hold.)

MR. WILSON: They wouldn't stand a chance and you know it. I'm stickin' with Boone. I figure if I'm gonna die, I'd just as soon go with people I know.

RUSSELL: Nobody knows Boone. Nobody ever will. He didn't come back to save this fort, he came back to give it to the British and walk away from it. If we get out of this, the first thing I'm going to do is charge him with high treason.

MR. WILSON: You're just scared, is what you are. Why don't you crawl back into your little rat hole and stay there til we get through here.

(Russell, filled with disgust and hatred of this newcomer, turns and leaves. And Mr. Wilson sights down his rifle and repeats his little speech, sounding like every hero he ever heard.)

MR. WILSON: You're just scared, is what you are. Why don't you crawl back into your little rat hole and stay there til we get through here.

AT THE INDIAN BLANKET
Boone is seated on the blanket opposite Blackfish.

BLACKFISH: So. You've finally decided to surrender.

(Boone laughs.)

BOONE: We have actually.

(From behind him, Hilly gets into the spirit of things.)

HILLY: But everbody's so excited to meet you, we're kinda havin' some trouble gettin' 'em to line up right.

(Boone has a look of great relief. Like finally, he's got some help.)

BOONE: Yeah, you should see them. Me first, no, me first.

HILLY: So while they're workin' that out, in there, we thought we oughta come out here and talk about how're you're gonna torture us after we give up.

(Boone laughs and motions for Hilly to come sit down beside him.)

BLACKFISH: A worthy discussion. Every tenth man I will give to the warriors to do with as they like. The others I will turn over to the British. As for the women, there will be no torture for the women. The women I will keep all for myself.

BOONE: That sounds good. *(He turns to Hilly.)* That sound good to you?

HILLY: Except for Florence.

BOONE: Well of course except for Flo. *(He looks back at Flo.)* Flo you must save for me.

HILLY: *(Looking back at Flo.)* No, no. Florence you must save for me.

(Boone immediately seizes on this as a delaying tactic.)

BOONE: He will not. This woman is mine. If you need a woman, you can have my daughter.

HILLY: I want Florence. I came here to get Florence, and I'm not leaving without her. You'll have to kill me to get that woman and I'm ready to fight you any time you say.

BOONE: *(Enjoying this immensely.)* You little thief. I don't even know you. I never walked any path with you. You just show up here aimin' to take my whole joy in life away from me, in front of my friends.

(Hilly stands up.)

HILLY: It's not my fault she's all you've got. If you hadn't always been runnin' around tryin' to be the first man to see every tree…What are you afraid of anyway, that if you stay put they might find out about you?

(Boone stands up.)

BOONE: Find out *what* about me, you little…

BLACKFISH: We will do no more talking until this matter is settled. You will fight for her.

FLO: No you will not. I am not some prize that…

(Boone has already stripped off his shirt.)

BOONE: Just stand back, Florence.

FLO: Hilly, this is ridiculous. All they need is to see Daniel Boone worn out from beating you up, and they'll start the attack right now.

HILLY: No they won't either. As soon as I whip his ass, they'll know we're every one of us as tough as Daniel Boone, and if that's true, they can never beat us. They'll light out of here as fast as they can.

(Flo turns to leave.)

FLO: I'm having no part of this. None of this…has anything to do with me.

BLACKFISH: Go then. Remain with the women. I will send a messenger when you are needed.

(Flo leaves. Hilly takes off his shirt. And as Boone and Hilly are circling each

other, Flo joins Squire, Russell, and Mr. Wilson who are watching from the front gate.)

AT THE FRONT GATE
Russell stands with Squire and Mr. Wilson.

RUSSELL: What is all that about?

SQUIRE: Looks like another one of Daniel's little tricks to me. Have a little fight. Waste a little more time. Well, what can it hurt. When the Indians see how Daniel humiliates this man they'll know who they're up against anyway.

MR. WILSON: Hey now. Don't count Hilly out, here. He's not as slow as he looks. *(The fight begins.)*

FLO: I can't watch.

MR. WILSON: Come with me to the east palisade, then. There's somethin' funny goin' over there.

(Flo and Mr. Wilson exit. A circle of light forms around Boone and Hilly. Hilly takes the first swipe. Boone counters well and Hilly goes down. An Indian pitches Boone a large staff. Boone looks at it, pitches it to Hilly. Hilly holds it, looks at it, and pitches it back to the Indian. And the fight begins.)

SQUIRE: Uh-oh.

JEMIMA: Daddy.

RUSSELL: What'll we do now.

SQUIRE: Not a thing. One move from us and the whole thing could start right here.

(We hear the sounds of cheering, the thumps of the blows. Boone seems winded and out of shape, compared to Hilly. But Boone is sneaky. There are some moments when we think they are just playing with each other, but then Boone begins to take it seriously, and finally, wrestles Hilly to the ground and forces him to give up.)

BOONE: Say it, You thief. Flo is mine.

HILLY: I won't. You're dead.

BOONE: You will. The man hasn't been born that can beat me, at this or anything else. Now say it.

(Blackfish lets out some kind of warrior cheer. But Hilly will not give in.)

HILLY: You've *got* a wife. If she still wants anything to do with you. What about her? Florence is mine.

(Boone looks up, seeing someone arriving in the Indian camp.)

Boone: Well. I'll be…

HILLY: What.

BOONE: It looks like the folks old Blackfish has been waitin' for, have arrived.

HILLY: Who are they?

BOONE: The British one is new to me. But the Chief standin' beside him is a real mean character. When he shows up, you know the talk is all over. *(Blackfish approaches.)*

BLACKFISH: I must go and greet my brothers. As for you, my son has beaten you. The woman he calls Flo, and you call Florence, is his. You will leave the village by sundown.

HILLY: I won't.

BLACKFISH: You will.

BOONE: He can't.

HILLY: I won't.

BLACKFISH: Whatever. *(Blackfish begins to walk away.)*
(Boone stops him.)

BOONE: Hilly can't leave the camp because I need him. And Flo can't be mine because I've got a wife. And the way we do things is a man can only have one wife. Now we enjoyed the fight and all, but this thing's not settled yet.

BLACKFISH: Very well. I will take the woman back.

HILLY: No! Now I've told you how this thing has to go.

BLACKFISH: All right. If my son does not want this woman he has won, he can give her to you.

BOONE: Good. That's what I'll do then.

HILLY: All right.
(Blackfish starts to move away again. Boone catches him.)

BOONE: But I would ask for the son's privilege of having the marriage performed in the lodge of my father.

BLACKFISH: And I would agree to anything to end this conversation.

BOONE: Done.
(Blackfish leaves. Hilly grins at Boone.)

HILLY: Done.

BOONE: *(Looking after Blackfish.)* I'm gonna miss him.

AT THE EAST PALISADE

FLO: I'm sorry I got so mad at you, when you asked me out to dinner.

MR. WILSON: Why shouldn't you be mad? I didn't give one thought to what you might be feeling.

FLO: The truth is. I had such a crush on you when I first came to work at the museum. I thought you were the handsomest, the smartest, the most charming man I'd ever seen. And it took me so long to accept that you would never be interested in me, that last night, when all of a sudden, you were interested in me...

MR. WILSON: For a minute.

FLO: I could've killed you.

MR. WILSON: No, I know.

FLO: I wanted to knock you down and jump on you. Throw you into the Boone street and crash my cart into you. Yell horrible things at you, tie you up and swat you with my mop and...

MR. WILSON: Go on.

FLO: You're not mad?

MR. WILSON: Of course not. I like you. I want you to be happy. If it would make you happy to hit me with a mop...

FLO: *(Laughing with him.)* Stop.

MR. WILSON: Come on. You have to see this.

(They duckwalk up to the edge of the palisade.)

FLO: Where?

MR. WILSON: See that little mound of dirt at the edge of the forest. So are you serious about this Rick?

FLO: He's very sweet. But if I had known he was married, I would never have started seeing him.

MR. WILSON: Well, of course you wouldn't. So is there anybody else? Now what about Hilly? I mean, I like him. And it's obvious he's crazy about you. And you know what? I think my therapist is crazy. I don't want to get married, I'm fine just the way I am.

FLO: Of course you are.

MR. WILSON: Maybe my therapist wants to get married.

(Squire approaches with Boone and Hilly.)

MR. WILSON: *(Referring to them.)* There they are. Squire? Daniel? Come see what you make of this. It looks like the Indians are digging a tunnel. I think they're trying to tunnel under the fort.

SQUIRE: I think you're right.

BOONE: Goddamn the British anyway. Whoever heard of an Indian digging a tunnel?

Squire: What should we do?

MR. WILSON: I say we start a tunnel of our own, aimin' to cross theirs, but underneath it, so where the two tunnels meet, theirs will collapse.

BOONE: You think that would work?

MR. WILSON: I know it would.

SQUIRE: O K., then. Get some of the boys and get on it.

BOONE: Where's your rifle, Wilson?

MR. WILSON: I had to give it to that Timmy. In the blockhouse.

BOONE: *(Hands his rifle to Mr. Wilson.)* Here. Take mine, then. Good work.

(Mr. Wilson takes the rifle with a look of absolute awe. Flo is not eager to hear about the outcome of the fight.)

BOONE: Now. Flo.

FLO: If it's anything to do with that fight, I don't want to hear about it.

BOONE: You're Hilly's woman. Fair and square. Blackfish says the two of you will spend the night in the lodge of his sons, and in the morning, you'll be man and wife.

FLO: That's what you think. *(She leaves.)*

HILLY: Florence...

(Boone grabs him to keep him from running after her.)

BOONE: No sense chasin' the girl. Where's she gonna go?

(Hilly isn't so sure of that.)

BOONE: She'll come around. You'll see. I'll talk to her. First time I ever saw her that scared though.

HILLY: That's because I'm so mean.

BOONE: Well, what do you say we go back out there and hear what kind of treaty the *British* have dreamed up.

HILLY: O.K.

(They turn and walk offstage.)

BOONE: You know, if you haven't got any place special to go after this, why don't you come on back to North Carolina with me.

HILLY: Thanks.

BOONE: So you'll come?

HILLY: Probably not. *(A moment.)* No offense.

BOONE: None taken.

BACK AT THE FRONT GATE
Flo stands at the front gate fuming.

JEMIMA: Did your mind just go blank again?

FLO: Your Daddy's tryin' to marry me off.

JEMIMA: That's nice.

FLO: I won't do it.

JEMIMA: But if you don't get married, where will you go after this? Cause you can't come home with us, you know. Mother is there.

FLO: No, I'm not coming home with you.

JEMIMA: Oh, that's right. I forgot. We don't *have* to go *anywhere* after this. We're going to die. *(Greatly relieved, she waves.)* O.K. Good luck.
(Jemima exits and Flo looks up and sees Rick enter dragging the carcass of a buffalo.)

RICK: So. What do you think? Pretty good, huh? Lotta damn meat, on this thing.

FLO: Uh-huh.

RICK: What's the matter?

FLO: I want you to take me home.

RICK: *(Speaking so no one else will hear.)* Take you back to the museum, you mean? I can't. Not for a while, anyway. I saw a coupla more of these dudes down there at the spring, and I figure I might as well get them too while I'm at it.

FLO: Oh, forget it. I'm beginning to understand why the rest of the women left already.

RICK: Besides, it's perfectly clear to me I'm out of the running here.

FLO: What running? What are you talking about?

RICK: For you, Flo. These guys have got it all over me, any day. Hilly fighting Daniel Boone. Mr. Wilson figuring out about that tunnel. What have I ever done? Kept the garage open so people can get another two years out of their old car?

FLO: What's wrong with that?

RICK: I know, I know. Dad would love it if he saw the thing was still going. The kids like to come over and crawl under the cars. I mean, I guess I'm proud enough. Lot of other guys went under the last ten years.

FLO: That's because they don't know what they're doing.

RICK: Look, Flo. You want a hero. You deserve a hero. Now, I'm a nice enough guy and all, but I'm the first one to say it. Fixin' a guy's transmission isn't exactly a heroic act.

FLO: It is if it's really fixed.

RICK: Thanks.

(She looks at him a moment. Then down at the buffalo.)

FLO: They owe you the tongue for killing it.

RICK: That's O.K. They can have it.

FLO: No. You eat it. Or dry it, if you want to. Doubled over, a dried buffalo tongue would make a nice pouch for a wrench, or something.

RICK: O.K. Great. I'll do that.

(Squire comes up to Rick and Flo.)

SQUIRE: Looks like Daniel and Blackfish are about finished out there.

FLO: But the Virginia regiment isn't here yet.

SQUIRE: They're not. We just received word that they turned back.

FLO: They're not coming?

SQUIRE: Nobody's coming. This treaty better be good. God help us.

THE CABIN

Seeing Boone and Hilly returning from the Indian encampment, Jemima, Russell and Mr. Wilson come up to where Squire, Rick, and Flo are standing. Rick has still not adopted the use of a frontier dialect.

JEMIMA: They're coming in. Open the gate. Open the gate.

RUSSELL: So what do we think this treaty says? We all agree to become Indians and tear the fort down for 'em?

(Rick and Mr. Wilson move slightly apart from the others.)

RICK: What's his problem?

MR. WILSON: Who cares? What's that all over your shirt?

RICK: Blood of the buffalo, man.

MR. WILSON: Wait a minute. That's not your shirt. That's *our* shirt. You took that shirt right out of the case.

RICK: And shot your dinner in it, yes, I did.

MR. WILSON: What are we having?

(Hilly and Boone come up to the group.)

BOONE: O.K. It looks like we got somethin' to talk about anyway. *(He hands his handwritten paper to Squire.)*

MR. WILSON: *(To Rick.)* Do you have any idea what that piece of paper would be worth?

(As Flo moves to avoid standing near Hilly, Squire reads from the paper.)

SQUIRE: "There will be no battle. There will be peace between the white men and the red men forever." *(He looks up.)* I don't understand.

JEMIMA: Does that mean we can we stay here? They'll all go home and we can stay here?

RUSSELL: No, it does not. It means there's somethin' he's not tellin' us.

BOONE: I don't know what it means. Except that Blackfish isn't calling the shots any more.

SQUIRE: Who is?

BOONE: Some Frenchy lieutenant in the British army, and Chief Moluntha.

FLO: What's *he* doing here?

BOONE: No, I know, it's not a good sign. But what they *say* is that they don't want to fight us.

RICK: *(To Mr. Wilson.)* They must've heard *we* were here.

BOONE: They want to set the Ohio River as a boundary. South of the Ohio would be Indian land. North would be white man's land.

SQUIRE: And if we sign this treaty, they'll go home?

BOONE: And we'll go home. That's right. Alive.

RUSSELL: And what else do we have to sign?

BOONE: An oath of loyalty to King George.

RUSSELL: I knew it.

SQUIRE: You're already a subject of King George just by virtue of bein' born in Virginia, Russell.

RUSSELL: I won't sign. I won't. Virginia is at war with the British.

SQUIRE: We have to sign it. It doesn't matter what it says. That or be slaughtered.

RUSSELL: I told every one of you what I thought we ought to do, only now it's too late.

MR. WILSON: *(To Rick.)* I worked for a guy like him once.

BOONE: I figure we should, you know, take a vote on it, get some sleep, and then, if everybody is agreeable, in the morning, eighteen of us will meet eighteen of them under the sycamore at dawn and sign the treaty.

RUSSELL: And then they'll kill us. Its a trick.

BOONE: No, I know it's a trick. But we'll have a pretty good idea by then what they plan to do.

RUSSELL: And just where are we gonna get an idea like that?

BOONE: Flo and Hilly are spendin' the night in their camp.

FLO: We are not. I told you that out there.

BOONE: Blackfish has the lodge all fixed up, Flo. Besides, it's just too good an opportunity to pass up. You'll spend the night spyin' out the situation, and just before dawn, you'll sneak back inside here and tell us what's going on.

FLO: I can tell you right now what's going on, in case you've forgotten. That's a war chant, they're singing.

BOONE: No, I remember. So at least we know they won't start anything til morning. That damn song goes on forever.

FLO: And what if this is a trick, too? What if all Blackfish wants is a couple of hostages to bargain with tomorrow.

BOONE: He doesn't. He likes Hilly, here. He's just trying to help him out with you. Besides, you know how he likes weddings.

(Flo walks away a little.)

BOONE: So, now. Like Russell says we have to assume that the attack will start right after we sign the treaty. So between now and then, I want every gun oiled, every knife sharpened, and buckets of water placed every five feet along the palisade.

(Squire, Rick, Mr. Wilson, and Jemima all leave with Boone, as he continues to talk.)

BOONE: Every man's gonna have a bandage or somethin' he can use for a bandage in his pocket or somewhere. And I want a list drawn up of who's reloading who's gun so when we get out there in the morning, everybody's gonna be in position.

(Russell has remained behind, standing between Flo and Hilly. Now, he regards Hilly with suspicion.)

RUSSELL: You won't really be married, you know.

FLO: *(Genuinely to Russell.)* Thanks.

(Russell exits and Hilly looks at Flo. She turns away from him.)

HILLY: This lodge business wasn't my idea, Florence, you know that. The only reason I even fought with Boone was to buy us some time. That, and I didn't want him takin' you away without a fight. But…

FLO: But since you won, and since we're back here in the wilderness, you'll just act as wild as all the rest of them. *(She grabs her hair.)* "Come on, girl."

HILLY: No, Florence. That's what I was trying to say, if I could finish my sentence please. I didn't win. Boone did.

FLO: What do you mean?

HILLY: I mean, he won the fight. I lost.

FLO: You mean he lied to me?

HILLY: And he wanted some spies in their camp overnight, so he thought up this lodge thing. (*A pause.*) But I'm not going to force you to spend the night with me. If you'd rather just go get a burger or something, let's go.

FLO: No. He's right. Somebody should be out there.

HILLY: So should I go get your stuff?

FLO: I don't have any stuff to get. But if you lay one finger on me out there, I'll kill you.

HILLY: Fair enough. So are you ready now?

FLO: I'm ready.

(*As the sound of drumming increases, they approach the teepee, and night falls.*)

AT THE ENTRANCE TO THE TEEPEE

HILLY: The only thing I'm worried about is what happens if we step inside this teepee and wind up back in the museum?

FLO: That would suit you just fine, I bet.

HILLY: How does it work anyway? Me and Wilson didn't have to say any magic words or anything. We didn't do anything except step inside. And you didn't either, I bet. So how did we get here?

(*An owl hoots in the distance.*)

FLO: (*Suddenly very tired.*) I don't know, really. The first night I did it, I was just standing there in the museum feeling like there was nobody in the whole world I wanted to see. Nobody I wanted to call. And nobody I wanted to call me.

HILLY: Because you already knew what they were going to say?

FLO: More like we'd had our chance, you know, and we blew it. Like we'd already decided it wasn't going to work, so why go on with it. Like it was just easier to give up. Nobody even blames you for giving up anymore. It's like being in love is something people used to do. When they had more time.

HILLY: So you said, the hell with that. I'm in love with Daniel Boone.

FLO: I did. I didn't even care if it was crazy. Suddenly, I knew exactly what to do, break all my dates, stop seeing people I didn't care about, and just love Daniel Boone. Then I picked up my broom and walked into the teepee to sweep it out, and here I was. I mean, there he was. Standing right in front of me.

HILLY: That's how I felt, too.

FLO: You did?

HILLY: About you. Not here though. Back there. At the museum. I'd known for a long time who I was looking for, and all of a sudden. There you were. As soon as I saw you, I knew I was gonna end up loving you.

FLO: How did you know that?

HILLY: *(A moment.)* You're a believer, Florence. *(A moment.)* A man needs a woman like that.

(The sounds of the war chant get louder.)

FLO: I hate that sound. I hate it.

HILLY: *(He holds the flap of the teepee open.)* It's O.K. We'll be O.K.

FLO: You go on in. I'm just going to walk around a little out here. See if I can learn anything.

HILLY: Do you want me to come with you?

FLO: I want to know why you're not scared by any of this.

HILLY: I've been in situations a lot tougher than this.

FLO: Back there, you mean.

HILLY: Sure I have. Everything is harder back there.

FLO: It's O.K. Blackfish is watching us. You go on inside. I'll be back in a little bit.

(Hilly steps inside the teepee, as Flo walks away.)

HILLY: Just be careful.

FLO: Thanks.

(Flo walks away and Hilly enters the teepee.)

INSIDE THE FORT

Boone is cleaning his rifle and talking with Jemima.

BOONE: I know somethin' is eatin' at you, Jemima. You might as well tell me what it is.

JEMIMA: I think Flo is an Indian. I think she's your Indian wife. *(Her anger rising.)* I think you brought your Indian wife back inside this fort with you, like nobody would even notice. What if mother had still been here?

BOONE: She might be an Indian. I don't know. I don't have any idea who Flo is. She told me she was married to a trapper and she got tired of him always smellin' of dried blood and wet fur and run off.

JEMIMA: Well, she told me the Indians killed her man and her child.

BOONE: No, I told you that to keep you from thinking she was my Indian wife.

JEMIMA: *(Furious.)* Is she your Indian wife?

BOONE: Not any more, no. Looks to me like those times are all gone.

JEMIMA: Are you gonna ask me not to tell mother about this?

BOONE: You're a grown woman now, Jemima. What you tell your mother is between you and her.

(Jemima softens considerably toward him.)

JEMIMA: Are we going to die tomorrow?

(And Boone hugs her, suddenly seeming like an ordinary good Dad.)

BOONE: No we are not. If we made it this far we'll probably live forever.

(Flo approaches. Jemima clings to Boone for a moment.)

BOONE: Florence, what are you doin' here?

FLO: I wanted to tell you what I heard.

JEMIMA: I'll be inside, Daddy.

(Jemima leaves and Flo watches her go.)

FLO: Is she all right?

BOONE: She's just scared, that's all. How's the enemy doing?

FLO: Well, Blackfish wants to go home, but Moluntha and the British feel more like a massacre.

BOONE: O.K. Thanks. You go on back out there now, and I'll see you in the morning.

FLO: I'm...uh...not going to be here in the morning. I'm going to walk on down the path, I think.

(He takes a moment.)

BOONE: Gonna miss all the excitement if you leave now.

FLO: I can't shoot worth a damn. You know that.

BOONE: You're runnin' from that man out there. Aren't you.

FLO: What if I am? You've done it enough.

BOONE: Yes I have. So I can tell you right now, it won't work, Flo. Rebecca done the same thing to me, got it into her mind that I was hers. You'll never get away from him, and you wouldn't be happy if you did. Best thing for you to do is give up and grab a hold.

FLO: I can't. I hardly know him.

BOONE: How much do you have to know? He came here to find you, he told me that himself. Then he fought me for you. Not a lot of men would do that. Give him a chance.

(Flo doesn't answer.)

BOONE: I mean, how're you supposed to know *what* you think, standin' around here waitin' to get shot? Maybe if you just went back out there and spent one night with the man, you'd feel different about it.

FLO: Never.

BOONE: People aren't like the country, Flo. You and me, we can walk away from all the fine places we've ever seen cause we know there's always gonna be a nicer place further on. But you walk away from a man like this, and chances are, you'll never see his like again.

FLO: It's not just him. It's somethin' about you, too.

BOONE: No, I know. I'm not gonna be much fun here for a while.

FLO: It's not that.

BOONE: Well. Maybe not.

FLO: Don't you want to know what it is?

BOONE: No, I don't think I do.

FLO: See. That's it, exactly.

BOONE: Well, I can't help that. It never *did* matter to me what other people did. Not that I wouldn't have an opinion about it. Cause I've known some people done some things I didn't like at all… *(A slight pause.)* But I would never try and stop 'em from doin' it, whatever it was. Never. It wouldn't be right.

FLO: Where are you going to go after this?

BOONE: Back home, I guess. It's time I went back to civilization and tried to redeem myself somehow.

FLO: Did you ever write to Rebecca, to tell her you were alive?

BOONE: No, I don't think I did.

FLO: Why not?

BOONE: I don't know. Nothin' out here to write on except the trees. And I'm sure as hell not going to do that. *(A moment.)* You go on now. If you're determined to lose this man, you'd better get goin' before he comes lookin' for you.

FLO: Not one for a sentimental farewell, are you, Daniel Boone.

BOONE: Nope.

(She just stands there a moment. And then suddenly, is very angry.)

BOONE: I'll see you again sometime.

FLO: No. I don't think you will.

BOONE: Well. Maybe not.

(She turns away.)

BOONE: You watch yourself, now.

(Flo walks away from him and over to the palisade behind the cabin and turns on the lights and she is...)

BACK IN THE MUSEUM

She takes off her shawl and whatever other articles of frontier clothing she is wearing and hangs them back up where they belong. She goes into the back room for a minute and comes out with her purse. She gets out a piece of paper and sits down to write a note. As she is writing, Hilly comes out from the back room and stands and watches for a moment.

HILLY: You must think I am the dumbest man on earth.

(She turns around, startled.)

HILLY: You didn't think I would know what you were doing? "See you later, Hilly, I'm just gonna go check on the Shawnee."

FLO: I did check on the Shawnee. And then I told Daniel Boone what I saw.

HILLY: Give me a break.

FLO: That's what he said.

HILLY: What Boone said?

FLO: Yes, he did. He likes you. He said I should give you a chance.

HILLY: Well then?

FLO: So. I'm leaving you my phone number.

(He takes the paper from her.)

HILLY: You are not. You're telling me *(He reads.)* "thanks for helping out at the fort, but I'm not ready for a relationship right now." What is it, Florence? Am I goin' too fast for you?

FLO: Yes, you are.

HILLY: No, I'm not either. You've been prayin' that somebody with some nerve would come along, and here I am. Now. What else is it? Is it Linda? Are my jeans too tight? What?

FLO: It's not Linda.

HILLY: It's my jeans. I knew it was my jeans. Well that's just too bad. This is exactly what I like in jeans. Every pair I have is just like this.

(Suddenly, Rick and Mr. Wilson burst back into the room from the door of the cabin. They are covered in blood and dirt, and look like hell.)

RICK: Jesus, God. What happened to you guys? We thought they captured you. Boone made us search the whole camp just to make sure you didn't get scalped.

HILLY: You mean it's all over?

RICK: What a battle. They went out to sign the treaty, and one minute, they were all standin' there, shakin' hands and everything, and the next minute there were guns goin' off, and tomahawks flyin' through the air…

MR. WILSON: Nobody even knew who started it.

RICK: And then they all rushed back into the fort and it was two really tough days, I'm here to tell you. Boone got hit, Squire got hit. Jemima got shot in the butt.

MR. WILSON: Kids reloading rifles, and Indians climbing up the walls, and fire arrows landing on the roof, and all the time we're trying to dig this tunnel…

RICK: And tryin' to stay awake and not go crazy from all the screamin' and yellin'.

MR. WILSON: And then it started to rain.

RICK: The one thing that could save our ass actually happened. Middle of the day, this mother of a storm hits. We thought, great, now we're gonna fuckin' drown here.

MR. WILSON: But when it was over, the Indians were gone.

RICK: Boone said Blackfish would see the rain as some kind of a sign.

MR. WILSON: I don't know. I saw a couple of Indians pretty close up that last day. They weren't really into it.

HILLY: So Boone is all right. That's good.

RICK: Except right as we were leavin', that little jerk Russell got Colonel Calloway to arrest Boone for treason.

HILLY: For treason? That's ridiculous. They'd all have died if it hadn't been for Boone.

RICK: So where were you guys?

HILLY: I wanted to stay. But Florence was tryin' to run away from me again.
(Rick and Mr. Wilson begin to take off their frontier clothes.)

RICK: I'm glad I'm not gonna have to explain to anybody what happened to these clothes.

MR. WILSON: They're not too bad. I'm very good at this sort of thing. We'll let them dry overnight, then I'll brush them off and put them back in the cases. No one will ever know.

HILLY: What finally happened to Boone? Did he go to jail for treason?

MR. WILSON: *(Now speaking as a historian.)* No. He beat it. But just barely. And then he went to North Carolina to find Rebecca and the children, and it took him almost a year to get back to Kentucky. Where he fought the

Indians some more, and they killed some more of his family. Until finally he got chased out of Kentucky because he'd lost all his land, and owed so much money. So he went with two of his sons to Missouri where he lived 'til he died. *(A pause.)* And then he stayed buried a while, until they dug him up and brought him back to Kentucky and buried him again.

HILLY: At least you think it was him.

MR. WILSON: That's right. Well. I'm going home.

RICK: Yeah. Me too.

MR. WILSON: Flo? Are you still leaving us?

FLO: I am.

MR. WILSON: But am I ever going to see you again?

FLO: I don't know.

RICK: Well, *(Indicating Hilly.)* he's gonna keep workin' here, isn't he?

MR. WILSON: He is, if I have anything to say about it.

RICK: So, you can just ask *him.* He'll know where she is.

MR. WILSON: Well good. That's what I'll do.

(And Mr. Wilson and Rick walk out together like old army buddies, remembering the old stories.)

RICK: So, did you see when that tomahawk landed in Boone's neck?

MR. WILSON: It was amazing. Like all he was worried about was where the next one was comin' from.

RICK: Never saw anything like him. Standing next to Boone, I even had the feeling those two dead guys might pull through.

MR. WILSON: He could've never done it without us, though. Two less men, and who knows what might have happened.

(They exit and Flo and Hilly are left alone.)

HILLY: So. Where were we?

FLO: Your jeans.

HILLY: O.K. You don't like my jeans. I don't like that long skirt.

FLO: *(Very tired.)* It's not your jeans. It's your whole attitude. You think you ought to have what you want just because you want it.

HILLY: It's not just because I want it. It's because I'm willing to pay for it.

FLO: What do you mean, pay for it? Are you buying me now? What do I cost, Hilly?

HILLY: I don't know, Florence. Maybe everything I've got. Maybe my job. Maybe my whole way of lookin' at things. Maybe you're gonna drive me crazy. Maybe Linda won't like you and I'll lose this thing I have with her. Or maybe she'll like you better than me, and I'll feel like a jerk for bringing you in there. Or maybe it'll be wonderful and I'll love you to the end of the earth and you'll have a heart attack and die. Or you'll run off with somebody else and *I'll* have the heart attack and die. I don't know what you'll cost me, Florence. And I don't care.

FLO: But what do you know about me?

HILLY: A lot.

FLO: Do you know I get depressed?

HILLY: I figured you did.

FLO: Do you know I don't want to work? That all I really like to do is read? Do you know that I hate my hair and spend a whole lot of time thinking about it? What about my folks? Wouldn't you like to know they're not insane or something?

HILLY: Not unless they're gonna live with us.

FLO: No. They're not.

HILLY: O.K., then. Marry me, Florence. Come and…be with me. Be whatever you want. You want to go invent electricity, or pan for gold, whatever it is, I'm in. *(A moment.)* I love you.

FLO: No, I know.

HILLY: So what do you think?

FLO: I think you're the first man I ever knew who actually just…heard what I said. *(Flo stands there a minute.)*

HILLY: You're tired, aren't you.

FLO: I am. I think I'm almost asleep.

HILLY: Tired is O.K. Sad is O.K. Running away from me again is not. O.K.? *(Flo stands there a moment.)*

FLO: O.K.

(And he opens his arms to her, and slowly she walks into them and he holds her. And after a while, he speaks.)

HILLY: It's gonna be great. I promise. I mean, it won't be great every damn day, but overall, it's gonna be great. You'll see. I'm the best man ever lived in Kentucky.

THE END

THROW OUT THE LIFELINE
Keynote speech for the Kentucky Arts Council's 25th Anniversary Celebration
Conference—Connections in the Arts. December 8, 1995.

It is my very great pleasure to come give this address. For it was this very orga-
nization, The Kentucky Arts Council, that saved me, as a young Kentuckian,
throwing out a veritable lifeline that would pull me forever into the safe harbor
of the arts, keeping me away from the dangerous shoals of a career in advertising.

Not that I could actually have had a career in advertising, of course. But I
thought I could, I mean, I hoped I could. I mean, after I realized I was unem-
ployable, advertising seemed my only hope. How had I learned I was unem-
ployable? By barely surviving a succession of jobs, where as a serious claustro-
phobic, I was horrified to learn that employers expected me to come in at a certain time in the morning and stay there all day. Thank my lucky stars, at just
exactly the right moment, the Kentucky Arts Council appeared, and here I am
today.

Before I begin, please forgive the death-obsessed, Pentecostal nature of the
title of this speech. I'm always asked for the title months before I've actually
written the speech. So when I get around to writing the speech, in this case, last
week, I have as little idea what this title might mean as you do.

But I suppose Throw Out the Lifeline might have something to do with
the fact that right now I'm working on a musical about Aimee Semple
McPherson, the American visionary/healer who one day in 1926 walked into
the sea and disappeared. Or it could have to do with that Stevie Smith poem
I've always loved, the one about the woman out in the water with her arm in
the air. I wasn't waving, she says, I was drowning. Or I guess, when asked for a
title, I could've just been obsessing about how I was going to die, which I've
always been convinced would be by driving off a bridge and drowning.

Or. Or. Throw Out the Lifeline could be what I imagined Nash Cox said
to Jim Edgy all those years ago, just before she hired me. For I was sinking all
right. I was drowning in a sea of misconceptions about what an artist was, what
an artist did, and who could play a part in the cultural life of our time. At the
time, I thought of artists as a rarefied group of very special individuals. Like the
best club in the world. And the hardest to get into. I didn't know I was already
in. And I wouldn't have believed it, if the Kentucky Arts Council hadn't told
me so.

To go back to the early seventies. I had a degree in philosophy, which
meant I could do nothing. And I had a teaching certificate, and two years of

experience teaching severely disturbed children in a state mental hospital. My future was not, as they say, bright. I had transferred to a job teaching gifted children, hoping to cheer myself up, hoping maybe that was where I belonged, but I had gotten involved in a huge argument with the director of the program about which biography of George Washington Carver we should read to the kids. And I had lost that argument. And I had decided not to return in the fall. So I was deep in despair. I was looking at the ads for advertising trainees. I had no idea what to do.

Yes, I wanted to write for the theatre. Yes, I had won all kinds of writing competitions. But I did not believe it was possible to be a woman playwright from Kentucky. The reason I thought this, was that in the early seventies, there weren't any. There were writers, all right, wonderful writers, a few of them women, but those writers were all from the mountains. So naturally, I thought being an artist was a matter of where you were born. If you were born in the mountains, you could be an artist. If you were born in Louisville, you had to go into advertising.

Further, I thought that to be an artist, you had to be born into an artistic family. If you wanted to be a writer, you had to have a father who founded the New Yorker, or an aunt who owned the *New York Review of Books*. I thought you had to live down the road from Wendell Berry. I thought you had to already know Harriet Arnow.

I thought, if you were an artist, the Arts Council would already know about you and already be giving you grants and already be helping you get in touch with your audience, so I would never have presumed to call and invite myself over. But one day—just to prove that all luck isn't bad—one day the esteemed Arts Council, in the person of Nash Cox, called me. "Who did you say this was?" I asked? She laughed, and then asked if I would come talk to her about being Filmmaker in the Schools. "But I don't know anything about film," I said. "Oh, that's O.K.," she said. "We'll send you to New York to study. Would you think about it?"

Did I say yes? How fast did I say yes? I met Nash. We talked, and as I listened to her, I felt the door opening. The door I had always been looking for. I had no idea what Nash saw in me, but when I asked her about it later, she said she just knew I was going to do something, and she wanted to watch.

And so I went to work for the Arts Commission in 1972, and stayed until 1976. And in the beginning, I felt like such an impostor. I wondered when they were going to find out I didn't know anything and start laughing. Or worse. Sometimes I lied and said I had read certain poets I hadn't read, or seen certain films I hadn't seen. But if they knew I was lying, they didn't tell. They simply kept listening for what I was doing, and pretty soon, I was actually doing things, the kind of things an artist does. I was actually making films with kids, actually working in the National Association of Media Educators, actually writing a big grant proposal to put artists in the schools, and then for two years, actually administering the grant. I had a new life. I knew a lot of people in the arts in Kentucky. I participated in conferences held by the Kentucky Arts Commission, and at one particular conference, I found myself actually walking the slippery ledge that leads around and behind...Cumberland Falls.

If you suddenly have the feeling that we've been headed toward this story the whole time, you're right. This story is why I'm giving this speech.

It was just after lunch that day, in the summer of 1973, and Jim Edgy, who was then the Director of the Arts Commission, and Steve Todd, a fellow filmmaker in the schools, and I were all feeling restless. We had all heard that there was a path that led you back behind the falls. We had also heard it was closed, prohibited, extremely dangerous, etc., etc. So we had to go. And we set off without telling anyone.

Down the walk we went to the overlook, then on along the edge of the cliff to the falls. We were feeling so calm, so...adventurous and superior. We were so cool. Even when we reached the huge barbed-wire gate, marked with a big sign prohibiting any kind of access any time for anybody, even then we were still cool. And even when we saw a man coming up from the other side of the gate—having just been behind the falls, his shirt ripped in four places, his face covered in blood...Even then, we were cool. Oh sure, he fell. But we wouldn't.

So we climbed the fence and made our way, single file, along what could only be described as a ledge, being very careful not to look down at the churning water and rocks some 200 feet below. Closer and closer we came to the falls, the spray now soaking us. And the ledge began to slope down in its final approach to the falls. We could see where the path disappeared behind the falls. But we couldn't get there yet. Well, I couldn't.

Steve and Jim were both taller than I was. And there was this...drop-off, I guess you could call it, a space between rocks along the ledge, a space too large for me to step across. Steve had gone first, then Jim. But there I was. Stuck. I wasn't about to go back, but how could I go on? Well. Can you hear my heart pounding? Can you hear the billions of gallons of water crashing over the falls about twenty feet...over there? Good.

Jim saw my predicament and held out his hand. "You'll have to jump," he said. Well. I knew it was stupid and dangerous. But it was also thrilling and necessary, so I did it. I jumped. And I did not fall into the river and drown. I landed quite near Jim, but without pushing him over either, and we continued around the jagged corner and…

Arrived…in the dark, safe, strangely dry chamber directly behind the falls. We sat down cross-legged, and stared out at the falls. And said things like "Oh my God," and "Wow," and "Oh man," for about a minute. And then we fell silent and just watched. And listened, of course.

And suddenly, it didn't look like we were behind a falls at all, but rather inside a drum of water. From inside the drum, it looked like the same water flowed eternally around and around—taking the same rippling path, making the same patterns.

After a while, we started to talk again, and strangely enough, our topic was the nature and purpose of art. It may have been the most high-minded, serious conversation I've ever had. Maybe we were afraid we'd all die on the way back from the falls, and we wanted our last conversation to be a good one. Maybe we were high on fear, or were in the presence of ancient spirits, I don't know. But here is what we said as we sat behind the falls.

The purpose of art is to express what we have in common, the life that we have in common, the life we could live in common if we could just escape our skin, our time, and the particularities of our experience. People who have strong religious beliefs can escape their individuality through rituals and rites, we said. But for those without faith (as we proudly claimed to be at the time), for us nonbelievers, art is our only way out, our only way in, our only way back to where we really live—in our senses, in our bodies, in our connections with each other. And by each other, I mean those with whom we have shared a victory, a defeat, or a purpose—regardless of whether we have shared a house or a bed, or even a century.

Somebody, I think it was me, said that art asked the question, "Do we have a common language, you and I?" And Steve said he thought art invented humans so it would have a way of passing itself along. Then Jim said it was time to go back to the conference for the session on ticket sales. So we stood up and looked around, knowing this was the definition of a once in a lifetime experience.

The return trip was quite uneventful, except that when we reached the barbed-wire gate, climbed over it and headed inland again, we got the giggles. We laughed like fools, like crazy people. We laughed til we cried, over nothing, over having survived our ordeal. We had taken a big, completely irresponsible risk and we had made it back safely. Except that none of us ever spoke about it again, not to each other anyway.

Then, two year later, on a day when Jim and I weren't there, a day that must have been much scarier, Steve Todd killed himself. Nash Cox called to tell me. And in my sadness over his death, the strangest protest kept going through my mind, as if I were arguing with him. "But Steve, we sat behind the falls together, we made it back. We're going to be O.K. How could you kill yourself? Why would you kill yourself?"

And eight years later, Steve's death would be one of the suicides I would try to understand by writing 'Night, Mother. I would try to save him, and the others, and myself, by saying in the play, "I see you. Grab hold. I've got you." Steve would not hear my offer of help. But others would. Other people would stop me in lobbies all over the world and say, "Thank you very much, my sister killed herself last year."

So in the same way that the Arts Council threw out the lifeline to save me, my plays and musicals are lifelines I have thrown out, to anyone who needs them. And I can't begin to count the evenings when I have grabbed the lifeline thrown to me by someone else—another artist, a friend, or someone in a dream, a Mozart, a Rilke, a Robert Penn Warren, a Jean Ritchie, a Lily Tomlin.

Art saves people. It saves us from our singularity, from our separateness. Art both documents our differences and saves us from them. Art is how a culture records its life, how it poses questions to the next generation, and how it is remembered.

Art is our common language. It is the connection we have to each other. It is how we say what it has felt like to be alive in our time. It is how we examine what has mattered to us, how we study the things that have held together, and mourn the things that have fallen apart.

Two of the things that have not fallen apart, in my experience, are my love of Kentucky, and my attachment to the Kentucky Arts Council. So let me conclude by thanking you for this connection, for this lifeline thrown to me so many years ago. Let me celebrate our connection in the conversations we will have over the next few days. And let me hope that the storehouse where you keep these lifelines is still full, because young artists need them. And we need our young artists. More than anything in the world. Let me say that again. We need our young artists more than anything in the world.

Thank you very much.

TIME AND LEARNING HOW TO FALL
Originally written for the Bingham Distinguished Lecture Series, 1986.
This version was given at Kenyon College, May 1988.

It is my great pleasure to be with you tonight. I do not, however, have the faintest idea why I am with you tonight. In the past, prior to giving a lecture, I have spoken with someone from the institution and asked some good-natured, but basically self-protective questions. You know, like Who Is Going to Be There, Who Do They Think I Am, and How Long Can They Just Sit There and Listen.

But this time, my agent simply said Do You Want To Go To Kenyon, and I said Sure, I like Kenyon, and he said Great, I'll Send You The Tickets.

Actually, I know someone who went to Kenyon. Kathy, her name was. We were poor counselors together at an expensive girls' camp in Tennessee. She taught archery and I taught astronomy and both of us were bluffing.

Anyway, we played bridge every night for nine solid weeks, and we were pretty good together. We won nine extra days off and nine bottles of bad bourbon. On the days off, we'd go into town and drink the bad bourbon, and talk about our troubles, which all started because our parents didn't have enough money to send us to a camp like this. It wasn't a complete waste of time, though. Because I learned a valuable lesson. You should never drink bad bourbon. Bad bourbon makes you blame your parents.

So now that I've explained my close connection to Kenyon, we're free to launch right into the speech. I've given a fair number of speeches in my life and listened to a very unfair number of them. The good ones are all the same. They start from something very specific, like how do you write a play, and end up telling you something very general, like what is the meaning of life.

I'd do that for you if I could, but the truth is, nobody knows how to write a play. Walter Kerr wrote the only book on writing plays that I ever read. It is called *How Not to Write a Play.* And Walter Kerr has hated everything I've ever written, so that just shows you how much he knows, doesn't it.

Now then, the title of this speech is Time and Learning How to Fall. You can write it down or not, it's up to you. I do not, in truth, know if there will be a quiz. But if I were in the audience, I would write it down. It is my experience in life that there is always a quiz. Time and Learning How to Fall.

A more descriptive title would have been The Life of the Dramatist in the Contemporary Theatre. But nobody wants to hear that. Some people might even tell you there aren't any dramatists in the contemporary theatre. But believe me, there are, and The Life of the Dramatist in the Contemporary Theatre is...yes, you guessed it, Time and Learning How to Fall.

The phrase is not original, I'm afraid. I've stolen it from what is known as a lesser, in fact, a vanished Marsha Norman play, *Circus Valentine*. You can always tell which plays are not going to work, because your friends come up to you in previews and tell you the work is ambitious. Deadly, that word, ambitious. Ambitious means, Well, sweetheart, you tried.

The play is about a small family circus, so small, in fact, that they perform in shopping center parking lots and everybody is related, somehow—though the relations are all pretty distant. The play takes place just outside the main tent. When characters go offstage in the play, they go on in the circus. They tame the lions or walk the tightrope or whatever. So, every character has a moment when he or she is performing, doing an act. But they don't fly the trapeze, or whatever, they do their own personal act, they say who they are, what they need, what they are afraid of...you know.

Anyway, this is part of Trina's act. Trina is the daughter of Fred and Goldie Valentine who run the circus, and the protege of Eva, the aerialist. Trina is in training for the trapeze. And the circus is all she's ever known. This is what she has to say.

"You can't just decide you want to be circus people. If you're not born to it, you won't ever be it, really, no matter how hard you try. I was born to it. And when you're born to it, you don't ever have to worry about what you're going to do because it's going to be the same thing you've been doing since you could ever remember doing anything. Sometimes I think it would be fun to go to high school, but my arms are real muscular, you know, so I might feel funny out taking pictures for the yearbook or something."

I'm learning the trapeze now, from Eva. Eva and Mama did a great double trap turn when they were young The Sparrow sisters! Da-Da. Eva even did a triple somersault once. It was in practice, but she did it just the same. The trapeze is pretty hard. It's all time, see and knowing how to fall.

"Cause you're going to fall, that's for sure." She goes on. "Most of the time, something breaks and that's why you fall. But sometimes people just let go. It's casting, that's what we call it. And nobody knows why people do it. One minute they're fine and the next minute they just let go. Their fingers open up, that's all. Their fingers just unwrap and straighten out all relaxed and they've let go only they didn't mean to. It's not a mistake, they don't lose their concentration or anything. It's weird. They just let go."

"If they tuck and fall right, they'll be O.K. though. You have to know how to fall. Oh," she says, "I already said that."

There's more, but that's enough. That's where the title comes from—Time and Learning How to Fall. Life-saving information for aerialists of all kinds, and that includes high-flyers in the theatrical circus.

Time First.

Aristotle said it, of course. Time, Place, and Action. The classical unities which must be observed in the theatre. Aristotle has his detractors, of course, but I am not one of them.

If you are going to write for the theatre, you must come to terms with time. Novels are about place. Movies are about action. The theatre is about time. Two hours, give or take ten minutes, is how long you have to play. Two hours of audience time, two hours of character time.

Now the audience time is chosen in an absolutely random fashion. You go to the theatre on Thursday the eighth at eight o'clock because that's when they have seats, or you have the babysitter, or you have to work late anyway so why not just stay in town.

The character time, however, is anything but random. It is, perhaps, the most important decision a dramatist makes. If I am going to show you an entire life in two hours, then I must select the precise two hours in which the entire life is visible.

I want you to know where she came from, what she has seen and done and what she makes of it. If I choose two hours too early, the problem will just be surfacing. Two hours too late and the problem is solved. I must chose the moment when the main character sees the problem, sees how big it is and where it came from, and decides what to do about it.

Because it is the essence of a lifetime, what happens in this two hours can be said in a sentence, but it must be seen in order to be believed. This is the theatrical moment.

There is, I think, just such a theatrical moment in every life. And I encourage you to exercise your latent playwriting talent and look for it in your own life. Just look, please. Don't write it. The field is over-crowded already, and it's never a good idea to write about yourself.

So, now, you've picked the two hours. Fine. Are you through with time for the evening? Oh no. It's even more important now. So important, in some plays, that you even put the clocks onstage.

When Frank Rich first reviewed 'Night Mother, it made him angry that there were six clocks onstage, all keeping real time. He thought we were overdoing it. So we cut two of them for Broadway and he liked it much better. What I was doing with all those clocks was just passing along something I believe about the theatre. The only way to keep the audience from looking at their watches, is to keep the clock running in the play.

Now, what this too-clever little phrase means is every second counts. The play must be in constant forward motion, like a ski lift. You pay your money and you sit down. The lift starts, and the ideal journey is straight to the top, nice and smooth. If it stops mid-air, half-way up the mountain and just hangs there, if you hear disturbing grinding noises, if the motor suddenly jerks you forward, you panic. You look around, you realize where you are and you wonder if you are ever going to get out of there. Plays are exactly like that. They must keep moving. And you have every right to complain about them if they don't.

Now, there are certain critical moments in this two-hour trip. One of them comes at the end of about eight minutes. The audience will give you eight minutes to start the engines. If you'll think about your last airplane ride, you'll see what I mean.

You pay your money and you get on. But pretty soon you want to pull away from the gate and shortly after that, you want to hear the captain tell the cabin attendants to sit down. And real soon after that, you want to be first in line for takeoff and start that rush down the runway and feel the nose lift off the ground and then hear the landing gear fold into place and then have the Seat Belt sign go off.

You want it all to happen that way because you want to go somewhere. A playwright has eight minutes to convince you that 1) you are going somewhere, 2) that she knows where you are going, and that 3) she knows how to fly this thing.

In that eight minutes, you should find out who the main character is and what he or she wants. That is, you should learn what is at stake here. And you should learn how you will know when you can go home

Going back to airplane talk for a moment. I'm sure you've seen plays that say they're taking you to Columbus, but when you get there, it's not Columbus at all, it's Akron. That makes you mad. And you are right to be mad. The playwright cannot fool you about where you are. You know if it's Akron or not, and you don't want to go there, or else you wouldn't have taken this flight.

But let's assume, for the sake of this discussion, that you are headed for Columbus. Only it's not a through flight. You have to stop first in Pittsburgh. Fine. You can handle that.

Just before the stop in Pittsburgh, or intermission, as we call it, there is the forty-five minute moment. In a plane, the Seat Belt sign comes back on again and you know you're on the way down. Something must happen onstage so the audience knows that the orange drink or the bathroom is no longer a remote possibility.

I discovered this forty-five minute moment by accident one night when I was sitting in the booth (the sound and light booth) at the Victor Jory theatre secretly taping a performance of my play *Third and Oak*. I wanted to listen to it at home so I could try to clean it up for broadcast on National Public Radio.

I was using hour and a half tapes—that is, forty-five minutes to a side. When the tape ran out, in each act, I turned the machine off, turned the tape over, and turned the machine back on. When I got back home and listened to the tapes, I realized that in the thirty-seconds when I was turning the tape over, I missed the critical emotional speech in each act.

There it was, the big scene, right at forty-five minutes. I had written it there out of instinct or ignorance, or both, but it became, from that time on, a hard and fast rule for me. One of the two or three I never break.

In the second act, we have half of the eight minutes we had at the beginning of the first act. We have four minutes for people to get comfortable again, realize that they have the same characters on the stage, and remember where those characters were when they last saw them. At the end of four minutes, the audience must recover their deep desire to know what is going to happen.

The clock ticks a little louder in the second act. For now, there is not only something at stake for the character, there is something at stake for the audience. There is, of course, another forty-five minute moment in the second act, or as they call it in musicals, the eleven o'clock number, but the most interesting piece of time is that two or three second hush, just before the curtain, when the audience votes on the matter presented to them. Has it been the truth? Has it mattered? Have they wasted their time, or did they just gain some time by virtue of the new understanding they have?

Experienced dramatists know the sounds of each of the critical moments in a play. The sound of this last one, the audience voting, is the most powerful. It's not the applause, although it can be reflected in the applause. The sound of the reflection that dramatists recognize is the moment. It is the sound of arms opening for an embrace. It is the sound of welcome. And when you hear it, it means that you now have all the time in the world to go home and write some more.

Well, so much for the time inside the play. What about the time around the play.

How much and what kind of time does it take to write a play? How much times does the play require of you after it is written, after you've done the part you know how to do. And how much time do you have left over for what you like to think of as your life?

Well, let's take the last one first. I have no time left over for my life. There is virtually no time when I am not writing. Reading is writing. Cooking is writing. Listening is writing. But what is writing, exactly? Nothing more than getting things straight. That is the job of the writer—to get things straight—things that people say, things that people think, things that people feel. I might as well be working as the straighten-out girl in a room full of hand-knitters.

Here are all these ladies with their clicking needles and their casual chatter and they're humming little songs and thinking their private thoughts and I go around and pick up the stray balls of yarn on the floor, untangle all the knots, brush off all the sawdust and lint and wind the thing back up into a ball so it can be worked the way it should be.

What you see in the theatre is always an untangling of some knot or other. Of course, you must care whether this knot is untangled or not. And you have to see how it got that way and you have to know that life can't go on til it's straight—but it's a simple act, really.

But it takes time to write a play. A fairly special kind of time, time devoted exclusively to the play and it's people. It is, in a sense, like visiting a foreign country for six months or so. If you spend your whole time in Bora Bora talking on the phone to the folks back home, you're going to miss whatever it is you've come to this island to see.

Withdrawal from the normal routines and the normal conversations of your life is absolutely required to write a play. There is a point where the characters become real to you, and the real people in your life seem like characters in some story you read last year. And pretty soon, you are having real conversations with imaginary people and imaginary conversations with real people.

You disappear in the middle of dinner, and you start ten projects without finishing one of them, and you get to the fruit market and forget what you came for. But that's not so unusual. That's what always happens when you have houseguests.

And that's what the characters become. Houseguests. The first day they're living with you, you know how they take their coffee. And after the first week, you know how often they wash their hair. And after six months of having them underfoot, day after day, you know more than you ever wanted to know, and you wish they'd go home. And then one day you face the terrible truth that they live there. They're never going home.

If the world likes them, they will go out a lot. If the world loves them, they'll be gone all the time. They'll go to places you have never been and meet people who wouldn't recognize you on the street. They have, in fact, a great old time. Already, Jessie and Mama, from 'Night, Mother, speak Spanish, French, German, Swedish, Danish, Finnish, Dutch, Portuguese, Greek, Italian, Polish, Yiddish, Chinese, Japanese, and Afrikaans.

And I'm happy for them. But I have to tell you, I won't be completely fulfilled until 'Night Mother is translated into Latin.

The other side of this is that you do have character houseguests that nobody wants to entertain. They go out of the house once, and nobody ever invites them back. And to tell you the God's truth, you actually get quite fond of them, these rejects. They are poor things but your own. In an odd way, they come to mean more to you than these Miss Personality characters that everybody keeps asking you about. But…more of that later. I have a few more thoughts about time.

How much time does it take to write a play? Well, you can put the words on the paper in about six months. You can do it in three months if you go away from home to do it. If you're a Noel Coward you can do it in two weeks if you're sick in Hong Kong. And if you're Allan Ayckborn, you can do it in one week if your wife slips your food under the door and the internal revenue is coming to take you to jail if you don't.

I have come to believe that there is a statute of limitations on plays. That they must be written in concentrated periods of time, that they must be finished in two years. That two years is about as long as you can stay the same person, the person who started the play. Once some significant change has occurred in your life, you can no longer approach the problem in the same way you did when you began.

I'm sure you've seen plays that people have worked on for too long. You can tell these plays because the central problem keeps changing. As you watch it, the main character seems to stop worrying about sex and start worrying mid-life crisis, or stop worrying about mid-life crisis and start worrying about death.

This is the writer worrying, pure and simple. The writer has solved the character's problem in his own life and now has no idea why the character is so upset about it. So, in order to stay interested enough to finish the play, the writer decides the character must actually be worrying about some new problem, this new problem being, of course, the new problem the writer has. This is bad on the stage. This is confusing.

An audience wants to deal with one problem at a time. An actor wants to deal with one problem at a time. Writers must solve their problems one at a time and move on. But that is difficult in the world of the theatre.

In Shakespeare's day, his plays were performed as soon as the ink was dry, and he went right on to writing the next one. In today's theatre, the writing is just the beginning of the Time a play takes. After you have written it, you let people read it. That's another two months, depending on how fast they read and how quickly they open packages from you. Then you go back to the type-writer for a second draft, or a third draft and that can take anywhere from one day to six months.

Then, you need to arrange a production. You send the script out and you wait. And if you get an offer, you wait until the day rolls around for the rehearsals to start. In the meantime, you're talking with the director and casting for the company and trying to determine if the set and costume designers are doing the same play you wrote. That's another six months or so.

These terrible delays between the writing of a piece and its final production cause terrible problems. One of which concerns publicity. By the time they get around to interviewing you about it, the writing is in the very distant past. It feels like someone saying to you, I loved that pumpkin mousse you had for dinner two years ago. How did you make it? Well, of course, you barely remember.

So when they ask you about this two-year old play, you read the script and you make your guesses about what the author thought, what the author was trying to do.

And, in truth, you have no better ideas about it than the people who are asking you. But since you're the author, they tend to take your word for it.

We're now at the eighteen-month point in our timetable. Rehearsals begin, that's a month, and the opening comes. The opening seems to last five years, but it's actually just a matter of hours. During which time, your physical and emotional health, your financial security, and your self-esteem are all taken up in front of the high priests like some still warm pigeon heart just cut out of some newly dead but raised-for-the-purpose sacrificial bird.

You try to stay calm while the priests chant their chants and slice open your heart and look for the signs. Now, nobody quite knows what they're looking for. Even they do not know what they're looking for. But what they see is effected, of course, by what they've had for dinner and what their wife or husband said to them on the way to the theatre and what they saw the last time your heart was there for their inspection.

The night does pass, however, and you try not to think about it, you go out and drink with your friends and you try to go to sleep and all the time you're waiting for the papers. Playwrights who tell you they're not waiting for the papers are lying. It's just that simple.

You may not care what they say, or you may not have any respect for them, but you do wait to see what they say. You cannot go on without knowing what they say. If they like it, you're free. If they don't, then you don't have a very nice day...for a long time. With *Circus Valentine*, it was almost three years before I had a nice day.

Now, we have sneakily worked ourselves around to the second part of the title of this speech, which is not as long, I promise you. Time is longer than just about anything. Learning How to Fall. When the critics don't like it, you fall, right there in front of everybody.

But there is no way to do significant work of any kind without falling. Falling, is, actually, the most important part of this life. If you don't fall, then you aren't working close enough to the edge. Then you are secretly holding on, then you're not really flying, you just fooled everybody for a little while.

Falling, then, is necessary, but dangerous. People can get hurt in a fall. People can die from a fall. Well, what they die of is the internal injuries, of course.

Tennessee Williams was, without doubt, killed by the critics. They kept after him and kept after him and finally, he'd just had enough. They kept thinking he owed them another *Streetcar*, another *Glass Menagerie*. Well, just for the record, he didn't. And they had no right to expect that of him.

It was in their power to save him and they didn't. They were holding his tie lines and they dropped them. He went up on the wire and they screamed and he lost his concentration and he fell, over and over again.

And only on the day after he died, did they give him what would have kept him alive—assurance of his rightful place as one of the most important playwrights in American or indeed World History.

If Tennessee Williams had lived, we might have seen what trick he was working on that required all that falling in practice. That is a problem, for playwrights, we have to practice in public.

And we must fall. You cannot do this work if you cannot live the life. There is an exchange from my new play, *Traveler in the Dark*, that sums up what playwrights must know. If they cannot know it and continue to work in spite of it, then they must quit. They will quit. They will have to quit.

In this exchange, the surgeon, and his father, the country preacher are arguing about how the surgeon has raised his twelve-year old son. The surgeon says, "I have spent my life straightening out the lies people have told him. No Stephen, there is no Santa Claus. No Stephen, when you die, you do not go to Heaven. No, Stephen, people won't like you better because you're smart, they'll be afraid of you because you're smart. No, Stephen, love is not forever, and God is not good, and Tomorrow is not Another Day. Tomorrow is this day all over again."

And the preacher says, "Well, wasn't he lucky to have you around."

Obviously, I agree with the surgeon. Those are the things we must know. And we must work in spite of them.

The higher you go, the further you have to fall, the stronger your nets have to be, the better your catchers have to be. The one thing you cannot be is afraid to fall. You will fall. And other people may be surprised, but you must not be. You can be surprised by which plays they knock you off the wire for, but you have to be prepared. It is a high-risk occupation.

So, how do you learn how to fall. Well, as anybody knows who has ever fallen from anything, even the dining room chair, you must relax. If you stiffen up and try to catch yourself, you're going to get hurt. If you relax, you'll just fall. Falling is not so bad. Getting hurt is bad. Deciding never to sit at a dining room chair again is bad. Being embarrassed, falling in front of your friends, is a waste of time.

Your friends react strangely to a fall. They actually think, most of them, that you won't fall. That you can't fall. Susan Stamberg said to me on National Public Radio in a series of interviews we did during the production of a new play in Cambridge, "Marsha, I can't imagine the critics not liking a play of yours." Ha-Ha. I told her it was altogether possible, but she didn't believe me. Then four weeks later, she was reading the negative reviews over the air for all the public radio's public to hear.

Even the *Courier-Journal,* which I regard as my friend, sent its own critics to see this new play of mine and they both loved it. Raved over it, in their reviews. Then this same *Courier-Journal,* three weeks later printed a collection of the terrible reviews from other papers around the country.

Now why did this paper, this friend of mine do this? And why did fifteen people from Kentucky call me to tell me what a terrible thing the *Courier* had done "to me" as they put it, and offer to read the article to me? I don't know.

Apparently, my falling off the wire has become news. Well, it's not news to me. There is a line in *'Night, Mother* about this. Jessie says to Mama, "Epilepsy doesn't mean anything. It just is." And that's what I have to say about negative reviews. They don't mean anything. They just are.

Negative reviews, they don't mean anything important, really important. They mean how much money I'll make off the play. But they don't mean anything about the play itself. History will decide that. Unfortunately, I will not live long enough to hear what history has to say. That is as it should be. History may be on their side. But I am on my side. And I know that all the plays I write are important, whether they are received well or not. That they are all a part of a body of work, which can only be evaluated at the end of the production of the complete work, not after the opening of any single production.

History may reverse itself completely about my work. It may eliminate me from consideration altogether. Then again, it might decide that even my address book is museum quality. I don't know. And I will die not knowing how this all turned out, so I am a damn fool if I spend my life worrying about something none of us in this room will ever know.

It is my work to write, and I will work until I find that, like John Fetterman said, being a character pays just as well.

I quoted from *Circus Valentine* at the beginning of this talk because *Circus Valentine* was how I learned to live this life. If I hadn't written it and hadn't fallen for the first time, I would be standing here today wearing my Pulitzer armor.

In writing another critical disaster, *The Holdup,* I learned how to contain the action of a play, to cause the piece to erupt and resolve without bringing in a character from the outside. That technique was at the heart of *'Night, Mother.*

Learning How to Fall is learning how not to get hurt, how to see the falls as proof of your courage, proof of your growth, learning not to be afraid of them, stretching beyond what you could do yesterday, and taking the chance that you will fall.

Learning to fall is looking for things you're not even sure you have, like wings, for example. And if you don't find them, well, at least you looked. So you fall, so what. The only way not to fall is not to move at all. I urge all of you to fall often and land hard if you have to, or gently if you can. And then show your scars to everybody.

Thank you very much.

HONOR IS NOT ENOUGH
New Dramatists luncheon
honoring Pulitzer Prize Winners 1987

David LeVine, Milton Goldman, Ron Lee, Tom Dunn, fellow Pulitzer winners, colleagues, friends and family of the American theatre:

It is my great privilege to speak for this valiant band of survivors up here. What I have been asked to say, is Thank you, on behalf of all the Pulitzer winners; those who have already thanked you by their presence at this table, those who are unable to be here because they are in rehearsal, and those who have found something more entertaining than either rehearsal or this luncheon. God only knows what that might be.

We thank you not just for honoring us, but for finding our current address, and sending us something other than a request for an autograph, or a letter asking where we get our ideas. (Actually, you know, those people never really want to know where we got our ideas, they want to know where they can get some ideas like ours, but better.)

We want to thank New Dramatists for arranging this event, for, in fact, discovering that so many of us are still alive. And we thank all of you for joining us today in shrimp salad. Of course we cannot forget to thank the people who dressed and designed this set, the person who costumed this cast, the lighting engineer, the director, wherever he is now, and the people who set up the tables, each of whom will receive 5 percent of our future earnings from this lunch.

Winning the Pulitzer Prize changes your life. And it is unfair, but true, that not winning the Pulitzer Prize changes your life too. There are important dramatists and magnificent plays which have slipped through the Pulitzer net. Many people who deserve to share in the honors of this day are not sitting at this table, but rather in the audience. I want to thank them for suffering our presence up here, when we know, and they know, that they should be here with us.

In truth, you cannot honor Pulitzer winners without honoring the entire community of dramatists. It takes, all of us, working carefully, obstinately, in good faith...all of us, working full-time to produce the two or three plays which will survive from any given season in this country. And although we write our plays alone, we are not alone in writing them. It is one of our few consistent comforts to know that other playwrights, people we respect and cherish, are just as depressed as we are.

Speaking simply then, as a member of this national community of writers for the theatre, this community you honor by honoring us flagbearers, I must stand here a little longer and say more than Thank You.

I am afraid, you see, it is not enough for you to honor us. Or rather, we need more than honor. We need for each of you, acting in whatever capacity you can, to act now to save us. We need you to defend us and protect us from a theatrical world that is increasingly ambivalent, at best, about the contribution of the dramatist.

American dramatists of another age would have howled in laughter at that very phrase. "The contribution of the dramatist? Hah!" they would say. "Makes the play sound like a donation!" "What is the play, for God's sake? A donation?"

Yes, I'm afraid it's beginning to feel exactly like that. A donation. And we all know, that there is a limit to the amount a person can afford to give to charity.

For reasons all too familiar to all of you, you are living with a generation of writers forced to find other markets for their skills. I think I can safely guarantee you that all dramatists, given a choice, would rather be writing a play. But we don't have that choice today. Not if we want to eat and read books and buy tickets to see our friends' plays.

Now, if you think we will always write plays just because we just like to do it, you are wrong. When it stops being merely impossible, and becomes absolutely insane, we will quit. We won't want to quit, and we won't give a press conference saying we've quit. No, when that day comes, we just won't have any more ideas. Even now, we know that to have an idea for a play is to submit to what can be a very long, very brutal process.

If you think that there will always be good new plays, because, well, anybody can write a play, you are wrong. I don't really believe you think such things, but I know that dramatists are under siege, and I know that some of our beseigers, if there is such a word, are the very people we work with year after year.

Some of these people are members of our fellow craft organizations. What they want is to "share" with us, or rather, demand from us their share, of the money we had hoped to live on while we write another play. We have not asked them to share the money they earn while they are out doing other people's plays for the next three years, or a share of the money they make in the movies because Universal saw them in our play. But maybe we should.

Plays take years to write, and writers take a lifetime to develop. Many people, yes actors and directors, but also our parents and children, our teachers, other writers and our friends, make valuable contributions to our work. The only way writers can and should repay these people is by continuing to write. For only when living writers continue to write can the theatre provide a healthy life and a decent livelihood for all its artists.

If the theatre comes to believe that the writer's work is no more important than any other member of the team, then we will just have to see you in the movies, or in novels or columns or maybe we will see you at the Xerox place down the street where we will be sitting behind a word processor correcting some adorable young actor's resume.

There are, however, ways you can help. First of all, you must allow us our careers. You must support the plays that don't work, so we can stay alive to write the plays that do. This is how the British do it, and we would do well to copy them. When Tom Stoppard writes a play nobody likes, everybody goes to see it anyway. They understand over there, that the so-called bad plays are where the so-called good ones come from.

Liz McCann, a person for whom I have enormous respect in this business, likes to say "What Broadway needs is more bad plays." And I agree. Actors and directors need to learn, and dramatists need to practice. And once upon a time, we had a theatre that trained its stars, instead of stealing them from the movies. There was a time, when, in order to try your hand directing a musical, you didn't first have to prove that you could be trusted with four million dollars.

Yes, I agree. We need more bad plays and more bad musicals, because if artists don't have the opportunity to work—well, it's like the athletic department telling its runners that they can't even get onto the track until they've won a big race. That athletic department isn't going to do very well. And that university should probably consider firing the coaches.

So, you can help by allowing us our careers.

You can also help by helping us clear up this confusion about what writing is. Asking questions is not writing, making suggestions is not writing. Directing is not writing. Acting is not writing. Designing and lighting are not writing. And people should not get writing credit or royalties for not writing.

Writing is what dramatists do. It is so mysterious and glorious, so dangerous and so costly. At its best, it is transparent, yet detailed, enduring, but ever accessible. Pulitzer winners make it look easy. Whatever else writing is, it's not easy. Writing only happens when it is welcomed, into the life of the writer, and into the world the writer lives in. Writing is, finally, so precious to you, that you have come here today just to look at a table full of people who can do it.

Writing is an act of faith. You do not have to thank us for writing these plays that have become a part of your life. We wanted to write them, we believed that they were stories worth telling, believed that there was a chance for them to find their audience, and believed that they might make a difference. And believed that maybe, just maybe, these plays might support the writing of other plays.

What we need, in order to keep writing, is to live in a world, in a theatrical community where it is still possible to believe these things.

If you want to honor us, the community of writers for the theatre, the past and the future winners of the Pulitzer prize, you must show us that we mean something to you. This luncheon is a good sign, and we thank you for it. Now, you must stand guard, and fight, if necessary, for an American theatre that writers can believe in, a place where we are safe, not from the critics or the fates, but safe in knowing that we are and always have been the primary life force, the constantly beating heart of the theatre.

MARSHA NORMAN won the 1983 Pulitzer Prize for her play *'Night, Mother*. The play also won four Tony nominations, the Dramatists Guild's prestigious Hull-Warriner Award and the Susan Smith Blackburn Prize. A feature film, starring Anne Bancroft and Sissy Spacek, with a screenplay by Ms. Norman, was released in August 1986. *'Night, Mother* has been translated into 23 languages and has been performed around the world.

Her first play, *Getting Out*, received the John Gassner Playwriting Medallion, the Newsday Oppenheimer Award, and a special citation from the American Theatre Critics Association. Her two one-act plays, *Third And Oak: The Laundromat* and *The Pool Hall* premiered at Actors Theatre of Louisville. Her play *The Holdup* was workshopped at ATL as well. *Traveler in the Dark* premiered at American Repertory Theatre and was later staged at the Mark Taper Forum under the direction of Gordon Davidson. *Sarah and Abraham* premiered at Actors Theatre of Louisville in 1987 and was produced at the George Street Playhouse in the fall of 1991.

Ms. Norman received a Tony Award and Drama Desk Award for her Broadway musical *The Secret Garden*. Her play *Loving Daniel Boone* had its premiere at the 1992 Actors Theatre of Louisville Humana Festival, and her latest play, *Trudy Blue*, premiered in the 1995 Humana Festival. She wrote the book and lyrics for *The Red Shoes,* with music by Jule Styne.

Marsha Norman, Four Plays, was published by Theatre Communications Group in 1988. Her first novel, *The Fortune Teller,* was published in 1987.

Ms. Norman has worked in television and film, including most recently, *Face of a Stranger,* starring Gena Rowlands and Tyne Daly.

Ms. Norman has received grants and awards from the National Endowment for the Arts, the Rockefeller Foundation, and the American Academy and Institute of Letters. She has been playwright-in-residence at the Actors Theatre of Louisville and the Mark Taper Forum in Los Angeles, and she has been elected to membership in the American Academy of Achievement. She serves on the boards of the New York Foundation for the Arts, the Independent Committee for Arts Policy, and the Council of the Dramatists Guild. She is the recipient of the Literature Award from the American Academy and Institute of Arts and Letters. Since 1993 with Christopher Durang, she co-chairs the Playwriting Department of the Juilliard Drama School.